LIGHTNING FROM THE SKY
THUNDER FROM THE SEA

by
Thomas Petri

authorHOUSE

AuthorHouse™
1663 Liberty Drive
Bloomington, IN 47403
www.authorhouse.com
Phone: 1-800-839-8640

© 2009 Thomas Petri. All rights reserved.

No part of this book may be reproduced, stored in a retrieval system, or transmitted by any means without the written permission of the author.

First published by AuthorHouse 10/21/2009

ISBN: 978-1-4389-4595-8 (sc)
ISBN: 978-1-4389-4596-5 (hc)

Library of Congress Control Number: 2009904666

Printed in the United States of America
Bloomington, Indiana

This book is printed on acid-free paper.

CONTENTS

Prologue	vii
Acknowledgments	xv
Good Ole Boys	1
Blue Dragons	11
Super Grunts	19
Hyong-je Haebyong	33
Nam Doe Khe Be	39
The Lost Platoon	47
The Friends	67
Will the Last Man Standing Please Call a Medevac?	85
What the Hell Happened to You?	101
Transition	113
You're Here to Deliver a Valentine from Ho Chi Who?	119
Rampage of the Giant Dragon	139
An Incident on Mui Ba Lang An	157
Unruly Party Guests	169
Different War, Same Mess	201
The Big Hurt	211
More of the Same	227
Solitary Refinement	249
The Last Tango in Quang Tri	257
Not on My Watch	291
Not One More Inch	305
Whoop Ass in Tiger Stripes	323
Shut It Down When?	351
Epilogue	357
Addendum I Anglico in Vietnam	377
Addendum II Korean Involvement in Vietnam	381
Addendum III 1st Anglico Honors	383
Addendum IV	387
Glossary of Military Acronyms and Terms	389
Glossary of Korean Terms	391
Bibliography and Documentation	393

PROLOGUE

Most written histories of man's advancement to the current era are basically highlights of event-makers. Those of accomplishment and leadership are the recognized names we know through the chronicles of time. Familiar names of our forebears are by and large political noteworthies, military leaders, people of wealth, and those in general who are perceived to have exerted some degree of measurable influence on events leading to the present.

I fully recognize the impracticality of assigning recognition to every soul who inhabited the earth. But yet, the greater portion of mankind in every era of history has always been populated by millions of unknowns who played no small role in bringing us to where we are. These were the people who eventually reaped the benefits of successes or suffered the consequences of failure attributed to historical personages of prominence. Just as no Hollywood production can offer much entertainment value without a good supporting cast, so too could transcriptions of history have significant meaning if viewed from a narrow perspective focused solely on acclaimed event-makers. We all know, for instance, that Winston Churchill, a man who commands and surely deserves great respect, didn't fire one shot during World War II, yet he is given a good deal of credit for the Allied victory. He was one of the greatest leaders this world ever produced, but his statesmanship would have gone to waste without millions of British citizens that embraced his leadership, carried out his vision, and did the actual fighting that saved England.

Where, for instance, would the hordes of Genghis Khan have ridden without their great leader? A better question still: Who would have ever heard of Genghis Khan if it weren't for the horde? The Great Khan wasn't killed realizing his ambitions. It was thousands of members of the horde who made the sacrifice for Genghis Khan to achieve empire. They were in actuality the ones who did the conquering. Genghis Khan was just someone born into a family that gave him the right to inherit a position that gave him the wherewithal to acquire a horde. Inasmuch as he was a prominent figure of his era, we all know the name of Genghis Khan. How many members of the horde who actually guaranteed the Great Khan historical recognition have been recorded for posterity?

Many centuries after the death of Genghis Khan, a modern horde led by General William Westmoreland struggled in the jungles of Southeast Asia, not for a place of recognition in the saga of man, but for a variety of reasons, and mostly for each other.

About thirty members of that horde met in Washington, D.C., on Veteran's Day 1989 for the first time since that war. It was a joyful reunion in the true spirit of friendship. For a three-day weekend we partied, saw the sights, and honored our fallen brothers. We conducted our own ceremony at the Vietnam Veterans Memorial, toured Arlington Cemetery, and socialized with veterans of other units. Not once that entire weekend did anyone discuss personal combat experiences. To an observer, we could have been former college friends gathered together to relive old times.

I never realized until that weekend how Vietnam has always been a very private part of our lives. Even in the company of those with whom I was privileged to share one of life's great adventures, little was ever exchanged concerning personal life-and-death struggles in a faraway corner of the world.

Many years ago, we fought our own little corner of the war in a most anonymous comportment. Being remote from each other, a majority of us had no idea the trials and dangers faced by others. We were in the same unit. We did the same job, operating in small groups from as many as thirty locations. For the most part, we partnered with just one other man. On some occasions, three of us might be in the same place at the same time. For extended periods, we would find ourselves as the only person of our own cultural experience amid 200 or more souls we didn't have that much in common with. Yes, the foreign troops we supported were our friends. We were well accepted and felt very welcome, and we did form an attachment to them. Our hosts were as cordial as they could be. But living under primitive conditions for protracted periods can be a very lonely existence when there is no one else to hang with who was brought up with similar customs and traditions to relate to. Not until I sat down to write this book did I really find out from personal interviews just what experiences were encountered by my friends.

Most the battles we fought received not the least recognition. In most of the actions where we participated, not more than one or two of us were involved. Not only did the press ignore us, we were also persona non grata in the Marine Corps. Oh, our unit colors received many battle streamers and honors, and many of us were well weighted down with personal decorations. But we were there, and we made a difference well beyond our small number. And only very few souls have any cognizance of the contribution we made.

The Korean Marine Corps' Blue Dragon Brigade points with pride to a 25:1 kill ratio run up at the enemy's expense. Did each Korean Marine personally dispatch twenty-five North Vietnamese soldiers? Or is it possible for one to believe that maybe a few unheralded Marines, having some expertise in controlling air strikes, artillery, and naval gunfire might have exerted some influence on those casualty figures? Well, it happened that way.

Here then is a story born of my heart in a spirit of tribute to a few men not known in history that answered a call and made a difference.

If not one other soul on this earth ever recognizes our contribution, we will always know. A lack of recognition cannot diminish our deeds or our courage. Not being acknowledged for our daring will never make us less than what we are. Our accomplishments will not fade from our memory, nor will our respect for each other ever grow dim with time.

There are some episodes of our experience that really need to be told in order to keep this history moving in context and impart central understanding to our overall experience. Some of the heroes depicted in the accounts herein either could not be contacted for an interview or were lost in combat-related circumstances, thus their perspective of events can never really be known. In those cases, the author has taken the liberty to tell their stories for them in collaboration with those of us who were able to be contacted. Between us, we put together an account of their deeds as best we could, and we apologize to them if our depiction of their daring is not 100 percent correct. I know in my heart they will understand. God bless all of them and their loved ones.

In some instances, the author has taken further liberties to infer mindset and thought processes of key players on the other side. Be it understood, at no time did the author have access to or conduct interviews with Viet Cong or North Vietnamese commanders or members of the units we opposed. Knowing the turn of events after the fact and having had plenty of time to reflect on how our former enemies might have reacted to situations and circumstances described in this work, the author makes an attempt to offer the reader some insight into combat action depicted in this book from the perspective of the opposition.

Research for compiling the historical facets surrounding the activities of Sub Unit One, 1st ANGLICO were gleaned from several U.S. Marine Corps publications produced by the History and Museums Division of Headquarters Marine Corps in Washington, D.C. These documents provided backdrop on overall tactical situations and imparted some understanding of how Sub Unit One fit into general schemes of several large-scale operations from a wider angle view of activities than we, for the most part, had understanding of at the time. More detailed, albeit sketchy and incomplete, narratives provided by Command Chronologies of Sub Unit One, 1st ANGLICO provided some commentary on specific unit involvement, but without personal interviews by participants, a cohesive account of the actions of this unit may not have been possible. By cross referencing Command Chronologies and Marine publications with personal interviews, the author was able to meld the following sources into a valid account of that unit's history:

Marines in Vietnam 1954-1973: An Anthology and Annotated Bibliography, 1974.

U.S. Marines in Vietnam: An Expanding War, by Jack Shulimson, 1982.

U.S. Marines in Vietnam: 1967, Fighting the North Vietnamese, by Major Gary L. Telfer, USMC, Lieutenant Colonel Lane Rogers, USMCV, and V. Keith Fleming, Jr., 1984

U.S. Marines in Vietnam: The Defining Year 1968, by Jack Shulimson, Lieutenant Colonel Leonard A. Blasiol, USMC, Charles R. Smith, and Captain David A. Dawson, USMC, 1997.

U.S. Marines in Vietnam: High Mobility and Stand-Down 1969, by Charles R. Smith, 1988.

U.S. Marines in Vietnam: Vietnamization and Redeployment 1970-1971, by Graham Cosmas and Lieutenant Colonel Terrance P. Murray, USMC, 1986.

U.S. Marines in Vietnam: The War that Would Not End 1971-1973, by Major Charles D. Melson, USMC, and Lieutenant Colonel Curtis G. Arnold, USMC, 1991.

Documenting the history of a unit over the course of eight years requires quite a bit of sleuthing. Extracting combat experiences from participants to gain eyewitness account values of actions depicted in this work really should be amplified with political and tactical posturing to acquire an overall perspective of events.

Because of the very fluid and confused tactical situation surrounding the 1972 Easter Offensive in I Corps, the author relied on several sources to put this episode of the war into perspective for accurately describing activities of Sub Unit One during those tumultuous times.

In the opinion of this author, *The Easter Offensive,* researched and written by Colonel Gerald H. Turley (Presidio Press, 1985), is the primer for recounting events in I Corps from 30 March through 2 May 1972. Every other source referenced for researching the last four chapters of this book employed Colonel Turley's work as a base reference for presenting their own examinations, each with its own unique insight and details.

Vietnam's Forgotten Army (New York University Press, 2007), a well-researched account by Andrew Wiest following the careers of two prominent Army of the Republic of Vietnam (ARVN) officers, provided a unique insight from the view of Vietnamese warriors that is sadly overlooked by many authors and historians.

As very little official documentation centering on ANGLICO's early war record exists, it was necessary to place heavy reliance on personal interviews and my own experience to document the first several chapters of this work. Command Chronologies from May 1965 through December 1967 were found to be incomplete and very scattered, offering only minute scraps of information. Other official

Marine Corps publications and documents placed ANGLICO in the category of "other Marine activities," covering one or two pages in very broad dissertations that more or less grudgingly make a statement almost as an afterthought: "Oh yeah, these guys were there too."

To understand the ANGLICO experience, the mode of operation forced on this unit needs to be explored. In Vietnam, Marines and Naval officers of Sub Unit One were parceled out, primarily to Vietnamese and Korean Armed Forces, but also supplied teams for U.S. Army activities as well. In spite of their small numbers, many ANGLICO detachments were required to provide naval gunfire support services for more than one divisional-size unit. As such, fire control teams of this organization by necessity evolved into a highly mobile force, sending personnel into the field with supported units on short notice. Early on in Vietnam, in order to cover demand for support, innovative commanding officers having never before employed this tactic: sent naval gunfire spotters aloft, flying back seat in mostly unarmed spotter craft. This pioneering initiative allowed spotters the mobility needed to cover large areas of responsibility, while ground spot teams from several central locations, providing support for infantry battalions, remained in the field for the duration of any given combat operation active at the time. When the operation was complete, the teams were often pulled from that unit then reassigned to a different unit taking the field. As an example: The team located at Hue City (June 1968) supported the 1st ARVN Division and the 37th ARVN Ranger Group with only five enlisted Marines and one U.S. Navy Liaison officer. In Quang Ngai at that same time, three enlisted Marines provided gunfire coverage for the entire 2nd ARVN Division. This same general scenario with location-specific variation was generally employed by most detachments, while a few locations were strictly airborne spotter operations. This mobile deployment concept served the Sub Unit well but left one drawback, as this mode of operation was not congruous for bonding with the supported units except at command level.

As there are exceptions to every rule, men working with the Korean Marine Brigade, by contrast, became permanent fixtures with their counterparts at company level eating, sleeping, and dying side by side, forging close personal relationships among Marines in the units they were assigned to.

Enlisted men operating remote from formal command structures more often than not assumed officer-level responsibilities, while junior-grade officers in the same situation on a daily basis dealt with command decisions usually reserved for more senior ranks. To make the point, on several occasions, lance corporals, for instance, found themselves preparing fire control plans and briefing field-grade officers on the use of naval gunfire or tactical air support availability. A small segregated detachment isolated from a central command structure will tend to promote a culture of independence, fostered by an environment of self-reliance. Operating in an atmosphere of self-sufficiency allowed creativity to flow, thus giving rise to one of the most innovative and leadership-rich units to see action in Vietnam.

In order to fully document histories and accomplishments of each detachment, a monumental task demanding two decades of research would surely be required to produce a work thousands of pages in length encompassing several volumes. This work as it is consumed almost nine years (albeit a leisure-time project) to complete, and this is about all I have in me.

It is with deep regret that this work does not contain accounts of all the detachments, as each one contributed in no small way to combat efforts conducted in their areas of operation. As each individual war experience is especially cherished by those who lived it, I am sorry I could not bring personal recognition to each and every detachment of Sub Unit One. If there is a desire harbored by someone else to take up this project, it will be my pleasure to make all my acquired documentation available.

May God bless each and every man, Navy and Marine, who had the honor of serving Sub Unit One.

ACKNOWLEDGMENTS

During my search to find the words for telling this story, I discovered the beginnings of this book started long before sitting down at a computer to sort out events and build a narrative. By now it is probably a worn-out concept that leaving a war zone is an experience in accelerated maturity that one didn't realize was growing while coping with the stress of combat. I believe it is also the beginning of a new war waged in the confines of one's own conscience.

What values one brings to a battlefield, one retains. Even those values that were compromised now return with new understanding of why they were so central to the makeup of a complete being. Now, for possibly the first time, full realization of the importance of those values is completely understood, and for the first time, knowledge of what was lost is lamented.

Waging war with one's own conscience is not a conflict easily resolved when you consider who the enemy is. The battleground where the war of conscience is waged involves those values that were retained versus those that were discarded. If the war then is not won, there will only be one casualty.

It is said we are the sum product of our total experience. If that is true, I'm very glad war was not my only experience.

The first battle over my values was fought by Andrew and Penelope Petri, a couple of kids just finding their own way in the world at that time. Growing up during the Great Depression, when prospects of a cozy future seemed like an unobtainable goal, they managed to reach maturity and dared to dream the dreams of youth. Just when prospects for higher expectations appeared on the horizon, they anted up with their peers of the Greatest Generation, putting their dreams on hold to save the world from Hitler and Tojo.

The perils of childhood can in many ways be as dangerous as a battlefield. They may not kill or cripple, but directions taken in youth can take a man down as fast as a bullet.

I am very grateful for the Catholic education that my mother insisted on. Not only did I receive discipline that would carry me through life, I was also taught the virtue of Christian values that have guided me through this world. I turned my back on my faith for several years, but largely through the love of my mother, my adoration for my daughter, and those brutal nuns that force-fed me an education, I returned.

Andy and Penny guided me through childhood and sent me on life's journey with many of the values they held most dear. Although some of what they tried so hard to thump into my head was lost, I'm sure they don't love me any less.

I must also say a few words about my younger brother, Al, who through it all has always been my best friend. I think we raised each other, almost matching Mom's effort in that endeavor. We had more than our fair share of fights, but always hung together when it counted. The year 1988 was a watershed year for us. We were together at my father's bedside when he passed away in January. We also formed a partnership of two within a core group of less than ten people that staged an event in Cleveland, Ohio, to pay tribute to the heroes of Vietnam, whom the citizens of this country never could bring themselves to properly honor.

Very blessed am I with a beautiful daughter who more or less forced me to walk the straight and narrow. Sheila Denise has been my hero since the day she was born. She also had as much a hand in raising me in my thirties and forties as I did raising her in her childhood. I have no idea what I might have become if she hadn't happened. Watching her grow into a woman is the greatest enterprise I've ever participated in. Seeing her now raising her own child is a source of satisfaction too overwhelming for mere words to adequately address. I am very greatful to my son-in-law, Paul for providing them with a secure environment and providing a base for a safe and prosperous future.

An old proverb states that the friends of youth are among the truest people you will ever know. I have found that it is possible to tell more about a man during one moment of crisis than you will ever find out through a lifetime of peace and tranquility. The incredible guys I was privileged to know and serve with in Vietnam are indeed the truest friends I've ever had. Every one of them would do anything at all for the rest. Not only were they my friends, but they were each other's friend as well. We all took great risks in looking after each other. Several made the supreme sacrifice in seeing to the welfare of their friends. One of us even sacrificed his sanity for a while to do the right thing for a friend in need. They held nothing back.

In St. Augustine, Florida, resides a lady who recognized the writer in me from letters and poetry composed just for her. She encouraged me to write something. This story has been in me for a long time. It took Linda to bring it out.

There are many others who deserve mention for contributions made, assisting me in finding my way through this world. In the interest of not offending some of them through acts of omission, I chose to limit this acknowledgment to those now closest to me. Those persons not acknowledged here know who they are, and I thank them from the bottom of my heart.

Forty years have gone by since the actions described herein actually occurred. Although we still carry fond memories of our gallant allies, many names of the Korean and Vietnamese we served with have long since lapsed from our recollection. Because of distance, language difficulties, and passage of time, some names of prominent Korean participants have been purged or blurred from our memories and regrettably are not within the confines of these pages.

The men of the Blue Dragon Brigade (2nd Brigade, Republic of Korea Marine Brigade) are a true credit to their nation whom the people of Korea have every right to be proud. We who had the privilege of serving with them salute those brave warriors from the land of the morning calm whose steadfast professionalism and courage command our respect and admiration. We will always regard them as brothers

The Marines of South Vietnam as is the case with Marines all over the world were not without honor and courage. These incredible men formed the backbone of South Vietnam's armed forces seeing action in every corner of the war. Had South Vietnam not had a Marine Corps, the country would not have survived as long as it did after U.S. Forces pulled out. In 1975 with their backs to the wall during the final days of the war, these Marines stood and fought with a resolve of unparalleled tenacity; many units fighting to the death of the last man standing. They also have earned our respect and we likewise regard them as brothers

Sadly, I cannot close this exposition without acknowledging those friends whose spirits are never far from us. Most of them never experienced marriage or the joys of raising children. They've never held memberships in country clubs or enjoyed satisfying careers in their fields of choice. Getting together with surviving members of our small band of brothers, one cannot help but notice how the years have transformed once-youthful features to maturity, complemented by too many birthdays. The fallen, however, will always remain young. I remember them at their peak, and I still think of them as indestructible. They too had a hand in shaping my life; they are still my good friends, and always will be.

Throughout the long history of U.S. involvement in Vietnam, jungle fighting and violent firefights carried on by tough-as-nails grunts dominated most publicized events in that faraway war.

Sailors of the U.S. 7th Fleet also played a major role in that struggle. Although not as well exposed or romanticized, naval involvement in Vietnam was far from a minor sideshow. Nearly every day of that war, several ships remained occupied in at least one or more war activities while plying the waters off North and South Vietnam.

Most of us who haven't been there regard sea duty off the coast as a relatively safe experience. Sure. For the surface fleet, a typical tour of duty in the combat zone was measured in weeks or months. As ships require yard time for maintenance in between combat excursions, it isn't possible to remain on station indefinitely. Three meals a day, clean sheets, soft mattresses, and frequent liberty at exotic ports of call isn't exactly a Spartan existence, but safe duty? Hardly. Of 2,555 Navy men who did not survive their tours, just over ten percent, 288, were serving aboard surface vessels off the coast when their young lives came to a tragic end.

Almost on a weekly basis, at least one ship came under fire from North Vietnamese shore batteries, several sustaining hits while exchanging high-explosive ordnance in lethal artillery duels. On more than one occasion, North Vietnamese aircraft did in fact challenge our fleet; one ship was actually bombed. Although none of our ships were lost in these encounters, a determined adversary was not deterred from trying.

Typically, ships assumed assignments of duty on Yankee Station—waters north of the demilitarized zone (DMZ)—providing essential services to fleet activities. Taking position on Positive Identification Radar Advisory Zones, guided missile armed destroyers and cruisers functioned as a buffer between North Vietnamese aircraft and fast carriers of the fleet. Plane guard, interdiction, Search and Rescue (SAR), and escort responsibilities rounded out a normal tour in the Gulf of Tonkin. Gunships on a regular basis moved close to shore, shelling defense installations and other targets of strategic intent.

In October 1966, Operation Sea Dragon was launched, whereby destroyers and cruisers ranged the North Vietnamese littorals, seeking out and destroying barges and sampans heading south with war supplies. These same ships also shelled shore installations such as radar sites, coastal artillery positions, and other military targets of opportunity.

Rotating to and from station in the north, many ships would also assume position on the gunline off the coast of South Vietnam for fire support duty. This was the war contribution that most endeared the Navy to us land-locked grunts.

Throughout this book, a few of the many ships that stood watch on the gunline are spotlighted with an abbreviated history of their Vietnam War activities. A unit of naval gunfire spotters would obviously be useless without gunships to deliver ordnance on observed targets. So, to those gallant crews who were ever-present to answer our endless calls for fire, this is our salute to a group of men who have earned our respect but have not received recognition in proportion to their contribution. It is with deep regret that there is not enough space within the confines of this book to make mention of every ship that manned the gunline. To those crews not mentioned here, please be assured that all of you have our deepest appreciation for a job well done.

GOOD OLE BOYS

Abandoned by retreating tides of untold millennium, coarse black sands of Batangan Peninsula glide beneath an ever- advancing surf from the South China Sea. Clear blue waters frame Batangan with rocky shoals and sandbars, creating daunting hindrances for hand-hewn fishing craft ever present in the cool morning calm.

When transcribed by French map makers, Batangan was erroneously translated from the Vietnamese Ba Lang An, or Three Villages of Peace, as the region was dubbed in times long past. Hamlets of My Lai, Song My, and An Ky, the current population centers, are believed by many to be the original Ba Lang An of old.

Just north of Ba Lang An, Tra Bong River empties its debris-laden cargo into the sea separating Chu Lai from Van Tuong on its south bank. Van Tuong is a swamp-infested neighborhood bordering the peninsula. Several fingers of backwater tributaries sluice away from the river, following natural depressions in the earth, creating clusters of brackish marshland. During the dry season when Tra Bong's outflow is not strong enough to hold back the sea, great quantities of salt water invade these fingers, rendering this land a mixture of mud and salt-laced sand.

Due south of Ba Lang An, Tra Khuc River terminates its endless journey from the mountains, depositing sand and silt into the sea before its muddy waters merge with gentle breakers born of its own outflow.

The realm between the rivers hosts traditional life styles long-established throughout all coastal lowlands of Vietnam. Hundreds of streams and rivulets meander through the area, serving as natural sources of irrigation for rice paddies that dominate the landscape. Occasional acres of high ground, sparsely wooded and lush with tropical flora and fauna, offer numerous oasis of dry land amid oceans of flooded earthwork levies. These islands serve as a refuge when rice paddies occasionally flood, offering safety to stranded farmers. Rice paddies bind the people together and define them as farmers. Rice fields dictate seasonal activities such as planting, irrigating, fertilizing, and harvesting. They provide a source of social interaction and foundation for celebration. It yields the staple that sustains them, as well as presenting opportunity for commerce in times of surplus.

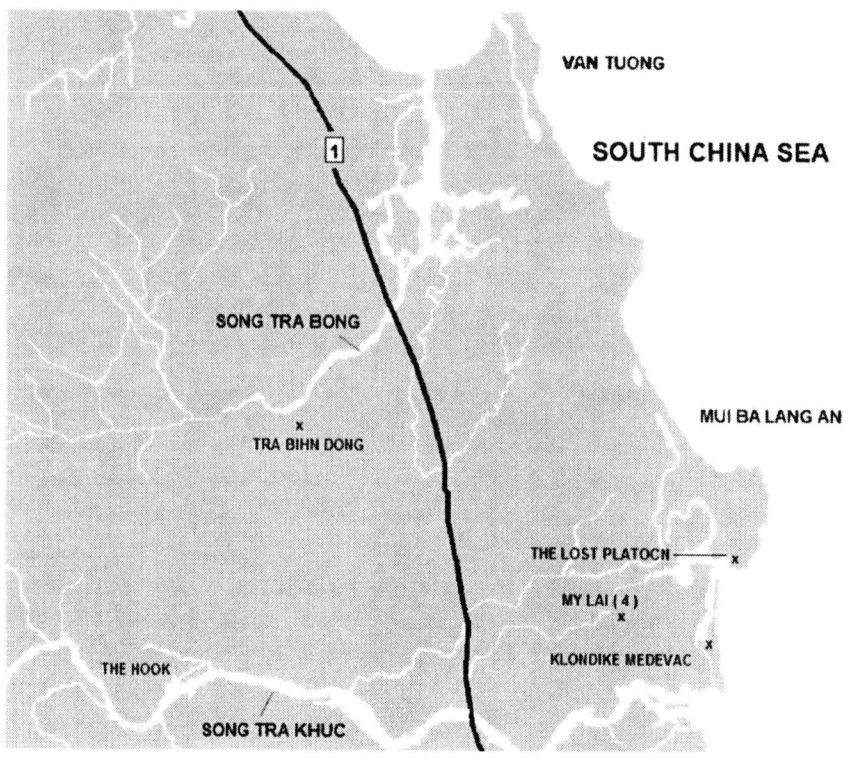

Bihn Son District, Quang Ngai Province

National Highway 1 parallels an unkept railroad line some six miles inland from the coast, winding its way north from Saigon to Hanoi. A mile or so west of the highway, rice fields take on irregular boundaries acquiescing to tropical woodlands and elevated topography. The lowlands also give way to foothills, gradually at first, then sharply rising to well over 8,000 feet the next seventy miles.

Mountains of the Anamite Range present a panoramic backdrop of primitive splendor. Magnificent cloud-clustered crests pierce the sky and spill over the border into Laos and Cambodia. Long rolling valleys rich in tropical vegetation represent the only practical avenues of navigation through these jungle-choked heights.

About 30,000 people live between the highway and the sea, on the land bound by two rivers. All in all, it is home to about fifteen percent of the rural population of Quang Ngai Province.

Life in that small coastal region changed very little over the past 2,000 years. Among the peasants that toil in the fields and fishermen who dwell in coastal settlements are found very few souls without deeply established ancestry on the land they call home.

Aside from knives, bicycles, and cooking pots, few metallic objects exist in this Stone Age economy. Everything needed to coax a living from the soil is fashioned by hand from wood, stone, or clay.

People age fast and die young in this economy by the sea. They marry early and never retire. Very few holidays are expected from the drudgery of their mundane labor. Young couples bring forth as many field hands as possible during childbearing years. Mortality rates are high among the children; a significant number of newborns never reach puberty. Malaria, infection, gangrene, and a legion of other maladies constantly stalk the young, the weak, and the careless.

Cognizance of the world around them is learned by experience and from primitive but practical wisdom passed on from ancestor to ancestor to the current heirs of the tillage. Art, philosophy, and literature have little time to compete with the curriculum of survival.

Genealogy of this people is lost in a confused chronology of Chinese, Cham, and Malaysian migrations up and down the coast of Indo-China. They have been conquered, reconquered, subjugated, and colonized to the nth since outside civilizations became aware of their existence. The peasants who live on the plain have been kidnapped, murdered, raped, looted, and taxed by every officialdom and pirate who had the strength to do so. Yet still they continue… little influenced, little changed by the cultural eccentricities of the processions of incumbencies who have sought dominion over this land. Like the biblical Jews, these are also a rebellious people; proud and defiant in the face of any "-ism" that deemed itself master of this land. A strong sense of culture bound them as a society embedded in tradition.

After Viet-Minh forces ended French colonial rule in 1954, a shifting of people from North to South and the traverse occurred in order to accommodate individual political preferences. Official estimates of Emperor Boa Daih fixed the number of South Viets who moved North at approximately 100,000. About sixty-five percent of those migrants pushed north from Quang Ngai Province.

Revolution against French rule took root in the early 1930s. Viet Minh from Quang Ngai were counted among the leaders of this uprising as young men local to this area flocked to champion the cause of nationalism. This locale also played a major role in efforts right after World War II that eventually brought the French to their knees. During the French Indo-China War, the area in and around this province was known as Inter Zone V and dealt more than one humiliating blow to the European power.

After a hard-won victory over France, Ho Chi Minh went about the business of exterminating his former allies, the nationalists. The Vietnam Doc-Lac-Dong-Minh (Viet Minh) was made over into the Vietnam Cong San (Viet Cong) in order to legitimize Ho Chi Minh's transformation from nationalist to communist.

Campaigns of terror were unleashed in the south aimed primarily at the regime of President Diem. The strategy was not to engage Diem's army but rather to discourage Southerners from participating in his government. Anyone having official status in the countryside was encouraged to resign or swift execution would follow.

Owing to deep-rooted sympathy the people held for Ho Chi Minh, the Viet Cong were entrenched in Quang Ngai right from their inception as a popular political and military force.

The area resisted all attempts by the South Vietnamese government at pacification. Strategic hamlet programs, for instance, initiated in 1962 to provide protection for rural populations, were an utter disaster in Quang Ngai, never gaining much of a foothold and never really achieved much in the way of popularity.

Western war managers divided Vietnam into four military tactical zones. Five northernmost provinces were designated as I Corps. Quang Ngai among this grouping was thus militarily categorized into a wartime subdivision.

By 1963, the Viet Cong boasted in-country strength of 25,000 hard-core guerillas and 80,000 regional and village militiamen. In that same year, Viet Cong were strong enough to ambush two battalions of government troops in Quang Ngai, inflicting over 300 casualties while suffering little damage of their own. This incident established the 1st Viet Cong Regiment as the dominant military power in the area. Early in 1965, they were reinforced by elements of the North Vietnamese 36th Regiment (36th was not at full manning levels in the South until 1966). At that time, the strength of the Viet Cong was estimated at 200,000, with fully one third operating in I Corps.

The 1st Viet Cong Regiment established its headquarters close to the coastline on Ba Lang An. It was a three-tier underground facility with a labyrinth of connecting tunnels. To ensure security, the vaunted 48th main force battalion garrisoned and protected that complex. From here, Charlie (the Viet Cong) held the land between the two rivers and governed the people of the lowland, who in turn were obliged to pay taxes in the form of rice, fish, and a supply of young men to fill the ranks of the regiment.

North Vietnam's 36th Regiment operated in Southern Quang Ngai and Northern Bihn Din Province while the North Vietnamese Army (NVA) 21st Regiment set up shop between the mountains and Highway 1 just north of Tra Khuc River.

Forces of the Republic of South Vietnam also competed for sovereignty over the people of the plain, but lacked sufficient manpower and strong leadership. Corruption and incompetence did very little to impress the locals of the government's commitment to their well-being.

Viet Cong, on the other hand, were a well-acknowledged part of mainstream life on the peninsula, living among the inhabitants, as most were native born to the locality of the regiment's area of responsibility.

In addition to taking care of the regiment, Charlie looked after the needs of Northern troops operating due west of Ba Lang An.

Sampans from North Vietnam regularly called on the fishing villages of Song My and My Lai (1) with weaponry, ammunition, and an assortment of supplies needed to support combat operations. Charlie established several overland routs and made extensive use of the rivers to channel the imports to his Northern cousins.

Arrayed against the forces of Ho Chi Minh in I Corps were two divisions of government troops, consisting of 20,000 ill-equipped regulars as well as undermanned and undertrained local and regional militia numbering less than 25,000. Owing to total lack of mobility, these troops were primarily garrisoned in large cities and provincial capitals, taking on defensive postures, rarely going on offense. This defensive nature of government strategy left the communists free to further consolidate power in the countryside.

Reports of Viet Cong activities were not lost on the 1st Marine division newly arrived in Chu Lai just north of Tra Bong River. Reliable information had pegged 2,000 men as the strength of the 1st Viet Cong Regiment, who with a sophisticated political infrastructure was boldly enforcing the will of Ho Chi Minh throughout the lowlands. Further intelligence obtained in late summer indicated an assault on Chu Lai base camp; the probable target was the airstrip within its perimeter. Marine patrols ferreted out prepared positions from where the attack would launch, and the cat was now out of the bag.

Operation Starlight was launched on 18 August 1965. It was a converging maneuver, closing in on Van Tuong from three sides. Tra Bong River was forded using LVTPs opposing Charlie from the North, while an air assault landed troops to the west. A battalion landing team of 3rd Battalion, 7th Marines (3/7) made an amphibious assault on the southeastern beaches of Van Tuong to complete the maneuver scheme. When the battle ended 24 August, the 1st Viet Cong regiment had been badly mauled, sustaining 964 dead.

Survivors of the regiment limped back to Ba Lang An only to face the Marines again on September 7th in Operation Piranha. Charlie took it on the nose once more, surrendering 249 more men to the hungry guns of the 7th Marines.

Still, the government of Vietnam was content to concede control of the area to the insurgent faction, making no attempt to garrison troops of any consequence on the land between the rivers. Sporadic small units of popular forces (local militia men) occupied positions either side of the highway, but made no serious effort to challenge Viet Cong or North Vietnamese troops.

Through the remaining winter and into spring of 1966, a series of sweeps west of Highway 1 were conducted by South Vietnamese Army troops and U.S. Marines.

Operation Utah resulted from information received by the 2nd ARVN Division from North Vietnamese Army prisoners taken near the village of Chau Nhai, not far from the abandoned rail line.

South Vietnam's 1st Airborne was helo-lifted into position on March 3rd. 2nd Battalion 7th Marines followed in midmorning, taking positions on the right flank. Just before noon, 3rd Battalion 1st Marines landed a few kilometers north. A regiment of the 2nd ARVN Division committed two additional maneuver battalions to complete the encirclement. Most of the action was over before dark on the 6th; leaving the roster of the 21st NVA Regiment reduced by 586 able-bodied men.

Still persistent to show the Western powers they were not just going to fade away, a battalion of the 1st Viet Cong regiment attacked a regional forces outpost at An Hoa late on the night of March 19th. The outpost, dug out of the top of hill 143 just 1,000 meters south of Tra Bong River, near the base of the Anamites, resisted fiercely and held its antagonists outside the wire all night. Early morning brought 3/7, Charlie's old nemesis from the previous summer, along with the 5th ARVN Airborne to within a kilometer of An Hoa. 2nd Battalion, 4th Marines took position some seven miles northwest, effectively trapping Charlie between the mountains and river. In four days of intense fighting, the ranks of the Viet Cong were trimmed by an additional 405 troops.

Except for large-scale operations of the Marines and ARVN troops, Charlie did enjoy some measure of success. The VC had few problems politically, extended their sphere of influence, bringing more Vietnamese under their control. Smaller units of the regiment ambushed RF and PF troops at will. The government suffered at least two attacks per week on outposts straddling Highway 1. This tactic effectively restricted troop movement off the base camps, limiting patrols to just a few hundred meters beyond the perimeter.

Lack of control over the status of the Viet Cong had become intolerable. It was very evident that that the local population in the surrounding area was filling the ranks of the 1st Viet Cong regiment, as replacements were needed. Each time the regiment went on offense it always had the numbers to do so in spite of the large toll of casualties suffered in the few successful government campaigns.

The 2nd ARVN Division was operating out of Quang Ngai City, but it did not have sufficient manpower to hold down garrisons and present a permanent government presence in the countryside. Quang Ngai is one of the least-populated provinces in Vietnam; therefore, placing very low on the priority list.

Not so with the Viet Cong, who was an established entity of mainstream life in the villages. Most of the people accepted him. In reality, the greater portion of the population supported and aided his cause. So as not to create any misunderstandings, the people of Quang Nhai Province not only supported the Viet Cong, they were, in fact, the Viet Cong.

Strategic necessity demanded a strong resident military presence in the area to maintain continuous contact and establish a visible component of government authority.

Arrival of Korean Marines in August 1966 kicked off a new era in the long history of local conflict The 1st Viet Cong Regiment could now expect a much more aggressive adversary. An unfamiliar power would now be in search of his base camps, supply lines, and storage depots. A relentless military machine had come to hunt the 1st Viet Cong Regiment.

The sons of *Dae Hon Mihn Guk* were novices in these latitudes but, so eager to learn, and equally as determined to dominate the land between the rivers.

USS Henry B. Wilson
(DDG-7)
Charles F. Adams Class Guided Missile Armed Destroyer
Call Sign: Black Velvet

USS *Henry B. Wilson*, then one of the new Adams Class guided missile armed destroyers, carried a variety of weapons and sensors, giving her ample capability to effectively deal with threats on high seas. Her powerful sonar, Anti Submarine Rocket (ASROC), and torpedo installations equipped her to fight submarines at extended ranges. Her supersonic guided missiles had the capability of destroying aircraft and warships many miles away. This tough customer was also equipped with five-inch/54 rapid-fire guns, having a twenty-round-per-minute nominal rate of fire with a range of thirteen miles, providing the ship with flexibility needed to engage surface, air, and shore threats, making her a formidable fire support platform. USS *Henry B. Wilson* had a 1200 PSI engineering plant, which produced 70,000 shaft horsepower to drive the ship at sustained speeds of over 30 knots. Each of her four boilers was equipped with a completely automatic combustion control system.

At 0934, Saturday 6 January 1962, she became the first DDG to make a Western Pacific (WestPac) cruise. USS *Henry B. Wilson* enhanced her reputation, proving the value of DDG-2 class ships during the subsequent six-month tour. She conducted fleet antisubmarine warfare (ASW) and antiair warfare exercises and performed plane guard, lifeguard, as well as Search and Rescue

(SAR) missions, conclusively demonstrating her value to the fleet in a most convincing manner.

Since her commissioning in December 1960, USS *Henry B. Wilson* has participated in twelve cruises to the Western Pacific. She fired over 50,000 rounds in several hundred fire missions against North Vietnamese and Viet Cong targets from 1965 to 1973.

USS *Henry B. Wilson* was back on the gunline in July 1972, providing devastating gunfire support in Quang Tri Province for offensive operations to retake fallen territory from the North Vietnamese. From 22 August through 2 September, in support of Vietnamese Marines, her accurate fires destroyed or damaged forty-four enemy structures, causing nine secondary explosions and an undocumented number of North Vietnamese casualties during the final chapter of VNMC's epic assault on Quang Tri City.

Once the battle for Quang Tri settled down, she steamed to southern Military Region 1 (MR1), firing in support of the 2nd ARVN Division in Quang Ngai Province, taking a terrible toll on communist forces. From 3-15 October and again from 25-30 October, her accurate fires in support of combat operations destroyed eighty-one enemy bunkers and structures while damaging an additional ninety-six. Her devastating fires caused an incredible eighty-one secondary explosions, resulting in twelve confirmed enemy KIAs and twenty more estimated communist fatalities. It was a great comfort to still have her on the gunline at the turn of the year, firing in support of offensive operations.

While on a 1975 cruise to the Western Pacific, the ship participated in the Cambodian and Vietnam evacuations and in the recovery of the USS *Mayaguez* from Cambodia. As a result of her ability to perform under pressure, USS *Henry B. Wilson* was awarded the Combat Action Ribbon, Navy Unit Commendation, Meritorious Unit Commendation, Navy "E", National Defense Service Medal, Armed Forces Expeditionary Medal, Vietnam Service Medal, Humanitarian Service Medal, and the Vietnam Campaign Medal.

We, who once found refuge under the protection of her guns, salute this valiant ship and her gallant crew.

BLUE DRAGONS

By any interpretation of the definition, third-party nationals equipped and financed by one foreign power to fight on the soil of a sovereign nation, having no common cultural affinity to either, can only be viewed as "mercenaries." All allied affiliations considered.

Under such an arrangement, the 2nd Brigade (Blue Dragon Brigade) Republic of Korea (ROK) Marine Corps presented itself for combat in Vietnam.

From homeport of Pusan, South Korea, the Blue Dragons embarked for combat duty with its brother Marines from America.

Trained and equipped by the United States in years following the Korean War, Blue Dragons were as disciplined, skilled, and professional as any military in the world. A seasoned core of combat-hardened veterans from a war that raged fiercely on their own native soil established an experienced cadre of leadership who knew well their chosen profession.

Little more than a decade earlier, the Korean people had fallen victim to an attempted communist takeover of their own homeland. During a short-lived occupation by North Korea, people of the South endured extremely harsh treatment by would-be conquerors. Events of recent history still burned in their hearts and haunted their dreams. They were mostly all children at the time, but scarcely a man was left untouched by personal tragedy as could only be forged in a crucible of terror. Many were orphaned, and all shared a thirst to settle a score that only those who drink deep from the same cup of dread can truly understand. Sadly, for many, it was the defining experience of childhood. It's not difficult to understand how quite a few of them grew up too fast and were forced to carry a burden that couldn't be hauled without help. They drew strength from each other, these Blue Dragons, and were always willing to lend a hand with each other's burden. In the true spirit of the phrase, these were a band of brothers, each dedicated to the welfare of his companions.

These were men of honor who said what they meant and meant what they said. Good times with good friends and a little *maek-ju* (beer) always brought just the right end to any kind of day.

They were a microcosm of their countrymen and very proud of self-directed accomplishments that propelled South Korea from third-world status to an emerging economic power in less than fifteen years. We perceived a lot of us in the men from *Dae Hahn Min Guk*. Young men mostly, just out of school, embarking on life's journey that started in service to their country, all now gathered together on the field of honor. The pride of 30 million people making its debut on the international stage, attempting to show the world that South Korea was now ready to assume a place in the governance of global affairs. Prior to service, some were students, while others dragged themselves from one job to another trying to find a vocation that suited them. A few signed on looking for adventure. Moreover, some found a home in *Haebyong Dae* (the Marine Corps) and would someday lead the Blue Dragons as tempered veterans.

All Marines of the Blue Dragon Brigade volunteered for duty in Vietnam. The officer Corps viewed combat assignments as opportunity for career enhancement. They were professionals who understood that combat situations and the business of war is the only reason for being on the payroll. Those with experience are more valuable assets than those without. Considering the fluid situation on their North border, combat experience was deemed a quality of immense value. Posted on a sand-bagged wall at Khe Sanh, a handmade poster by an unknown author proclaimed, "For those who fought for it, freedom has a flavor the protected will never know." That flavor was still fresh on their palettes, as the Korean people just a few years removed gained first-hand experience with the alternative. The instinct to remain free is credited with helping engineer the economic and social triumphs of the recent past. Almost the entire Korean Marine Corps was on the waiting list for posting to Chung Yong Bodae.

Republic of Korea Marines arrived in Vietnam in September of 1965, then redeployed to Quang Ngai Province in August 1966. Combat operations commenced almost immediately.

A society that lives in such close proximity to a culture totally dedicated to its demise must by necessity accentuate the virtues of discipline and preparedness.

Discipline as established in the ROK Marine Corps might have fomented grounds for mass desertion in the armies of ancient Sparta. There were no wimps in this outfit.

Early one morning, the author observed a personnel inspection. As the company commander was examining a weapon, he suddenly turned to his platoon leader. He was noticeably very irate. Shoving the rifle in the face of his junior officer, screaming at the top of his voice, he pointed to a spot on the receiver, slapped the lieutenant in the face, pointed back to the rifle, and slapped him again. After thrusting the rifle into the officer's chest, he stormed away from the platoon at a brisk pace, still screaming as strong as his lung capacity would permit. The lieutenant stared at his commander's back just seething, trying to think of how he was going rescue himself from this embarrassment. Being dressed down in front of the troops was an affront to his honor and damaged his personal pride.

Once the captain cleared formation, a squad leader ran up to the lieutenant, snapped to attention, and waited for what he knew would not be a pleasant experience. Bringing his face within inches of the NCO, the rifle was raised up between them to eye level. Not a word was spoken as the officer pointed to the rifle and waited for response. Both men remained motionless, staring at the tell-tale aberration several minutes. Just as the sergeant opened his mouth to suggest an explanation, the lieutenant tossed the weapon into the air high above the NCO's head. As the sergeant extended his arms to catch it, a hard right fist was driven forcefully into his gut. Without flinching, the rifle was caught and smartly maneuvered to port arms position in a single movement. The staring contest resumed until the officer walked away.

Dropping his right foot back one pace, rising one inch on the balls of his feet, the sergeant executed a perfect about-face pivot. Snapping his left foot forward, the maneuver was completed, bringing both heels together with a distinct click. He was now face to face with the poor slob who owned the weapon still held at port arms.

In all this time, the rest of the platoon remained standing at rigid attention. Every eyeball in formation strained hard for a side-glance look at the drama unfolding to his left or right.

Once again, the ritual of reviewing the offending discrepancy was played out, this time with a lot more animation, as the private was beaten to the ground. For a while, it looked as though the poor grunt would have that rifle shoved up his ass. This is but one example of a form of special discipline referred to by its slang expression, *Kkolabaga* which defies translation. It's just one of those words found in any given language whose meaning is understood rather than defined.

This is how business was conducted in *Haebyong Dae*. Paying homage to the proposition that shit rolls down hill, a cult of payback was developed and institutionalized into a reinforcing structure of hard discipline. Not even staff officers were immune from this rigorous code of ethics that drifted down through the ranks, solidifying the chain of command. Every Marine knew what was expected of him and carried out orders without question or reservation. It bound them together in an unbendable team void of weak links.

In the beginning, the ROKs interacted with the local population like big brothers who stopped by the playground to chase away bullies. But soon, that attitude turned to scorn as reality of the disposition and conspicuous political allegiance of these people became obvious.

Blue Dragons quickly developed a reputation among allied troops as being hard-nosed. The battle for the hearts and minds of men soon held little application for the Korean concept of pacification.

To this day, they still deal with a communist persistence to subjugate their own homeland, and the ROKs knew only too well the true nature of the prey they hunted in Vietnam. Men of the ROK Marine Corps were not nearly as motivated to offer protection to villagers who didn't appreciate the security the brigade represented, as they were immersed in an all-consuming suspicion of anything communist. They were very familiar with the jaundiced view of the world as preached by those who worship at the altar of Mao Tse Dong. There were no illusions concerning the ultimate aspirations being pursued by North Vietnam, nor were there any reservations regarding the job needing to be done. The utter insanity of these peasants inflicting communism on their own countrymen was very difficult to comprehend. If the people of Quang Ngai Province would not be disposed to help them root out Viet Cong, they would do well to just stay out of the way.

A brigade is about the size of an infantry regiment, consisting of three maneuver battalions and one supporting artillery battalion, forming a core structure of South Korea's best knock-out punch, which is a mirror image of a U.S. Marine infantry regiment. The Koreans, however, did not appoint their line companies alphabetically, as in the tradition of American regiments, but gave them numerical designations instead. The 1st, 2nd, and 3rd Companies fell under command of the 1st Battalion. 5th, 6th, and 7th Companies operated out of the 2nd Battalion, while the 9th, 10th, and 11th Companies were attached to the 3rd Battalion. The Korean word for the number 4 is *sa*. As the Chinese language is to most Asian dialects as Latin is to Western tongues, "sa" in Chinese means "death." As such, no unit in the Korean Armed Forces contains the numeral 4.

The Blue Dragon Brigade was strictly an affair for grunts, lacking even the most basic air assets. Not only were armored vehicles nonexistent, but also at that time Korean forces were still armed with World War II vintage M-1 rifles as the mainstay infantry issue. Considered by many to be the most accurate and reliable shoulder weapons ever developed, it was no match for the firepower of Soviet-made AK-47s. Plans were under way to refit the brigade with M-16s, but that was some months off. A lack in modern armaments was more than compensated for by training and discipline. Doing anything the hard way never became an obstacle or an excuse for failure.

Additionally, a reinforced motor transport company and logistics support group was attached to brigade, as well as extra infantry personnel for internal security. Other units as needed were assigned as support troops for special assignment. This was a showpiece operation for the Korean Marine Corps as well as a testing ground. Within reason, Brigade Commander General Lee Byong Chul could have anything he needed to insure success.

Korean Marines had never been in combat outside their own borders before. Vietnam would be much more than just a thermometer for evaluating training and preparedness. This is a political statement for their cousins across the border who had been swallowed up in the Iron Curtain. Demonstrating how South Korea was now militarily strong enough to send troops abroad was a message aimed at the leadership of North Korea. This was much more than just a propaganda crusade or a demonstration of strength. It was a deliberate in your face, rub your nose in shit type maneuver to let the North know, in no uncertain terms, that killing communist lowlife's anywhere on the planet is now our national past time.

They were loaded for bear and eager for the hunt.

Under an arrangement with the U.S. Marine Corps, air assets would be provided to the brigade and assigned the same priority for available aircraft as are American units. A team of experts would be assigned and charged with the mission of keeping an air umbrella over the Blue Dragon Brigade in and out of the field.

USS Berkeley
(DDG-15)
Charles F. Adams Class Guided Missile Armed Destroyer
Call Sign: Bright Penny

In March 1964, USS *Berkeley* made her first deployment to the Western Pacific as an operational unit of the U.S. Seventh Fleet. She was awarded the Navy Unit Commendation for the role she played in the Tonkin Gulf PT boat incident, the first attack on a U.S. warship operating in the gulf, which made her the first guided missile destroyer to be awarded this commendation.

During her second deployment in 1966, USS *Berkeley* participated in a SAR mission involving an F-G4 and an HU-16 Albatross in the gulf between Hon Me Island and the North Vietnam coast. During the rescue effort, USS *Berkeley* silenced enemy shore batteries with accurate counter battery fire.

The period of 1967 to 1970 proved to be very busy years for USS *Berkeley*, as she was repeatedly called to action in Vietnam, participating in numerous Naval gunfire support missions.

USS *Berkeley*'s last deployment to the Western Pacific during the Vietnam era began with just seventy-two hours' notice in April 1972. During this cruise, she was directly involved in the mining of Haiphong Harbor, providing a protective barrage of fire while carrier-based aircraft covered the harbor with mines. Remaining under enemy fire from shore gun emplacements for over a half hour, USS *Berkeley* delivered over 280 five-inch rounds before clearing the harbor at 32 knots. USS *Berkeley* became a fixture on the gunline, responding to calls for fire around the clock for stressed ground units fighting off

North Vietnam's Easter Offensive. For the entire deployment, she expended over 11,000 rounds of five-inch ammunition.

We, who once found refuge under the protection of her guns, salute this valiant ship and her gallant crew.

SUPER GRUNTS

Looking windward from atop the Koolau Mountains, Kaneohe Bay, silhouetted against the blue Pacific, offers scenic expression to a classic statement of paradise. Anchoring the Makapu Peninsula just twelve miles across the mountains from Honolulu, Marine Corps Air Station Kaneohe Bay is upscale by comparison to other stations of the Corps. It's considered good duty among Marines fortunate enough to draw posting to the facility. No one could argue with the great liberty and diverse activities available. It was a terrific place to live and a very inexpensive way to experience all Hawaii had to offer.

Several turns past the main gate, nestled in the far west corner of the base, three isolated barracks and a headquarters building house the 1st Air Naval Gunfire Liaison Company, a furtive organization whose existence is not commonly known, even among most Marines. ANGLICO was not nor was ever meant to be a secretive institution, but the nature of its tactical posture does not promote contact with other Marine combat units. In fact, throughout its sixty-plus-year history, ANGLICO is effectively unknown to the American public.

Tracing its proud lineage back to the bloody island-hopping campaigns of World War II, the unit experienced its first trial by fire while executing its assigned mission of directing infantry-based close air and naval gunfire in support of U.S. Marine and Army Divisions conducting amphibious operations in the Pacific. Designated as

Joint Assault Signal Company (JASCO), these Marines directed and controlled the first modern use of close air in support of infantry. They landed, fought, died, and bled on Iwo Jima, Okinawa, Tarawa, and Saipan, participating in most of the island fights. Their story has never been told. As support troops, their exploits took back seat to those magnificent trigger pullers who overran the Pacific, stacking up one victory after another. The war would have still been won without JASCO, but at what additional cost?

The organization was dissolved at the end of WWII as providing these services to the U.S. Army was no longer required. War on the Korean Peninsula precipitated reactivation in 1951 as 1st ANGLICO. Their organizational assignments were extended during the Korean conflict to provide support for participating allied units as well. A new era of engagement began as the unit gained hard-won experience working with Royal Marine Commandos, South Korean armed forces, and most other allied troops serving in theater. New chapters in the history of close air support were written as jets and helicopters first appeared in combat over the skies of Korea. More lessons were learned and experience was gained, which laid groundwork for more efficient use of close air support. With each subsequent conflict, knowledge was gained that would be passed on to successive changes of the guard, who would in turn put this information to use and take it to the next level. Geographically, Korea, being a peninsula, also allowed naval gunfire spot teams ample opportunity to direct ordnance on enemy positions. In each combat situation where the unit was deployed, it evolved a little further into the entity it is today, shouldering a larger role each subsequent time it took the field.

Between Korea and Vietnam, mission roles and training regimens were expanded to allow for potential involvement in support of more elite U.S. Army and allied units in non-amphibious circumstance.

Field radio operators and naval gunfire spotters composed the military occupational specialties of the tactical membership of this unit. Both professions were cross-trained in each competence, and each in turn were further qualified as infantry-based Tactical Air Controllers (TACs). An airborne-capable platoon was established, which mandated many ANGLICOs attend jump school and undertake other specialty training in the event they were called to enter combat by unconventional means. Not knowing who they may be called on to support, training was pushed to the level of the most elite units in the free world. The 1st ANGLICO was as highly trained and motivated a group of professionals as existed in the Marine Corps. They were prepared and ready to accompany any U.S. Army or allied element into harm's way anywhere on the globe.

Officers assigned to ANGLICO came from the air wing. All were experienced pilots charged with providing leadership and training for an organization with a very familiar mission assignment. Having officers qualified to fly helicopters, attack and fighter jets, and cargo and transport planes promoted comprehension of aircraft capabilities, ordnance, and tactics. Pilots were a natural selection for the job at hand and served the unit's tactical requirements as Air Liaison Officers (ALOs).

From mighty warships of the U.S. Navy, gunnery officers also drew posting to ANGLICO, applying their knowledge and experience to train enlisted Marines in the finer points of naval gunfire application and control, as well as taking active roles and command responsibilities in the field as Naval Gunfire Liaison Officers (NGLOs).

Several differences exist between land-based artillery and the big guns of the Navy. The primary distinction between the two concerned the fact that naval gunnery was adapted, not designed, for shore bombardment. These are rifles with flat trajectory designed for engagement in ship-to-ship combat, as opposed to higher angle field pieces. Elevated ground, for instance between ship and target, would require altering trajectory angles as would targets on reverse slopes of hills. A condition known as "danger close" would alert shipboard batteries that naval gunfire was being employed closer than 600 meters to friendly troops due to this flat trajectory having a larger range of probable error with long or short rounds. When navigating rough seas, it isn't always possible to keep guns oriented at the same elevation calculated for fire solution data. Gun mounts obviously will roll and sway with the ship, causing a round or two to go astray on occasion.

In spite of the differences, naval guns are fairly well automated and can deliver more rounds on target over a sustained period. They travel at faster velocity than ordnance fired from field pieces, conveying more devastating impact, thus bringing more destruction to bear on target. Shells from these guns don't just fall on target;

they slam right into it...and hard. Having personally witnessed the USS *New Jersey* in action, the author can honestly state with no uncertainty, outside of missiles and high-capacity bombs, there is no comparison to demolition caused by a sixteen-inch gun.

Throughout the Vietnam War, rapid fire five-inch/54 caliber and five-inch/38 caliber guns of U.S. destroyers responded to the majority of calls for fire in support of ground troops. These weapon systems boasted a sustained rate of fire of twenty and fifteen rounds per minute, respectively, and were capable of putting ordnance on target up to thirteen miles away.

The U.S. Navy employs a variety of ships that are very capable and well suited for shore bombardment. In Vietnam, most ships on the gunline offshore fell into the following categories:

Light cruiser (designated as CL; if armed with missiles, CG or CLG).

Light cruisers in the Vietnam area were used primarily on naval gunfire support, Operation Sea Dragon, and in support of amphibious landings. They carry eight- or six-inch guns with a range of sixteen miles and five-inch guns with a range of thirteen miles. In addition, these ships are equipped with surface-to-air missiles (SAMs).

Guided missile destroyer (designated as DDG)

Guided missile destroyers are among the most versatile ships in the Navy and were employed for many jobs in the Tonkin Gulf and South China Sea. In addition to surface-to-air missiles, they carry rapid-fire five-inch/54 caliber guns and excellent sonar systems, and were used extensively for naval gunfire support, Operation Sea Dragon, carrier operations, and antisubmarine patrols. Ships of the Adams class were the most sophisticated destroyers of the time.

Destroyer (designated as DD)

Destroyers of World War II vintage in the Vietnam area, all of which received extensive rehabilitation and modernization, were well suited for a wide variety of operations. Their five-inch/38 and five-inch/54 guns are used daily on Operation Sea Dragon and naval gunfire support, while their speed and maneuverability are used to advantage on Search and Rescue duty and carrier operations. These ships were the backbone of the destroyer force of that era.

Destroyers of the Forrest Sherman and Farragut classes at that time were the newest destroyers in the Navy and are similar to the guided missile destroyers in hull design, gunnery, and sonar. They were utilized extensively for Operation Sea Dragon and naval gunfire support because of their capable five-inch guns.

Note: Naval guns are designated by the diameter of the bore or caliber and by the length of its barrel in multiples of its bore. Therefore, a five-inch/38 caliber, for instance, fires a five-inch-diameter round from a gun having a (5x38) 190-inch-long barrel. Five-inch/38s were the mainstay of World War II Naval gunnery and were the finest seagoing artillery pieces of their time.

Shortly after midnight on 16 July 1927, thirty-eight Marines and forty-seven Nicaraguan *Guardias* under their command became trapped, sustaining repeated attacks by a force of 800 Sandinista rebels in the small mountain village of Ocotal. Sandino himself was reported to have been in command of the operation. Sandinistas assaulted the small provincial capital throughout the night and well into late morning, giving the defenders all they could handle. Substantially outnumbered, Captain Gilbert D. Hatfield ordered emergency signal panels deployed at daybreak. A daily patrol of two Marine planes led by Lieutenant Hayne D. Boyden spotted the panels displayed in the courtyard. Boyden reported the development upon returning to the airstrip in Managua; a mixed flight of five DH4B and O2B-1 biplanes, armed with machine guns and four twenty-five-pound contact bombs each, took off to support the garrison.

Major Ross Rowell arrived over Ocotal in midafternoon and made one pass over the town for orientation and to gain perspective on friendly positions and potential targets. From 1,500 feet, Marine war birds lined up and dove on enemy troops exposed in the streets. As each aircraft pulled out of its strafing run, the rear-seat observer delivered a parting shot group with his swivel-mounted Lewis machine gun. A second pass at lower altitude sent the attacking force running from town. With the fleeing rebels now exposed in the open, Marine pilots exacted a heavy toll on them. All told, the air attack lasted about forty-five minutes and wrote the first chapter in the long history of Marine close air support. Rebel casualties from the action were never fully documented, but estimates of up to 300 were claimed by Marines in Ocotal.

Early the following year, Marines and *Guardias* on patrol sustained a large number of casualties in a well-laid ambush. Over the next few days, the Marines and insurgents exchanged gunfire in several running skirmishes. Lieutenant Christian F. Schilt made repeated landings in the streets of Quilali, Nicaragua. Flying a Vought 02U-1 Corsair, Schilt brought in needed supplies and hauled out wounded while under fire, marking the first aerial resupply and medical evacuation in support of combat infantry. For his actions at Quilali, Lieutenant Schilt received the Medal of Honor.

The Ocotal and Quilali episodes propelled combined arms action from theory to application. It was not the last time this tactic would be employed in Nicaragua, allowing air/ground coordination to take root in the jungles of Central America.

Well established as the premier air/ground team, the Marines pioneered close air support during low-intensity conflicts of the Central American "Banana Wars" in the 1920s. Doctrine and tactics developed just prior to World War II were elevated to a science in Korea. With the emergence of U.S. combat troops in Vietnam, no other power on the planet possessed the combat experience and know-how of air/ground effectiveness anywhere near resembling the United States Marine Corps.

Watching made-in-Hollywood versions of war, one comes away with the notion that once a decision is made to employ close air support, the planes arrive on station immediately and just start bombing. Pilots always appear to instinctively know exactly what to bomb without one word of briefing from anyone on the ground. Right from the first bomb and every bomb thereafter, each sortie is a perfect bull's eye. If only it were so.

The basic technique for bringing airborne ordnance on target is a very involved and serious business. A Tactical Air Controller (TAC), by virtue of the destructive power he brings to bear in any given battle, holds the key to life and death for many on both sides. As in any war, but particularly germane to Vietnam, the TAC needed to be certain beyond any doubt that supporting aircraft completely understand where the target is located, and just as important, know the positions of friendly troops, their formation, and distance from the target.

From 2,500 feet and greater over a battlefield, pilots do not have the same view as Marines on the ground. In thick-canopied jungles, pilots cannot see anything moving on the surface, and traveling at 400 to 600 miles per hour doesn't help the situation. Even having an exact fix on grid coordinates, azimuth and distance readings for both factions in most instances will only narrow the target to a general location. If the pilot does not interpret his map exactly as described to him, or if the TAC erred in his map reading, no one will have a clue as to where that first bomb will come down. The process is keyed to verbal communication and comprehension of visual references. To further complicate matters, aircraft cannot keep circling an objective while TAC and pilot reach consensus on where to drop ordnance, thus affording enemy troops opportunity to disburse or even set up to bring down the aircraft. At a minimum, infantrymen owed it to the men who were saving their asses to protect those pilots. Mutual respect and teamwork were prime elements for success of the best one-two punch on the planet.

Typically in Vietnam, when requesting air support, map coordinates were passed on to the air wing along with a brief situation report. Radio frequency and contact call sign of the requesting unit was also provided. This would bring the jets to the general objective area. Once the flight leader was on station, he would contact the TAC for a situation briefing and the two would get together on how the friendly position and target would be identified before the aircraft became visible to enemy troops. Marking your own position was swiftly accomplished by different combinations of colored smoke that would filter up through the treetops and be easily recognized from the air. Azimuth and distance call-outs in relation to the smoke would provide a rough target location. To be absolutely sure of correct target recognition, mortars should mark the target with white phosphorous rounds or similar. To be on the safe side, it's always desirable for aircraft to approach the target parallel to friendly front lines so ordnance is not released over the good guys or toward friendly troops when coming in on the enemy's rear. On the other side of the coin, making use of predictable approach and exit vectors could spell disaster to the aircraft, alerting gunners to obvious flight patterns. Using the point of impact of the first payload as a reference, subsequent bomb runs are adjusted by directing preceding sorties to put their loads north, east, south, or west by whatever distance the initial ordnance missed its mark.

In Vietnam, we were fortunate to have witnessed the emergence of airborne Forward Air Controllers (FACs), who flew conventional aircraft capable of operating at lower altitudes and slower speeds. Being closer to the action and having better perspective of the terrain, communication of enemy locations from ground to air was transferred much easier, taking a lot of guesswork out of target identification and recognition of friendly troop positions. Once the airborne FAC was sure of the target, he would brief the support aircraft from the same view they both held from above the battlefield, speaking in descriptive terms familiar to both. When all was ready, the airborne FAC would then fire a marker rocket at the target. Observing the FAC make his marking run, the support pilots had much improved opportunity of getting on target quick, which greatly reduced the possibility of both friendly casualties and shoot-downs.

Reading maps, taking compass readings, and doing math while people are doing their damnedest to kill you is not an easily accomplished chore. Dodging bullets and explosions while trying to focus on the methodology of this enterprise can create enough stress to enable horrible possibilities to develop into very real events. Just the slightest lapse of concentration can bring unthinkable consequences to men who are expecting help from above.

Training and practice developed familiarity with established procedures, instilling second-nature reaction to known and anticipated situations, aimed at promoting confidence and understanding of the job at hand.

Partnered with today's technology, proficient personnel have transformed close air support into a science of surgical precision. Computers, lasers, and global positioning systems make short work of target acquisition and identification, but aren't worth spit without dedicated men to pull it all together.

In recent times, you will recall how special operations personnel were dispatched to Afghanistan, providing air support for Northern Alliance troops that brought a swift end to the ruling Taliban. Three generations of ANGLICO Marines bequeathed their blood to provide modern tacticians an ample supply of ink to dip their quills while writing doctrine on these high-tech support operations.

With deployment of Marine combat units to the Republic of Vietnam in early 1965, 1st ANGLICO activated Sub Unit One for overseas duty on 19 May that same year. Headquarters remained at Kaneohe Bay, where worldwide assets of the organization were controlled and managed. The parent organization also instituted an extensive training program oriented for service in Southeast Asia and managed rotation of personnel in and out of Sub Unit One.

Hawaii was a perfect place to train for operations in Vietnam. Climate, terrain, and general field conditions were a close approximation to what was actually found in Southeast Asia. Field training and tactical exercises were generally conducted on Oahu and Molokai, while live-fire naval gunfire training and close air support skills were honed on the island of Kahoolawe, a lesser-known island tucked between Lanai and Maui. It is a military reservation employed by the U.S. Navy for gunnery practice and aerial bombardment exercises.

Sub Unit One, 1st Air Naval Gunfire Liaison Company arrived in Vietnam on 29 May 1965 with two naval gunfire spot teams, establishing its headquarters in a small villa within the Military Assistance Command Vietnam (MACV) compound near the Saigon racetrack. History has recorded it was the only U.S. Marine unit to be tied directly into the command structure of MACV. From here, the commanding officer, Major Richard E. Romine, and his successors effectively provided management of all Sub Unit One tactical assets and fire control teams in-country.

Since most of the fighting in Vietnam was concentrated around heavily populated coastal regions, naval gunfire was a ready and flexible means of support. Shipboard batteries were well capable as a general rule of reaching targets up to ten miles inland, depending on how far off the coast the support ship was stationed. Mobility and speed of naval ships allowed for rapid massing of fire at any given point. Naval gunfire was available around the clock and, unlike air operations, was relatively unaffected by foul weather. The mainstay of naval gunfire support throughout the war remained the five-inch gun batteries of American destroyers.

Naval gunfire teams routinely accompanied U.S. Army and Vietnamese units in the field, while others patrolled the skies flying back seat in spotter planes, applying their deadly trade over larger areas. One Naval Gunfire Liaison Officer, either U.S. Marine or U.S. Naval officer, normally commanded one or more spot teams. By January 1966, ANGLICO assets in-country grew to fifty-five men in eleven detachments, distributed in all four tactical zones. Lieutenant Colonel Carroll B. Burch relieved Major Romaine in February. From its initial deployment to Vietnam, ANGLICO fell under operational control of III Marine Amphibious Force (III MAF) but operated as a separate command under MACV. In September 1966, operational control of Sub Unit One was formally transferred from III MAF and integrated into General William Westmoreland's headquarters.

Throughout 1966, naval gunfire teams of Sub Unit One observed and controlled more than 5,000 naval gunfire missions, racking up over 3,000 confirmed kills and destroying more than 20,000 enemy structures with no small amount of credit due from the accurate fires of those magnificent gunship crews.

August 1966 saw deployment from Kaneohe Bay, the first rotation of ANGLICO Marines destined to support the Blue Dragon Brigade under the able command of Captain Stephen W. Pless; this was officially designated internally as the ROK Marine Detachment. Before the year ended, table of organization strength of Sub Unit One escalated to 146 men, organized into thirteen detachments. Only in the ROK Marine Detachment, however, did the unit perform in its dual function of air-liaison, controlling fixed wing support and providing the full range of helicopter combat mission capabilities. Each ROK Battalion was assigned an Air Liaison Officer, who commanded two-men Tactical Air Control Parties (TACPs) assigned to each Korean company. Each TACP contained one ground FAC and one field radio operator, both of whom were enlisted men capable of performing in either function. Patrolling the skies over the Koreans, at least one naval gunfire spotter and one FAC in the same aircraft was airborne at all times while troops were in the field.

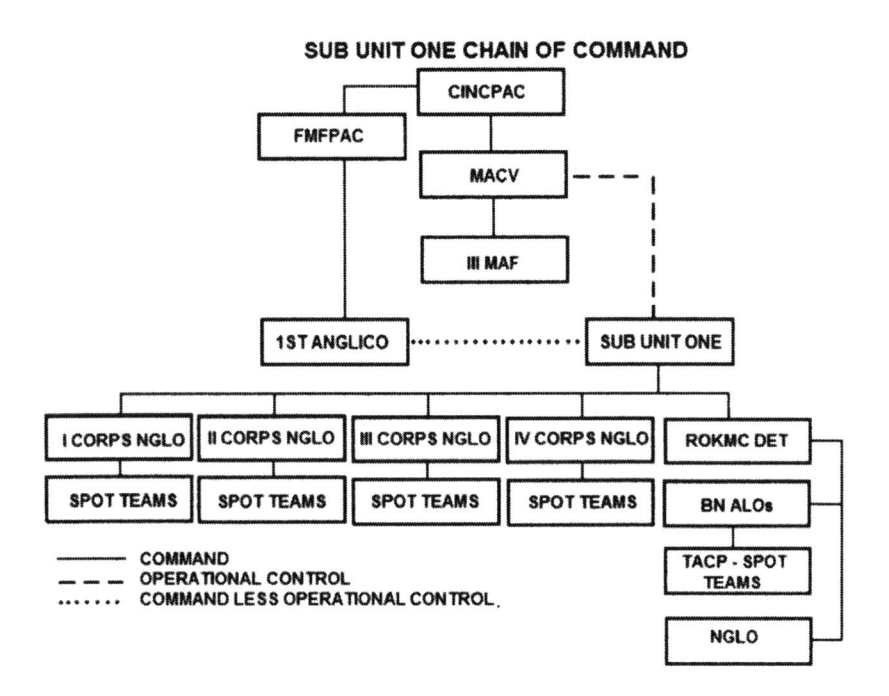

SUB UNIT ONE CHAIN OF COMMAND

```
                        CINCPAC
                           |
         FMFPAC            |
           |             MACV  - - - - - - -
           |               |                |
           |             III MAF            |
           |                                |
       1ST ANGLICO  ................  SUB UNIT ONE
                                            |
   ┌──────────┬──────────┬──────────┬──────────────┐
I CORPS    II CORPS   III CORPS   IV CORPS    ROKMC DET
 NGLO       NGLO       NGLO        NGLO            |
   |          |          |           |          BN ALOs
SPOT TEAMS SPOT TEAMS SPOT TEAMS SPOT TEAMS        |
                                              TACP - SPOT
                                                TEAMS
                                                   |
                                                 NGLO
```

――――― COMMAND
― ― ― OPERATIONAL CONTROL
……… COMMAND LESS OPERATIONAL CONTROL

USS Buchanan
(DDG-14)
Adams Class Guided Missile Armed Destroyer
Call Sign: Sharp note

On station off the DMZ 30 March 1972, USS *Buchanan* was the first gunline ship to fire on North Vietnamese invasion forces during the Easter Offensive. During those first hectic days of April, USS *Buchanan* provided gunfire support for evacuation of ANGLICO Marines at forward ground observer post, Alpha 2, the defense of Dong Ha, and the evacuation of the Vietnamese Naval Base.

At the Cua Viet River on numerous occasions, USS *Buchanan* took enemy troops and tanks under direct fire and was credited with destroying four enemy tanks at the DMZ and killing numerous enemy troops massing at the Dong Ha Bridge.

USS *Buchanan* embarked on 5 April with Commodore T.R. Johnson, COMDESRON 31, leading an operation into North Vietnamese coastal waters. That afternoon, she fired the first rounds into North Vietnam since Sea Dragon operations ceased in 1968.

On 10 April, USS *Buchanan* was directed to proceed to Da Nang Harbor for regunning alongside the tender USS *Samuel Gompers* (AD-37), marking the first time a U.S. Navy ship was assigned tender availability in a forward combat area during the Vietnam War. With regunning complete, USS *Buchanan* once again put to sea, continuing operations off the coast of North Vietnam. Several times per day, her guns hammered supply routes, surface-to-air missile sites, enemy troop concentrations, and coastal defense sites.

On 16 April, she led the first strike against the Do San Peninsula off Haiphong Harbor in company of the Seventh Fleet Command ship USS *Oklahoma City* (CLG-5), USS *Richard B. Anderson* (DD-786), and USS *Hamner* (DD-718). On the following day while engaged in a brutal exchange of gunfire with hostile shore batteries, one enemy shell found its mark. The shell penetrated the superstructure, killing SN Leonard R. Davis and wounding seven others. Material damage was quickly isolated. Three hours later, USS *Buchanan* was again striking enemy targets until 18 April, when USS *Buchanan* retired to Da Nang for battle damage repair.

After a brief four-day period as plane guard for the attack aircraft carrier USS *Kitty Hawk* (CV-63), USS *Buchanan* returned once more to the gunline. Ordered to the northern reaches of the Gulf of Tonkin on 8 May, USS *Buchanan* participated in operations near the Do Son Peninsula. One of these operations involved suppression of hostile shore batteries, providing protection to other U.S. Naval forces mining the entrance to Haiphong Harbor.

On the night of 10 May, USS *Buchanan*, in company with USS *Newport News* (CA-148), USS *Providence* (CLG-6), USS *Oklahoma City* (CLG-5), and USS *Hamner* (DD-718) once again returned to Do Son Peninsula as part of the most formidable cruiser-destroyer strike group assembled in the Pacific since World War II. Striking against military targets in the Haiphong Harbor area, she was the only U.S. Navy ship to participate in every surface strike off Haiphong Harbor since operations were initiated on 5 April.

In sixty-three days, USS *Buchanan* struck North Vietnamese targets forty-nine times, delivering over 7,700 rounds on target against enemy emplacements while receiving fire on almost every mission.

We, who once found refuge under the protection of her guns, salute this valiant ship and her gallant crew.

HYONG-JE HAEBYONG

Positioned in Bihn Son District just south of Chu Lai, the Koreans established Brigade headquarters astride National Highway 1, about halfway between the rivers. A sequence of company-strength outposts were strung out on Van Tuong and Ba Lang An Peninsulas, continuing across the highway to the foothills of the Anamites in a circular formation. Two remote outposts a little further into hill country were occupied by *Suesecdae* (Recon Company).

The ANGLICO Detachment's late-afternoon arrival at Brigade headquarters terminated an uneventful forty-minute truck ride from the airstrip in Chu Lai. They were shown to a small clearing near the parade ground, where the new arrivals pitched tents in a driving rainstorm, beginning a most unceremonious start to a very hazardous assignment.

Soon after breakfast on day two, the Americans were parceled out to Battalion command groups. Two-man fire control teams found their way to the company-strength outposts, where the acquaintance process with the Hyong-je haebyong (Brother Marines) was inaugurated.

The host Marines were found to be an austere but cordial bunch, showing more than ample enthusiasm for making their brothers from the United States feel welcome. A great deal of concern was displayed for the safety of the fire control teams. The Hyong-je haebyong couldn't do enough to ensure their comfort. Plenty of thought was unmistakably applied in determining where ANGLICO bunkers should be placed, so as to allow quick access to the company command structure if need arose for the TACPs to bring their talents to bear on any threat to the outpost.

Typically, a Korean outpost wore the look of a World War I battle scene. The entire perimeter was lined twenty or so feet thick with coiled concertina wire, straddling an irregular mesh of tanglefoot. The concertina was strung with empty C-ration cans laced with pebbles so as to create a hollow rattling sound that would alert the watch should some portion of wire be disturbed or cut. For good measure, antipersonnel mines were salted very liberally throughout the barrier. A sandbag-reinforced trench line defended the concertina frontier with machine gun bunkers positioned to provide interlocking fire in support of small arms defense laid down by infantry. Bunkers housing troops assigned to perimeter defense were located in close proximity to their respective areas of responsibility and were tied into the line with yet other connecting trenches so troops could gain access to their fighting stations without exposure to enemy fire. It was possible to use this mode of travel for most destinations within the compound.

Acknowledged and avowed as an assault-oriented institution, the U.S. Marine Corps does not provide much in the way of practical instruction on how to build defense-biased structures for prolonged service, such as bunkers. It's a lot of shovel work. Digging out a foundation and filling sandbags is not exactly the no-brainer a mental image of these activities would bring to mind. Several of the *Hyong-je haebyong* donated labor and know-how, assisting in erecting as much of a water-proof, mortar-proof, home away from home as could be assembled with the limited materials at hand. Several days of uniform-soaking sweat and sore muscles yielded a log and terra cotta construction that remained about seventy percent underground, a new concept in living that took plenty of getting used to.

Still getting acquainted with the Hyong-je haebyong, the Blue Dragons were as curious about the Americans as the Americans were of them. In many instances, Marines often found themselves cast in the role of English teacher, among other things. Everyone wanted to engage them in conversation to practice his language skills. This in turn presented the Americans with bountiful opportunity to absorb some *Hahn Guk Oh* (Korean), improving their ability to communicate with the Hyong-je haebyong. From the start, it became evident that these good-natured cohorts were not without quality expertise in horse-trading skills. Emblems, equipment, uniforms, and anything of official Marine Corps issue was on the trading block. Problem is, with only two Americans among 200 or more avid traders, demand far exceeded supply.

Normally, trading government issued anything is not condoned by the Marines; however, sporting occidental features amid a groundswell of Asians would not well serve the purpose at hand. Obtaining Korean field uniforms also promoted a comfort level, allowing the Americans to blend in, particularly out in the field. Talking the talk and walking the walk didn't come easy but it came. Some became fairly proficient in the language, but all made an effort.

One of the more problematic barriers to a life of luxury in Vietnam was chow. The Hyong-je haebyong ate rice and cabbage soup three meals a day, seven days a week. *Kimchi,* a pungent cabbage dish (Korean coleslaw) fermented in fish oil, was occasionally available at dinner. It took a while to develop a taste for kimchi. It has an aroma that defies description, but it did add some zest to the evening meal. The Americans alternated their gourmet dining obsession between Korean mess hall chow and C-rations. C-rations offered only twelve possible meal choices, half of which are not edible.

As a side note: The cook would make kimchi in a fifty-five-gallon drum. Once the ingredients were added, the concoction was covered and kept away from light for ten days; usually this meant burying the kimchi pot in the ground. There is an oft-told story of a company cook having recently prepared a drum full of this celebrated brew. It had been underground about eight days when a single incoming mortar round scored a direct hit on the caustic salad. Before the smoke settled, every nose in the company quickly discerned who the casualty was. Many swore that the ever-present rats deserted the compound for several days.

As a matter of etiquette, if one is to gain acceptance in the high-testosterone zone of grunt cultures, by necessity one must become master of the ritual, *maek-ju monta mashida,* (the drinking of massive quantities of beer) or *so-ju.* Now, so-ju is a very interesting drink.

It has no equivalent in the Western world. Not an exact match, it is more or less akin to Japanese *sake* than anything else. Resting on the bottom of the jar is a fairly large root. Once the so-ju is consumed, the root is cut into equal portions and divided among all who shared the so-ju. It had its intended effect.

Having limited prospects for leading fascinating leisurely lives with few pressing engagements on their social calendars, the TACP teams acquired an appetite for kimchi, developed a thirst for so-ju, and learned to speak Hahn Guk-Oh. And…bonded with the Hyong-je haebyong and became friends, became a team, became…Hyong-je haebyong, and trusted them with their lives.

USS Waddell
(DDG-24)
Adams Class Guided Missile Armed Destroyer
Call Sign: Frogman

USS *Waddell* made her Vietnam debut on Yankee Station off the coast of North Vietnam in November 1965, taking part in Search and Rescue operations through the end of the year. She returned in January 1966 for a second deployment in that same capacity.

In February, USS WADDELL took her turn on the gunline, providing reliable fire support to ANGLICO NGLO teams in II and III Corps tactical zones before returning to her homeport of Long Beach, California, in April for a brief stand-down.

Early in 1967, USS *Waddell* was once again busily engaged off the Vietnamese coastline. From 2 March to 21 May, the ship displayed exceptional readiness in all tasks assigned, including gunfire support off South Vietnam, interdiction of North Vietnamese offshore traffic, and gunfire missions directed at select targets in North Vietnam. Occasionally coming under fire from shore installations, USS *Waddell* skillfully returned fire, employing counter battery measures, inflicting maximum damage on enemy shore batteries. The good ship emerged from the actions unscathed. During this deployment, the USS *Waddell* expended over 2,000 rounds of ammunition while earning the reputation as the busiest ship in the Tonkin Gulf.

Returning to Vietnam on 1 August 1968, she took three turns on the gunline in both North and South coastal waters and completed one assignment as plane guard for the attack carrier strike group around USS *Coral Sea* (CVA-43) and USS *Ranger* (CV-61).

Back on her fourth tour of the combat zone on 12 December 1971, USS *Waddell* resumed gunfire support station off the coast of the demilitarized zone, functioning in a dual role, as she also interdicted water traffic from North Vietnam as well before departing for assignment in the Indian Ocean.

Her timely arrival off the coast of South Vietnam on 1 April 1972 brought USS *Waddell* on the gunline off northern I Corps, where she participated in counter battery fire against invading North Vietnamese rockets and artillery. She was also kept busy answering call for fire around the clock in target-rich Quang Tri Province, contributing significant results.

From 3 to 9 April, USS *Waddell* encountered daily counter battery fire from communist gun emplacements around the Cua Viet River. In most engagements, the fighting was so close the USS *Waddell* was able to observe her own fall of shot. On 8 April, locked in a duel with a high-priority target, the USS *Waddell*, while having the better part of the fight, did incur damage to her ASROC launcher system. Continuing on with the fight, she was able to cause secondary explosions in the impact area ashore, generating good effect on target.

USS *Waddell* fired so many rounds on 9 and 10 April, she required two underway replenishments of ammunition. The pace of activity from 11 through 21 April did not allow much downtime, as the ship interdicted and destroyed several sampans ferrying troops across the Ben Hai River, which runs through the center of the DMZ. The ship remained on task over the next few days, firing on and destroying several antiaircraft sites and coastal gun emplacements. So many rounds passed through her five-inch/54 bores that she needed to withdraw to Subic Bay to renew her guns.

USS *Waddell* finished her involvement in Vietnam on 13 April 1973 in Operation End Sweep, removing mines salted into Haiphong Harbor.

We, who once found refuge under the protection of her guns, salute this valiant ship and her gallant crew.

NAM DOE KHE BE

Captain Albert J. Ransom deployed to Vietnam in year eight of his career. Entering service in 1958 as a slick sleeve private, Captain Ransom worked his way up through the ranks to earn his commission in the school of hard knocks. From an early age, he was caught up in a passion to fly, trying unsuccessfully to penetrate flight training programs through the U.S. Air Force before enlisting in the Marine Corps. After two years of service, the enlisted Marine exploited an opening in the Naval Aviation Cadet program to secure his long-sought entry to flight school.

Known as a man who would get the job done, Captain Ransom was a career-minded officer bringing natural enthusiasm to every assignment. Constantly on the prowl for new experiences, he volunteered for jump school in Kaneohe, took jump master training, and eventually ran the ANGLICO jump school. A seasoned fighter and attack pilot, Al Ransom was considered an expert on aircraft ordnance and capabilities. Coupled with ANGLICO and grunt experience from his enlisted days, this Marine was very familiar with workings on both ends of close air support and well positioned to influence the outcome of any conflict from the cockpit or the mud.

Commanding the 1st Battalion team, Captain Ransom led from the front, pushing himself and his team hard to earn the respect of troops they supported. Ever the diplomat, building relations with the ROKs came easy to this Pennsylvania native, who was raised across the United States. Friendships of a lifetime were established with many Korean staff officers.

Summoned to a briefing one mid-September morning, details pertaining to tactical objectives of Operation Dragon Claw were presented to battalion staff officers. Fresh intelligence gained from

ARVN military sources concerning communist activities on the coast presented an opportunity for Brigade to strike a blow at local guerillas. An area on southern Ba Lang An would be the objective. Troops would be set down by helicopter in three waves just west of the objective, while a land force converged from the northwest in a maneuver designed to isolate enemy troops, cutting them off from expected avenues of retreat. South Vietnam's 2nd Division would supply a blocking force positioned on the south bank of Tra Khuc River near the coast. Maneuvering plans in sequence to preordained locations were calculated to channel enemy troops and trap them between South China Sea and the river.

Early morning of 17 September, a flight of UH-34D helicopters from HMM-361 set down on the battalion landing pad. Teams of Koreans in full combat dress sprinted to awaiting choppers and scampered aboard. In keeping with his long-established style of leadership, Captain Ransom positioned himself to set down with the first wave. The first flight was composed of headquarters and service company command officers and two platoons of grunts. Within minutes, lead elements lifted off and circled until the entire flight was airborne, then banked right on a southeast heading.

UH1-E gunships of VMO-6 joined the armada a few minutes into the flight, as the armed expedition closed on objective.

As per plan, transport choppers skirted west of the objective, taking a long approach, keeping distance, while Captain Ransom went to work coordinating impressive landing zone (LZ) prep. Through a communications hook-up in the chopper, the 1st Battalion skipper was in contact with the flight leader, who confirmed attack jets were now on station working over the landing site. Monitoring the action over the squadron tactical (TAC) net, Captain Ransom thought to himself, "This is just the way it's supposed to go."

Observing his first for-real LZ prep perched next to the door gunner, Captain Ransom watched dive after dive of fast movers producing plumes of black smoke, billowing in and around the area where he'd soon set foot. As the last sortie began his approach, assault craft started their descent on a heading toward the LZ. Seeing the objective getting closer with each passing second, the skipper became fixated on gunship escorts applying finishing touches just a few hundred meters distant. He knew this was it. Trying to control a pestering fear suddenly erupting from the nether reaches of his mind, the Marine clicked on his handset, thanked the escort choppers, and steeled himself for life's next adventure. No sooner had the words cleared his throat, a light jolt shook him alert as landing wheels making contact with the ground intensified adrenaline levels now racing through his veins.

Small arms fire kicked up dirt a few feet ahead as Captain Ransom bounded from the aircraft, sprinting toward a bomb crater several yards to his front left. Right on his tail, Lance Corporal Robert J. Sherwood, carrying the radio, kept pace with his C.O., dodging poorly aimed rounds that were now increasing in intensity.

Securing protection offered by the crater, Sherwood passed the handset to his skipper, who immediately established contact with the flight leader. Bobby Sherwood observed nearby Koreans pumping fire to the east and followed outgoing tracers with his eyes. Seeing what the Marines were shooting at, Sherwood was astounded at the number of muzzle flashes blinking back from a tree line barely 400 meters away. Like a bloodhound on the scent, the scrappy lance corporal pointed out his find. Captain Ransom had a target.

Unexpected resistance this soon into Dragon Claw posed threatening consequences to landing craft bringing in the next troop insertion. A decision was made to hold back the second wave until suppressing fire eliminated resistance. Taking the same westerly holding pattern as the first wave, UH-34 pilots were delighted to allow ANGLICO to bring in an additional flight of A-4s to quiet things down.

Lance Corporal Sherwood pulled pin on a smoke grenade and tossed it twenty or so feet in front of the crater. Captain Ransom used the ballooning red smoke as a beacon to call ordnance on target, scotching everything within a hundred meters of where defiant defenders of Batangan lay in wait.

Calling the next flight down, the skipper turned over communications to Sherwood, who talked the teardrop-shaped UH-34s to ground, while Captain Ransom hunted down the 1st Battalion C.O. to coordinate a quick move off of the LZ.

Il (pronounced ill) *Chungdae* (1st Company) came in on the next wave and immediately fanned out to provide security for the last flight, which arrived without incident a half hour later. Each company in turn moved out, taking its position for the drive to the coast. Battalion HQ hiked eastward to an imposing hill overlooking immediate objectives of Dragon Claw. Having a great field of fire and easy helo access, HQ remained in place through day three.

Over the next few days, Korean Marines pressed forward toward the objective, under constant harassment from snipers. Several promising firefights broke out but did not yield results on par with Brigade's expectations.

Monsoons come to Quang Ngai every year about this time. This year was no exception. Rains pound southern I Corps in massive torrents from September through January, and it started falling with a vengeance on day three.

By evening of day four, all three line companies maneuvered to position for completion of the final phase of Dragon Claw. Headquarters Company caught a helicopter ride to a commanding peak overlooking real estate where the battalion would see action just a few clicks west of South China Sea.

Late in the morning on day five, small arms fire sent HQ personnel scrambling for cover.

Spotters observed muzzle flashes originating in a village at the northern base of the hill they currently occupied. *Som Chungdae* (3rd Company) just cleared that village yesterday and reported it deserted. With all the grunts further out on Batangan, it fell to HQ people to solve their own problem. Well-aimed fire soon made movement on the north perimeter very hazardous. Lacking sufficient manpower to actually go down and assault the village, Captain Ransom's advice was sought.

Calling upon his friends at the air wing, a flight of two F8U Crusaders arrived on station twenty minutes later.

The Koreans studied this situation and expressed concern that at less than 300 meters they were indeed too close and might be sprayed by fallout from the exploding bombs.

A stand-off discussion continued five more minutes while the A8Us impatiently circled overhead, awaiting instructions. After winning a hard-won approval, from the reckless depths of his psyche, Captain

Ransom descended fifty meters downhill for no better reason than to prove a point.

Once in position, smoke was popped for reference and the show was on. Confident in his decision, the skipper brought down the first pass right on target, standing in the open, putting on a display of bravado for an audience gathering at the crest overlooking his target. Having requested 250-pound snake eyes, the captain was shaken when he realized the first bomb down was a 500-pounder. Dull thuds of heavy shrapnel and debris coming to ground close by told him things are not going exactly as planned. Already too committed, the captain put his fears aside, stood his ground, swallowed hard, and called down the next sortie.

Showing his following on the hill that close air support is nothing to fear, Al Ransom brought his hands over his head in unison with the next detonation as if simulating an explosion. A smile crept onto his face as each subsequent sortie brought cheers and laughter from he didn't know where. Hoping he could get through this without becoming a casualty of his own stubbornness, the officer kept up his charade through a torrent of errant missiles and debris until the A8Us expended all ordnance and headed home.

In Korean folklore, there is a legend of a laughing ghost who is large in stature and fearless. From that day forward, Captain Ransom was dubbed in Hahn Gook-Oh as *Nam Doe Khe Be*, the big happy ghost.

Nam Doe Khe Be was not allowed much time to reflect on his colorful new nickname. Unfolding events on Ba Lang An would come to a head within weeks and would dominate Brigade's agenda for the next several months.

Unrelenting rain became the dominant event of the last day of Dragon Claw. Low ceilings and foul weather kept all but emergency flights on the tarmac and precipitated 1st Battalion's two-day walk back to command post.

Without resupply by air, headquarters personnel lived off the land, scrounging wild rice and whatever water they could collect from the downpour. It was a sorry looking parade that finally came through the wire after almost forty-eight hours on the hoof with precious little results to show for their efforts.

USS Saint Paul
(CA-73)
Baltimore Class Cruiser
Call Sign: Tornado

The Fighting Saint returned to her home away from home, the Western Pacific, in 1966, for combat operations off North and South Vietnam. During five annual deployments to Southeast Asia, she supplied gunfire in support of allied troops, interdicted supply lines, and struck enemy installations, leaving in her wake heavily damaged coastal defense sites and destroying several North Vietnamese Naval craft. In her 1966 deployment, she had fired more than 10,000 rounds in support of allied troops south of the DMZ. Prior to that, it was in Korea that CA-73 had last fired her big guns at hostile forces, and it had been more than twenty years since the "Snooky Poo Maru," as she was affectionately known to her crew, had participated in World War II.

USS *Saint Paul's* second Vietnam deployment began 3 April 1967, when she steamed west from San Diego. It would be seven months and 20,000 rounds later before the Fighting Saint would return. This time, USS *Saint Paul* would be taking part in a new phase of the war...Operation Sea Dragon...firing upon military targets located inland, on the coast and off the shores of Vietnam. The most important objectives were the interdiction of supply routes and Wiblics, waterborne logistic craft used by the North Vietnamese to transport military supplies to the Viet Cong and other elements operating in South Vietnam.

These large junks and barges that moved stealthily along the coastline were protected by a network of costal defense guns capable of ranges from ten to twelve miles. It was these guns that USS *Saint Paul* braved to halt trafficking of supplies. More than once she felt the sting of their shrapnel as she charged in to fire on targets.

The Fighting Saint worked hand-in-hand with spotter aircraft from naval carriers and land-based ANGLICO spotters, making use of their eyes to destroy her targets. At other times, when the use of aircraft was not practical, she would zero-in on targets using computer coordinates or visual sighting by gun director personnel.

USS *Saint Paul* did not return from this combat unscathed. On 1 September 1967, she engaged in her toughest battle of the deployment. Accompanied by two destroyers, she moved in to attack waterborne logistics craft when no less than twenty-five coastal defense sites opened fire. She immediately returned fire and a running battle ensued with shells falling all around the ship.

More than 500 rounds were fired at *Saint Paul* that morning, and one round found its mark. A shell entered near the starboard bow and damaged a storeroom and several staterooms. There were no personnel casualties. Continuously firing, the ship maneuvered to safety and retired to sea for repairs. Working all night, crewmembers pumped the damaged area dry and welded a patch over the hole. The patch held during high-speed turns, and the next day, the Fighting Saint returned to the gunline.

USS *Saint Paul* later steamed to Subic Bay for permanent repairs. (She had been in Subic Bay just a month earlier to have all of her eight-inch guns replaced.) She returned to Sea Dragon, where she destroyed six more waterborne craft, two concrete blockhouses, and two costal defense sites. She also heavily damaged railroad yards at Cong Phu and the shipyards at Phuc Doi. She was relieved by USS *Newport News* (CA-148) in October and headed to San Diego.

In May 1968, on her third Vietnam deployment, USS *Saint Paul* returned to Sea Dragon operations. She picked up right where she left off, shelling enemy targets on call for fire missions around the clock. She silenced North Vietnamese Army gun positions and sank three thirty-foot logistics craft while damaging two fifty-foot motorized tugs. The ship again took a brief mid-deployment break, regunning in

Subic Bay. In over 1,300 missions, she was credited with 380 enemy killed and 800 military structures destroyed or damaged. She was relieved in October by USS *New Jersey* (BB-62) before pointing her bow east for San Diego.

During her 130 days on the gunline on this deployment, the Fighting Saint fired a total of 64,055 rounds, making a total for the Vietnam conflict of more than 93,000. These figures established the twenty-three-year-old USS *Saint Paul* as ANGLICO's "Top Gun," having fired more rounds during a single deployment, and more rounds in all of her deployments, than any other warship. She was awarded the Navy Unit Commendation for her exceptionally meritorious service during this deployment.

Although the Fighting Saint had been decommissioned by the time the Vietnam conflict ended, she holds the distinction of two famous gunfire "lasts." As a member of Admiral "Bull" Halsey's Third Fleet, she fired the final round on the home islands of Japan on 9 August 1945. She followed up that notoriety by letting go the last salvo of the Korean War on 27 July 1953, just two minutes before the armistice took effect.

In more than a quarter century of service to her country, USS *Saint Paul* earned eighteen battle stars and fired more rounds of ammunition than any other U.S. cruiser in history. She hosted eight heads of state. A total of eighteen of her commanding officers and executive officers ascended to flag rank. The Fighting Saint was truly a cruiser among cruisers. Her likes will not be seen again.

We, who once found refuge under the protection of her guns, salute this valiant ship and her gallant crew.

THE LOST PLATOON

Viet Cong militia wisely avoided all possible contact with the Koreans during Dragon Claw, taking this opportunity to observe Korean tactics and formations. The few firefights that were initiated satisfied regimental command's curiosity about the effective firepower of World War II vintage weaponry fielded by their new adversary.

About four weeks after Operation Dragon Claw ended, Lieutenant William E. Thomas, Jr., recently commissioned from staff sergeant, already airborne on his daily mission received direction from Brigade HQ to contact a U.S. Navy destroyer off the coast. Flying back seat in one of two USAF spotter planes from the 20th Tactical Air Control Squadron (TASS) assigned to Brigade, Lieutenant Thomas was one of the most experienced naval gunfire spotters in the Corps. After making contact, the O-1 altered course toward the ship's position. In flight, they were notified by the destroyer of a sampan that had run aground and detonated itself. Arriving over the last reported position, the sampan was observed to have gone aground on the north shore of Ba Lang An. Both crewmen confirmed there was nothing left of the sampan except the hull resting on ocean bottom near the coast. Closing on the wreck, debris was seen to be strewn all over the beach. After a couple of low passes over the beach, that debris was identified as small arms and assorted munitions.

As leaving this weaponry laying about overnight to be gathered by the local VC would sooner or later come back to bite someone in the ass, a company from the 5th Marines was dispatched to police up the cargo later that afternoon.

Approximately one month later, around midnight, Lieutenant Thomas and one of the Air Force FACs were scrambled from Quang Ngai airfield to investigate yet another sampan reported to have run aground near the mouth of Tra Khuc River Delta. Arriving on scene using limited available moonlight, the craft was observed to be stranded.

Coming up on the Dixie Station frequency, Lieutenant Thomas put out a broadcast seeking any ship in the vicinity. A U.S. Coast Guard cutter came online, responding enthusiastically. Armed with one five-inch/38, the gallant ship was anxious for the mission. After establishing the ship as being illumination capable, target acquisition data was relayed to the gunboat. Once illumination was on station, Lieutenant Thomas adjusted that five-inch/38 on target, severely damaging the craft.

At first light, a team of Koreans accompanied by USN Lieutenant C.J. Baumrucker, Brigade NGLO was dispatched by helicopter to determine the sampan's cargo. After boarding the vessel, the ship was confirmed to be carrying AK-47s, RPGs, and 12.7mm machine guns. More Korean Marines were brought out by helicopter to remove the weapons.

Some ten weeks later, a sweep conducted by *Il Taedae* (1st Battalion) brought the Koreans out to Ba Lang An not far from the beached sampan. With all the clandestine shipping activity occurring in that area, the Koreans were more than curious about support activities essential for keeping this supply route open.

All events of that day have never been quite clear to us and cannot be totally documented as we did not have access to the few survivors for an account of all the actual occurrences. With bits and pieces of incomplete information from others who where involved in this action, the author believes he is close to a fairly accurate depiction of those events. The end results and overall scope of this operation, however, have never been in question.

Midafternoon on the last scheduled day of that sweep, a reinforced platoon from *E Chungdae* (2nd Company) was conducting a clearing operation near the outskirts of a village not far from the coast of an inland waterway that separated Ba Lang An from the mainland.

Mortar section personnel split off, establishing a firebase on a small knoll just north of a dirt access road skirting the waterway's north bank to support the operation.

Operating solo with 2nd Company, Sergeant Kenneth C. Campbell consulted his map for orientation and drifted sixty or so meters further south across the access road toward the coastline to slightly higher ground for a better view of the surrounding terrain, with a group of six Marines providing flank security. This left a fairly wide expanse between the security detail and platoon.

Togo 88 (eight, eight), a USAF Forward Air Controller, Captain George Buckner, piloting a O-1 bird dog, approached from the northwest on his daily patrol of ROK real estate. He was on his way back to the airfield for refueling. The O-1, a militarized version of the Cessna L-19 flying out of Quang Ngai airstrip, was one of two airborne FACs assigned to Brigade. Lieutenant William E. Thomas, Jr., USMC, in his familiar back seat position as naval gunfire spotter, watched the Marines several hundred feet below maneuver on mission.

Som Sodae (3rd Platoon) executed a clearing operation that brought them to the outskirts of seemingly deserted An Hai (1) village. Approaching in wedge formation, the platoon entered the settlement on an eighty-meter front from the west, well dispersed and very apprehensive. A commanding hill some 140 feet high pierced the sky less than a hundred meters south of the village.

An uneasy feeling gripped the platoon as a foreboding sense of danger matched their every step. Moving cautiously through the village, one squad provided cover for two alternating squads, utilizing fire-team rushes in a hooch-to-hooch search.

After a 100-meter penetration, an armed guerrilla suddenly ran from the rear of a hut as a fire team approached to search it. He ran toward village center, drawing fire from everyone who had an eye on him. At full sprint, several bullets slammed him to the ground, killing the man before his lifeless body finished tumbling in the dirt.

Under the watchful gaze of the rest of the squad, two Marines approached the dead VC with deliberate caution. Poking him with rifle barrels, the carcass was turned over onto its back, revealing a youth sporting a haircut in the tradition of Viet Cong soldiers. His temples were shorn close to the skin halfway up to his crown, leaving a medium-length tuft of hair on top brushed to one side.

Silently, every eye in the village nervously scanned nearby structures and landscape, looking for evidence of other phantoms that were surely lurking unseen somewhere nearby.

A second man bolted from behind a straw-laden cart some thirty feet from where his comrade was gunned down and disappeared behind a hut, pumping his feet for all they could function. No one had a chance at drawing a bead on him.

Cautiously, a squad advanced toward the last sighting and peered down a deserted twenty-foot-wide dirt avenue that ran through the center of the village. Two other squads fanned out in opposite directions. One squad crossed the dirt pathway under cover from the others, taking up position on the east side to observe both ends of the road.

Fanning out thirty meters on each side of the main drag, employing fire-team rushes, the platoon advanced on village center, checking each hut en route and posting two-men stationary security posts at strategic intervals along the way.

Twenty minutes of hut hopping brought the platoon to a sixty-meter-square dirt plaza intersected by three roads. A fifteen-foot-diameter stonework water trough fed by a hand pump occupied the center junction in front of a thirty-foot-tall bamboo structure that spanned the entire width of the square at the far end.

Assessing the situation, the platoon leader ordered a halt. With hand signals, he motioned one squad to advance on the building from the right. Every other grunt in formation assumed firing position, training their weapons on the large building, straining hard to detect any movement, listening intently for tell-tale sounds that would signal a call to action.

Slowly, *Som Pundae* (3rd Squad) advanced on the structure, every eye scanning each opening on the building. Breaking into a sprint from thirty feet out, two fire teams took up firing positions at the bottom of the steps while a third, never hesitating for a second, vaulted the stairs, crashing through a double-wide front door.

Even as Som Pundae advanced on the building, one fire team from II Pundae (1st Squad) rushed the trough, taking up firing positions, while the remainder skirted left, taking cover behind huts lining the plaza.

Not more than two minutes after entering the structure, a grenade blast followed by fifteen or twenty seconds of rapid-fire rifle reports echoed from inside.

After an anxious ten minutes, grunts who'd been inside the structure re-emerged through the same door from which they entered, dragging what remained of the VC who bolted from the platoon some twenty minutes earlier. The building was secure. There were no more threats inside.

With a collective sigh of relief, a ten-minute stand-down was ordered to give troops a brief respite from a merciless sun. Flies gathered on the dead Cong left on the steps as most of the platoon gravitated toward the trough for a splash of cold water on sun-beaten faces. Cigarettes were lit while small talk was exchanged and gripes aired. Men dropped backpacks and loosened cartridge belts in anticipation of as much relaxation as could be gleaned from a short rest. This being the last objective, the platoon would hook up with E Chungdae for the night after finishing the search operation in the village, then hump back to command post in the morning.

From a camouflaged position on the commanding hill overlooking the village, the VC commander observed relaxed Marines in the square through field glasses. He was in communication with a swarm of his troops quietly infiltrating on the unsuspecting Koreans from the direction of the village that had just been cleared. Other elements emerged from a tree line on the eastern outskirts of the settlement just beyond sight of the security posts left behind on the press toward village center. Two full companies of the 48th main force battalion were cautiously taking up position to entrap the unsuspecting Marines in the plaza.

From his lofty perch on the hill, the VC commander was anxious for his troops to complete their advance while his quarry remained at rest. He had not expected to find his target so off guard. From his command center, he ordered more speed, cajoling his charges to move faster.

Seeing an officer barking soundless invectives, the commander watched from the heights as men slowly gained their feet, groping for equipment, signaling an end to a windfall opportunity to catch his prey in such slack posture. After careful deliberation, the VC commander immediately ordered the attack before his troops inside the village were fully in position.

Now at 500 feet, almost directly overhead of E Chungdae's firebase, Lieutenant Thomas was stunned to see mortar detonations suddenly churning up earth amid Marines who were in a scramble for cover.

Sergeant Campbell, some 100 meters from the village, was caught by complete surprise as were nearby Marines on flank security. Cut off from the firebase and sweep platoon, being unaware of the magnitude of the tactical situation playing out around him, Sergeant Campbell contacted Togo 88 in a frantic attempt to find out what was going on.

Even as Campbell's transmission was still coming over the O-1's radio, Lieutenant Thomas at 400 feet overhead was horrified to see several black-clad figures popping up from spider trap holes shielded from Campbell's view by foliage not twenty feet away, postured between the entrapped NCO and firebase.

"Ya Ja Su One 14 (one, four), this is Togo 88. Turn right and get the hell out of there fast, over! You have VC to your immediate front at close range."

Before Sergeant Campbell was fully able to digest Togo's broadcast, twelve to fourteen black-clad figures opened up from a thick island of jungle growth to his left, taking both him and the security detail under fire.

Reacting on instinct, Sergeant Campbell emptied a magazine in the direction of the interlopers while angling back toward the security detail who had established a base of fire in a shallow depression some thirty feet away just off the road. Once the magazine was deplete of ammo, the NCO turned and moved quickly, closing distance with his fellow Marines as fast as he could pump his legs, zigzagging, diving, and rolling several times. Twice in his sprint to safety, the sergeant was involuntarily knocked from his feet. Finally, the Marine reached the depression, diving head-first over prone riflemen behind the rise that now formed the front line.

Turning toward the enemy, raising off the ground just enough to peer over the rise in an attempt to sort out the calamity, Sergeant Campbell anxiously hailed Togo in an attempt to get more detailed insight on the confused tactical situation. Something was wrong. The handset was not crackling when he released the key. Lowering his head, the NCO pulled the radio from his back in a single motion to discover what the hell was interfering with communications. In quick order, the sergeant checked the on/off switch, frequency dial, and volume setting. Campbell did not notice two bullet holes in the casing until he attempted to unlock the battery compartment.

"Ya Ja Su One 14, this is Togo 88; over." Lieutenant Thomas tried several times to contact the earthbound sergeant. "Ya Ja Su One 14, this is Togo 88; over." Scanning the landscape below, Lieutenant Thomas diverted his eyes from time to time, consulting his map. He couldn't understand why he was not able to see muzzle flashes from those VC mortar tubes. The eastern tree line and hill just south of the village, being the most dominant terrain features, were the only tactical vantage points to launch an attack. As such, the calculating lieutenant deduced these terrain features to be the only logical source of the problem. The O-1 pilot observed several Viet Cong approaching the village access road from direction of the tree line, confirming Lieutenant Thomas's suspicions. The bird dog was now circling at 1,500 feet. A call went out from the pilot over UHF requesting diversion of any aircraft in the area even as his back seater was still attempting to re-establish his link to Sergeant Campbell.

Frantically working to expose the circuitry, Campbell hoped the problem could be solved by simple wire splicing. Fire volume suddenly accelerated far beyond anything yet encountered.

Marines around him furiously pumped round after round toward the VC. Sensing the urgency of the vigorous activity, Sergeant Campbell leveled his rifle over the rise to add more fire. From the number of muzzle flashes now blinking back from the overgrowth, the sergeant deduced several more enemy troops had augmented the assault force in the brush.

Orders barked in Korean brought the security force to their feet, still firing frantically as they back-peddled toward a tree line some sixty meters behind them on the north side of the road.

Campbell forgot about the radio and started falling back with the ROKs, snap shooting his M-14 from the shoulder until his head dipped below the rise. Turning, the NCO took his first step in an all-out life-and-death sprint for the tree line.

Mortar crews at the firebase experienced a deluge of mortar rounds while machine gun and AK fire seemed to erupt from all directions.

Togo 88, still in a wide circle overhead, lost track of Sergeant Campbell toward the last leg of its loop. Lieutenant Thomas experienced piercing trepidation over lack of response from the silent radio below. A feeling of helplessness settling over the lieutenant quickly accelerated to dread over the fate of his NCO. Adding more anxiety to an overstressed crew, the bird dog was now dangerously low on fuel. They could not remain on station any longer, having already exceeded safe fuel levels. Torn by loyalty and common sense, the O-1, having no other choice, reluctantly cleared air space. Togo 87, scrambling from Quang Ngai airfield, became airborne. While still in his initial ascent, Togo 88 transmitted updated situation reports to the relief craft, along with coordinates for an air strike once jets arrived on station. A detailed description of terrain and tactical situation was exchanged to the extent that both pilots agreed on this course of action. Togo 87 was also advised there would be no one on the ground to identify and confirm targets. This would be an air strike in the blind unless 87 was able to identify firm targets.

In the village, Marines meandering around the plaza were stunned by an overwhelming opening volume of fire that came without warning from seemingly everywhere. Four Marines were cut down before reaching their feet. Men grabbed what gear was close by and gravitated as best they could to their assigned squad leaders, in a confused drill of bedlam, not really knowing from where the attack was launched. A half dozen more sustained wounds of varying degrees. Others dropped in place and returned fire. Still taking casualties, all over the plaza men returned fire without direction, reacting on instinct.

Three of four, two-man security posts fell to superior numbers while a fourth, undetected by the invaders, donned a cloak of invisibility by remaining motionless in their harbor among the huts while assault teams streamed past them on all sides. Lacking communications, they had no other option available but to hunker down and await an opportunity to rejoin the platoon.

In the plaza, a furious exchange of fire developed as Marines scurried for cover offered by huts lining the junction. Looking around, the platoon leader could see his men clustered in small groups. Shouting orders to form fire teams, the lieutenant, unconcerned with his personal safety, hustled about to the closest groups, directing fire where it was most needed and moving men around, building improvised units. Calling out to men not possible to reach, he encouraged them to withdraw from the open and form up with others close by.

The lieutenant knew he needed to get his men out of that village before it was closed off. The sooner he made his move, the better. He wasn't sure which avenue was the best way out but he did know it wasn't possible to leave the way they came in. He needed help fast. The only units close enough to pull his bacon out of the fire, were likewise pinned down and unable to advance. That aside, squad leaders following orders collected what men they could to concentrate fire and prepare for a breakout.

Before anyone went anywhere, the casualties in village center needed to be evacuated.

With Marine machine guns now in action, the collective firepower of every weapon in the plaza laid down enough suppressing fire for a makeshift rescue force of several Marines braving an attempt at recovering the dead and evacuating two wounded, who lay where they fell near the trough.

On orders, eight men broke cover, rushing the trough. The plaza was raked with so much fire, bullet strikes kicked up a dust cloud that both partially shielded the Marines and obscured their vision as well. Upon reaching the objective, vigorous automatic fire from atop the commanding hill forced the squad to abandon the trough. Managing to drag both wounded with them, the rescuers fell back to the huts lining the western perimeter of the plaza.

Two pockets of resistance some forty meters apart formed on either side of the plaza opposite the bamboo building. Elsewhere, Marines unable to hook up were engaged in an unorganized "every-man-for-himself" defense of the ground he currently occupied. Pinned down and hard-pressed just to stay alive, uncoordinated movement in the court was almost impossible as small arms fire and grenades blanketed everything in the square in a shower of steel. Each man dreaded the thought, but also understood necessities of reaching an organized unit to get out of this alive.

Six Marines lay trapped in the plaza. It was only a matter of time before all life in that fire-swept square was extinguished. Encouraging his men to join the closest squad, the lieutenant shouted above the calamitous roar of battle at these men to make their move on his command. Calling to the squad on his right, the officer ordered everyone to lay down a heavy base of fire when he gave the word. His own group composed of Som Sodae received the same directive.

On signal, accelerated fire erupted from two bases. Four of the six stranded Marines sprang to their feet. One was cut down before taking his first step. A dust cloud rose about the remaining three who, in full stride, were ripped by AK fire, each felled by multiple hits of flesh-tearing cones of hot metal.

Sensing what was going on, Viet Cong concentrated fire at the remaining two until they also succumbed to the murderous deluge of a cruel rain.

Demoralized and horrified by the grisly sight of his men so mercilessly snuffed out by an unrelenting horde of demons, the officer forced his attention away from the remnants of the macabre ballet of death and turned to the task of saving what men he could. Reinforcements could not be counted on. He had only what assets he brought into the village, and he needed to make the most of them. His radio operator had not been seen since the opening volley, leaving the platoon hopelessly alone.

Weapons personnel on the knoll were hard-pressed to sort out events. No one really had a handle on where the mortar fire was coming from. Multiple counter battery fire missions called in to Brigade artillery were haphazardly pounding suspected positions with negative effect. All contact with Som Sodae in the village had been severed. Incoming mortar and automatic weapons fire was restricting the mortar crew's ability to perform their mission, but no attack materialized on their perimeter.

Only a few meters from the tree line, the platoon corpsman attached to the security detail was knocked from his feet, felled by AK fire. Two Marines grabbed him on the run, dragging the wounded man a final few feet into the tree line. One Marine attended the injured corpsman while Sergeant Campbell and remaining Marines turned to face their pursuers. A line of Viet Cong spaced out over a sixty-yard front at fifty meters distant were firing across open ground and closing fast. One hundred meters east, eight or nine black-clad figures were observed entering the tree line, attempting to flank the trapped Marines.

After a token expression of fire at the attackers in the open ground, the NCO in charge ordered his team to withdraw further into the overgrowth, taking the wounded corpsman with them. Once out of sight, the Marines changed course to a westerly heading, then turned south after 200 meters in an attempt to circle and hook up with the firebase.

In the village, realizing how untenable his position was, the lieutenant sent one fire team back in among the huts to establish a base of retreat. Met with the same tenacious fusillade as faced in the plaza, the fire team was taken under fire by two squads waiting in ambush.

Hearing the mayhem from among the huts, another fire team was dispatched to help out and was greeted by the same frenzy of fire that pinned down the first team.

What still remained of the platoon struggled to keep what precious little grasp they had on a not-very-promising position. Without cover and outnumbered by who knows how the hell many, a move away from the plaza offered the only sensible course to follow.

Calling over to *E Pundae,* the officer shouted a basic plan of fire and maneuver to reach a more defensible position. Not knowing where that position might be, if it even existed, was more of a prayer than a plan.

He had entered the village with forty-six men. Ten were now dead, twelve wounded, and his radio operator and the eight men on security posts were unaccounted for. Counting the walking wounded, twenty-three able-bodied Marines would have to be enough for the task.

Only twenty minutes into this mess and he'd already lost half his command.

Not having been able to close the gap, both squads some forty meters distant from each other moved into a narrow alley behind the huts lining the plaza, taking their wounded with them, only to face a tenacious foe in close confines of constricted passages not more than six feet wide.

Som Pundae joined the fight in progress immediately upon entering the alleyway. It was much more intense than what was experienced in the plaza. Both fire teams first into the alley had been badly mauled, sustaining six casualties. The machine gunner and his aide never fired a round as they were taken out before the big gun could be brought to action.

E Pundae did not fare much better. Engaged in a running gunfight at six feet with a well-prepared adversary, they sprinted through a maze of passageways entering the alley, taking casualties with each step.

Seeing no way out and not willing to abandon their wounded, each squad planted their feet and fought to the last man as the sun prepared to set on a disquieting day of bitterness.

After an hour of struggling through a dense rain forest, flank security became bogged down in thick jungle growth. Feeling somewhat safe in fading daylight, the NCO in charge ordered a rest. Satisfied they were no longer being followed, the team lingered awhile, giving some attention to the wounded corpsman, who by now had lost a lot of blood. Spirits lifted as the drone of Togo 87's engines filtered through the jungle canopy. They also experienced a little unease as jungle cover also made them invisible from the air. Within minutes, the high whining sound of jet engines punctuated with explosions let them know someone was hard at work cutting down the odds. With all this activity, something must be afoot. A decision was reached to seek a position near open ground that would permit Sergeant Campbell to flag down something with wings or rotors. Having been turned around in the overgrowth, being unable to see landmarks, the detail angled further west and cleared bush well over a mile from where they entered.

Togo 87, now in contact with a flight of A-4 Skyhawks, systematically directed sorties on the troublesome tree line near the village, planting napalm the entire length and depth of the forest. He then shifted concentration to the high hill. For twenty minutes, he worked over both targets with 250-pound snake eyes and napalm. When ordnance was expended, both war birds cleared air space over Ba Lang An.

Just before dusk, a drumbeat of rotor blades slapping at air over the buzz of helicopter engines cut through the dim glow of fading light. With no one on the ground to direct them in, the flight leader was totally reliant on coordinates provided earlier by Lieutenant Thomas. Togo 87, still on station, would control the landing, having just released the flight of A-4s.

Setting down on the high hill overlooking the village, *Yuk Chungdae* (6th Company) hit the ground looking for blood. Sergeant Lawrence C. Smith, landing with the first wave, set up shop, preparing for the next flight. Assault troops were surprised at the lack of opposition as not one shot greeted their arrival. Considering the events of just one hour past, this troop insertion was expected to be anything but easy.

Once Yuk Chungdae reported the hill secure, the main body of E Chungdae, newly arrived on location, moved in. Entering the village from the same direction as did Som Sodae earlier that afternoon, everything seemed quiet. Out of place quiet. Nothing stirred. Not a sound interrupted a graveyard silence, which held everyone's imagination captive.

Not long after threading through the monotonous maze of bamboo and thatch huts, the point squad happened upon a carnage scene in the alleyway behind the plaza and followed it into the courtyard beyond.

The body count didn't add up to a full platoon. More bodies were found outside the village but still fell short of a full platoon of men. An in-depth search of the village revealed more cadavers, but still did not account for all hands.

Several of the bodies, although void of fatal wounds, were rich in cuts, welts, and burns. Some were posed with testicles and penises stuffed in their mouths. Agony was so frozen on these lifeless faces that one could almost hear the last death screams that had yet to clear their throats.

Several times in their sojourn through a hostile countryside, the security detail could not help but notice UH1-Es coming and going. Knowing a relief force was now on the ground heightened their hopes for a happy ending. Search craft could also be seen drifting overhead, but too far east. While seeking an avenue closer to the aircraft activity, several times the team observed locals scurrying around. In order to minimize risk of being observed, the team moved slowly and deliberately. Of prime concern, the wounded corpsman needed hospitalization, and quick. Moving him around this much wasn't doing the injured man any favors. With darkness settling in, the team decided to set up a night logger while there was still enough light to select an advantage position.

Finding a small recess at a tree line border that guarded access to a larger field, the tired men stopped to survey the adjoining area. It looked to be as good a spot as they were likely to come across, and it suited their purpose.

Once the team slipped into position, a quick inventory of gear turned up nothing in the way of illumination. Brainstorming their options, Sergeant Campbell convinced the NCO in charge of the security detail that a signal fire was the only way to attract attention of anything in the air. It was a major risk but the reality of going undiscovered in the middle of an area so well populated for one more day was not a promising strategy to pursue. Chances of the wounded man surviving the night were even slimmer.

As soon as the sun dipped below the horizon, Marines quietly ventured a few yards into the open. A fire pit was prepared, while others gathered fuel. As a precautionary afterthought, a poncho barrier was erected around the fire pit, anticipating it would provide a blind, shielding firelight from any potential ground-level observation.

Close to midnight, unmistakable but faint sounds of helicopter engines brought the silent campsite to life. Off to the southeast, running lights of two aircraft still some distance off appeared to be on a heading that might offer an opportunity to employ the signal fire. Marines at the campsite held their breath, hoping the aircraft's trajectory would hold. Once they were sure, a Marine quickly lit a heat tab, gently placing it on the prepared tinder. As soon as the flames gained enough strength, Sergeant Campbell and one Korean in very deliberate motions began waving a poncho over the fire, reminiscent of long-ago American Indians forming a smoke signal. All in attendance hoped like hell that the tempo of their efforts would be recognized from the air as a Morse code S.O.S.

At 2,000 feet, a gunship pilot hailed his wingman, directing his attention at 10 o'clock. Altering course to take his flight directly over a glowing beacon, each pilot wondered if this could be the men they were searching for, or a clever attempt by the enemy to lure a helicopter close to the ground. Reducing altitude to 500 feet, the gunship loosed an aerial flare. On his next pass, the co-pilot, observing the site through field glasses, confirmed the presence of at least one Caucasian and four Asians, all dressed in American-style field uniforms, euphorically jumping around and waving. Still not certain of what they were walking into, the wingman was ordered down as the gunship circled just out of rifle range, ready to answer any threat. Setting down at night without ground contact is, to say the least, extremely unnerving.

Jubilant, four Marines put the wounded corpsman on a poncho and carried their colleague out into the field, where Sergeant Campbell and the team sergeant were waiting.

Not more than twenty seconds after touchdown, all passengers having been safely pulled aboard, the rescue craft broke contact with earth, once again ascending to safer heights.

Next morning before the sun peeked over the eastern horizon, search parties continued taking the village apart. Every Marine sifting through that village on this grim recovery detail had been absolutely enraged all night. As fierce and brutal as the Koreans developed a reputation for being, they are also very folksy people with a down-home protective reverence for their own. In solemn sadness, they gathered their dead and searched for the living, just seething and crying unashamedly. Now they understood the rules of this game. If that's how they play, bring it on! Those heartless, soulless *Kae Sa Gya* (just what you think it means) would soon be introduced to Korean-rules ass-kicking.

From that day on, Brigade adopted a mindset of payback that would go far beyond vengeance. An eye for an eye and a tooth for a tooth fell far short of the accounting procedures demanded of the Hyong-je haebyong.

USS Ozbourn
(DD-846)
Gearing Class Destroyer
Call Sign: Spreadeagle

In 1965, USS *Ozbourn* took her turn on the gunline, providing fire support on a variety of missions. She returned to Vietnamese waters again in August 1966 as a unit of Amphibious Ready Group (ARG) 76.5. For her steadfast performance during Operation Deckhouse III, 24 through 29 August, USS *Ozbourn* was commended for excellence by COMUSMSCV, COMSEVENFLT and COMPHIBREADYGRU. Returning to gunline duty on 31 August, she disengaged from one mission to render support in the Vung Tau area. Despite monsoon weather and limited visibility, USS *Ozbourn* responded by crossing Lagi Bay at maximum speed. While dodging shoals and shallows in the bay, enemy tracer fire was sighted between breaks in the weather. Open fire was ordered at maximum range, directly into enemy positions where the fire was emanating from. The shore fire control spotter's first call for correction was, "Great! More of the same."

Throughout the remainder of 1966, USS *Ozbourn* remained on the gunline, transferring to Task Group 77.8 as an escort to USS *Enterprise* (CVN-65) in January 1967, then once again reassigned to the Amphibious Ready Group, where she lent her guns to U.S. Marines involved in Operation Beacon Hill in March. USS *Ozbourn* on 25 March was hit by two rounds fired from enemy shore batteries, damaging her fire control radar room and igniting two ASW missiles. In spite of the damage, USS *Ozbourn* continued on mission, responding with effective counter battery fires, silencing enemy shore installations before retiring for repair.

During May in three separate actions, USS *Ozbourn* was fired on by enemy shore emplacements. She responded to each occasion with counter battery measures, quickly silencing those enemy guns.

On 4 December, USS *Ozbourn* was taken under fire once more, sustaining a direct hit, disabling her aft gun mount. Two men, CS3 Raymond L. Cork, Jr., and SN Edward S. O'Brien, were killed and three injured. The gallant ship continued fighting while dodging over a hundred enemy shells.

USS *Ozbourn* through most of 1968 participated in Operation Sea Dragon. While operating off North Vietnam, she was twice taken under fire, exchanging rounds with enemy gunners.

Throughout 1968, USS *Ozbourn* expended 16,777 rounds of five-inch ammunition. Gun damage assessments confirmed eighty-eight enemy KIAs, 379 structures destroyed, and 422 damaged.

USS *Ozbourn* appeared in Vietnamese waters next on 24 October 1969, firing over 6,569 rounds of five-inch ammunition. During her 1971 deployment, she fired an additional 3,850 rounds.

On 30 April, USS *Ozbourn* once again navigated waters of Vietnam, providing support for USS *Midway* (CV-41) aircraft flying targets over South Vietnam. On 1 May, USS *Ozbourn* proceeded north to join guided missile cruiser USS *Chicago* (CG-11) on station in the Gulf of Tonkin.

For the remainder of the year, she was in and out of the war zone, performing assignments as directed. In early September, USS *Ozbourn* assumed post on the gunline off Quang Tri Province, furnishing Naval gunfire support for troops ashore until 22 September, when she was reassigned to the Hon La Island group, where she took part in sinking over fifty tons of enemy supplies.

Finishing her last duties of the war on 11 October, USS *Ozbourn*, via Hong Kong and Subic Bay, returned to her homeport of Long Beach for a well-earned stand-down.

USS *Ozbourn* officers and crew received the following decorations for heroic and meritorious action: four Purple Hearts (two posthumously), three Bronze Stars with combat "V", fifty-five Navy Achievement Medals, five COMSEVENFLT Commendations, and twenty-three COMCRUDESGRU SEVENTHFL Commendations. In addition, USS *Ozbourn* was awarded the Meritorious Unit Commendation for actions on 25 March 1967 and 23, 24, and 25 May 1967.

We, who once found refuge under the protection of her guns, salute this valiant ship and her gallant crew.

THE FRIENDS

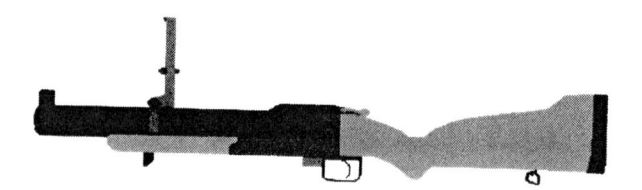

Corporal Willis Leonard McBride hailed from Tazewell, Virginia, epitomizing those values of a working-class community that typify Middle America. He was a married man with a well-developed moral compass. No one could remember hearing of Will ever being in the least bit of trouble.

PFC Maurice (John) Biehn was raised in Gregory, Michigan, a small rural town northwest of Ann Arbor on State Route 36. He loved having fun and rarely passed up a chance to flirt with mischief. Like McBride, he kept pretty much to himself and got along with everyone.

They came of age 800 miles apart, raised on ethics and virtues found in every corner of America, each in the tradition of his own family's observances. Not having much in common, the pair did not run together in Hawaii. Will, being married, stuck pretty close to the barracks, while John hung out in Waikiki, living the single life as could only be experienced in a bachelor's paradise.

Once in Vietnam, these two strangers were paired as a fire control team with 3rd Battalion and dispatched to an outpost where necessities of survival in very dangerous surroundings were deciphered together. Having been newly posted at Kaneohe shortly before drawing assignment to Sub Unit One, PFC Biehn missed out on opportunities at live fire control on Kahoolawe. In truth, there were a lot of gaps in his training. Taking inventory of the junior man's skills, Willis McBride took on the role of trainer, rounding out absent knowledge Biehn would need to function on his own. At nineteen, PFC Biehn was most grateful for the personal tutelage. He looked up to Corporal McBride, three years his senior, not only as a mentor but as a friend as well. McBride recognized and respected Biehn's desire to shoulder his part of the load. He took Biehn on as a project and appointed himself his brother's keeper. They labored long and worked hard to bridge a gap that needed spanning in the shortest time possible.

Living among foreign troops, observing customs in a culture shared by people of a common heritage not of your own acumen, is a difficult way to spend a year of one's life. Holidays, entertainment, and social activities are all clustered around protocols of unfamiliar tradition. Under such circumstances, people tend to gravitate to the only other person of their own cultural experience present.

McBride and Biehn looked after each other and learned the ways of the Hyong-je haebyong. Thus a friendship was born that would endure through some harrowing times.

Not long after posting to *Ship Chungdae* (10th Company), the pair found themselves on day patrol in the foothills west of National Highway 1 just south of Tra Bong River. Ship Chungdae drew perimeter security for Battalion, routinely conducting platoon sweeps around the command post. This particular patrol would see double-duty as the entire company took the field to act as blocking force for *Ku Chungdae* (9th Company) driving east from the Anamites toward National Highway 1.

Before the sun peeked over the horizon, Ship Chungdae was on approach to their assigned location, three platoons online in file.

Poised at a valley access several clicks west, Ku Chungdae was in jump-off position, point platoon already on the march. With a hundred-meter interval established, the remaining two platoons saddled up, forming the base of a company wedge formation on a 200-meter front. Corporal Calvin A. McGinty, Jr., and Lance Corporal Terrence J. Perko composed the Tactical Air Control party and stepped off with Headquarters Platoon, experiencing apprehensive reactions that accompany every sojourn into peril. A steady drizzle keeping pace all through the night had just ceased one hour before launch, creating an uncomfortably damp and chilly morning. Water still clinging to jungle growth wasted little time soaking their uniforms, causing involuntary shivers coursing through their bodies.

By 0545, the first rays of a hot morning sun, blending with damp atmospheric conditions, summoned a thick rolling fog, gliding down the slopes from the high ground, swarming onto the valley floor below. Lazy billowing wakes of earthbound clouds curled behind random formations of legless men slowly cutting a swath through a ghostly landscape in total silence.

Eight hundred meters ahead, some 300 members of a Viet Cong logistics caravan making a supply run to Tra Bong were preparing to break camp. Unable to make much speed through the downpour, they spent the night in the valley and were planning to linger in the area till darkness so they could slip past Korean outposts and travel undetected by American aircraft.

This particular campground was a prepared stopover often utilized by Viet Cong travelers moving to and from Ba Lang An, and was chosen for its favorable topography. It was at this location where a gully cut into the north hill boundary, offering the only other exit from the valley. Hidden by a thick canopy of vegetation, the campground and gully could not be seen from the air. Once through the gully on the other side of the hill, six or seven mini-canyons offered escape into the surrounding high country. Just in front of the camp, the valley widened to its largest expanse. Two fingers of high ground branching from the south slope on both sides of the gully channeled all who traveled the valley toward the northern end, providing a barrier on either side that could be defended by minimal force for short periods, enabling the main body to escape. A small unit of old men provided a permanent garrison for the campground, making sure the area remained free of debris keeping up appearances of a deserted mountain valley.

That same morning fog shieling them, also kept them unaware of *Ku Chungdae's* approach.

Near the eastern end of the valley where intersections of three well-worn footpaths formed a Y-shaped junction, Marines of *Ship Chungdae* quietly split into two groups. *E Sodae* (2nd Platoon), providing security for H&S and weapons platoons, assumed position in the center of the split, while the remaining two platoons took to high ground on the north slope. John Biehn made the ascent with the flank platoons while McBride, shepherding the radio, remained close to the command structure.

Seeing his men correctly positioned, at 0615 the company commander notified battalion he was in place and ready.

By 0730, the cloud cover parted, giving promise to one of the few sunny days of a tenacious monsoon season. Slowly dissolving into a mist, the fog was completely dissipated by 0800. Seeing no other way around the finger hill, *Ku Chungdae's* lead squad gravitated toward the northern slope of the valley.

From his sheltered position well camouflaged by thick vegetation on the western slope outcropping some 100 meters in front of the camp, a sentinel looking up from cleaning his weapon was startled to see a formation of enemy troops not sixty meters up the valley. Sending his runner into the camp to sound a warning, the sentinel quickly reassembled his weapon and drew a bead on the point man.

News of the interlopers instigated a rushed flurry of activity as men scrambled about the camp, sounding the alert as quietly as possible.

An additional three-man cell crawled into place just in front of Ku Chungdae, who had now advanced to within twenty meters of the VC listening post.

Gathering their weapons and what supplies they could manage, Viet Cong gravitated toward the gully and began to stream out of the valley as silently as the urgency of this maneuver would allow. Cracks of rifle fire from the listening post negated any further need of stealth as the flow of men accelerated to a hell-bent for leather race to exit the valley.

Meeting the opening volley with return fire, the point squad went to ground, relaying a situation report on this turn of events back to Ku Chungdae Actual (Company Commander). A heated exchange continued for five minutes then tapered off, as the point squad had little trouble establishing fire superiority. While a support squad maneuvered just south of the altercation, the point squad poured on coordinated fire while the enveloping squad assaulted the knoll, driving the VC cell back toward the camp. No casualties on either side.

Upon hearing gunfire, VC work parties throughout the valley, not knowing what events were taking place near the gully, were forced to fend for themselves. A few groups darted in different directions, while most remained in place, relying on training to seek as much concealment as this jungle-choked valley could afford.

Advancing through the camp, Marines of Ku Chungdae wasted little time discovering abandoned supplies scattered here and there. Supplies consisted for the most part of grenades, small arms ammo, and RPG rockets. A little more probing revealed a gully saturated with trod-down vegetation and scores of footprints trailing off into the canyons just beyond.

Ku Chungdae sent two platoons into the gully while the remainder of the company sorted through the supplies, looking for documents and preparing to destroy the ammo. Corporal McGinty accompanied the pursuit platoons, while Lance Corporal Perko took charge of the radio, remaining with 9th Company command elements.

Upon receiving news of the find, battalion ordered pursuit of the fleeing Viet Cong, directing Ship Chungdae into the valley.

Ship Chungdae recalled half its force from the heights, leaving John Biehn on the crest with one platoon. Corporal McBride moved out with the main body toward center valley. A different atmosphere is present when heading into a known danger zone than when on patrol, just hoping to ferret out an unseen adversary that may or may not be in your path. Senses heightened and adrenalin levels elevated as men moved forward in anticipation of contact somewhere up ahead.

A handful of VC work parties trapped in the valley, aware that Ku Chungdae was sweeping in from the west, headed east, not knowing of Ship Chungdae's approach. Gathering at a listening post on the eastern outcropping, they mapped out an impromptu escape plan to infiltrate to the footpath junction on the east end.

As lead elements descended the finger outcropping, a lookout on top spotted a column of Koreans in a small clearing some eighty meters distant. The small band scurried back over the finger and down the reverse slope. A VC sniper further south sent a round down range toward the clearing.

Will McBride's body convulsed involuntarily as a sharp snap from a bullet cracked through vegetation just inches over his head. Machine gun chatter erupted on the flank while men hustled forward to confront the threat.

Regaining his posture, Corporal McBride jumped on the radio, hailing Terry Perko to make sure none of his people were in the area. Digesting Terry's situation report, McBride regained his feet, following Headquarters group toward the supply cache. Just a few yards from the edge of the clearing, a second round slammed into one of the thin border trees at shoulder height less than a foot to Will's right. McBride came to ground a half second ahead of a dead branch knocked loose from the bullet impact, shattering on contact with his back. McBride crawled the last few feet into the bush and just lay there, trying to catch his breath, shaking off the fear.

It's not a comforting thought to know someone has you in his sights and is following your every movement. Corporal McBride collected his wits and applied commonsense reasoning before moving one more inch. Glancing at the spot where the first round almost found him, McBride traced the back azimuths of the assumed trajectory toward the finger hump. He repeated the exercise with the second bullet strike to triangulate and gain perspective on the general direction of his stalker. His attention settled on an area some 200 meters high on the finger outcropping, where it tapered off the south valley slope. Scanning an area thirty meters in each direction from where his seat of the pants triangulation told him the sniper was anchored, the corporal centered his attention on likely places of concealment he would choose were he that sniper. After about five minutes of intense eye search, McBride thought he saw movement. Rising up on his elbows, the NCO rested his cheekbone on his thumb, cradling the small of his rifle stock, and lined up his sights on the suspected lair. After four or five more minutes of concentration, McBride was sure he saw something but didn't have a clear target.

Looking around, he found himself all alone. It seems no one else noticed his predicament. McBride was so intense and scared he didn't notice that the command group had moved out. Grabbing his map, Will fixed the grid coordinates and raised Perko on the radio, asking him to arrange a mortar round on his map fix. Lance Corporal Perko ran down the Korean weapons platoon commander and requested a fire mission. Within minutes, McBride heard the report of an outgoing

81. He observed a round impacting forty meters short and some twenty meters or so too far right. McBride was about to make a round adjustment when a lone figure broke cover and sprinted toward the south slope. Quickly shouldering his weapon once again, the Marine centered his sight picture and pumped four rounds down range, dropping the fleeing sniper on the last trigger pull.

Raised on time-honored Christian principles that all life is sacred, a crisis of conscience had just invaded that place in his heart that stood guard over the essence of who is Willis McBride. Not having time to deal with it, the Marine hustled off in search of his command structure.

Ship Chungdae entered the base camp around 1030. After a brief meeting with *Ku Chungdae,* the latter's skipper took his remaining troops and followed his two line platoons into the gully.

After a brief exchange of pleasantries, Perko bid farewell to McBride, falling in with *Ku Chungdae*. After just a hundred meters or so, the gully ended, forming a junction of two shallow canyons that split east to west. Knowing from reports of the pursuit platoons now ninety minutes ahead that several other branch canyons meandered through the area, *Ku Chungdae's* skipper decided to keep his force intact and follow his pursuit platoons up the east canyon. Diluting his force in this maze made for ambush had the earmarks of disaster. The only blocking force in the area was the platoon from *Ship Chungdae* ridge hopping from the east. If they were to trap anyone, this was the only logical heading to take. If, on the other hand, they ran into trouble, help would be close by.

Over the past half hour, Corporal McGinty's apprehension level accelerated as the canyon began to narrow. The terrain inside the canyon he was currently traversing was only about eight feet wide. Thick jungle growth on the canyon walls draped the canyon in a canopy that shrouded the area in an almost twilight quality of visibility. It was like walking through a cave being drawn to a dim light at the end of the tunnel. McGinty was fighting so hard to control his uneasiness he didn't realize how quiet things were around him.

Calvin McGinty was born and raised in Tallassee, Alabama. Tallassee is a small rural town halfway between Montgomery and Auburn, in a field-and-stream environment on the Tallapoosa that provided downstate Alabama boys a sportsman's paradise. All his outdoor experience had never prepared him for this much darkness so close to noon. A few hundred meters later, his spirits lifted as a glimmer of light from up ahead showed they were coming back to the natural world of sunlight once again. It was at that point a halt was called for a few minutes' stand-down in protection of the overgrowth before venturing into open light.

Once progress resumed, it didn't take long before the tree canopy gave way to a hot midmorning sun. It hurt his eyes. Calvin removed his glasses to wipe tearing from his eyes, trying hard to adjust from one extreme to another. A Korean behind him found some humor in his observation that almost everyone was squinting and tripping over roots while trying to regain their sight after being so long in darkness.

From up front, report of a small explosion signaled an end to the cakewalk. Two Koreans on point tripped a booby trap, leaving both with shrapnel in their legs. Almost immediately, small arms took the point under fire in sporadic random bursts that were more nuisance than threat. Deducing this to be a delaying tactic, a fire team was dispatched with an artillery FO up the canyon wall to seek an advantage position and bring fire to bear on the holding party.

Once in position, artillery batteries from *Som Taedae* (3rd Battalion) began adjusting on the ridge line to the patrol's immediate front. One gun fired adjusting rounds until the FO talked them on target. Needing only two adjustments, fire for effect salvos impacted some 100 meters from the platoon, 20 meters from the top of the ridge. A second fire for effect order sent six more rounds slamming into the ridge line. The smoke had not yet settled before the ROKs moved out.

Two squads assaulted the heights in quick order soon after the last round impacted on the ridge, only to find nothing. When the all-clear was given, the remainder of the platoon scaled the canyon, bringing up both wounded men. Orders came in over the TAC net to hold in place and await the skipper.

A work party began clearing out a landing zone while McGinty borrowed the platoon tactical net radio and relayed through Terry Perko coordinates and request for Medevac of two routine WIAs.

One hour later, Klip Klop Medevac arrived on station and lifted off with the two wounded without incident.

Once joined with the main body, Ku Chungdae headed back out to the valley the way they came in, with nothing to show.

Ku Chungdae re-entered the camp near sunset while Will McBride was directing the last sortie of evening aerial resupply operations. Both company command groups settled in close proximity to each other to take advantage of a common perimeter. This gave Willis a chance to network with Perko and McGinty, whom he hadn't seen since posting to the bush.

Still making headway from the ridge-hopping excursion, John Biehn and the flank platoon of Ship Chungdae could see the combined Korean force in the valley below about a half mile west. Night was already settling in. Making a steep descent down vine-laden slopes in the dark and feeling their way through that valley was deemed more risk than necessary. Settling in on the ridge line for the night was a sensible decision.

Som Sodae Jung (3rd Platoon Commander) selected a narrow plateau protected by two steep inclines north and east. A gradual slope to the west descended to the valley floor. Taking nothing for granted, he personally assigned each man a defensive position and ordered the platoon to dig in. As a precaution, artillery was registered on all four sides of the summit. Storm clouds gathering overhead shielded defensive positions on the plateau from a half moon drifting in and out of overcast skies, instigating a gentle rain to disrupt any thought of spending a comfortable night in safe harbor.

McBride, McGinty, and Perko enjoyed the novelty of having the company of someone other than his own teammate in the field, getting caught up on the latest scuttlebutt and just enjoying the moment in spite of the rain now coming down in torrents. A sudden automatic rifle burst from just ten feet away sent the three face down in the mud. Another burst of fire erupted to their left, then yet another somewhere close by in the half light. Not having a clue as to what was going on, the three formed their own private perimeter, trying to sort through the confusion and fight down fear abruptly creeping into their throats.

Slipping and sliding through the mud, a Korean splashed down beside the trio, informing them as quietly as he could that VC were emerging from the tunnels, popping up through spider trap doors. He left instructions for ANGLICO to remain in place and be sure of their targets before shooting, then scampered off in a different direction before any questions could be asked.

After what seemed like fifteen minutes or so, fire teams of Marines gravitated toward known spider traps in the last remaining minute of twilight. Two Marines would establish guard position, training their weapons on the hole, while two others approached the spider trap. One man pulled up on the cover while the second tossed hand grenades into the opening then closed it up in quick fashion. This procedure repeated itself simultaneously in several places inside the perimeter for the next half hour.

Adding to the chaos inside the perimeter, snipers initiated sporadic fire from outside, creating a tenuous situation for anyone moving about. If this wasn't enough to worry about, some VC managed to make it to the surface after dark, emerging from undiscovered subterranean earthworks slinking about the campsite. Word was passed down to discard ponchos. Medical adhesive tape was passed around with orders for everyone to apply a strip down the center of his helmet. Anything moving without a strip display was fair game.

About this time, things really got spooky. The ANGLICO Marines could hear and sense movement all around them, not knowing who it was that was coming or going. With a lack of moonlight and the ever-incessant rain, visibility was no more than five feet. All eyes were agape in wonder as shadowy figures darted this way and that. Periodically, sporadic clusters of fire would erupt here and there in no particular pattern. Each man rehearsed in his mind "*Mi Guk Haebyong, so-ji mara!*" ("American Marine, don't shoot!"). Not one of the three had the least notion to breathe any more than necessary, let alone move. Waiting in the dark, afraid, wet, and miserable, each conjured visions of unknown horrors lurking just out of sight, but drew strength from being near close friends they knew to be totally reliable.

In the silence, Will McBride's thoughts drifted to John Biehn. Hindsight being 20/20, Will wished he would have left the radio with John instead of having both team radios in the same location, leaving his friend without communication. He knew no one planned it this way, but couldn't help but wonder how his buddy was making out.

Without warning, a furious exchange of gunfire erupted to the trio's left rear, snapping Will out of his distraction in startled bewilderment. Muffled but unmistakable Vietnamese voices interrupted by rifle report appeared to be coming from the direction of the gunfire. Muzzle flashes dulled by rain blinked from several positions not more than twenty feet from where they lay, half submerged in mud and water.

From seemingly out of thin air, two apparitions materialized in front of Terry Perko, running at sprint speed and just about ready to step on him. With no time to think, Terry held his rifle up at port arms from prone position, thrusting his weapon forcefully into the shins of the first phantom to reach him. At full sprint, he tumbled into the trio. Quickly rising to one knee, Corporal McGinty brought his rifle butt up from the ground, breaking the levitated specter's jaw, showering McBride with blood and teeth.

Not being able to comprehend what just happened but fully realizing he was in serious trouble, the second phantom fell right on his ass as he tried to reverse course on mud-slicked soil. Only when his ass hit the deck did he see an American not two feet away. The last recorded memory of his short life was a muzzle flash from Terry Perko's rifle—right in his face.

Fearing the commotion may draw fire from the Hyong-je Haebyong, McBride raised his voice in the darkness: "*So-ji mara, so-ji mara, VC KIA!*"

That same shroud of darkness enveloped the flank platoon on the small plateau. Now waste deep in water, Marines peered out of their fighting holes, trying to filter out rain chatter, listening intently for tell-tale decibels of disturbance that didn't belong in the natural surroundings. Sheets of water cascading off rocks and overhangs mimicked the roar of whitewater rapids rushing down a river canyon, filling the ears of every man present.

Eighty or so meters from the summit on the west slope, Viet Cong emerging from a tunnel complex initiating a slow excursion toward the flooded encampment struggled with the same problem of limited visibility and rain clatter. As if these handicaps weren't enough, sloppy soil conditions imposed an added impediment of poor footing. Although not the most ideal conditions for attacking up hill, the VC commander rationalized poor weather conditions favored his troops over blind defenders. After all, he was the only commander of the two who knew something was about to happen. Taking almost a full hour to close within thirty meters of the plateau, lead elements of the attacking force paused to allow rear units ample time to get in place. Within half an hour, the attack went forward.

Two Marines in the center left foxhole almost went into cardiac arrest upon hearing a dull thud of something splashing into the mud from what seemed to be right in front of them. A brilliant flash followed by a deafening explosion temporarily blinded the duo. Muzzle flashes flickered in the darkness as the sound of gunfire muted the soft roar of the foul weather serenade enveloping every man facing the west slope.

Return fire from manned fighting holes sent tracers racing down hill. Forward observers contacted Battalion. Seconds later, star shells burst overhead, lighting up the deluged landscape in a sinister radiance, silhouetting the attacking force in a backdrop of exaggerated shadows. Artillery from 3rd Battalion began pounding the west slope. Ordnance arched in on pre-registered coordinates—a wasted effort, as the enemy was already between the registration point and summit. The forward observer tried everything he knew to adjust rounds onto the attacking force but dared not bring the big guns any closer.

Front line grunts exchanged grenades with forward elements of the attackers, dotting the perimeter with flashes and smoke. Twice the VC came to within eight or so feet of the defenders before being driven back at point-blank range in a savage fusillade of fire. After twenty-five minutes of concentrated fighting, the west slope went quiet as half-visible antagonists melted into the shadows.

Artillery mercilessly continued pounding the west slope. For good measure, the valley floor at the base was generously pulverized to cut off escape routes. But the Viet Cong did not descend too far from the summit. Crawling back inside their subterranean refuge, which provided protection from the barrage of whistling death, they hunkered down, waiting for calm to return.

Men on the plateau breathed a sigh of relief, enjoying the spectacle of Brigade howitzers working over the hillside below. For fifteen more minutes, the earth shook under a constant deluge of 105 and 155mm explosions. When the barrage lifted, the men of Som Sodae found themselves once again alone with the sounds of nature. A feeling of elation earned in victory settled over the platoon. They forgot about their discomfort for awhile. The platoon corpsman reported four minor and two moderately wounded Marines. Squad leaders all reported being low on ammunition! In the confusion of recalling the other platoon that ascended the heights with them, it took most of the reserve ammo when they rejoined the company. At the time, it seemed like a good idea, considering they needed to move quickly over rough terrain. There was no thought of spending the night isolated from Ship Chungdae.

John Biehn, feeling useless without a radio, pulled his poncho hood over his helmet and dropped his head forward, shielding as much of his body as he could from the rain in a vain attempt to try for some sleep. Radio or not, this weather wouldn't permit air activities tonight anyhow, he thought, and quickly let go of his regrets. More than discomfort, the excitement of the attack pushed his adrenaline level over the top. Sleep would not come to PFC Biehn that night.

The low-ammo situation played on the mind of Som Sodae Jung. If they were attacked again, he needed some type of advantage. Squad leaders were called to a meeting in the center of the perimeter. In his estimation, there was not enough ammo to repel another assault of the same intensity. His plan was to move the platoon off the plateau some thirty feet. If an attack materialized, they would counterattack right through it. The objective was to reach the valley and head west toward where the combined companies were bivouacked. Once the platoon was a reasonably safe distance from the hill, artillery would be loosed behind them to cover their withdrawal.

Packing up their gear, and discarding ponchos, Som Sodae moved slowly in absolute silence downhill and stopped at the new designated defense line. Looking back to the plateau, the lieutenant could see the dim outline of the crest silhouetted against darkened skies. He felt a little more comfortable about his move, but doubt still tugged heavily at his heart.

John Biehn could not remember ever being so scared. On the side of a hill with no fighting hole, no definable perimeter, and nothing but pitch blackness any direction, he turned his head. It felt like being alone and naked in a haunted house. He was sure he once had a dream along that scenario.

Just before dawn, the rains abated to a slow drizzle. From out of the darkest part of night all along the front, muted sounds of movement filled the hearts of every man with dread. Up and down the line, each man steeled himself, waiting for the call to action. Following progress of their opponents' advance, by recognizing incrementally louder and more distinct sounds of men struggling uphill, was a test of fortitude and a tribute to discipline. Gunfire erupted on the right flank, initiated by grunts at point-blank range. Reacting at lightning speed, the lieutenant gave the word to attack. All along the front, men sprang to their feet, lurching forward, firing from the hip. Two men needing help, supported by a Marine on each arm, followed a phalanx in front of them. Within the first four strides, Marines were mingling with Viet Cong who were caught totally off guard.

Marines charged headlong into their attackers, violently colliding with the enemy: shooting, slashing, and screaming. Shrill invectives clearing Marine throats seemed reminiscent of Indian attacks in grade B Westerns.

John Biehn bumped into an oncoming attacker, glancing off the man's shoulder. No sooner had he regained momentum, another loomed in front of him. Thrusting his rifle out in front of him, the second man was shoved out of the way with a vicious clip under his nose.

Being thrown off balance in the scuffle John lost his footing, hitting the deck hard. Holding onto his rifle, John slid for a distance of what seemed like eight or ten meters. His momentum was abruptly stopped when he slid into the legs of someone running uphill, causing the man to tumble right over him. Gaining his feet once more, John pumped two rounds into the interloper and continued his maddening downhill slalom.

Forward momentum picked up speed as no wanted to be cut off or fall behind. Each contact was as brief as possible. Viet Cong were totally confused. As Marines rushed through their ranks, attackers turning to fire stopped short, knowing they could be shooting their own further downhill. Those guerillas in front, not knowing what the hell was going on uphill, became entangled in the same situation as soon as Marine forward motion penetrated their ranks.

Not known at the time (and this is still conjecture on part of the author), most of the attacking force was still inside the tunnels, waiting their turn to exit the narrow passage under the night sky.

Reaching the bottom of the slope some 110 meters from where the downhill assault began, squad leaders turned and started organizing their fire teams to face the enemy. Each squad leader had to account for all his Marines. Somehow, within seconds of arriving on the valley floor, a quick head count under a chaotic cloud of confusion confirmed all personnel amazingly accounted for.

Three squads hurriedly formed up, unleashing a full clip of ammo uphill. Reloading while turning to run, the whistling rush of incoming artillery prompted a quicker withdrawal than anticipated. The forward observer wasted little time in passing on fire orders to Battalion.

USS Providence
(CLG-6)
Cleveland Class Guided Missile Armed Light Cruiser
Call Sign: Firefighter

In May 1957, the twelve-year-old light cruiser USS *Providence* (CL-82) was reclassified as a guided missile light cruiser (CLG-6). Taken out of the Atlantic Reserve Fleet, she soon began conversion at the Boston Naval Shipyard. This massive project stripped away all but one each of her four six-inch gun turrets and six five-inch gun mounts, as well as virtually all of her original superstructure. In their place, the ship was given a twin-armed launcher for the newly developed Terrier guided missile, a large missile magazine, and associated control systems. A greatly enlarged superstructure, enhanced radar, and extensive communications electronics were also installed to fit the cruiser for employment as a fleet flagship. *Providence* was recommissioned in September 1959 and joined the Pacific Fleet in July 1960.

In October 1960, *Providence* steamed across the Pacific to begin her first Far Eastern deployment, which lasted until March 1961. She returned to Asian waters in May 1962 to become flagship of the Seventh Fleet. Homeported at Yokosuka, Japan, she remained in that job for more than two years, until July 1964, and then cruised back to the United States by way of Australia and the Southern Pacific. Providence's third Seventh Fleet tour of duty, her second as flagship, took place between December 1966 and December 1968. In an era dominated by the conflict in Southeast Asia, she was frequently called upon to operate off Vietnam, where her advanced electronics were employed to control air combat operations, while her guns shelled enemy targets ashore. During the Tet Offensive, in February 1968, she provided bombardment support for the U.S. Marines' intense fight to recapture the city of Hue. Shortly before that, in January 1968, she made a fast run north to Korean waters in response to the seizure of the U.S. intelligence-gathering ship *Pueblo*.

During the early 1970s, Providence served as flagship of the U.S. 1st Fleet, operating in the Eastern Pacific. North Vietnam's 1972 offensive sent her back to the Far East in April. For nearly all of the rest of that year she delivered six- and five-inch gunfire against enemy forces, including a number of raids against the port of Haiphong and other areas in North Vietnam. Returning to the United States in December 1972, Providence almost immediately began preparations for inactivation. She was decommissioned at San Diego at the end of August 1973 and placed in reserve. Later towed to the Puget Sound Naval Shipyard, at Bremerton, Washington, she was redesignated CG-6 in mid-1975 but had no further active service. USS *Providence* was stricken from the Naval Vessel Register in July 1978 and sold for scrap in 1980.

We, who once found refuge under the protection of her guns, salute this valiant ship and her gallant crew.

WILL THE LAST MAN STANDING PLEASE CALL A MEDEVAC?

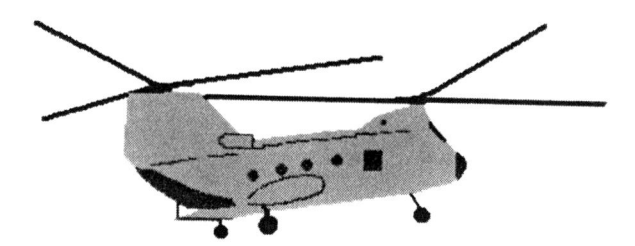

Through the rest of that autumn and early into winter, monsoons continued pelting Quang Nhai Province without mercy. Brigade, still intent on settling old scores from events after Dragon Claw, kept aggressively to offense. Search and destroy operations continued unabated. When Brigade was not in operation mode, platoon-size patrols and company sweeps continued probing for an elusive adversary that always managed to avoid contact whenever possible. Plenty of small skirmishes were initiated by both sides, but large, "kick ass, grab some glory" battles long sought by Brigade never materialized.

Early January 1967, 3rd Battalion took initiative in the foothills just south of Tra Bong River to disrupt supply activities recently brought to General Lee's attention through intelligence gathered one week earlier.

Captain Larry Oswalt, commanding officer, 3rd Battalion ANGLICO team, was informed by Colonel Park (not his real name) *Som Taedae* C.O., to prepare for a search and destroy operation in the far west reaches of the territory. Operational plans called for battalion command personnel hitching a chopper ride to 9th Company outpost, situated on a small hill a few clicks west of National Highway 1. Per plan, two line companies on command moved out from their respective base camps in a hammer and anvil tactic, calling for *Ship II Chungdae* (11th Company) to sweep south from the river, pushing enemy troops into the waiting gun sites of Ku Chungdae.

While Brigade continued turning Ba Lang An inside out, intelligence suffered from a tunnel vision of vengeance. Unknown at that time, elements of the 21st NVA Regiment were converging toward the Korean area of responsibility and were now filtering into operational boundaries of that planned sweep.

Operation Swift Dragon (unsure of actual name) was launched on January 5 with an Airborne troop insertion on a company outpost deep into Indian country. After four days of busting ass through mud, in a rain-soaked jungle, a brief firefight was initiated by Marines of Ku Chungdae. Enemy soldiers observed traveling a footpath heading east were taken under fire. After a brief skirmish, Ku Chungdae managed to secure two prisoners. They were sporting AK-47s and wearing khaki NVA field uniforms. This event marked the first known contact between Koreans and North Vietnamese troops, causing a rush of excitement as word of this coup made its way up the chain.

Evening of day four bore witness to Swift Dragon being officially declared a big disappointment. Headquarters and command personnel planned on being airlifted back to Battalion CP. Unsuccessful in securing a ride due to heavy rain, Captain Oswalt delivered the bad news to Colonel Park, who was in a hurry to get back to the office. Not a man to be put off, the 3rd Battalion C.O. immediately ordered a march back to the CP so he could get at those prisoners. He had a strong sense these captives represented something of value in need of exploiting as soon as possible.

A small column comprised of battalion command officers and a reinforced platoon moved off the hill under a steady downpour around 1230 on 10 January at a brisk pace. Captain Larry Oswalt, Lance Corporal David Lucht, and Lance Corporal William F. Croney fell in close to the rear of the formation. Having served a prior tour with 3rd Battalion, 7th Marines, Lance Corporal Lucht was an experience jungle fighter from Operations Starlight and Piranha, but was new to ANGLICO. He was on his maiden voyage with the ROKs going through on-the-job training supervised by Captain Oswalt, who always reserved replacement orientation for himself. The captain was a stickler that Marines new to ANGLICO learn what they needed to learn the right way. Since 1962, Larry Oswalt had been flying some of the most lethal war birds in the U.S. arsenal, being very aware of how wrong things could go if things weren't done right.

An hour into the march, the Marines followed a small clearing to an irregular-shaped flooded rice paddy approximately 100 by 150 meters in girth, hemmed on three sides by thick tree lines. Two large hills running north and south bracketed the paddy, creating a miniature valley. The column followed a footpath sitting atop a wide dike with a drainage ditch on the right side that skirted around the eastern perimeter opening up to a large field of dense scrub brush on the other end.

Surveying his surroundings, Lucht became uneasy with noticeable absence of Vietnamese working the field. Something just didn't seem right. Flipping off his M-14's safety, Dave followed his two companions into the rice paddy, eyes darting from one side to another, looking for signs of danger he felt sure were all around him.

As the point squad reached midway across, ANGLICO started into the paddy and had only moved thirty or so meters into the open when a furious exchange of rifle fire exploded from up front of the column. Lead elements came face to face with a dozen or so North Vietnamese at no more than ten paces. Both factions opened fire simultaneously. Koreans having the better part of it chased the Vietnamese from their harbor. Quiet returned to the landscape for a few seconds until flanking squads moved into the paddy to cut off escape routes. In unison, the far tree line ignited in a calamitous roar of gunfire. Six Koreans in forwardmost positions were taken out within seconds. NVA from entrenched positions engulfed the entire paddy in a rain of steel.

Other Marines along the column, caught by complete surprise, fell at random from the wide dike. The flanking squad in the paddy was hammered, taking heavy losses. Men at point and middle of the column returned fire while rear elements hustled forward to close ranks with those further in the paddy, casualties mounting with every step.

Sprinting to catch up with the main body through a torrent of small arms fire, the ANGLICO team accompanied by the rear guard loosed a lethal barrage of their own at the forward tree line. A second front burst open from behind about thirty or so meters left of where they just entered the rice paddy, shooting a number of the rear guard in the back. Oswalt, Lucht, and Croney dove behind a paddy dike thirty meters or so in front of a cluster of Marines midway in the procession, which was feverishly pumping fire in all directions. As if the horrific volume of small arms fire wasn't enough, mortar detonations started churning up the paddies, flinging mud and rice stalks everywhere. Even the rain was now coming down harder than it had all morning. The rice paddy was alive with millions of splashes, large and small, natural and man-made. It wasn't possible to distinguish bullet strikes from raindrops.

Defensive actions took both tree lines under fire, while individual Marines rushed forward, pulling dead and wounded behind the dike away from murderous torrents of fire. Injured Marines drawn out of danger were left to care for themselves until a corpsman could reach them, as every rifle on the line was needed for suppressing fire to answer incoming bedlam.

Exposing himself for a better view, the forward observer was cut down in the act of adjusting artillery on the tree line. As he was thirty or so feet out into the paddy, his body was not visible above the water line. No one could locate him or the radio still strapped on his back. Loss of that radio severed all communication links to artillery support. There was no one left alive in the rice paddy who knew the radio frequency of battalion artillery. Not knowing the fate of his gallant FO, the battalion commander was heard shouting over the din for artillery, but there was no answer.

Mounting problems plagued the defenders as almost every other field radio in the column was quickly put out of action or submerged in the rice paddy on the back of the man who carried it.

Lucht and Croney worked their M-14s hard in a futile attempt to match fire volume coming in on them from two sides. Captain Oswalt tried to establish contact on the TACP net but hills on either side were interfering with his transmissions. NCOs struggling to get a grip on the situation shifted troops here and there to establish a base of fire in two directions. Officers barked orders, sending runners up and down the line. Other officers consulted maps to establish their exact position, trying to get a handle on the confused events.

Lance Corporal John Houghton at Ku Chungdae's base camp, little more than an hour's march away, picked up Captain Oswalt's frantic voice over the team radio. Located on higher ground, he had clear voice to Brigade as well as Captain Oswalt and was in position to relay transmission. Captain Oswalt quickly called out his position and requested air support as fast as it could get there.

At the same time, Ku Chungdae's commanding officer was in communication with his boss, who was fighting for his life in the rice paddy a few meters up the column from Captain Oswalt. What radios the Koreans had left experienced the same problem of transmissions being blocked by topographic interference.

Five minutes later, a reinforced platoon-size reaction force was assembled on the fly to mount a rescue mission for the beleaguered Marines desperately trapped in a cross-fire ambush. Lance Corporal John Houghton would accompany the reaction force, leaving the radio with his teammate, Lance Corporal Patrick P. White, who took over conversation with Captain Oswalt.

Tracing footfalls of the Headquarters party, Koreans moved out downhill on an eastward heading toward a shit sandwich somewhere up the trail. Mindful of the oft-used tactic of pinning down a small unit, hoping to draw rescue forces into ambush, the reaction force proceeded as fast as they dared without throwing caution to the wind.

Seeing anything through blinding sheets of rain was almost impossible. No one really noticed exactly when, but a frontal assault on the paddy dike materialized as NVA soldiers suddenly appeared no more fifty meters in front of the defensive fires laid down by confused Marines along the footpath.

Confident that help was on the way, Captain Oswalt took initiative, relaying coordinates to Lance Corporal White for artillery support. White in turn passed on the information to Korean FOs on the hill who had link to Brigade batteries.

Startled at unfolding events to their immediate front, Dave Lucht and Bill Croney poured round after round into the attacking force. Captain Oswalt pulled out his .45 for only the second or third time in-country. Surprised at how calm he was as the automatic jumped in his hand after each trigger pull, the officer quickly emptied a magazine into the oncoming attackers. As he reached for another magazine, grenades began falling abundantly among the trio.

One grenade landed eight to twelve inches to Dave Lucht's left. Running on instinct, Lucht picked up the grenade, flipped over on his back, instantaneously flinging it into the paddy. As he rolled back over into firing position, nearby explosions sent shrapnel cutting deep into his back.

Captain Oswalt, seeing how intense the fight had become, ordered Lucht and Croney to higher ground, hoping more elevation would overcome frequency interference. A steady flood of small arms fire and grenade explosions stalked their every movement, hurling mud and debris in their path kicking up water spouts on all sides. A bullet glanced across the face of Lucht's watch, stopping the timepiece at 1400 hours. Almost simultaneously, both legs were ripped by rifle fire. Not having time to deal with the pain, the Marine wiped the cobwebs from his eyes, trying to recover his senses. Knowing he wouldn't last long if the bleeding wasn't stopped, the wounded man quickly pulled his belt from his waist, tying off his left thigh.

Four feet away, Captain Oswalt felt a terrible sting in his leg. His mind went blank as pain shot rapidly through his body. Letting go of the radio handset, he hurriedly tried to evaluate the damage. Discovering a shredded mess covered in blood, he knew he was in trouble. As his leg was half submerged in water, now dark with blood, the officer could not determine the severity of his wounds. He attempted to shrug it off but the pain wouldn't let go. No matter which way he moved, agony kept him pressed flat to earth.

Through a dense fog of torment, Dave Lucht heard Captain Oswalt call out he was hit. Crawling toward his C.O., dragging his legs behind him and firing over the wounded officer's shoulder, Lucht caught glimpse of two snipers a hundred or so meters away high in the right tree line about six feet apart. Rising up on his elbows, aligning his right eye behind the rear sights, he intuitively sensed that he and Captain Oswalt occupied all their attention. Bullet strikes kicked up mud all around him as he fumbled with his rifle. Flipping the selector switch to rock and roll, Lucht loosed a burst of automatic fire, sending both soldiers plummeting from the trees.

Not realizing his two teammates were hit, Bill Croney reached the ditch and turned to face his attackers. Seeing the plight of Oswalt and Lucht, Croney laid down cover fire to draw heat from his two companions, now sprawled in the paddy struggling to keep their heads above water. Several times when incoming fire slacked off, Bill Croney tried to reach the stranded duo but was driven back by accelerated fire once he exposed himself. A machine gunner had his range, stitching up soggy earth all around him, keeping Croney close to the dike. There was no cover whatsoever between him and the casualties. He became fearful he might be drawing too much attention to the men in the paddy but he had to try.

With searing pain spreading through his body, Dave Lucht repositioned his rifle over the paddy dike and continued his one-man vendetta, concentrating on nearby attackers coming at him and Captain Oswalt from the immediate front. Still trying to assess the extent of his wounds, Captain Oswalt looked up to see NVA closing in. Leveling his .45 at the attackers, the officer fired nonstop, exhausting all his ammo. The onslaught caught the NVA by surprise. Coupled with Bill Croney's cover fire and renewed concentration of fire from Marines along the dike, several North Vietnamese fell to newly incensed gunfire, stalling the assault and causing some confusion among the attackers. If there was any thought of celebration, it was soon thrown aside as determined attackers quickly recovered, pressing the attack with renewed vigor. NVA in both tree lines firing from entrenched positions piled it on thick, reducing what little firepower still poured from the dike down to a pitiful trickle.

Feeling useless without ammo, Captain Oswalt turned his attention back to communications. Pulling on the cord, threading it through his half-closed palm as best he could, the handset was yanked from the water. To his left and right, Koreans loosed a furious volume of fire. Unable to move, the captain held his ground, re-establishing the wireless link to Lance Corporal White, reporting the deteriorating situation.

Pat White passed on news of two American casualties to Brigade.

At Brigade headquarters, *Nam Doe Khe Be* received word of Oswalt and Lucht with much consternation. Now in charge due to temporary absence of Captain Pless, Captain Albert J. Ransom, monitoring one ANGLICO and two Korean TAC nets, scurried about the Fire Support Control Center (FSCC), attempting to sort out the confused state of affairs and trying to get a handle on events. Togo 87 and Togo 88, the only assets under his direct command that could provide visual narrative on the tactical situation, were grounded due to poor visibility and low ceiling.

Reports coming in from Koreans in the paddy and from radio relay by Pat White did not paint a clear picture of events at the point of crisis.

Once the coordinates reached his ear, Captain Ransom wasted no time in requesting choppers from Ky-Ha. The trouble was weather conditions were keeping everything on the ground.

Days of earth-soaking rain raised water levels in the paddy to almost topping over the dike. One of the few paddies not completely awash in water was occupied by Captain Oswalt and Lance Corporal Lucht. There was just enough space above the water line to keep their heads partially behind cover without drowning.

Over the next half hour, the marooned pair lay dodging bullets, pressed close to a dike wall that afforded precious little shelter. Dave occasionally pumped a few rounds down range to keep the NVA at a distance, hanging onto a belief that somehow this would all soon be over. Captain Oswalt still worked the radio, attempting to get artillery into this battle. Having been in constant use, he hoped the battery would hold out a little while longer.

Lance Corporal Croney, keeping watch over the stranded Marines, made two or three more attempts to evacuate his teammates but was still plagued by that damned NVA machine gunner, narrowly escaping with his own life.

The ambush ordeal, now an hour and a half since the first shots rang out, seemed like days. Bleeding, in unspeakable pain, and now numbing-cold and miserable, Dave Lucht and Captain Oswalt each wondered inwardly to himself how long before a random shot would take them out of this war. They were both amazed to have survived this long in the open.

By 1500, the Koreans managed to established a solid radio relay of their own and finally had artillery working over both tree lines and the attacking force in the paddy.

In all that time, no place in the rice paddy was spared for one moment from concentrated torrents of incoming fire. Not only were the ROKs outmanned, they were outgunned as well. M-1s could not keep pace with the magnitude of fire being poured out by enemy AK-47s. There was little chance the Koreans would ever gain fire superiority with weaponry at hand. Discipline and training were the only weapons keeping the NVA from overwhelming these courageous Marines. Individual Marines reacting as a team made all the difference in the world.

Artillery finally found the mark and forced NVA advancing in the paddy to pull back fifty or so meters, taking away some of their advantage. Heavy volume of fire, however, was still coming in. Because of the downpour and wet landscape conditions, many of the 105mm howitzer shells armed with contact fuses were not detonating. Calling back to Ku Chungdae, Captain Oswalt requested air bursts, which of course had no effect on the entrenched troops, but they did stalemate the tactical situation and raised hell with all the NVA above ground. Enemy troops in the paddy were stalemated, stalling any further advance.

Putting his fears aside, Bill Croney steeled his mind. Leaving the protection of the dike once more, taking advantage of newly intense artillery bombardments, the kid from Detroit crawled through a torrent of bullets, half submerged underwater, to reach the wounded Marines. Summoning what strength was needed, Croney managed to reach Dave Lucht, who was the closer of the two. Lucht vaguely recalled many years later telling Bill, "I didn't mind dying so much, but I don't want to die over here." Bill Croney was a quiet kid who came to Vietnam from Hawaii with the first rotation attached to Captain Oswalt's team. In a gallows humor retort, attempting to bolster everyone's confidence, Bill couldn't resist responding to Dave with, "Well, OK! Let's get the hell out of here!" Pulling his friend across the paddy through a maze of fire, Bill was able to haul Dave over the dike into the ditch.

Taking inventory of his courage, Bill Croney psyched himself for one more foray into the open, going back out after Captain Oswalt when two Koreans dashed into the paddy ahead of him through a hellstorm of fire and dragged the officer back behind the somewhat-safe haven offered by the dike.

Hopelessly outnumbered, the Koreans did not have enough manpower to concentrate fire at every NVA strong point at the same time.

At the forwardmost position, at point-blank range, six Marines exchanged fire and grenades with a rush of NVA who, out of the blue, appeared undetected, coming at them from the right flank. Quickly advancing to within twenty feet, the Marines refused to give ground, chasing them off in a fury of fire with their reliable but old M-1s. Firepower diverted to halt the attack was exploited by enemy in the tree line to strengthen the right flank and move even closer to the Marines. Grenades lobbed from the tree line only a few meters away drove the point squad from their position. In order to avoid being cut off, the squad pulled even closer to the center of the dike and thus further away from the only escape route. Two more Marines were killed withdrawing. Orders were given to fix bayonets.

Captain Oswalt was in bad shape. Now in better position to evaluate the damage, the officer's leg turned out to be much more severe than thought. Weak from loss of blood, the captain was in and out of consciousness several times over the next hour, but kept up on events as best he could. Bill Croney did what he could for his ailing skipper, but did not have the required medical skills beyond slowing blood loss and treating for shock.

Lance Corporal John Houghton, on the march without a radio, was unaware of the casualty situation he'd have to deal with at the paddy. Slipping and sliding through ankle-deep mud at a fairly quick pace, the rescue party was making good headway. John hoped like hell the hard rain would muffle their approach.

With the attack temporarily in check, Korean leadership stabilized the situation by pulling the column closer together in a more manageable formation. Dogged determination and courage were among the few resources the ROKs commanded in abundance. Directing defensive fire and repositioning troops in a more organized structure, Marines tried desperately to gain an upper hand against a determined adversary. The battle for gaining fire superiority was still out of reach. In spite of being outgunned, defensive fire from Marines along the paddy dike was having some effect, limiting the maneuverability of their antagonists. Artillery through a jury-rigged system of radio relay was showing more result in restricting volumes of incoming fire.

Taking advantage of a slightly more improved tactical situation, a triage area was set up in a small clearing behind the ditch. The Battalion surgeon and surviving corpsmen went to work providing as much care as possible to casualties who were filtering in. Several wounded Marines were already being attended to when Croney pulled Captain Oswalt and Lucht into the clearing. The Battalion surgeon gave both Americans a shot of morphine and a quick examination. Gathering his equipment, the doctor turned to render his services to another Marine when a single well-aimed round from the left tree line ended the valiant doctor's life.

Some of the bravest men ever to appear on a battlefield are medical corpsmen, who on a daily basis risked life and limb to save the lives of wounded Marines. It was no different in *Dae Hon Haebyong Dae*. Every man in that paddy felt his loss, knowing that someone special had been taken from them that day.

Marines who were able made their way back to the dike once medical treatment was applied. Even severely wounded Marines who were able took up rifle to defend the dike. Every weapon online counted. One third of the Marines entering that paddy lay dead or wounded. Loss of firepower from these silent warriors was swiftly taken advantage of by North Vietnamese soldiers, who were inching closer to the trapped Marines on both flanks under cover of the tree lines. Ammunition was running low and if something was going to happen to save the trapped Marines, it better happen fast. Improved weather was the only good omen for the desperate defenders. Rain showers began trickling off to a heavy mist, allowing somewhat better visibility, but that worked both ways.

At around 1600, radio transmissions from Ky-Ha alerted Captain Ransom at Brigade of impending launches of Medevac flights as improved weather conditions in southern I Corps would now permit emergency missions. Reports coming in from the paddy, however, confirmed heavy fire in such volume as to make landing attempts impossible.

Korean officers at the FSCC concocted a plan for every tube within range, mortars and howitzers alike, to concentrate fire on the affected area, bringing overwhelming fire to smother those two tree lines in high-explosive rounds.

For the next half hour, artillery shells fell on both tree lines at a rate of twenty or twenty-five per minute. Not long into the barrage, incoming fire slacked off to a dribble, then died out all together.

Dave Lucht heard the radio crackle. A flight of UH1-E gunships, call sign Klondike, from VMO-6 escorting Medevac choppers were hailing "*Sip-Ja Song* 14," and that was him. After acknowledging Klondike, Lucht wasted little time requesting artillery fires lifted.

Lance Corporal Lucht, propped against a tree and having clear view of his surroundings, broadcast a situation report directing an approach heading from the north. Bill Croney standing by with a red smoke grenade flung it as far into the paddy as his arm strength allowed. Moisture hanging heavy in the air kept the smoke from billowing too high off the ground but it did meet terms of intent. Anticipating the purpose of marker smoke, with artillery fire lifted, NVA troops in the tree line came back to life, pouring on fire as intense as anything witnessed so far that day. Realizing the implications, Dave waved off the landing attempt as incoming fire wouldn't allow safe touchdown. The last thing needed in that paddy right now was one more emergency to deal with. Medevac choppers acknowledged directive, moving off to circle northeast, waiting for instructions. With vicious intent, Lucht called down the gunships.

Bill Croney and Dave Lucht moved further down the dike for a better view of the strike zone, while the first UH1-E started his run, leaving Captain Oswalt on his own.

Spirits lifted up and down the dike as the first pass onto the right tree line brought cheers and shouts from grunts manning their position.

Pass after pass of concentrated rocket and machine volley poured into both tree lines. UH-1Es wreaked havoc on NVA positions, loosing massive amounts of ordnance. Smoke from WP rockets filled the valley, obscuring vision, offering a welcome smoke screen, and shielding the Marines behind a man-made smog. Incoming sorties were defiantly met with return machine gun fire. In spite of the horrific pounding meted out by the gunships, defiant resistance from the tree line still mocked the men trapped in the paddy. Several bullet holes pierced the skin of both war birds, narrowly missing crewmen.

After forty minutes of death-dealing airmanship and a valiant performance by both crews, ordnance was depleted and fuel nearly exhausted. Klondike had no choice but withdraw to rearm and refuel. The standby Medevac birds were also unable to remain on station due to fuel consideration. Air power did, however, manage to force the NVA to back off, giving the paddy dike defenders a little breathing room. Radio relay then ordered artillery back to work.

Elation turned to depression as the lifeline to the outside world departed. Looking skyward, the Americans wondered if daylight would remain with them long enough to bring the air wing back for another try. Koreans resumed a mask of defiance, bracing for a night of uncertainty.

Some of the wounded had been suffering for nearly four hours. Two had already died of wounds and several more were in very dire straits from loss of blood.

Captain Oswalt was already going in and out of shock from blood loss, and Dave Lucht was now experiencing terrible agony from too many holes in his body. He too was bleeding his life away. Bill Croney took charge of the radio, did what he could for his wounded teammates then waited for what seemed like hours.

USS Goldsborough
(DDG-20)
Charles F. Adams Class Guided Missile Armed Destroyer
Call Sign: Running Trace

In February 1966, USS *Goldsborough* made her second deployment to Asia. She provided gunfire support for Operation Binh Phu I, firing nearly 600 rounds. *Goldsborough* also screened attack carriers on Yankee Station in the South China Sea. She participated in SEATO exercises in May and was station ship at Hong Kong in June. On 26 June, she was again off Vietnam on picket station.

In 1967, she participated in Operation Sea Dragon, designed to interdict the North Vietnamese lines of supply into the Republic of Vietnam, and provided naval gunfire support along the DMZ. During this deployment, USS *Goldsborough* fired nearly 10,000 rounds in support of allied forces and avoided over 800 rounds of hostile fire without damage to the ship. Upon her return to Pearl Harbor, she was awarded the Naval Unit Commendation for exceptionally meritorious service in Vietnamese waters from 29 August 1967 to 17 February 1968.

In November 1968, USS *Goldsborough* made her fourth Western Pacific deployment in five years, participating in eighty-eight gunfire missions in support of Vietnamese, Republic of Korea, as well as U.S. Marine and Army forces.

After a yard period in 1970, USS *Goldsborough* made a fifth WestPac tour, departing Pearl in August and arriving off the coast in February 1971. Again she provided naval gunfire support for allied troops and carried out carrier escort duties in the Gulf of Tonkin.

In September 1971, USS *Goldsborough* departed on her sixth deployment to the Western Pacific, providing naval gunfire support for allied ground troops and performing carrier escort services. In early 1972, she was assigned to the recovery task force for Apollo 16. *Goldsborough* departed again for the war zone on 13 October 1972 for her seventh deployment to the Western Pacific. This would be her last trip to the gunline. On 19 December, while engaging targets as a tactical unit of Operation Linebacker, USS *Goldsborough* was hit by coastal artillery fire. The shore battery put a hole five feet wide through an upper deck. HTC Donald A. Dix and BM1 Robert M. Dow were killed in the resulting explosion, and HT3 Gary L. Boyce died of wounds received that day on 1 January 1973. Continuing the fight, *Goldsborough* avenged her gallant crewmen, facing off with those coastal guns and pounding them into silence. The ship's crew received a Meritorious Unit Commendation for service between October 1972 and February 1973. Making her last departure from the war zone, the ship returned to Pearl Harbor in May 1973.

We, who once found refuge under the protection of her guns, salute this valiant ship and her gallant crew.

WHAT THE HELL HAPPENED TO YOU?

Moving off trail into the jungle, orders to swing wider south for an approach on the trapped HQ party from a different direction passed through the unit. Decibel levels of battle clatter had been growing in intensity the past 200 meters. A strong wind hurling rain at their backs made battle sounds in the rice paddy seem more distant than it really was.

Having only sketchy details of the tactical situation up ahead, a morbid fear settled into a deep knot in Lance Corporal John Houghton's stomach. The volume of fire coming from up ahead was much more concentrated than he'd expected. Growing up tough in a downtown neighborhood of Philadelphia, John had a sense of survival that would not go untested before the sun went down that day.

Twenty minutes later, the platoon closed on the southern valley entrance, then halted to organize formation. After a brief radio conference, orders were given to move out. From fifty meters, the platoon broke into a run, piercing the rice paddy in squad rushes parallel to and sixty meters in front of the HQ party. Caught by complete surprise, twenty or so NVA were gunned down from behind. Marines at the paddy dyke laid down a heavy base of fire, expending most of their ammunition, enabling the reaction force to drive NVA attackers further back into the near tree line. Dazed and exhausted defenders along the dike, almost completely out of ammo, were content to slink down in the ditch, turning the fight over to these newcomers.

At a low crouch, Lance Corporal Houghton broke into the paddy, wasting little time scanning the landscape for his teammates. He was astounded at the lack of organization and leadership providing direction for the confused men lining the dyke, just sitting there with thousand-yard gapes on their faces. Houghton could feel a total breakdown in morale. No one really looked at him, they looked right through him. There were no cheers, no rejoicing, nothing at all to indicate presence of emotion.

Spotting Bill Croney, Houghton moved swiftly to his location and received an update on the situation. Croney pointed out Captain Oswalt sprawled in the triage ditch several meters away. The two Marines sprinted over to him on the double. Quickly down on one knee and looking into Captain Oswalt's eyes, he asked in typical John Houghton humor, "What the hell happened to you?" which brought out a stalled laugh long missing from Larry's throat. As expected, Captain Oswalt was shivering, cold, and not very lucid. John did what he could for his C.O., then started looking for Lucht, promising to come back. Seeing the object of his search some fifty feet further ahead, John gravitated to where he was holed up. By this time, Dave Lucht's entire body was racked in pain. Every time John touched him, Dave would wince in agony and pull away. After several attempts, Houghton and Croney managed to resettle the wounded Marine on drier ground. The Duo went back for Captain Oswalt and carried him to the small patch of semidry ground now occupied by Lucht. Making sure the trio was comfortable; Houghton took the radio from Croney and went to work seeing what he could do about getting a chopper on the ground.

Looking around at the intense firefight raging up and down the paddy, Houghton realized there wasn't a chance of bringing anything safely down with fire volume this heavy. Lance Corporal Houghton immediately jumped on the net, calling for more air support.

Reports of Ku Chungdae's breaking through to the trapped HQ party triggered a celebration at Brigade. *Nam Doe Khe Be* was still very concerned for his two Marines at the paddy. For the past hour he'd been making arrangements for more than just another air strike. If the weather wouldn't cooperate and allow air rescue, then more boots on the ground should settle things down. Captain Ransom ordered Corporal Jeffery M. Daggett to mount up and be ready for a chopper ride out to the rice paddy. If they couldn't land in the paddy, they would come down close by and force their way in. One way or another, Captain Albert J. Ransom would have the all wounded, to a man, tucked in at Charlie Med that night.

One hour remained before this gloomy light of day would retreat before oncoming darkness. John knew he'd only have one shot at getting wounded out before morning. As it was, rain already limited visibility, and heavy cloud cover would not allow much moonlight. Helicopters wouldn't be capable of seeing anything in this soup once the sun went down, assuming of course they'd be allowed to fly at all.

"*Sip Ja Song* 14, this is Klondike One dash Two, are you still there? Over." John was ecstatic. "Roger that, Klondike"! What'd you bring us? Over." "I've got the same bunch of pirates as last time and some extra help." The reply reached his ear. "Has your situation changed? Over." "Negative on your last!"

Informing the senior Korean officer of the impending air support, John requested artillery fire be lifted. Once accomplished, John came back up on the net. "Come on down."

Rearmed and refueled, VMO-6 returned with an attitude. Major William B. Dodds and Lieutenant David A. Ballentine were back to work, and they weren't leaving till the job was finished. Explaining the situation to Houghton, the gunship pilot lined up his flight and came in hot.

Retracing moves from an hour earlier, the UH1-Es poured it to the right side and closest tree line, setting it ablaze with rockets and machine gun fire. Run after run drove the North Vietnamese from their foothold close to the paddy. After twenty minutes of hard work, return fire slacked off to a trickle, then died our entirely.

After a conference with the flight leader, the first Medevac chopper was called down. Wounded Koreans with the aid of their buddies were helped to the waiting helicopter and shoved aboard.

John Houghton was everywhere, dodging bullets, moving quickly from one location to another behind the ditch, securing good views of the air show from different angles: providing feedback, locating targets, directing strafing runs, and bringing down Medevacs. NVA gunners did their best to take Lance Corporal Houghton out of the fight. Years later, John couldn't begin to guess how many rounds just narrowly missed putting him face down in that paddy.

The next chopper in was a CH-46. The Sea Knight landed seconds after the lead helicopter was airborne. As soon as the ramp came down, wounded HQ personnel were loaded on. Dave Lucht found himself hurriedly carried aboard by two ROKs and roughly dropped on the deck, landing hard on some other poor grunt. Dave painfully repositioned himself and watched the ramp being drawn up, only to see Captain Oswalt roll onto the ship's deck with help from the crew chief as the ramp angled steeper toward the closed position.

Both gunships now turned their attention to the left tree line with as much enthusiasm as displayed for the right side as the Medevac bird lifted off.

With the sun setting, muzzle flashes from both tree lines were much more pronounced, blinking all around the paddy. Several close misses damned near took out John Houghton as he moved about the flooded landscape.

Now well out in front of the dike, shifting position for a better view of the air assault, John Houghton almost tripped on a wounded Korean who'd been lying half submerged in water for who knows how the hell long. His leg had been badly lacerated, making movement painful and difficult. With bullet strikes coming to ground within inches of the gutsy lance corporal, John stopped long enough to tie off this Marine's badly shot-up limb and do what he could to stop blood loss.

Coming in empty, the third chopper, a UH-34D piloted by Lieutenant Steve C. Wilson, swung wide over the paddy, drawing a bead on the LZ. Strong fire from the left tree line opened up at close range, scoring several direct hits as the UH-34D passed overhead. The helicopter started losing airspeed and began spiraling in on a collision course with the rice paddy. Lance Corporal Richard N. Soukup, the door gunner, sustained a bullet wound low on his stomach about one inch above his groin. With great skill, the pilot fought the controls, set down soft, and cut power.

Not realizing the UH-34D had been knocked out of the sky, Houghton thought it a strange place to land. He knew he didn't direct him there, and as far as he knew, he had the only radio in the field. Trying to hail the rotor craft several times, John Houghton was unable to raise a response.

Looking around for options, there was only one course of action left open. "If someone doesn't get over there quick and tell him he's in the wrong place," Houghton thought, "he's going to be in deep shit'.

Pulling the Korean to his knees, Houghton threw a shoulder into his waist, hefting the man into a fireman's carry and began a headlong charge across 100 meters of soggy rice paddy in pouring-down rain. Showers of bullet strikes kicked up water spouts on all sides, every step of the way. This was the last helicopter in the flight, and John wanted to put the injured Marine on board. Slogging through a wet paddy was not easy, to say the least. Pumping his painfully tired legs as fast as he could, a man cannot run through this crap. As deep as the water was, each step required him to lift his foot above the water line in order to make headway. John thought his lungs would collapse before reaching the chopper. As one totally exhausted John Houghton neared the teardrop-shaped craft, AK rounds could be heard above the deafening battle clatter, snapping through the fuselage.

The crew was already assembling outside the cargo door when John stumbled into the area, letting his passenger slide off his shoulder into the murky brown water. He wasn't moving. Frantically checking the Marine, he found the reason why. John didn't know where, but someplace between ship and staring point, the Marine he tried so hard to rescue took a bullet in the back. Torn with emotion at the Marine's death, and stunned that his new friend stopped a bullet that would surely have killed him, John had more than enough to think about and his mind wouldn't allow him enough peace to deal with it. Would have, could have, and should have. It was enough to drive you crazy. This maddening situation already had him climbing half out of his skin.

Staying on task, John turned to the crew and laid out the situation, pointing across the paddy to where the good guys were holding the line. The injured door gunner was mobile and, with help from pilot and crew chief, was able to negotiate his way back to the dike and await rescue.

The five Marines stepped out for the dike, John Houghton leading the way. Keeping the damaged ship between themselves and the tree line, the three-minute sprint to safety was launched through one hellacious fusillade of gunfire.

Klondike, with his remaining ordnance, covered the earthbound Marines, seeing them safely reach protection of the perimeter. With nothing else to throw at the North Vietnamese and running low on fuel, both gunships once again headed for home.

There were still wounded ROKs in the ditch, and now an injured door gunner needed care just as urgently. Mobile at first, the crewman was now in bad shape. His crewmates did what they could, then settled the gunner in the ditch. A Korean corpsman administered morphine and a pressure pack, then left him in the care of his fellow Marines.

A reaction force of some twenty Marines assembled on the Brigade parade ground now boarded a CH-46 Marine Sea Knight, dripping from the same heavy downpour showering the miserable grunts stuck in the paddy. Gunship escorts were already inbound to the rice paddy. Once the reaction force climbed aboard, the pilot wasted little time getting up and on the way. Contacting his escort, the big chopper settled into a westward heading and pulled throttle.

In the rice paddy, nobody really noticed the fast-fading light; every one just suddenly realized the sun was completely below the horizon with darkness settled firmly on the paddy. Incoming fire tailed off to sporadic sniping and soon faded into complete silence. Rain still came down in buckets. Cold and worn out after five full days of chasing Charlie in the rain on very little sleep, John had one more crisis to deal with before calling it a day.

How the hell was he going to get one more helicopter into this shit soup? It was quiet now; he just wanted to grab some sleep.

Bringing the handset slowly to his ear, one tired Lance Corporal John Houghton put out a broadcast on current developments. Brigade acknowledged transmission then inquired about the condition of the ship and crewman. Once John completed his report, *Nam Doe Khe Be* advised him to expect company.

Within ten minutes, his radio came back to life. He was being hailed by Captain Kenneth D. Waters of VMO-6, flying escort for a CH-46, announcing he had cargo to offload and he also understood some friends of his needed a ride.

Hauling out the wounded Marines occupied center stage in everyone's mind. John had hoped this could've been accomplished before dusk. With such low visibility, the only way to mark his position would show every trigger-happy gunner in the valley exactly where he was.

Houghton hustled over to the Korean lieutenant and asked him to have the wounded staged for very quick evacuation. The ROK officer assigned two men to each injured combatant and pulled them all together in an area John designated. The helicopter crew then carried their injured man to where the Hyong-je haebyong staged their own wounded.

All heads down, John moved as much of a safe distance away from the LZ as he dared, pulled pin on an illumination grenade and set it on top of the dike, then held his breath.

Unable to discern or communicate landmarks in these blacked-out conditions, John requested gunship escorts forego strafing runs. Without being able to provide visual reference beyond the illumination grenade, risk of causing friendly casualties in his judgment was too great.

Houghton hailed the CH-46, transmitting landing instructions and steering his heading into the landing zone so his flight path would not traverse the valley. Using the illumination as a beacon, John directed the big chopper to set down fifty meters west of the glowing grenade. Seeing anything was almost impossible but the drone of the engines and whoop, whoop, whoop of the blade slap directed his eyes toward the descending aircraft.

Lowering the cargo ramp while still ten feet from touchdown, the pilot set up for a quick exchange of passengers. As soon as the twin-rotor craft made contact, troops scampered down the ramp and drifted toward the dike, passing through teams of Marines shuttling wounded en route to the waiting ship.

It occurred to John that he didn't have a full load going out. He knew Bill Croney had been though hell, spending the entire afternoon in a miserable and very stressful situation. As an afterthought, John put Bill on the chopper and told him he'd see him back at battalion. This was one of the few perks enjoyed by ANGLICO.

Corporal Daggett bounded down the ramp, blending in with Marines trying to get acclimated in their new surroundings. He spotted John Houghton walking back from the CH-46 now building up RPMs, creating a prop wash, pelting his face with stinging drops of rain. Waiting for the engine roar to fade, the two friends greeted each other with a handshake.

Both Marines had come over from Hawaii with the original rotation. They knew each other well, sharing many good times chasing wahines all over Waikiki.

Anyone who knows John Houghton also knew better than to hand him a straight line. Daggett wasn't thinking when he asked, "Where we gonna bed down?"

John looked out to the rice paddy, fixated on a downed CH-34.

"John! Where're we sleeping tonight?"

Without saying a word, Houghton started slogging through the rice paddy with a blank look on his face just staring at a nice warm, dry, comfortable place to rest.

Koreans, fearful the NVA would mortar that airship sometime during the night, begged John and Jeff to stay away from it. They had every reason to be concerned. That ship presented a very tempting target, and it stood far outside the perimeter of the force in the rice paddy.

John Houghton would hear none of it. He hadn't been dry for five days. He hadn't slept for four nights. He hadn't given a shit for the past twenty-four hours. If he died in his sleep, well?

Taking the door machine guns off their mounts, staging what linked ammo they found, both passed the night, blissfully uneventful, in a nice dry, warm helicopter. It wasn't exactly home, but it felt great.

USS Turner Joy
(DD-951)
Forrest Sherman Class Destroyer

While engaged in watchdog patrols in the Tonkin Gulf, USS *Maddox* (DD-731) on 2 August 1964 sent out a call for assistance when she became the target of an unexpected attack by three North Vietnamese torpedo boats. Aircraft from USS *Ticonderoga,* responding to the crisis, destroyed two of the bothersome craft. When USS *Turner Joy* arrived on the scene, things had already quieted down. The destroyer duo continued patrols when, on 4 August, both ships were once more under attack and took appropriate countermeasures, once more calling upon attack craft from USS *Ticonderoga*. Over the next two and a half hours, a running sea battle continued, claiming two enemy craft sunk and two badly damaged.

The now-famous "Tonkin Gulf incident" precipitated retaliation with USS *Constellation* joining USS *Ticonderoga* in launching sixty-four sorties at targets near the coast. Planes of USS *Constellation* took out the torpedo boat bases at Hongay and Loc Chao, while USS *Ticonderoga* engaged the naval bases at Quang Khe and Phuc Loi as well as an oil storage depot at Vihn, setting ten percent of North Vietnam's oil reserve ablaze.

From that day through the end of the Vietnam War, USS *Turner Joy* became one of the most involved ships in the conflict, making appearances in the war zone in each year of the war from 1965 through 1973. She served tours on both Yankee and Dixie stations, performing a variety of missions that ran the full spectrum of destroyer capabilities. USS *Turner Joy* participated in Sea Dragon operations,

SAR, and plane guard duties off and on over the course of her many deployments, and received fire from shore batteries on many occasions. As a permanent fixture on the gunline, every spotter in the Marines Corps at one time or another had opportunity to adjust her accurate fires.

For her exemplary service in Vietnam, USS *Turner Joy* received nine battle stars.

We, who once found refuge under the protection of her guns, salute this valiant ship and her gallant crew.

TRANSITION

Events in the rice paddy were put under a microscope. 3rd Battalion received a new C.O. almost immediately. We never did know what happened to Colonel Park. He was replaced the same day. One thing, however, did stand out like a painted fart. M-1s were never going to measure up to AK-47s in an ass-kicking contest. In the first encounter with North Vietnam's well-equipped army, the ROKs experienced fire in volumes they could not begin to match. Korean troops in that firefight were for the most part experienced Marines who reacted as they were trained. Defensive fires were laid down in accord with sound military procedure. Discipline held the day and only courage saved their asses. The grunts were willing, but lacked sufficient firepower. Training and discipline is the only reason anyone made it out alive.

The old venerable Garande, as good as it was, just could not compete in the all-important race to achieve fire superiority over modern assault rifles. Thirty-round magazines versus eight-round clips. Automatic fire selection versus straight, semi-automatic fire. Short and easy to wield in the bush versus large, heavy, and unwieldy. The Koreans were totally outmatched in the paddy. Short-distance firefights negated the only real advantage the reliable old weapon held. If they were to face North Vietnamese troops in the field again, it was determined, they damned well better have more firepower.

Within a week, M-16s started showing up around Brigade. By the middle of February, at least half of all Marines in the line companies possessed these weapons. Gradually, M-16s started replacing all World War II shoulder weapons. U.S. Marine instructors held classes in Chu Lai, training ROK officers and NCO in the nuances of care, cleaning, and operation of the new infantry issue.

Claymore mines, Light Antiarmor Weapon (LAW) rocket launchers, and other newly developed weapons also found their way into Brigade arsenals.

General Lee, in a planned rotation, was recalled to Korea, where he would eventually become commandant of ROKMC. His replacement, General Kim Yon Sang, was cut from the same mold. A little younger perhaps, but just as grizzled!

All three maneuver battalions kept their line companies inside the wire throughout the last two weeks of January. In anticipation of monsoon season coming to the end of its cycle, prospects of better weather improved everybody's mood. Although never hearing this from official channels, it is believe the ROKs also wanted to wait on upgrading their firepower before continuing search and destroy operations. Brigade was in no particular rush for a repeat performance as experienced in the paddy fight of 10 January. It's also believed General Kim was hunting heads and putting the fear of God into his command staff.

As usual, a cease-fire agreement arranged by the feel-gooders was in effect for Tet holiday festivities, and as usual, the communists took full advantage of the cease fire to move troops and supplies around to improve their tactical posture.

Plans for humbling the Blue Dragons had been in the works for quite some time. Early in February, North Vietnamese tacticians of the 2nd NVA Division were assembling a regimental-size expedition composed of one battalion each from the 1st and 21st NVA Regiments and one battalion from the 1st Viet Cong Regiment. In addition to normal table of equipment gear, 120mm mortars and ammunition were transported to the province by elephant from the Ho Chi Minh Trail, down through mountain valleys west of Tra Bong. The author believes the HQ party blundered into lead elements of this force at the paddy fight on 10 January.

No one is totally sure what was and was not known at the time these events were unfolding, as this intelligence briefing was learned after the fact from NVA prisoners. This much is known. A reinforced regiment was moving against the 3rd Battalion's 11th Company, occupying a position near the village of Tra Bihn Dong about one mile west of National Highway 1, less than one click from the south bank of Tra Bong River.

On the night of 14-15 February 1967, all that planning loosed the hounds of hell.

USS Oklahoma City
(CG-5)
Cleveland Class Guided Missile Armed Light Cruiser
Call Sign: Fireball

On 14 December 1964, USS Oklahoma City began refresher training in Southern California waters to prepare for a lengthy deployment. She then departed for Yokosuka, arriving 7 July to assume her duties again as 7th Fleet flagship.

Shortly thereafter, North Vietnamese gunboats attacked U.S. destroyers in the Tonkin Gulf, and Oklahoma City quickly began a twenty-five-day alert in the gulf. Training exercises and operational visits to various ports in the Far East followed, and in June 1965, she began gunfire support missions off Vietnam. When the level of hostilities increased, she began to spend more and more time in the South China Sea and eventually participated in Operations Piranha, Double Eagle, Deckhouse IV, and Hastings II.

After serving as 7th Fleet flagship for two and one half years, USS Oklahoma City returned to San Francisco Bay Naval Shipyard 15 December 1966 for overhaul. Following her yard period, she began refresher training in the Southern California operating area in July 1967 and continued those exercises and intermittent calls to West Coast ports until she was deployed again to WestPac, 7 November 1968.

She arrived at Yokosuka 20 December and in August 1969 was again contributing to the strength of the 7th Fleet by participating in the varied assignments its units are called on to perform. *Oklahoma City* received two battle stars for service in Vietnam.

The ship provided naval gunfire support for troops in South Vietnam, gunfire operations against coastal targets, and antiaircraft operations in North Vietnam. In 1971, the *Oklahoma City* released the first successful combat surface-to-surface missile fired in U.S. Navy history, using the new Talos RIM-8H antiradiation missile to destroy a North Vietnamese mobile air control radar van. In 1972, the ship was attacked by North Vietnamese MIG aircraft but was not damaged. One of the attacking MIGs was shot down by an accompanying missile ship.

We, who once found refuge under the protection of her guns, salute this valiant ship and her gallant crew.

YOU'RE HERE TO DELIVER A VALENTINE FROM HO CHI WHO?

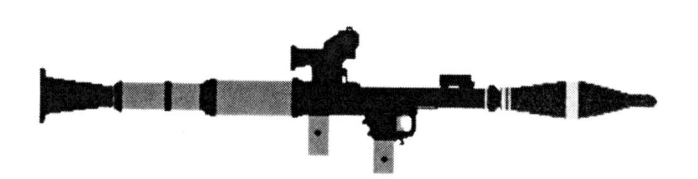

A steady drizzle contributed more discomfort to already high levels of humidity hanging heavily in the night air. Floating streams cascading from well-worn footpaths spilled over sand-bagged parapets, causing ankle-deep puddles of standing water to flood mud-encrusted defense trenches. Peering out over the bulwark, silent sentinels manning post with poncho hoods drawn loosely around unfastened helmets strained hard to see and listen through an offbeat concerto of discontinuous chatter.

Ship-Il Chungdae defended a 300- by 200-meter oval-shaped fortification straddling a small hill within sight of Tra Bong River. Captain Jung Kyong Jin, senior officer on station, commanded 294 Marines including an attached 4.2-inch (four-deuce) mortar battery. A graduate of the Korean Naval Academy, Captain Jung was in his sixth year of service. Having been in-country several months, he was already a seasoned pro. As was his custom, Captain Jung made rounds of post every evening before retiring. This night he bid his charges to be especially vigilant. Not that he had any special premonition, but he knew this weather was more helpful to those outside the wire.

Lance Corporals Dave Long and Jim Porta, having just finished checking in on the ANGLICO TAC net, secured their team radio and prepared to settle in for some well-earned downtime. It was normal for the talkative pair to idle away evening hours engaged in a trivia fest concerning nothing in particular and everything in general. Listening to Porta play his harmonica, Dave put pen to an unfinished letter too long postponed: Just another day at the office.

Under cover of darkness, NVA battalions took up assault positions several hundred meters outside 11th Company's wire. Mortar and recoilless rifle crews transported their lethal cargos to preordained locations and fixed them in place. Ammunition was staged, distance measurements and azimuth readings were taken, and last-minute weapon checks were performed.

A platoon-size reconnaissance approached the western perimeter, utilizing rain clatter to dull the sound of their movement. Some of them undoubtedly posed as villagers at Tra Bihn Dong to scout ROK defenses, but had never been this close before. Their mission: to chart assault zones through the wire. ROK Marines had a habit of changing machine gun positions and the NVA needed to know where these weapons were located that night. Very slowly and methodically, enemy soldiers advanced through the wire barrier, carefully avoiding mines and trip wires. Demolition men marked or disabled every antipersonnel mine encountered. Sand was poured into pebble-filled C-ration cans to eliminate threat of discovery from these jury-rigged alarm boxes. Moving very deliberately, exhibiting the cautious patience of a watch maker, forward progress was measured in inches.

That part of the perimeter was defended by *Som Sodae*, and they were hard at work. At 2330 a Marine at his listening post picked up movement and passed word back through channels. Captain Jung placed his entire command on alert, instructing his troops to hold fire. Very quietly, Marines gravitated to assigned positions and awaited orders. Every squad leader in the company supervised his charges, making certain nothing would occur to alert the unsuspecting survey party. Each Marine waited in silence; every breath measured, every ear tuned from behind sand-bagged ramparts in anticipation of pandemonium that was sure to follow.

Keeping informed on the probe's progress, Captain Jung allowed the recon team to close within five meters of his trench line.

"So-da!" ("Fire!")

Every Marine online opened up, sending a shower of red tracers into the wire and beyond. Flares lit up the night. Fire volume from Korean weapons increased as heartbeats quickened with each trigger pull. At that range, even in the dark, marksmanship came easy.

Bullets and grenades found their mark, tearing flesh and kicking up a mud storm engulfing the advancing sappers in a shower of steel. Not having a snowball's chance in hell of gaining fire superiority, Vietnamese were observed reeling back into the tree line, dragging several comrades with them, leaving one body behind, twisted in the concertina. As soon as the shadowy figures disappeared from view, fire discipline was restored. All was quite again.

Jack was out of the box.

Owing to the strength of the probe, Captain Jung realized this was just the beginning. He kept the company on alert. Additional Marines were assigned to listening posts, more ammunition was distributed, crew served weapons checked, and fire support plans were reviewed.

Lieutenant Kim Se Chang, the forward observer, having already pre-registered artillery on likely avenues of approach, contacted battalion to alert the batteries that fire support plans may have to be employed on this watch.

General Kim Yon Sang, newly appointed Brigade commander, called his staff together for review of every contingency ever considered by his planners if needed to mount a rescue mission to an outpost.

Harassment and Interdiction (H&I) fires were suspended so every artillery tube in Brigade could remain poised for concentrating fire in defense of *Ship-il Chungdae*.

Yuk Chungdae was brought to Brigade from *E Taedae* (2nd Battalion) and put on standby as a quick reaction force to join the fight should *Ship*-il chungdae need more boots on the ground.

Every line company in close proximity was also put on alert, ready to mount up.

Lance Corporal Long contacted Brigade, making sure he had air support on call should it be required that night.

Captain Stephen W. Pless, commanding officer, 1st ANGLICO, ROK Marine Detachment, having been in communication with Marine Air Group 13 (MAG-13), received a commitment for a fleet of transport helicopters and supporting gunships to carry Yuk Chungdae to the rescue. Captain Pless, a gunship pilot by profession, identified four possible landing sites in close proximity to Ship-il Chungdae. He hoped it wouldn't be needed, as night landings in virgin LZs are as good a recipe for disaster as it gets.

General Kim made sure everyone at Brigade from private to general understood completely: Ship-il Chungdae will not fall.

Upset at being discovered so soon, the NVA Regimental Commander was confronted with a dilemma. The regiment was too committed at this point, and it was no longer possible to turn away. If he ordered an attack forward, knowing the alert had been sounded heavy casualties could be expected, putting divisional planning in danger.

Not known at that time, but discovered later in a notebook pulled from the pocket of a dead NVA officer, North Vietnamese troops were poised to strike several targets in Brigade's area of responsibility. An all-out quick elimination of 11th Company was only the first objective in a night that would see massive destruction and loss of life among Korea's finest. According to plan, Ship-il Chungdae was to be dispatched within one hour along with Ku Chungdae and E Chungdae. A second unidentified regimental-size force was also deployed that night (not verified). Why this second force did not materialize (if it was deployed) is not known. Whatever the case, they were to roll over their first objectives and converge on the big prize. The final target was never identified, but Brigade headquarters was thought to be prime intent. Making a decision to attack or not attack wasn't his to make. The die now was cast, and he had to perform. How the hell would he explain himself?

He reasoned that if no other incidents occurred for a calculated interval, the Korean commander might consider the reconnaissance to be just a botched probe. The longer his prey remained on alert, the less alert he will be the longer nothing happened. So, he waited anxiously in the dark as ghosts of uncertainty clouded his once-clear vision of victory. Had he ever witnessed a KMC rifle inspection, he would realize hoping for sloppy discipline was a poor rack to hang his expectations on. But he held a detailed sketch of the objective in his hands, showing every bunker in the compound. He knew exactly what personnel were housed in those dugouts. He knew where Captain Jung lived and where Lieutenant Kim, all the platoon leaders, and the ANGLICO team were housed. He also knew these structures were targeted for destruction in the opening salvo. "What can they do without leadership?"

His confidence slowly returned as he correctly reminded himself he had better intelligence than his adversaries. Less than a month earlier, two of his men donned uniforms of his enemies and presented themselves as interpreters from the 2nd ARVN Division. For three weeks, the men inconspicuously sat atop a small ridge running through the center of the outpost, just looking around. Every destination they traveled was paced off and noted.

Five and a half hours later seemed like a good enough calculated interval. Assault elements were ordered forward to close on objective. At 0410 on the 15th a merciless recoilless rifle and mortar barrage was loosed on 11th Company.

A small flashlight bulb dangling from a beam inside the command post gave off a pale amber glow, projecting exaggerated shadows against sand-bagged walls. Men bending over a makeshift table watched Captain Jung trace topographical features on a map with his finger as he spoke in measured tones.

Lance Corporals Jim Porta and Dave Long sat several meters in front of the command structure, airing concern over M-16 rifles recently issued to 11th Company in limited quantities. Per plan, the ROKs were gradually replacing vintage M-1s as Brigade's prime infantry issue. Reports from U.S. Marines who had that damned weapon forced on them were not comforting. Inasmuch as the ROKs are not as familiar with M-16s; and inasmuch as these pieces of shit have a tendency to jam; and inasmuch as they are probably going to be hit tonight, things might…Conversation stopped in midsentence as the pair became alert to a series of dull thuds some distance beyond the frontier. Whispering whines from seemingly everywhere quickly accelerated to shrill whistles. Shouts of "Incoming!" from all over the compound sent men scurrying in chaotic scrambles for the nearest cover.

Every bunker on the NVA commander's list was hit. Two, three, four, and more shells slammed hard into the earthwork constructions, exploding them apart, collapsing roofs, and causing massive damage. Impact explosions dotted the compound, scattering torrents of shrapnel over every square foot of 11th Company real estate.

Minutes after the first shells fell to earth; an infantry attack was launched from southwest in battalion strength. *Il Sodae* (1st Platoon) met the initial thrust by unleashing a terrible display of firepower. Above the calamitous roar of battle, Vietnamese were heard to be blowing whistles, beating on drums, and screaming, *"Dae Han, ra di ra di"* ("Koreans, come out!") Flares illuminated the night sky; tracers darted every which way, putting on a light show the likes of which had never been seen in Quang Ngai. Fire volume from both sides of the wire was immense. Within five minutes, the remaining two NVA battalions were committed, hitting the north side with a vengeance. *Som Sodae* opened fire immediately, every bore online responding in a frenzy of fire, resounding in the night like thousands of runaway jackhammers.

Lieutenant Kim had artillery working, as 105 and 155mm howitzers feverishly added more lethality to the conflict, raining steel all around the outpost. The light show now boasted impact flashes generously dotting the landscape all around the complex as well as within the perimeter.

Weapons Platoon brought its mortars into action, adding yet more voices to this insane argument.

Communications notified battalion of the attack. It was a redundant report as deafening thunder could be heard from all over the Tactical Area of Responsibility (TAOR). All eyes turned toward the light show opened wide in wonder. The entire Brigade knew what was going down at Tra Bihn Dong, every heart frozen in fear for their brothers at *Ship-il Chungdae*.

Porta and Long shielded themselves as best they could from detonations impacting by the dozens all around them. The duo lay still, pinned to earth as shrapnel zipped to and fro just overhead. Deafening concussions shook the earth, raining mud and stone on their exposed backs. Feelings of helplessness gripped their minds in fear frenzies, with each screaming shell sounding as though it was heading right between their shoulder blades.

Now under attack from two directions by three full-strength battalions, Captain Jung moved about the perimeter, assessing the situation, shifting personnel, directing fire, and taking charge. The North Vietnamese had arranged a nightmare scenario, bringing nearly 2,400 seasoned troops against 294 sons of Dae Hahn Min Guk.

On the north perimeter, Som Sodae was stacking up bodies across their front, having already stalled two massive surges aggressively pressing toward the trenches. In spite of intense volumes of fire by the Marines, NVA troops continued closing on the defenders, now in human waves. With fresh meat constantly pouring into the fray, North Viets gained new momentum, managing to destroy several sections of concertina blockade with Bangalore torpedoes and satchel charges. On the backs of dead comrades sprawled on the concertina, with support from RPGs and machine guns, attackers moved forward, pouring into the trenches at 0422, barely twelve minutes into battle.

Staff Sergeant Bae Jang Choon's 3rd Squad bore the brunt of the incursion. Despite serious wounds to his right shoulder, Staff Sergeant Bae refused to abandon his position, ordering his Marines to stand their ground and prepare to meet the enemy *mano a mano*. The squad unleashed a terrible shit storm of fire, stacking up more bodies immediately in front of their trench line. The fight escalated from rifles to grenades as North Vietnamese forced their way into the outpost. Fighting digressed to pick axes, entrenching tools, fists, boots, bayonets, and teeth in an all-out brawl for survival now spreading through the trenches. Staff Sergeant Bae, brandishing an entrenching tool, defiantly faced the oncoming horde straddling the parapet, bludgeoning five Vietnamese to death, effectively blocking access to the trench line.

Faced with an overwhelming and relentless enemy, the squad fought back with an undaunted and ferocious tenacity. PFC Kim Myong Deok gunned down ten enemy soldiers at point-blank range as they tried to storm his position before he was himself wounded by grenade explosions. Staff Sergeant Bae picked up Kim's automatic rifle, shooting ten or twelve more to death. Seriously wounded, bleeding profusely, and out of ammo, Staff Sergeant Bae in his last mortal act exchanged hand grenades with the wall of human flesh pressing in on him; firmly standing his ground until the unshakable Marine finally succumbed to a never-ending shower of shrapnel.

PFCs Doh Sung Yong and Kim Dong Jei were hit by small arms fire. Ignoring their pain, both Marines continued fighting from their entrenched position. PFC Doh crawled to a sandbag rampart, where several NVA had taken refuge from the onslaught of 3rd Squad, lobbing a hand grenade over the top, killing five or six NVA soldiers. Doh rushed back for more grenades and repeated his attack of moments earlier under cover fire from his friend Kim Dong Jei. Unable to fire fast enough at the human wall pouring through the wire; both were overwhelmed by AK fire, going down like Marines, fighting to the last breath.

At this same moment just eight feet away, Corporal Kim Nam Suk manned his machine gun until a bullet sent him to his final rest. Assistant gunner Woo Choon Mae took over trigger position, working the M-60 a couple more minutes before stubbornly giving up his own ghost to an angry swarm of fire. The last surviving member of the machine gun team, PFC Song Young Sup, was already mortally wounded and played dead, allowing two grenades to roll from his hands while enemy soldiers filed past him in the trench. Song and the NVA were consumed in a maelstrom of flash and steel.

Further down the trench line, Sergeant Lee Hak Won, after dispatching four or five NVA with his bare hands, was mortally wounded by bayonet slashes to the point where he too could no longer fight. The tough-as-leather NCO pulled pin on two grenades and flung himself into his antagonists, taking his own life and four more North Viets with him.

PFC Lee Young Bok, defending his fighting hole, was the only squad member not killed or injured in the unfolding bedlam. The gutsy private lured North Vietnamese toward him, dropping grenades as he disappeared into one of the connecting trenches. When the grenades exploded, he reappeared and released several more into the dazed enemy, killing a number of his pursuers, temporarily stalling the attack.

First Squad also had its hands full, repelling a tidal wave of oncoming North Vietnamese. PFC Shon Soon Tae knew his resistance would soon be greatly diminished by loss of blood. Completely out of ammo, the intrepid Marine charged his antagonists at fixed bayonet, taking out two soldiers before going down for the last time as bullets from beyond the wire ripped through his body.

An entire squad was lost in a matter of minutes. The steadfast resistance and magnificent sacrifice of 3rd Squad was enough to slow the attack just long enough to allow arrival of several reinforcements to help plug the hole. *E Pundae* filled the void, hammering away at the encroaching mob.

Knowing they were needed elsewhere, Dave Long and Jim Porta sprang to their feet, breaking for the observation post. Firing as they ran, Dave dropped an NVA soldier to his near left, taking several others under fire while threading their way through a maze of tracers and explosions. Shielding the other flank, Jim Porta cut loose a well-directed volley, sending a small group of Vietnamese to ground. Seeing their plight, Marines manning the observation post provided cover fire until the pair safely entered the bunker. Both Americans immediately took up firing positions, adding two more trigger pullers to the embattled HQ staff.

Retrieving his radio, Dave Long tried contacting Brigade without success. A quick change to secondary frequency yielded negative results as well. Going back on primary, Dave picked up a transmission between Brigade and Spooky 1-1, an AC-47 gunship. How could he be this lucky? Circling west of location at 8,000 feet, Spooky was describing a battle raging below him as the biggest firefight he had ever witnessed. Stepping into the exchange, Dave informed all concerned it was his position under observation. Taking over the conversation, Dave relayed his tactical situation as he knew it, as well as coordinates and approximate dimensions of the outpost, preparing to get Spooky into this battle. Armed with 7.62mm miniguns capable of sustained fire of 6,000 rounds per minute, he could end this fight right now.

As soon as Dave's briefing was digested, Spooky moved in, dropping three flares over the northwest perimeter. The extremely bright flares lit the night like nothing anyone had ever witnessed. Captain Jung did not look favorably on his positions being that well lit up and directed Dave to stop the flares. In the excitement of the moment, Dave couldn't hold the C.O.'s attention long enough to explain the gunships capabilities. As Captain Jung was dealing with a crisis a second, he just didn't have time for classes on air support. The 11th Company C.O. then ordered artillery to pour it on.

In order to bring Spooky close enough to safely employ his weaponry, Dave needed to convince Captain Jung to lift artillery fires. Jung Kyong Jin would have none of it. With his defenses bending at point of attack on two fronts, he knew artillery was working; he wasn't sure what a gunship could do. As Spooky circled to bring his guns to bear on target, Dave had to call him off; fearing artillery fire might bring the big ship down.

Spooky took position north of Tra Bong River, watching the battle, hoping to get another chance at applying his weapon systems.

Outside the wire in front of 1st Platoon, North Vietnamese brought up mortars that were now firing and wreaking havoc on the company command post. Lieutenant Shin Won Bae, commanding *II Sodae,* spotted the gun emplacement. He impressed the closest Marines to him into a makeshift assault force. Organizing a classic Marine tactic, he ordered his rifle squads to lay down a base of fire, while he led a fire team assault on the mortar tubes some 100 meters in front of his position, shielded behind a rock formation. Platoon Sergeant, Gunnery Sergeant Kim Yong Kil, accompanied the attackers. When the team closed within twenty meters of the gun emplacement, Gunny Kim threw two hand grenades toward the enemy defenders. As soon as the grenades exploded, Shin and his fire team advanced on objective and repeated this tactic until they reached the rocks. In a brief but violent action, the survivors went down in a shower of rifle fire. Over twenty dead soldiers lay crumbled amid these three threatening tubes. As soon as the mortars were collected, Shin withdrew his force.

On the other side of the perimeter, Som Sodae was heavily engaged in hand-to-hand combat as they desperately fought to hold ground against an ever-increasing enemy, who were literally swarming all over them. Daily *Tae Kwon Do* (Korean martial arts) drills were currently demonstrating their worth. Every bone-crunching punch, kick, and head butt thrown at phantom antagonists thousands of times during early-morning workouts were now paying dividends. The grunts of Som Sodae were literally making the NVA eat their own teeth in a desperate free-for-all of biblical proportions. Many Marines put flimsy M-16s and bayonets aside in favor of entrenching tools and knives. North Vietnamese apparently did not possess hand-to-hand combat skills anywhere close to Tae Kwon Do. Their adversaries, however, thrived on this military discipline. The only thing keeping the Viets in this wild exchange of blows was overwhelming numbers. As soon as one attacker was killed, five more took his place. NVA strength seemed to be unlimited. The outnumbered defenders more than had their hands full, grudgingly giving ground to the human tide in a fighting withdrawal. By now the fight had spilled over the trenches and was extending into the compound's interior.

PCF Lee Ki On came upon two North Viets in the company's mortar pit. Lee, out of ammo, took his .45 by its barrel, brandishing it like a hammer, and beat the pair senseless. After hiding the tubes under some nearby debris, Lee killed the pair with a hand grenade and rejoined the punch fest, to die with the hyong-je haebyong if necessary.

In one of the four-deuce mortar pits, two artillerymen exchanging fire with several NVA soldiers were flanked by North Vietnamese; one, armed with a flame thrower, advanced on them. PFC Kim Bo Hyun and PFC Yung Sang Yul maneuvered against the thermal weapon under cover of suppressing fire provided by other Marines on their flank. As the cunning duo reached throwing distance, the flame thrower and several enemy troops were quickly eliminated in a huge firestorm when the fuel tank erupted.

Il So Dae experienced this same tactic as NVA sent two flame throwers to exploit a newly opened breach in the platoon's lines. Once again the aggressive Lieutenant Shin with Staff Sergeant Oh Sung Hwan hastened forward, confronting this threat with automatic weapons fire and grenades. The Marines killed the soldiers, seized the flame throwers, and rallied the platoon, re-establishing the perimeter.

Inside the observation post, Dave Long peered out from his sand-bagged firing port and noticed three attackers moving across his front at about 150 feet in single file. Taking aim by dim flare light, Dave recalled a tactic employed by Sergeant York a few wars earlier. Firing from back to front, he loosed three rounds, all of which found their mark, dropping men in the rear one at a time so those in front wouldn't realize somebody had them under fire.

Thinking the NVA was organizing a move on the structure, Porta and Long sprang to have a look outside. Explosions shook the earth moments after exiting the sand-bagged building. Several mortar and

RPG rounds bracketed the bunker, destroying the firing port newly vacated by Dave Long. The pair scurried off, advancing forward toward the secondary trench line, looking for some ass to kick. If they weren't going to be allowed to use their specialty, reverting to basics was all right by them.

Employing basic infantry tactics, unit cohesion kept NVA forces from overwhelming the determined defenders. Everywhere in the compound, squad- and fire team-size units held their ground, collaborating with fire support and maneuvering against a massive crush of enemy troops. *Ship-il Chungdae* refused to buckle, more than matching overwhelming numbers with mad dog ferocity of pissed-off grunts. As in the paddy fight a few weeks earlier, training and discipline became intangible weapons of unrivaled value.

Exhausted and battered after an hour of continuous energy- and emotion-draining combat, a foreboding situation confronted the embattled defenders. North Vietnamese unrelentingly continued to press their advantage from two directions, penetrating the perimeter at both points of attack, pushing 11th Company Marines closer to the center of the compound, and they were now in possession of about one third of the outpost. Mortar fire was still making life hazardous above ground for Marines not engaged in perimeter fighting, as shells were impacting in and around the Company command post and fallback positions.

Brigade artillery, ringing a wall of explosions around the compound, effectively isolated NVA units that breached the wire from succeeding reinforcements trying to force their way into the trenches, successfully stalemating the North Vietnamese incursion. By 0515 things were just a little more under control as Lieutenant Kim kept the big guns busy, working over every possible approach.

At 0530, with second effort NVA troops once again began encroaching further into the weakened 3rd Platoon sector, pushing outnumbered defenders all the way back to the fallback trenches. Fighting with desperate determination, *Som Sodae* refused to cave, making the attackers pay dearly for every inch.

Il Sodae likewise was forced by weight of numbers to give up some real estate. Lieutenant Shin, as he had done on several occasions that night, rallied his platoon, forcing the NVA advance to a grinding halt almost as soon as it began.

Not much has been said about E Sodae, as their sector was not under direct attack. However, they were under intense fire from outside the wire, being frozen in position to defend against an attack should one materialize. This in effect diminished available manpower for assignment to hot spots around the perimeter. All the H&S personnel, weapons platoon, cooks, clerks, and apple polishers were knee-deep in death struggles raging all over the outpost. However, that part of the perimeter was still intact. As unbelievable as it may sound, the bulk work of battle against 2,400 attackers was at this time being shouldered by just two measly platoons of Marines, assisted by gunners from the four-deuce mortar section and support personnel.

As had been the case all night throughout a very intense struggle, the tide of battle turned once more to smile on the stressed Marines. Captain Jung made a decision to pull one squad from his only reserve, *E Sodae,* to reinforce the hard-pressed 3rd Platoon. It seemed to work as the aggressiveness of the attack began to weaken at 3rd Platoon's sector, allowing his Marines to take advantage of the relaxed aggression. Over the next hour, the battle reverted pretty much back to a stalemate. Marines refused to give any more real estate. Defending the specific square foot of ground each Marine currently occupied, the 11th Company stubbornly held NVA advances in check, putting up furious resistance.

0630 brought the first faint rays of sunlight to eyes that gave little weight to ever beholding light of day again. An overcast misty dawn clouded with fog permitted just enough light to allow the eagle eyes of Lieutenant Kim Se Chang to locate the NVA Regimental command post. Finding his map, the aggressive officer quickly determined grid coordinates, calculated distance, and took an azimuth reading, then relayed data to Brigade artillery. Heatedly talking on his AN/PRC-10 field radio, he gave the order to "fire!" Lieutenant Kim, having sustained a bullet wound to the head right through his helmet a half hour earlier, struggled very hard to keep his concentration.

Every gun in the battery applied new elevation and direction data to their death-dealing delivery mediums. Having received the fire order, a gunner on gun three pulled his lanyard, launching its lethal sixty-five-pound consignment down range. "On the way" confirmation was voiced over the battery radio back to Lieutenant Kim.

"Roger, on the way," Lieutenant Kim acknowledged as he strained his eyes to observe impact from the adjusting gun. Seconds later, a round landed fifty meters short and an equal distance right of the intended location.

"Add five-zero, left five-zero, fire for effect!" Kim shouted into his mouthpiece.

Again, all six field pieces dialed in new adjustment data. When all was ready, "*So da,*" Each tube erupted in unison, belching smoke and flash, silhouetting the howitzers in the twilight against graying skies, adding more voices of encouragement to their brothers at Tra Bihn Dong. After all, they were the kings of battle and they were in this fight too. Reloading and firing as fast as the exhausted crews could work, round after round was launched down range.

All hell broke loose among the NVA command personnel as explosions swallowed senior regimental staff in earth-shaking flashes, flinging radios, maps, officers, and gear to the ground and through the air. White-hot shards of jagged metal shredded bodies and material alike into portioned and twisted imitations of what they once were.

Lieutenant Kim stayed on mission just long enough to see it through before surrendering to unconsciousness, knowing he'd made a difference that night.

Energized by newly available visibility, Marines manning the FSCC made the most of an opportunity to contribute their unique talents. Lieutenant Kim's assistant, Staff Sergeant Kim Hyun Chul, exposed himself to intense small arms fire and took charge, refusing to keep his head down as he obstinately scanned the landscape through field glasses, seeking out targets of opportunity.

The staff sergeant was rewarded for his watchfulness when he caught sight of NVA mortar crews that had been making his life miserable all night. "Payback is on the way," he thought, pointing out his observation. Jubilant, he plotted map coordinates and once more called in data to the battery, repeating the adjustment and fire for effect process. Kim watched through binoculars as brigade's howitzers extracted a terrible toll on Vietnamese mortar crews, eliminating any further threats from these high-angle harbingers of whistling death.

Cut off from command structure and now lacking supporting fire from mortars that had been causing mayhem and destruction all through the attack, the North Vietnamese incursion started falling apart. Casualties were escalating as their best ally, darkness, fled the field, exposing them to relentless firing from payback-hungry Marines. Payback was definitely on the breakfast menu that morning, and the dinner bell was ringing.

For the first time since hostilities commenced, Captain Jung had a clear view of his besieged base camp. He could see his units and their activities as well as his enemies, seemingly as through different eyes. The *Ship-il Chungdae* skipper now wrestled the fate of his company away from uncertainty, and took complete control of dictated conditions that he would now sure as hell influence. Captain Jung Kyung Jin was now fully established as the dominant tactician at Tra Bihn Dong. He put in motion a plan that would turn out to be one of the most crucial events of battle.

Assembling a makeshift force of a single squad from 1st and 2nd Platoons, Captain Jung ordered a counterattack designed to isolate North Vietnamese soldiers within his perimeter. Lieutenant Kim Ki Hong, Weapons Platoon Commander, volunteered to spearhead this innovative but dangerous exercise.

3rd Platoon Marines at this point had been pushed further back into the compound engaged in a running gunfight, making a stand immediately below the company's observation post, where FOs were still adjusting artillery fire. Som Sodae at this moment in time was on a personal basis with most members of the NVA assault battalions, having been in continuous brawls at nose length for going on three hours.

Lieutenant Kim began his assault at 0650, leading his squad on a complicated double envelopment maneuver against North Vietnamese, who were trying to get something working. Catching the NVA completely off guard, the assault force cut a swath through the NVA, violently mixing with confused enemy troops, shooting, slashing, and bludgeoning everything in their way. Kim personally killed five enemy soldiers with his .45, while his impromptu unit gunned down dozens more. Bullets, rifle butts, and bayonets took their toll as the squad aggressively pressed forward. The determined officer and his charges forced the Vietnamese back beyond the fallback trenches.

Emboldened by the attack, Staff Sergeant Kim Son Kwan, 3rd Platoon Sergeant rallied some of his men and joined the attack. Marines of *Som Sodae* began screaming and yelling insults as they fell violently upon dazed enemy soldiers. Surrounded by Lieutenant Kim's assault force, the North Vietnamese refused surrender and fought like hell to find a way out. The Koreans killed all that could not escape. Those that were able to retreat hooked up with NVA support units in the outer trenches who between them represented a company-size delegation.

Lieutenant Kim's enveloping force, now augmented by the dauntless Marines of *Som Sodae*, engaged the company-size support troops in a furious firefight but lacked manpower to execute further advancement against entrenched troops. As outnumbered as *Ship-il Chungdae* was, it would not help the situation to lose more Marines.

Pulling one last trick out of his bag, at 0725 Captain Jung ordered Lieutenant Kim's assault force to beat a retreat and withdraw to the observation post. His objective was to lure the North Vietnamese into attack mode and bring them into the open. It worked. Sensing an opportunity to salvage Tra Bihn Dong, the NVA commander ordered an advance on the company observation post. They came at the Marines beating gongs, screaming, and appearing to the whole world that they were finally going to get the job finished.

Allowing his adversary to advance within fifty feet, Captain Jung sprang the trap.

"So-da!"

Som Sodae cut loose with a murderous volume of fire, felling a number of attackers. On command, elements of 1st and 2nd Platoons executed a classic envelopment, surprising the NVA with this maneuver for a second time in less than an hour, cutting down most of the lead troops still standing. Survivors found the fastest ways possible out of the compound and never looked back. For all intents and purposes, *Ship-il Chungdae* had prevailed. With North Vietnamese in retreat under clearing skies, artillery fire was finally lifted so finishing touches could be applied.

Spooky 1-1, running low on fuel, had withdrawn to home base an hour earlier.

Togo 87 arrived on station just before dawn, securing a great view of events. In communication with Jim Porta, the airborne FAC was up to speed on who was where. He was also in contact with a flight of Marine F-4s and two gunships from VMO-6. All night long, Lance Corporal Porta harbored a burning desire to tattoo his name on someone's ass.

Bringing down the gunships, first to dust the perimeter, the UH1-Es brushed lingering NVA from the outer defense trenches. Not in a mood to do anything else but run, the NVA did not fire on the gunships. VMO-6 had a field day, expending all ordnance and racking up a good tally before departing.

As soon as VMO-6 cleared air space, Togo dove on target, sending a white phosphorous marker rocket into a large group of retreating NVA. An audience gathered on the southwest perimeter to witness napalm canisters chase fleeing battalions who not so long ago threatened to overrun them. Giving the F-4s a chance at the windfall of targets, Togo brought them in low, allowing napalm maximum spread. Remanning outer trenches, Marines of *Ship-il Chungdae* were inebriated with victory and cheered the punishment being administered to those NVA bastards.

There was never a formal body count taken to record the effectiveness of those air strikes, but Dave Long and Jim Porta estimate the toll at better than 200. Later that afternoon, Togo 87 reported hundreds of graves being dug in the foothill valleys due west of Tra Bihn Dong.

The world will never know the countless acts of valor displayed that night. Tra Bihn Dong found a place in Korean military lore as the greatest single victory of ROK forces in Vietnam, or anyplace else outside South Korea. Every clerk in Brigade worked overtime for months processing reams of paperwork for award recommendations.

Through the hell of it all, it's difficult to fathom only ten Marines of *Ship-il Chungdae* were killed in action that night. Most of the dead were members of the 3rd Squad, 3rd Platoon, who willingly laid down their lives during the first frantic minutes of a nightmare, buying time for their brothers and giving the company a few precious moments to react.

USS Higbee
(DD-806)
Gearing Class Destroyer
Call Sign: Truck

Ready for action 3 January 1964, USS *Higbee* trained on the West Coast until departing for Japan 30 June, reaching her new homeport, Yokosuka, 18 July. During the Tonkin Gulf incident in August, the destroyer screened carriers of Task Force 77 in the South China Sea. In February 1965, USS *Higbee* lent her guns in support of the 9th Marines at Da Nang. USS *Higbee* steamed in and out of Vietnam most of the year, providing fire support as a gunline unit.

Returning to South Vietnam in April 1969, USS *Higbee* bombarded enemy positions near Cape St. Jacques and the mouth of the Saigon River, re-establishing her position on the gunline.

On 19 April 1972, the USS *Higbee* became the first U.S. warship to be bombed during the Vietnam War. Flames and clouds of black smoke from leaking oil engulfed the deck as the crew fought the fire. A MIG 17 came out of the mountains, went "feet wet," and passed directly over the USS *Sterett* (DDG-31). It then made a turn up the track of the strike force that included the USS *Oklahoma City* (CG-5) and USS *Lloyd Thomas* (DD 764) and dropped two 250-pound iron bombs on the next ship in line, the USS *Higbee*. Mere moments before, the USS *Higbee* experienced a hot round in her after gun mount. This hang-fire condition forced evacuation of the mount as a precautionary measure. One of the MIG's bombs dropped on the vacated aft mount, as the second dropped into the water alongside her fantail. Just as the MIG pulled up from her bomb run and banked to starboard toward the safety of the mountains, the USS *Sterett* achieved missile "lock-on" and fired two Terrier missiles, one of which downed the MIG. USS *Higbee*'s steering gear was damaged by the attack. She encountered no fatalities, and damage control teams had the fires quickly under control. USS *Sterett* stood by, as USS *Higbee* fought her fires, completed her turn, and proceeded out of the area, still with her rudder inoperative. USS *Sterett* continued to stand by USS *Higbee*. On her own power, USS *Higbee* headed for Da Nang, the closest friendly port.

We, who once found refuge under the protection of her guns, salute this valiant ship and her gallant crew.

RAMPAGE OF THE GIANT DRAGON

Morning of the 15th, struggling to force its light through overcast skies, revealed a sight not easily looked upon by even the most hardened combat veterans. Emotionally spent and exhausted Marines, peering from behind bloodshot eyes, beheld a scene straight from hell. Bodies hardened in death poses lay strewn about the compound in a myriad of baroque positions. Mutilated masses of frozen flesh lay twisted amid pools of coagulated blood. Entrails trailing away from torsos torn half inside out, limbs and other body parts randomly littered the ground in no particular proximity to the bodies they were once whole members of. It was a grotesque landscape of horror that promoted a study in revulsion as could only be envisioned by a mad artist striving for the ultimate in surrealist expression.

Men combed the battlefield searching for survivors, frantically trying to locate buddies who didn't answer morning roll. Corpsmen and Marines alike feverishly cared for the wounded and sorted out the serious cases for immediate treatment and evacuation. Almost every man in the company had multiple wounds.

While air assets were working over the remnants of the 2nd NVA Division, Dave Long and Jim Porta, satisfied that Togo had a handle on things, began organizing ground preparations for Medevac operations that would be under way very soon.

Sixteen helicopters arrived on station, depositing a relief force of Yuk Chungdae who immediately began organizing for clearing operations as soon as air activities ceased. Corpsmen and doctors from the Korean field hospital at Brigade, among the first down the ramp, hurried to the triage area and rendered treatment and advanced medical assistance to those most in need of urgent care.

Wounded, staged in priority according to the seriousness of their injuries, were loaded on those same choppers for a ride to Charlie Med.

VIPs from all over I Corps came to Tra Bihn Dong that morning to congratulate Captain Jung and his Marines. General Kim and most of his senior staff came off one of the first choppers to set down inside the wire. Finally, he had the long-sought-after big battle that had eluded the Blue Dragon Brigade these many months.

Even III MAF himself, Lieutenant General Lewis W. Walt, commanding officer of every Marine in Vietnam, dropped in to survey the victory.

The Eleventh Company compound was indeed a very popular destination that morning. Like vultures drawn to a kill, reporters of various affiliations descended on Tra Bihn Dong to cash in on the headlines. It didn't really matter to them what happened. The heroic events of the past few hours didn't concern them, nor did the courageous sacrifice of the 3rd Squad hold any interest. They were there to take pictures and act to the whole world as though they really knew something. They seamed to us; self-serving, self-proclaimed experts who prized their media affiliation over American citizenship.

With Yuk Chungdae now in the field sweeping the entire perimeter for wounded NVA, survivors of the 11th Company busied themselves dragging bodies outside the wire and rebuilding their defenses. The intelligence commentary offered in the past two chapters concerning the battle of Tra Bihn Dong was recovered from prisoners taken in this clearing sweep as well as from documents found on the bodies of NVA officers generously decorating the landscape in and around 11th Company's perimeter.

Somewhere west of Tra Bihn Dong, remnants of a defeated regiment were reeling back toward the mountains. They were hurt bad. Undoubtedly they had significant wounded to care for, thus adding more of a burden on these escaping refugees.

All through the previous night up through midmorning of 15 February, the combined effort of the entire brigade was for the single purpose of saving Ship Il Chungdae. Now that a badly mauled regiment was at their mercy, no plan existed to capitalize on the situation. In hindsight, it was a complete surprise to learn an entire regiment participated in the Tra Bihn Dong attack. General Kim and his staff, however, did not want to let the North Viets off the hook.

Ku Chungdae based southwest of the battle sent out patrols in strength to cut off any elements filtering through their territory. E Chungdae to the southeast likewise sent out patrols in strength for the same purpose.

Operation Giant Dragon was born on the fly to pile on punishment and levy a heavy tax on the 2nd NVA Division. All three line battalions worked overtime, making preparations to go on offense.

On the morning of 16 February 1967, companies moved out from their base camps toward the high country southwest of National Highway 1. Two ARVN Airborne battalions moved into position along the Tra Khuc River to cut off and block sanctuary routes. One battalion of the U.S. 5th Marines set up shop in the foothills northwest of the river. Even if the operation came up empty, this area needed to be secured. In the past month, the NVA showed little respect for the Blue Dragons, as evidenced from their bold ambush on the 3rd Battalion HQ party in the paddy and now this regimental-size strike at Tra Bihn Dong. It was long past time for the NVA to learn who rules the roost in this part of the world.

Korean Marines tended to name their combat operations associated with dragon anatomy or character: Dragon Claw, Dragon Tooth, Dragon Fire, Happy Dragon, Mad Dragon, this Dragon, and that Dragon. The one entity all these snappy labels held in common was the simple truth that to a grunt, they all digressed to "Dragon Ass" before the sun set on day one.

Tactical planning for Giant Dragon was a simple hammer and anvil maneuver design to push south, attempting to drive North Vietnamese troops ahead of them toward South Vietnamese paratroopers at Tra Khuc River. If that didn't get the job done, the 5th Marines knew what to do. *Ku Chungdae* was the only company in position to cut off westerly escape routes. Their job was to channel hostiles toward the south.

E Chungdae and II Chungdae guarded easterly escape routes and likewise positioned themselves to turn any fleeing remnants south.

Second Battalion committed *Oh Chungdae* (5th Company) and *Cheel Chungdae* (7th Company) to join the 6th Company already at Tra Bihn Dong to function as the operational hammer of Giant Dragon, driving straight south.

Progress toward the river was swift but methodical, gathering no incidents worthy of comment. On the second-to-the-last day of Giant Dragon, 19 February, the Koreans closed on the Tra Khuc.

Within sight of Tra Khuc River at an area known as the hook, *Oh Chungdae* was in position to execute its last objective. Radio traffic had been alive all morning with news of contact reported by ARVN Airborne units posted on the south bank.

One quarter mile north of the river, a dirt access road branching off National Highway 1 cuts west for six or eight miles. Oh Chungdae was using that road to speed its arrival at an anticipated advantage location to launch an assault on the hook.

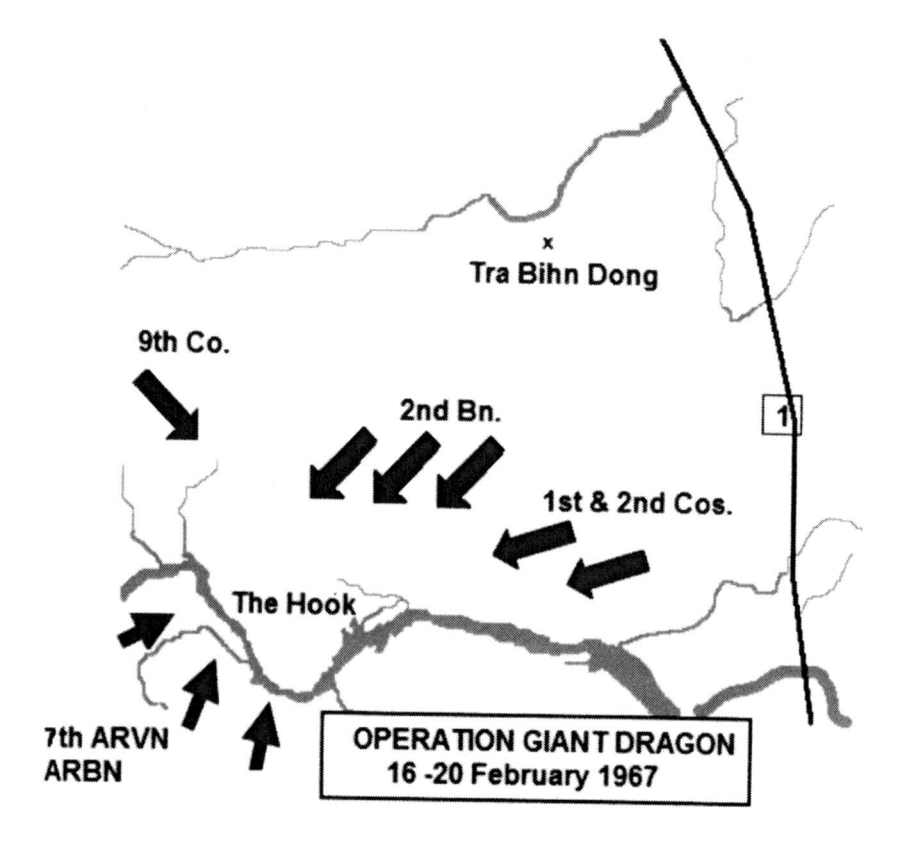

OPERATION GIANT DRAGON
16 -20 February 1967

Surviving elements of the 48th Viet Cong main force battalion, frustrated at finding the river crossing blocked by concentrated fire from ARVN Airborne troops, retreated north toward the access road in hope of finding a safe passage west. Lead scouts spotted Oh Chungdae on a collision course to intercept them. Not wanting to have his back to the river with hostile troops on the opposite bank, the VC commander made a hasty decision to confront Oh Chungdae and attempt a break-through. Arriving at the road minutes ahead of the looming contact, a spontaneous, albeit haphazard, ambush was organized on the run. With no time to brief their men, VC officers were still assigning ambush positions as the unsuspecting Koreans blundered into the kill zone.

Oh Chungdae, unaware of impending contact, continued forward on a timeline to be in jump-off position before an assumedly desperate adversary could react to its presence. From fifty meters, the hasty ambush was sprung. Not exactly textbook execution, as the bushwhackers' opening volley was not well coordinated. Forward elements opened up prematurely. Others down the line commenced fire in random sequence, negating the full advantage of surprise.

Koreans dropped in place, returning fire, while officers and NCOs struggled to get a handle on the crisis. The roadside offered very little cover as terrain on both sides consisted mostly of knee-high scrub vegetation sparsely distributed over a carpet of crabgrass and sand.

PFC Gary Fiedler, in the center of the formation, isolated by ten or twelve meters from other Marines, lay pressed to the ground, firing his M-3 grease gun at muzzle flashes barely within range of his vintage weapon.

Captain Oh Sae Chang, looking around to assess the situation, spotted a cemetery thirty or so meters west of the road right behind his company that was spread out some seventy-five meters either side of him. He ordered one platoon to establish position in the cemetery to provide cover fire for the rest. The burial plot was on higher ground and offered more protection than the barren roadside.

Once the VC established a sustained base of fire, a not-too-spirited assault went forward. Gary Fiedler, sensing something was afoot but not having clear targets, propped himself up on one knee for a better look. Shocked to see three VC in front of him at less than twenty meters, Gary quickly rose to his feet, spraying the trio and killing all three of them. Bullet strikes kicking up sand at his feet sent the confused Marine backpedaling quickly to his right. In the corner of his eye, Fiedler caught a glimpse of two more attackers bearing down on him from the oblique. Quickly pivoting to his left, Gary cut loose with another burst, stitching the chests of both men with hot .45 rounds.

Dropping on one knee to change magazines, Gary became suddenly aware he was alone. For a brief moment, confusion clouded his mind almost to the point of panic. Frantically snapping his head left to right, scanning the immediate area for signs of men who were just there seconds ago, he became acutely aware of someone calling to him through the din of fire. "Pilter, Pilter!" (There is no "F" sound in the Korean language; therefore, "P" is the closest substitute.) "*Edi wa!*" ("Come here!") Following with his ears the sound of that call to the edge of the cemetery, Gary was relieved to see the company only thirty or so yards away.

Springing to his feet, Gary set off on a serpentine course toward his buddies at a low crouch while cover fire zipped past him on all sides. Elated to have survived his one-man excursion from exile, the kid from New Jersey's blood pressure receded closer to normal levels now that he was secure in the presence of trusted companions. 5th Company continued pouring fire into the ambush area for two more minutes, and then sprang to assault.

Seeing no way past Oh Chungdae, and wanting no part in a sustained fight with the Koreans, the VC wisely pulled back to rethink their options. As quickly as it started, contact was broken. Luckily, the 5th Company sustained no casualties in five or six mad minutes of mayhem.

When Oh Chungdae's assault reached the newly vacated ambush site, the only thing still there was spent shell casings. Evidence indicated the unit was moving west along the river. As night was closing in fast, Oh Chungdae did not pursue, but waited for other Blue Dragon elements.

By early morning, with all ROK companies now in position, Brigade committed every unit in the field in an all-out drive for the river. NVA and VC units, wanting no part of the hyong-je haebyong, fled before the advancing Koreans, electing to push across the river.

It was an easy day for the ROKs, as they could not pick a fight. The brunt of the fighting that day was carried by the 7th ARVN Airborne Battalion, who racked up an impressive body count, performing valiantly. For their notable performance in that battle, the 7th ARVN Airborne Battalion was awarded the Presidential Unit Citation.

After the fight at the hook on 20 February, Operation Giant Dragon was terminated. Line companies departed the area on foot, making their way back to their respective base camps. An upbeat mood accompanied Yuk Chungdae on its way back to *E Taedae* base camp. Late in the afternoon, the company was traversing an open rice paddy when all hell broke loose. An undetermined number of NVA opened up with small arms and machine guns from 300 meters out, sending Yuk Chungdae into defensive mode. Mortars from an unknown location piled on more lethality to the unfolding movement.

Sergeant Lawrence C. Smith and Lance Corporal Terrance J. Perko, just as surprised as were nearby Koreans, hit the dirt hard. Caught in the open, Sergeant Smith ordered Perko to pull back to a paddy dike at their immediate rear. At the intersection of two paddies, Sergeant Smith dove behind the right side dike, while Lance Corporal Perko sought refuge behind the left embankment. Consulting his map, Big Smith fixed his position, as well as plotting NVA gunners. Needing radio access, Sergeant Smith, calling for Perko, noticed the lance corporal wasn't moving. The big sergeant called out several times, trying to raise a response, with negative results.

Reacting on fear, sensing all was not right, Large Larry vaulted the dike. Calling out to Perko once more, the sergeant stopped in midsentence as he noticed the junior man lying on his back, tunic saturated in blood. Crawling over to his radio operator, Sergeant Smith looked into Perko's eyes while reaching for the first aid kit on the wounded man's cartridge belt. A bullet had entered Perko's neck, causing blood to exit the wound at a high rate. In a very weak voice, Terry looked up and garbled, "Sergeant Smith!" The kid from Maple Heights, Ohio, closed his eyes, turned his head, and was gone.

Gathering his composure, Sergeant Smith pulled the radio from Terry's back. He had one more chore to complete now, a service he hoped he'd never be called on to execute. As circumstance would have it, the handset cord was severed.

Threading his way to the company command group, dodging rounds from every weapon in the NVA arsenal, Sergeant Smith found a radio operator who allowed him use of his equipment to get up on the ANGLICO TAC net. As senior man in the field, Smith called for the TACP team on his eastern flank to gravitate over to his position. He was confident one consolidated team could provide what air support might be needed for both companies. Sergeant Sheffield and Lance Corporal Lawrence .A. Smith, traveling with 7th Company, answered the call.

Cutting across the open paddy behind Marines pumping out suppressing fire at hidden adversaries, the team braved incoming fire, finding Sergeant Smith peering over the paddy dike next to Terry Perko's lifeless body.

Despondent and feeling helpless, the big Marine took the handset from Lance Corporal Smith. After hailing the proper call sign and establishing contact, Sergeant Smith continued in solemn voice, "Request a routine Medevac! Over. One USMC KIA!" The call went out over the TAC net.

Captain Stephen W. Pless, overhearing the Medevac request coming across the FSCC radio at Brigade, was heartsick at discovering he'd just lost his first Marine. Grabbing the handset from the radio operator, he anxiously requested initials of the casualty. "TANGO-PAPPA" the answer blared back at him.

Report of those initials hit everyone like a ton of bricks. All hands listening on the TAC net were totally demoralized at hearing this turn of events. That's one crumby way to receive high-impact news of that nature. Everyone to a man understood how lucky they'd been not to have lost anyone the first six months in-country. It didn't seem real that Terry had gone down. But it was true! Alone and in teams of two, the ROK Marine Detachment all came face to face with the reality of their own mortality that afternoon.

Looking around at the situation, Sergeant Smith realized he had some work to do before attempting to bring a Medevac into the shit sandwich he was now in the center of. Back up on the TAC net, Sergeant Smith hailed Togo 88, requesting that the O1 drift toward coordinates just provided.

Once Togo appeared over the battle, Sergeant Smith made sure his own position was recognized and directed the pilot's attention at a tree line on an outcropping of high ground to his north. After consultation with the 6th Company C.O., it was agreed to put an air strike into the tree line.

It was very evident an unidentified NVA unit filtered into the area after the Koreans passed some three days ago on their drive to the Song Tra Khuc. Within minutes of Togo's request for fixed wing support, Tarbush Medevac crackled over the radio, hailing "*Sa Ma Oul* 14 Bravo." A detailed situation briefing exchange between ground and air transferred smoothly. Lance Corporal Smith tossed a smoke grenade for visual reference. Sergeant Smith made sure Tarbush understood his position was under fire, directing the Medevac to approach from the east. Artillery and mortar fire were suspended as the gunship escort approached the high ground outcropping with lethal intent.

Incoming and outgoing small arms fire chattered incessantly as the team looked on, ready to adjust ordnance. Coming in at tree-top level, the UH1-E walked his full complement of rockets the entire length of the wood line. Green tracers arched up from several positions, barely missing the gallant war bird. Climbing out of his rocket pass, the UH1-E executed a tight turn, diving back on target, lacing the wood line with machine gun fire. Two more passes on the wood line exhausted every round on board, forcing the Medevac operation to abort. Heavy fire still poured from the woodland.

Medevac had no sooner cleared air space when Togo 88 hailed Sergeant Smith with news that a flight of A-4s was on station, ready to start work. Having observed the gunship rockets, Togo was already on objective. As soon as Togo finished briefing the A-4s, he dove on target, sending a marker rocket center mass of the wood line.

Defiant fire still streaming from the wood line alerted everyone watching the NVA were still there.

Sergeant Sheffield, behind Sergeant Smith, sat on the ground, locating targets on his map, calling out coordinates to Big Smith, who was now on his feet, relaying targeting information to Togo.

Adjusting bomb runs in relation to his marker rocket, Togo brought the jets down on a heading fifty meters east of the marker. As each attack craft approached target, outgoing fire slacked off as North Vietnamese gunners put their heads down, bracing for impact.

As each attacking A-4 released his load and started his exit vector, ordnance impacting on target shook the earth. Fire would once again pour out of the wood line before bomb shrapnel stopped falling. It was now evident the buggers were dug in.

Intently occupied observing each run, keeping Togo informed of ordnance effectiveness, Sergeants Smith and Sheffield soon became the focus of NVA gunners. Rounds started impacting on all sides. Standing his ground, Big Smith heard Sheffield scream a steady stream of vulgarity as bullets passing between the big man's legs stitched Sheffield's left leg.

Both Smiths laid him back to assess the damage. Calling for a Korean corpsman, Sergeant Smith continued the air strike.

Working over the target area for twenty more minutes with napalm and 250-pound snake eyes, the A-4s expended all ordnance and withdrew.

Smoke rose several feet over the wood line as fires, still smoldering from several locations, obscured observation of the target area. As things were fairly quiet, the Koreans ordered an advance, pushing forward on a wide front toward NVA positions. Almost as soon as the advance began, fire once more erupted from the wood line, killing three and wounding two ROKs. As night was settling in, the ROKs stopped their advance and called for artillery.

Sergeant Smith, after consulting with 6th Company Actual, dialed Brigade once more. His shopping list was getting larger. He still had wounded on the ground and insisted he really needed to get the Medevac back on station. Reporting he was now two men short, replacements were also requested. After a quick exchange of ideas, Brigade sent a request to Da Nang for an AC-47 gunship to suppress NVA fire.

Two hours after the sun went down, Spooky 1-2 hailed Sergeant Smith. Retracing the situation report, Spooky was brought up to speed on target data. With all heads down, an illumination grenade marked 6th Company's position. Once Spooky acknowledged the marker, Sergeant Smith directed the big gunship's attention to the wooded high ground 400 meters north.

Satisfied everyone concerned was on the same page, Sergeant Smith cleared the gunship to fire.

Spooky discharged one of its 2 million-candlepower flares over the wood line, illuminating the entire landscape.

On a circular orbit, the AC-47 cranked up its miniguns, sending a solid beam of orange tracers racing into the tree line. This ship was fitted with three 7.62mm Gatling-style miniguns mounted to fire from gun ports on its left side. Miniguns are capable of delivering up to 6,000 rounds per minute on target, every fifth round being a tracer. At 6,000 rounds per minute, it appeared to be a laser weapon right out of a science fiction movie.

Being as this occasion marked the first time a weapon of this sophistication was employed in support of Korean Marines, oohs and aahs expressed a reverent awe of approval up and down the ROK chain of command. Sergeant Smith, having never controlled or even observed this weapons platform perform before, was damned pleased with himself. Terry Perko wasn't able to answer for himself, but as long as it's within their power, the surviving team members were proud as hell to be the instrument of payback. Working over every spot where muzzle flashes were observed, Sergeant Smith didn't spare a one. Through brilliant flare light, the tree line looked to be denuded. Many of the trees weren't even standing anymore. Sergeant Smith, satisfied the job was finished, terminated the mission and released Spooky.

When Medevacs returned later that night, all casualties finally left the field.

Late spring and early summer of 1967 beckoned the winds of change, storming across I Corps in the form of a tactical realignment of force. The 1st Marine Division began pulling out of Chu Lai, relocating further north as fast as units of the Americal (23rd) Division turned up to settle into newly vacated Marine base camps. Task

Force Oregon was activated in April as an umbrella command of all newly arrived U.S. Army units operating out of Chu Lai. The Blue Dragon Brigade was scheduled to follow its brother Marines north in December and now fell under temporary operational control of Task Force Oregon.

Lieutenant Colonel Lavern W. Larson relieved Lieutenant Carroll B. Burch as commanding officer of Sub Unit One in March.

Ba Lang An Peninsula continued to be a meat grinder as operation after operation sought to break local force insurgents and draw main force elements into combat. During a chopper assault on 3 April, Lance Corporal Bobby Sherwood sustained a mortal wound from large caliber antiaircraft fire while on descent to a hot LZ not far from where E Chungdae lost one platoon so many months before. On 25 May, in close proximity to that LZ, small arms fire claimed the life of Lance Corporal Charles E. Thomas while conducting a sweep operating solo as the TACP for *Som Chungdae.*

In May, the Blue Dragon Brigade was formally incorporated into Task Force Oregon as a tactical asset of the new command structure. As quickly as the new arrivals became situated, combat operations commenced. In late summer, the Americal Division staff undertook preparations to assume control of the territory south of Chu Lai, now managed by the Korean Marine Brigade. A series of joint operations with the Blue Dragons was initiated on limited footing to acclimate Americal troops with their soon-to-be new area of responsibility.

In a planned change of command, Lieutenant General Lewis W. Walt was relieved by Navy Cross recipient and future commandant of the Marine Corps Lieutenant General Robert E. Cushman, Jr., as senior Marine commander in Vietnam on 1 June 1967.

At Sub Unit One headquarters in Saigon, Lieutenant Colonel Carlton D. Goodiel, Jr., having assumed command from Lieutenant Colonel Lavern W. Larson in August 1967, now managed all ANGLICO tactical assets in Vietnam, which now totaled 158 officers and enlisted men, Navy and Marine.

August was not kind to Sub Unit One. While on a joint operation with the 196th Light Infantry Brigade, Captain John L. Lavish, 3rd Battalion ALO, and his Tactical Air Control Party, consisting of Sergeant Calvin A. McGinty and PFC Stanley J. Seavers, accompanied 3rd Battalion

Forward Command Group, sweeping terrain west of National Highway 1. As this was Seavers's first time out with the Koreans, he was gaining practical experience and receiving field orientation from two of the best. Operation Dragon Head V gave both Koreans and men of the ROKMC Detachment their first experience with armor as a supporting arm. On 1 August, the U.S. Army armored personnel carrier (APC) they were riding tripped a jury-rigged eight-inch round buried in its path, tragically claiming the lives of all three Marines instantly.

The Shore Fire Control Party (SFCP) based at Hue City routinely sent spot teams into the field at battalion level to provide naval gunfire in support of infantry operations conducted by the 1st ARVN Division and 37th Ranger Group. Operation Lam Son-108 covered ground between Hue and Dong Ha close to the coastline. Corporal John W. Telford, recently reassigned from the ROKMC Detachment, teamed with Sergeant R.W. Heinz in his first outing with ARVN troops. On 17 August, a mortar attack on the battalion encampment took the life of Corporal John Telford.

In such a small organization, although spread all over the country and remote from each other, the loss of six men in such close proximity was felt by everyone. Telford, McGinty, Sherwood, and Thomas had all trained together in Hawaii with most surviving members of the Sub Unit. Six men in the larger scope of this war didn't make headline news. Other units on a daily basis lost many more in just a matter of minutes, but this loss represented close to four percent of a small force, and each one was regarded as family.

Coming out of the field on 5 October, the original ROKMC Detachment with replacements already on hand looked forward to departure from the war zone. PFC John Biehn, having extending his tour six more months, was recently arrived back in-country from thirty days' leave with his family in Michigan. His long-standing friendship with Corporal Willis McBride would have to be put on hold and be taken up again sometime in the future. McBride's mind was filled with joyous expectations of being reunited with his wife after such a long separation, and time couldn't pass fast enough to satisfy his longing to be in her company once more.

Monsoon season returned to I Corps late that fall, finally arriving on 8 October. With low ceiling and poor visibility, the resupply helicopters normally working Brigade were grounded at Ky-Ha, with no expectations of resuming operations until morning. McBride was counting on a ride to Chu Lai on one of those birds on their return flight. With orders in hand for a flight to Saigon then stateside, Will McBride was as anxious as a man can be to start the first leg of a long voyage home. One more day's delay seemed like weeks. Rain and low cloud cover continued to limit flight operations again on the 9th. John Biehn, feeling the apprehensions of his good buddy, sought permission and checked out the battalion team Jeep to help speed his friend's journey. Having a chance at being in position to board a plane in Chu Lai for Saigon as soon as the weather broke lifted Will's spirits. McBride's gear was in the Jeep before Biehn could say, "Let's go."

A heavy drizzle on an opened-top Jeep didn't make for a comfortable ride, as both men were soaked to the bone and freezing cold. McBride was completely oblivious to the discomfort, and Biehn was willing to suffer whatever it took to get his friend started home. The 400-yard access road from 3rd Battalion to Highway 1 was tire-high in mud but the Jeep managed to reach the main drag and turn north on the hardtop. At the bridge over the Song Tra Bong some 200 meters further ahead, what little traffic there was on Highway 1 was backed up on the south bank. Walking past a mixed line of civilian and military vehicles, the pair soon saw the reason for the traffic jam. Water rapidly gushing east on the Song Tra Bong was only about one foot short of cresting over the bridge. Two days of rain had filled the river gorge to its maximum.

Shrugging their shoulders, both men realized Corporal McBride would have to endure one more day of anxious waiting. Climbing back into the Jeep, Biehn turned around and made good progress back to the access road. Water covering the intersection hid the road surface, causing the Jeep to get bogged down on the apron. All four tires were hopelessly buried in mud.

No one really knows for sure the next sequence of events, but when the Song Tra Bong crested, a flood swept south from the river, sweeping both men into the rice paddies. Their bodies were found in close proximity to each other, suggesting that one was trying to save the other. There is no way to tell for sure who was trying to save who, but all who knew them are positive either one would have done all he could for the other.

Losing two well-respected teammates so close to rotation really took much of the exhilaration out of leaving Vietnam.

United States Coast Guard

During America's involvement in the war in Vietnam, a fact that is not widely known or appreciated is participation of the U.S. Coast Guard under operational control of the U.S. Navy. Patrol boats and cutters of the USCG made a large contribution, patrolling the waters surrounding that war-torn country to prevent North Vietnam from delivering war materials and food supplies to local and main force Viet Cong elements operating in the South.

Some 8,000-plus U.S. Coast Guardsmen manning fifty-six vessels navigated the waters of Vietnam's 1,200-mile coastline. Seven members of this service were killed in action while participating in seaborne operations assisting the war effort.

In addition to assuming station as units of Operation Market Time, many of the High Endurance Cutters took turns on the gunline, providing gunfire in support of allied ground operations.

Gunline ships of the U.S Coast Guard are sequentially listed below by hull number.

USCGC *BIBB* (WHEC 31)
USCGC *CAMPBELL* (WHEC-32)
USCGC *DUANE* (WHEC-33)
USCGC *INGHAM* (WHEC-35)
USCGC *SPENCER* (WHEC-36)
USCGC *TANEY* (WHEC-37)
USCGC *OWASCO* (WHEC-39)
USCGC *WINNEBAGO* (WHEC-40)
USCGC *SEBAGO* (WHEC-42)
USCGC *WASHUSSET* (WHEC-44)
USCGC *WINONA* (WHEC-65)
USCGC *KLAMATH* (WHEC-66)
USCGC *MINNETONKA* (WHEC-67)
USCGC *ANDROSCOGGEN* (WHEC-68)
USCGC *MENDOTA* (WHEC-69)
USCGC *PONCHATRAIN* (WHEC-70)

USCGC *YAKITAT* (WHEC-380)
USCGC *BERING STRAIT* (WHEC-382)
USCGC *COOK INLET* (WHEC-384)
USCGC *HAMILTON* (WHEC-715)
USCGC *MELLON* (WHEC-717)
USCGC *SHERMAN* (WHEC-720)
USCGC *HALFMOON (WHEC-738)*

USCGC *BARATARIA* (WHEC-381)
USCGC *CASTLE ROCK* (WHEC-383)
USCGC *GRESHAM* (WHEC-387)
USCGC *DALLAS* (WHEC-716)
USCGC *CHASE* (WHEC-718)
USCGC *RUSH* (WHEC-723)

We, who once found refuge under the protection of her guns, salute all the valiant ships and gallant crews of the United States Coast Guard.

AN INCIDENT ON MUI BA LANG AN

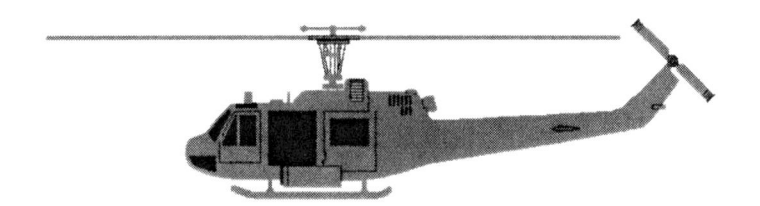

Born and raised in Noonan, Georgia, Captain Stephen W. Pless graduated from Georgia Military Academy and went straight to Parris Island, beginning his colorful career in the Marines as a slick sleeve private. Taking advantage of one of the many flight programs offered by the Corps, Steve Pless learned to fly helicopters and was never again totally content without a joystick in his hand. He'd found a home in the Corps and was fond of telling anyone who asked, he'd stay a Marine till he was too old to walk. Many men lay claim to it, but Stephen Pless is one of the few certified adrenaline junkies known to this author. A real family man who adored his wife and loved his children, he was also a man of action who lived for the hunt. He experienced life to the fullest and had a streak of loyalty a mile long. Having a career in the Marine Corps meant the world to him, and he wore it for all to see like a tiger wears stripes. Cut from the same mold as many legends of the old Corps, once you came to know him, it became only too evident that this was a man who would not die of natural causes.

Through spring and summer of 1967, Captain Pless earned a well-deserved reputation as a comer, distinguishing himself as a man on a mission. Flying in support of Marines committed to some of the fiercest and bloodiest fighting of the war in the hills around Khe San and other hot spots, this Marine was credited with saving many a grunt's ass, contributing to the body count in no small way. For his efforts and steadfast performance that summer, Captain Pless was awarded the Purple Heart, Silver Star, Distinguished Flying Cross, and numerous Air Medals. No effort was too great, no mission too dangerous. If there was a job to be done, he'd damn well do it, and that was that. Having once been a grunt himself, Steve had a fastidious empathy for mud Marines that defined his principles and cemented him to his earthbound teammates. In that year, Captain Pless racked up over 780 missions of various classifications.

19 August 1967 started out not much different from most late summer mornings in Vietnam. Captain Pless, having finished his tour as commanding officer of the 1st ANGLICO ROK Marine Detachment in early spring, now served with VMO-6 as assistant operations officer, resuming his love affair with helicopters.

VMO-6, a Marine UH1-E gunship squadron flying out of Ky-Ha, provided support for most destinations within I Corps. The author cannot begin to ponder how many times a month that particular squadron saved at least one of our asses. Gunships from this squadron had been in the paddy with Larry Oswalt, Bill Croney, and Dave Lucht. They were there for Johnny Houghton, Jim Porta, and Dave Long. *Nam Doe Khe Be* used their services, as did Larry Smith, Willis McBride, John Biehn, Kenny Campbell, Terry Perko, and everyone else in the detachment. There's not a man among us who is fully able to express proper gratitude for the pilots and crews who came to whatever shit sandwich we called them to, doing what it is Marine air crews do best.

That day he and his crew drew armed escort duty for Medevac operations, call sign Klondike Medevac. As circumstance would have it, they were summoned to *E Chungdae's* command post late in the afternoon to evacuate a Korean who injured himself while working on a four-deuce mortar. The assigned UH-34D Medevac chopper experienced some mechanical difficulty and would be a little late arriving at destination while the crew switched aircraft. Captain Pless decided to launch independently and meet the Medevac chopper on station, deducing his ship could have the LZ secured prior to its arrival if the situation warranted.

Staff Sergeant Lawrence H. Allen, a Canadian citizen who joined the U.S. Army to fight in Vietnam, was en route to Chu Lai aboard a U.S. Army CH-47 Chinook helicopter, ferrying a load of injured Americans between hospitals. Shortly before 1600, the craft came under direct fire from the ground, sustaining several hits, apparently to the extent where the pilot reached the decision or was forced (situation not known) to set down and assess the ability of the aircraft to safely continue in flight.

Immediately after the Chinook set down on the beach, Staff Sergeant Allen and three other NCOs formed a perimeter around the crippled bird, providing security, while the crew chief tried to ascertain the extent of damage and get the big chopper airborne once more. In short order, a grenade exploded at the front of the aircraft and automatic fire began pelting the ship. The four men on foot tried scrambling back aboard, but the chopper was already off the ground. They retreated to a sand dune to put up a defense with the limited ammo on their persons. Grenades and small arms fire pinned them down and restricted movement away from the dune. Grenades arched over the sand dune, dosing out generous rations of shrapnel, spraying all four men. A Viet Cong with an automatic weapon appeared on the flank, cutting loose with a burst, striking everyone but Allen, who played dead.

Klondike, while approaching *E Chungdae* from northeast, picked up an emergency broadcast over the "GUARD" channel. An aircraft identifying itself as Land Shark sent out a message: "My aircraft is all shot up and I have a lot of wounded aboard. I'm going to try to make it to Duc Pho." Then after a pause: "I still have four men on the ground. The VC is trying to take them prisoner or kill them; God, can somebody help them?" The last known position as stated by Land Shark was on the beach about one mile north of Tra Khuc River.

Knowing the area fairly well from his tour with *Chung Yong Bodae*, Captain Pless set course southeast and headed toward the general vicinity of Land Shark's last reported position near the old killing grounds of Dragon Claw. In an attempt to contact the distressed craft, Captain Pless tried hailing Land Shark several times. "We are a fully armed UH1-E gunship, and we are in the area. Can we give assistance?" There was no response.

Recalling the situation briefing just minutes ago with the ground TAC at *E Chungdae*, Captain Rupert E. Fairfield, co-pilot, advised the Medevac chopper over FM frequency the landing zone was secure and he should proceed with the evac mission without cover. He further advised they were pulling out of the current mission to see what they could do for the stranded crew.

Independently, U.S. Army Warrant Officers James P. Van Duzee and Ronald L. Redeker also departed Ky-Ha on separate missions shortly after 1600 on a southerly heading. Both heard the same distress call as Klondike and set a course for Mui Ba Lang An. (Both were flying UH1-Es, gunships or slicks not known.)

As Klondike reached the mouth of Song Tra Khuc, the crew observed explosions on the beach about a mile north of the river not far from a coastal village (Believed by the author to be My Lai [1].). As soon as the explosions stopped, thirty to fifty armed Viet Cong sprinted from the tree line, storming the beach and surrounding four Americans who were lying prone near water's edge. Polling his crew, Pless asked, "You all with me?" Captain Fairfield turned toward the crew with thumbs up. Crew chief Lance Corporal John G. Phelps and door gunner Gunnery Sergeant Leroy N. Poulson enthusiastically returned the universal go signal, each knowing it was not going to be fun.

Warrant Officers James Van Duzee and Ronald Redeker arrived over the beach within seconds of each other, witnessing the grenade shower and mob scene. Not being able to distinguish Viet Cong from American at that altitude, they circled, trying to ferret out who was who. Both were on the radio trying to get a reaction force on the ground and more assistance from the air.

From high above the action, both Army pilots were thunderstruck to observe a Marine UH1-E rolling in low on the hot, making a suicide pass directly over the VC, who were beating, stomping, and slashing at four hapless Americans. Sergeant Allen, seeing Klondike buzzing fifty feet overhead, waved an arm at the UH1-E. The Canadian paid for that act of defiance with a rifle butt to his face. Enraged, Captain Pless immediately ordered Gunny Poulson to fire into the mob. From his door gunner position, Gunny Poulson cut loose with a short burst, stitching up the ground around the perimeter, sending the Viet Cong in an "every man for himself, elbows over assholes" flight for the tree line.

Twenty or so feet past the mob, Captain Pless pulled the gunship into a hard climb, switching armament at the same time to rocket pods, then quickly nailed a perfect near wingover right, maneuvering the armed helicopter to line up on the enemy's rear at almost ground level. From a hover, Captain Pless cut loose a volley, sending all fourteen rockets center mass of the fleeing horde.

A UH-1E is also armed with four side-mounted M-60 machine guns, and Steve Pless knew how to use them. Displaying some of the most remarkable airmanship in the history of aviation, Captain Pless wasted no time making run after run at the panicked militiamen. Flying through dense smoke caused by the initial rocket attack, the determined pilot relentlessly hounded the retreating enemy. Flying as close to the ground as possible without going subterranean, mud and other debris began collecting on the windscreen kicked up from the UH1-E's own bullet strikes. An undetermined number of Viet Cong paid a hell of a price for pissing off Steve Pless. Phelps and Poulson added more fatalities to the lethal strafing runs, firing bursts from their respective door guns into the tree line and village.

Pulling out of his last run, the intrepid pilot threw the gunship into a side flare, continuously pouring fire from a hover into the VC-infested tree line only thirty feet away. After expending all ammo, Captain Pless pointed the nose toward the surf and set his ship down fifteen feet from the Americans. The ship was now oriented, leaving the machine gun of Lance Corporal Phelps to defend the crew. Defend them he did, methodically chewing up the tree line with controlled burst of 7.62mm.

Gunny Poulson unplugged his headset and gunner's belt, vaulting from the helicopter and coveried ground quickly, reaching Sergeant Allen. Poulson had him up on his feet post haste and moving toward the ship. Depositing Allen in the right door, Gunny Poulson returned to the sand dune for a second wounded soldier.

Phelps kept up cover fire as Viet Cong in the tree line, somewhat recovered from the gunship assaults, organized a bid to gain the initiative. Massive volumes of fire came streaming out of the tree line, striking the ground all around the helicopter. Lance Corporal Phelps found himself cast in the role of lead gunslinger in a stand-off duel at thirty paces with machine guns. And numbers were not on his side.

Braving sheets of fire getting back to the sand dune, Poulson was confronted with a large man. Adding to Poulson's predicament, the man was in a tidal depression, which made lifting him out difficult. Every time Poulson tried to lift him, his feet sank into wet sand.

Seeing Poulson's predicament, Captain Fairfield exited the gunship a few feet behind Phelps. Seeing three Viet Cong ten feet off his left rear, the co-pilot reached back into the helicopter, retrieved the door gun, and killed all three in one burst.

Upon reaching Poulson, incoming fire began making life very hazardous for the trio. Bullet strikes kicked up dirt uncomfortably close, inhibiting their ability to carry out this evacuation. Seeing several VC trying to outflank them, Captain Fairfield wasted little time ordering Lance Corporal Phelps back to his machine gun.

Arriving at his gun, Phelps noticed an undetermined number of armed VC making a move on the aircraft, firing as they advanced. Phelps opened up. The onslaught sent them all to ground, dead and alive. The survivors kept up firing. Lance Corporal Phelps couldn't see them, but their bullet strikes were kicking up sand all around the plane.

Fairfield and Poulson managed to lift the second casualty out of the depression, dragging the big man back to the ship under protection of Phelps's machine gun. Soft powdery sand and dozens of near misses didn't make the trip any easier.

Unknown to the Marine crew at this time, U.S. Army helicopters piloted by Warrant Officers James Van Duzee and Ronald L. Redeker, without being able to communicate with Klondike, began pouring fire into the tree line in support of the dauntless Marine crewmen.

Captain Fairfield and Gunny Poulson, making a third return trip toward the surf, discovered this man to be even larger than the prior evacuee. The soldier lying prone on the beach was not conscious and presented a dead weight load. Not for one second since Klondike set down was there any letup in fire volume being directed at the UH-1E or Marines in the sand.

As injured as he was, Sergeant Allen accepted Phelps's machine gun, cradling it in his injured arm while working the trigger with his good hand. Propping himself against the gunner's seat, Allen concentrated fire to the left side of the ship where Viet Cong were closing on the craft.

Phelps then sprinted to assist his two crewmates. With Fairfield and Phelps each lifting the injured American by his arms, Poulson picked up the big man's feet. Phelps and Fairfield, leading the way, fired their revolvers at VC popping up from behind sand dunes. Just feet away from the helicopter, Phelps let go of the wounded man to deal with a Viet Cong suddenly appearing from behind the aircraft, brandishing a hand grenade. Phelps emptied his cylinder into the attacker before the trio continued the last few steps through increased fire from all directions, pushing their heavy burden onto the ship's deck.

From the driver's seat, Captain Pless expended all his handgun ammo, dropping several assailants within arm's reach of his aircraft.

Captain Rupert Fairfield gutted out a fourth trip to the sand dune. Disheartened at observing that the last casualty had suffered a slit throat, the co-pilot quickly checked for pulse, heartbeat, and dog tags. Dismayed at finding no signs of life, he quickly returned to the airship that was already rolling in throttle, building up RPMs for takeoff.

As soon as the skipper saw everyone on board, Captain Pless performed a quick check of his gauges then pulled pitch. Still taking heavy fire, he became aware of a Vietnamese UH-34D suddenly setting down on the beach to his right. A U.S. Army gunship quickly materialized from the same direction, making a strafing run on the tree line and village. Realizing his ship was too heavy, Pless struggled with the controls, trying to get the UH1-E moving. After a few frantic moments, Klondike achieved liftoff, lumbering slowly across the surf line, bearing out to sea just barely airborne, automatic fire pushing up hundreds of water spouts either side of the ship.

Four times during a white-knuckle effort to gain altitude, Klondike's landing skids dipped into the waves. Captain Pless ordered everything not essential to flight dumped out. Rocket pods were jettisoned. Ammo cans, armor plate, and anything not bolted to the aircraft was pitched out. Slowly the war bird's tired engines built up enough torque to gain additional air speed. Gradually climbing, the aircraft banked north. After an anxious ride, the bullet-riddled gunship finally arrived at Chu Lai. Poulson and Phelps did what they could for the injured soldiers, keeping all three alive till touchdown at the 1st Hospital Company Helo-Pad.

After Action Report

The following is a verbatim statement given by Captain Donald D. Stevens, USAF, dated 23 August 1967. Captain Stevens was one of the invaluable pair of U.S. Air Force airborne FACs assigned to the Blue Dragon Brigade, identified elsewhere in this book as Togo 87 and Togo 88. In his statement, Captain Stevens provides insightful narrative on the strength of the force opposing Klondike Medevac during their daring rescue operation. Arriving minutes after Klondike cleared the area, Captain Stevens had this to say concerning the situation he walked into:

"On 19 August 1967, I was scrambled from Quang Ngai airfield. Upon getting airborne, I was advised by my ground control station that a helicopter had received enemy fire and made a forced landing on the beach.

"When I arrived over the scene, an Army 0-1 aircraft was directing a flight of F-100 aircraft against targets in the area. Since he was not a qualified FAC, he turned the air strike control over to me. I am a USAF FAC assigned to the 2nd ROKMC Brigade and fly under the call sign Togo 87. When I assumed control of the flight of F-100s, Cat Killer 39 [the Army 0-1] told me that the helicopter had received intense enemy fire after setting down and had managed to take off again but left four people on the ground. Three of these people were picked up by a U.S. Marine-armed UH-1E piloted by Captain Pless. During their pickup they received very heavy automatic weapons fire, small arms fire, and attack by numerous enemy at close range, throwing hand grenades.

"The fourth person was reported as a confirmed KIA. I could see the one body lying on the beach. I continued controlling the F-100s and followed this attack by controlling five other flights of U.S. Marine fighters and several U.S. Army helicopter gun ships.

"I could see five areas from which intense automatic weapons fire and antiaircraft fire came during each fighter pass. These positions were all within 200 meters of the body on the beach, and one position was only about 40 meters away. These positions were the targets of my air strikes. Throughout our attacks, we received intense ground fire.

"As a result of the air strikes by the fixed wing aircraft, armed gun ships, and the attack made by Captain Pless's armed UH-1E, there were three automatic weapons positions neutralized and over 50 enemy KBA [killed by air strike] confirmed by my body count.

"A U.S. Army command and control helicopter arrived on scene and asked me if I felt it was feasible to airlift a reaction force into the area. I informed him that only one body remained and that intense enemy fire still existed. He decided to try to put in the reaction force. Within fifteen minutes, the reaction force was inserted and the man on the beach was extracted. After the helicopters refueled, the reaction force was extracted.

"I continued to direct another air strike against the area in spite of heavy thunderstorms moving into the area. When the weather became too low, a 500-foot ceiling with one-mile visibility, I discontinued the air strike and returned to Quang Ngai to land."

Side Note

The reaction force never advanced beyond the beach because of strong enemy resistance. Continued heavy ground fire was encountered throughout the reaction force insertion in spite of heavy suppressive fire laid down by no less than six accompanying helicopter gun ships. During the insertion, Rattler 03 (the command and control helicopter) counted ten automatic weapons positions in action. The lead helicopter in the extraction reported twelve positions in action during one pass over the area.

Sadly, only Staff Sergeant Allen survived wounds received that day on the beach. His two gallant companions expired in the hospital before morning.

Thomas Petri

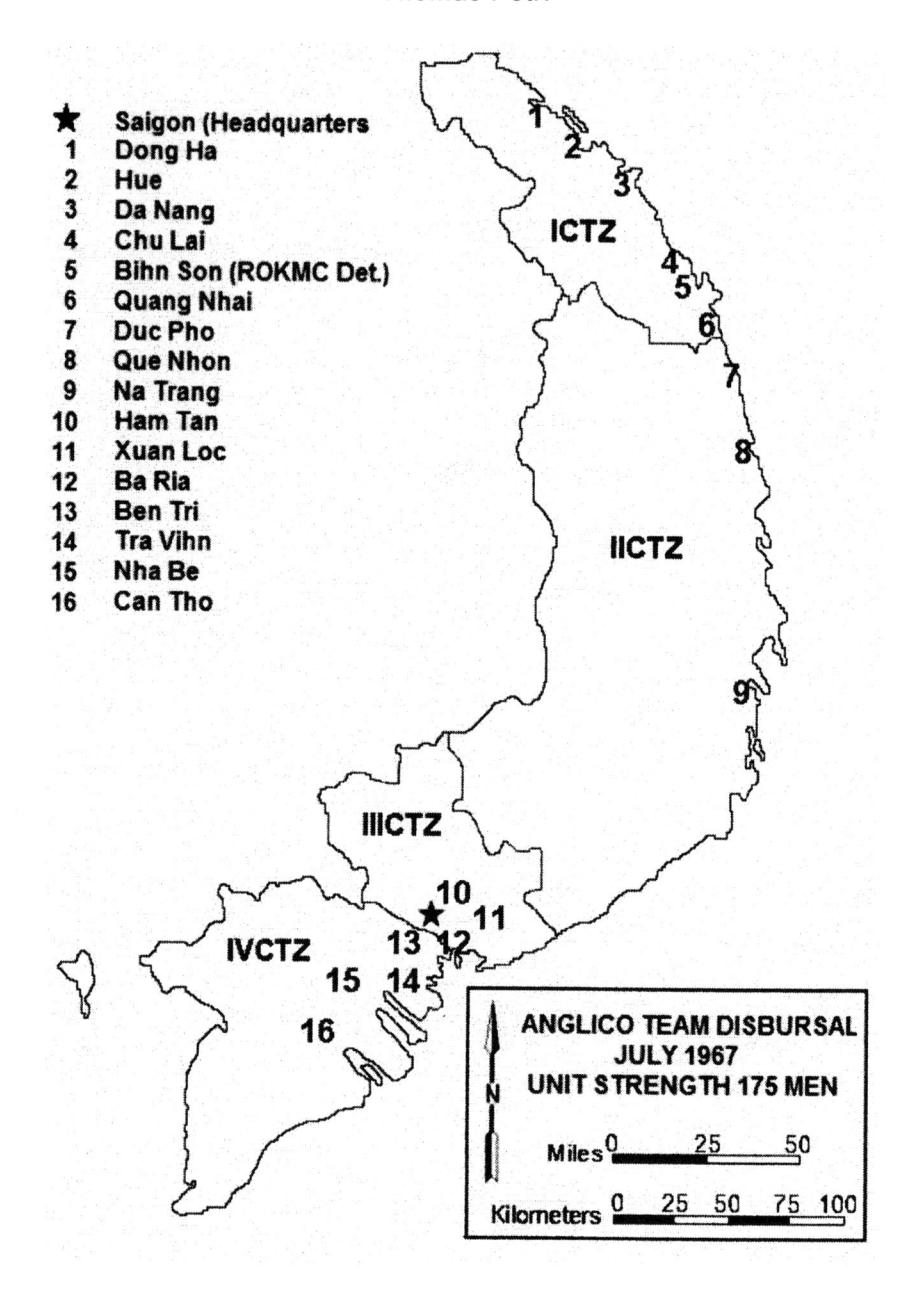

★ Saigon (Headquarters)
1 Dong Ha
2 Hue
3 Da Nang
4 Chu Lai
5 Bihn Son (ROKMC Det.)
6 Quang Nhai
7 Duc Pho
8 Que Nhon
9 Na Trang
10 Ham Tan
11 Xuan Loc
12 Ba Ria
13 Ben Tri
14 Tra Vihn
15 Nha Be
16 Can Tho

ICTZ
IICTZ
IIICTZ
IVCTZ

ANGLICO TEAM DISBURSAL
JULY 1967
UNIT STRENGTH 175 MEN

USS Mullinnix
(DD-944)
Forrest Sherman Class Destroyer
Call Sign: Disapprove

Between 2 August and 1 November 1966, the USS *Mullinnix* deployed off South Vietnam, ranging from the DMZ to Mekong River, providing valuable gunfire support coinciding with the Vietnamese Counteroffensive Phase II (1 July 1966–31 May 1967). During bombardment of enemy positions, she fired 13,702 rounds of ammunition in support of the First Marine Division, U.S. Army, and Army of the Republic of Vietnam. She departed the 7th Fleet on 17 November 1966, arriving in Norfolk, Virginia, on 17 December.

USS *Mullinnix* returned to combat for her second gunline patrol on 1 May 1969, spending most of her time on station just south of the DMZ, firing in support of the Third Marine Division. The USS *Mullinnix* completed her third and final gunline patrol during this WestPac cruise on 15 July 1969. During the eighty-three days on three gunline patrols in the I and II Corps areas, USS *Mullinnix* provided naval gunfire support to allied forces south of the DMZ around Da Nang, Cam Rahn Bay, Nha Trang, and Qui Nohn. During calls for fire in three patrols, she fired on 1,627 targets at an average range of nearly 17,000 yards. For her naval gunfire support performance for fiscal year 1969, USS *Mullinnix* was named "Top Gun" among the gunline destroyers by ANGLICO spotters. A proud crew returned to Norfolk on 3 September.

In 1972, the USS *Mullinnix* (DD-944) made her third trip to the gunline off Vietnam. The USS *Mullinnix* deployed from Norfolk on ninety-six hours' notice, along with three other destroyers, in response to the North Vietnamese Easter Offensive of 30 March 1972. She arrived in Vietnam with one twin-barrel three-inch/50-caliber and three modern single-barrel five-inch/54-caliber guns.

The Mighty Mux arrived off the coast on 16 May. In her first few hours on the gunline, the USS *Mullinnix* fired over 500 projectiles. With highly accurate precision and an experienced crew, *Mullinnix* was able to provide successful gunfire support of South Vietnamese ground troops. This performance was later recognized in a formal presentation of the Gunnery E for excellence to the Weapons Department.

On this tour, USS *Mullinnix* participated in the defense of Hue City and the campaign to retake Quang Tri. These campaigns involved the largest assembly of gunfire support ships in the Vietnam War and the largest amphibious landing since Inchon in the Korean War in support of Vietnamese Marines.

We, who once found refuge under the protection of her guns, salute this valiant ship and her gallant crew.

UNRULY PARTY GUESTS

On 10 November 1967, the Blue Dragon Brigade launched Operation Dragon Tail in coordination with U.S. Army units of Task Force Oregon. A fourth maneuver battalion (5th Battalion) recently activated for duty provided more flexibility to an already formidable field force, continuing to improve its resources and effectiveness as a light infantry asset. Dragon Tail terminated on 21 December, producing no appreciable results. At first light, 22 December, the brigade pulled out of Quang Ngai Province and moved to its new area of responsibility in the Hoi An Basin a few miles south of Da Nang.

At the airfield near Da Nang, the first Korean Marine Corps air assets, designated as Detachment 5, consisting of only two 01 Bird Dogs newly arrived in Vietnam, assumed spotter plane duties from the USAF FACs of the 20th Tactical Air Support Squadron. From day one of operations in Hoi An, the Korean spotter planes performed as airborne artillery spotters for Brigade gunners, carrying an ANGLICO spotter as back seat passenger to provide air and naval gunfire support. Kimchi 1 and 2 replaced Togo 87 and 88 in ANGLICO call sign address books.

Operation Flying Dragon began right after Christmas. The operation was more or less designed to familiarize the ROKs with their new TAOR, giving them a feel for the new environ.

Thomas Petri

The Sub Unit began 1968 with 230 men, both Marine and Navy, having added additional fire support teams in all four tactical zones.

In the northwest corner of South Vietnam just below the DMZ, the battle of Khe Sanh came to life on 21 January 1968, presenting an opportunity for dealing the NVA s crushing defeat. North Vietnam committed at least two and possibly three divisions against the combat base, manned by 6,000 U.S. Marines. Ten days later on 31 January, 80,000 North Vietnamese troops and an estimated 40,000 Viet Cong guerrillas surprised allied forces by launching an offensive, disrupting Tet holiday festivities in a bold countrywide surprise attack.

Tucked in among several barrier islands on Vietnam's central coastline, white facade buildings of Nha Trang silhouetted against the South China Sea portray a panoramic vista reminiscent of tranquil travel posters, beckoning vacationers to a relaxed tropical escape.

At 0015, Tuesday morning 30 January, mortar and rocket barrages from Viet Cong batteries west of town mingled with the sounds of pyrotechnic revelry that traditionally accompany lunar New Year celebrations. Unknown at that time, local force insurgents prematurely fired, for reasons that are still not clear to this day, the first shots of what history recorded as the 1968 Tet Offensive. Shortly after the shelling began, two full-strength Viet Cong battalions launched a ground assault into the city. An undetermined number of local force VC, having already been in Nha Trang several days, on cue, initiated attacks at several other strategic locations. Unprepared defenders of Vietnam's 91 Airborne Ranger Battalion, at only sixty percent strength, put up fierce resistance at the railroad station on the northern outskirts of Nha Trang, buying time for command officers to sort through the confusion and mount a counterattack. U.S. soldiers of the 272nd Military Police Company, one of the initial targets of the offensive, also scrambled to meet the threat. Fighting soon spread to the streets as allied forces struggled to get a handle on events.

Billeted in a contract hotel near town center, Lance Corporal James W. (Sam) Sandoz was awakened from a sound sleep around 0130, as were Lance Corporals Raymond R. (Dink) Roughton, III, and Jerry W. Becker in a room one floor above. Sensing all was not right, the trio quickly dressed and armed themselves, meeting on the fourth-floor rooftop patio. To the west and north, illumination flares silhouetting Nha Trang's skyline appeared to be much closer and more frequent than normal perimeter defense activity. In the crisp night air, distinctive AK-47 signatures filtering through festive sounds of firecrackers heightened everyone's apprehensions. Gunshot reports reaching their ears appeared to be originating just a few blocks west. Peering down from the patio, Nha Trang took on a surreal appearance under an amber glow of flare light. Civilians were moving about on foot, motor scooter, and bicycle as if nothing unusual was occurring. Seeing nothing at either end of the street below, after a while the trio decided nothing worthwhile could be accomplished from hanging out inside. The Marines exited the building around 0200 to find out exactly what was going on. If the city was in fact under attack, they reasoned, there must be some ass to kick.

In command of all II Corps ANGLICO assets, U.S. Navy Lieutenant William C. Vandiver, with five Shore Fire Control Parties under his authority, also made his NGLO headquarters in Nha Trang. The officer left the BOQ soon after hostilities started, making his way through the streets to II Corps Fire Support Coordination Element (FSCE) a few blocks away. Having the foresight to prepare a fire control plan weeks before with consent of the installation defense command, Lieutenant Vandiver felt confident in his ability to defend Nha Trang. With the USS *Mansfield* (DD 728) on station off the coast, he had just the tool to make life difficult for attacking elements. Thanks to reports coming in from Special Forces outposts strung around Nha Trang, the officer was able to dial in counter battery fire at several incoming mortar and rocket locations. Having direct communication with the ship, Lieutenant Vandiver and his team relayed adjustment data as received by observers at the outposts. Most of the incoming rocket and mortars fell silent soon after the big guns were adjusted on target. The USS *Mansfield's* formidable five-inch/38 main batteries were also brought to bear on likely avenues of approach to Nha Trang, interdicting troop movements and reinforcements, effectively cutting off access to the city. Throughout the long night and several hours into daylight, Lieutenant Vandiver and his team worked nonstop, answering demands for fire support.

Outside the hotel's main entrance, the trio couldn't help but notice the absence of the ARVN guards who manned building security 24/7. Once on the street, the team headed west, avoiding downed power lines randomly littering the streets. Spread out approximately one block apart, the patrol continued west to a junction of five roads. From somewhere up the street a machine gun opened up on a Filipino contract worker cruising by on his motorbike. The sudden burst caused him to lose control, wrecking his ride. Covering the man until he cleared the street, the Marines took shelter next to a building. An old Vietnamese man riding a bicycle ambled into the street and immediately came under fire. Several rounds tore through the unsuspecting man's body, almost cutting him in half. Several anxious minutes later, a Vietnamese male on a motor scooter with his son on the back turned onto the street from a side road. The Americans quickly blocked his path, ushering the man in a safer direction.

Lance Corporal Sandoz darted down a side street to see if he could maneuver into grenade distance behind or off to the side of the VC machine gunner. His two teammates remained in place, providing cover fire. Halfway down the street, he was confronted by three Vietnamese in black peasant attire, the eldest man armed with an M-1 carbine, the other two unarmed. They looked to be three generations of a family. The group approached to within a meter, speaking only in Vietnamese and using gestures to suggest Sandoz drop his rifle. Sandoz, sensing a feeling of uneasiness among the three, reassured them, "It's OK, I'm an American." On orders from the old man, the unarmed teenager began tugging on Sandoz's rifle. Sandoz, snapping out of his naiveté, finally realized what was going on; in a single motion, energized by panic-induced adrenaline, he kicked the boy in the groin and sprayed all three with his M-16, retreating back to the main drag. Finding Roughton and Becker, he quickly explained the situation on the side street.

Retracing Sandoz's footfalls, the trio came upon two dead Vietnamese. Lance Corporal Roughton policed up the dead man's carbine. Finding a blood trail not far from the cadavers, they sent a small civilian entourage on their way before following the crimson trace.

Observing the blood trail seemingly disappear over the wall of a modest house, Roughton and Becker scurried forward to the door,

Sandoz providing cover. Cautiously peering in at an angle from the door frame, Lance Corporal Becker caught sight of the wounded man by limited moonlight reaching for a grenade. Lining up his M-16, Becker fired into the room, killing the man before he could lay his hands on it.

Continuing down the side street, hugging houses lining the avenue, Lance Corporal Becker just by chance looked through an architectural slot on a concrete border wall and spotted a field pack propped against the house within its perimeter. Motioning for his companions, the trio gathered at the wall close to the entry gate.

Further up the street, a Jeep occupied by four U.S. Army personnel ambled slowly in the Marines' direction. Leaving the gate, Lance Corporal Roughton stopped the Jeep before it could pull in front of the house. Explaining the situation to the lieutenant in charge, he requested they remain and provide cover fire while the Marines assaulted the house. While still engaged in conversation, a twelve-man ARVN patrol approached from the same direction as did the Jeep. Enlisting the Vietnamese into the project, a basic maneuver plan was worked out between the three factions.

Once all was ready, Becker and Roughton entered the gate, taking up assault positions covering Sandoz as he too made his way into the courtyard. On cue, all elements opened fire. Sandoz ran forward, tossing a grenade through the open door, then dove for cover.

No sooner had the grenade blast subsided, the trio burst through the front door, rifles blazing. Nothing! After a quick search, it was evident their quarry managed to escape the house through another exit.

When the three Marines emerged from the house, their so-called fire support was no longer in the area. Both ARVN and Army troops had already melted away into the night even before the trio entered the home. They just ran off without so much as a "see you later." Years later, all three remembered a burning urge to hunt them down and kick their asses.

Cutting over to another major thoroughfare, the Marines continued their sojourn through Nha Trang. At a crossroad, the Marines found themselves in front of a U.S. Army MP compound at the southwest corner. Stopping for a cigarette break and an exchange of information, the MPs recounted a Viet Cong unit boldly marching past the compound in formation a little earlier. Someone shouted, "Halt!" in Vietnamese, which broke up the formation, sending the unit running down the street. Several soldiers were sure that a sniper was occupying a building across the street at the northwest corner of the intersection. Inquiring as to what the Marines were up to, one of the men at the gate wisecracked, "If you guys are so tough, why you don't take out that sniper?" The MPs further informed them that were under orders to remain inside the compound for defense and could not offer any assistance.

Having had enough of the Army, the Marines cautiously advanced on the house for a better look. A quick scan of the building showed it to be a two-story wood-framed structure with a chest-high concrete and stone retaining wall on all four sides. Access to the inner courtyard was provided by an iron gate on the right edge of the property. Sprinting across the street, the Marines caught sight of an enemy soldier standing in the front doorway, apparently loading his rifle. All three opened fire, taking cover behind the retaining wall.

Peering over the parapet, Sandoz was engulfed by AK fire slamming into the concrete wall, peppering his arm with bullet fragments, which attracted return fire from his two companions.

On the premises of the house immediately south of the structure now under attack by the Marines, a half a dozen or so Korean soldiers guarding the residence of Major General Choi Dae Myung, attached to the Republic of Korea Armed Forces Vietnam (ROKAV) field command, were startled by the commotion next door. Rushing to investigate, they learned from the Marines of an armed Viet Cong occupying the structure.

One soldier left and soon returned with a box of grenades; in these Koreans, the Marines found a willing ally ready to do battle. One Korean rolled a few grenades still in their cylindrical cardboard containers to the Americans. During the ordnance exchange, fire from inside the house directed at the transfer area killed the unfortunate Korean. Fire volume coming from inside the house added up to more than just a single sniper. Unknown to the attackers, reinforcements entering the home through the back door decided to make a stand at this house.

For the next two hours, against who knows how many, the Koreans and Marines engaged in a stand-off firefight. Grenade after grenade was lobbed through every opening in the house within throwing distance. Window and door frames were literally chewed apart by small arms fire but the attackers could gain no advantage. The allies had the home covered from the front but lacked manpower and weapons to generate enough firepower to risk a full-bore assault. As it became evident that firepower coming from inside was increasing, Becker ran back to the MP compound to see if he could borrow an M-79 grenade launcher and enlist some help. Once it became evident that no one was willing to do a damned thing, Becker raced back to his companions, where the siege continued.

As the early morning sum rose over Nha Trang, a unit from the U.S. Army arrived on scene with the M-79s requested earlier. An officer in charge of the newcomers took control of the fight. In spite of additional personnel and more sophisticated weaponry available, the firefight still continued to a stand-off, no one really pushing for an assault on the building. The MPs manning the compound across the street never did come over to help. Disgusted with the whole affair and seething with a major case of the ass for the MPs, the three Marines left the Army to do their thing, making their way back to the FSCE.

All through the day of 30 January and well into night, U.S., Marine, CAP units, and ARVN forces in the Da Nang Area of Responsibility experienced contact with NVA/VC units of various sizes. Ambushes, ground assaults, as well as mortar and rocket attacks occurred on several avenues of approach to Da Nang. Each enemy initiative was met by force and soundly defeated. Action was still ongoing into the first week of February. In all of these encounters, enemy forces did not come close to success. From all accounts and official sources, communist efforts at attacking Da Nang were either inept or poorly coordinated.

Just south of Da Nang, two companies of the Viet Cong 25th Battalion entered the city of Hoi An, resting on the north bank of the Song Thu Bon at 0300. One company quickly seized the German-run missionary hospital, while the second attacked the 102nd ARVN Engineers encampment and laid siege to the MACV compound housing Quang Nam Advisory Team 15. Caught off guard initially, the engineers then rallied. Determined resistance exhibited by the stubborn engineers stalled Viet Cong advances but not before giving up half their real estate. ARVN defenders managed to hold off further advance until reinforced by nearby artillerymen. Lowering their guns and firing point-blank into the attackers, ARVN artillery stalemated the tactical situation until sunrise.

Alerted by Korean elements billeted at the airstrip to unfolding turns of events now being played out in Hoi An, the Blue Dragon Brigade dispatched a two-battalion reaction force that rushed to surround the city at dawn. Elements of the 51st ARVN Regiment also scrambled to meet the threat, sending one maneuver battalion to reinforce the Koreans.

At 0730, lead elements of 5th ROKMC Battalion entered Hoi An. With deliberate caution so as to minimize damage and casualties among city residents, the Koreans slowly advanced on the MACV compound, meeting spirited resistance every step of the way. Radio transmissions from the entrapped MACV advisory staff reported enemy troops digging in at the occupied engineer's camp. Further reports told of reinforcements coming ashore from numerous boats operating on the Song Hoi An.

Fighting became more intense as ROKs neared the MACV compound; ANGLICO TACPs called in helicopter gunships to suppress fire from several fortified positions. At 1320, lead elements of 27th Company finally linked up with the besieged MACV advisory element. The Koreans consolidated their position then moved out for the hospital and engineers' compound. Although almost completely surrounded, enemy troops still managed to keep their southern flank open. In view of this situation, three Korean companies were dispatched to close the south flank.

Keeping one company at the MACV compound for security, the Koreans advanced to reinforce the engineers, who had not made much progress in expelling the enemy still holding half of their base camp. Facing well-dug-in opposition, the final assault was put off until morning. With dusk approaching, other elements, having not made anticipated progress toward the hospital, also remained in place at their furthest point of advancement until dawn.

Early on 31 January, in a fierce assault, the ROKs finally drove a stubborn enemy out of the engineers' compound and, after a brief scrimmage against a not-so-spirited defense, succeeded in taking the missionary hospital.

After action reports from Hoi An, as detailed by the advisory team and Vietnamese sources, listed allied casualties as 58 KIA and 103 wounded in action. Between the Blue Dragons and 51st ARVN, 358 enemy troops were killed and over 190 prisoners were taken. Of these prisoners, eight were confirmed to be enemy military personnel, eighty were confirmed as VC cadre, while the remaining were just Vietnamese citizens trying to evade the fighting (they were promptly released).

It wasn't over yet. Even though Hoi An was fully restored to allied control, the countryside north, south, and west of the city still hosted uncommitted NVA units. At 0930, elements of the 31st NVA Regiment attacked the village of Dien Ban some 2,000 meters due west of Hoi An in coordination with an attack on Duy Xuyen, located 2,500 meters southwest.

Reinforced by Korean Marines, the 51st ARVN Regiment's successful assault quickly turned the invaders from Dien Ban. The situation at Duy Xuyen was not as easily remedied, as communist forces occupied the town for most of the day, forcing the district chief to seek the protection of the Korean Marines.

From 1 through 5 February, Korean Marines teamed with the 51st ARVN Regiment, rooting out units of the 31st NVA before the area was finally under reasonable control. The Korean sector was the last area within the Da Nang TAOR to put down existing threats to the city of Da Nang.

According to an enemy prisoner from the 31st NVA Regiment taken in the fighting west of Hoi An, the mission of his unit was to attack Hoi An as many times as required, then set up a liberation government.

At 0233, 31 January, the 6th NVA Regiment, supported by local force guerillas already in the city, launched a coordinated attack on the ancient imperial capital of Hue, seizing several objectives in the northern portion of the "Old City" without much wasted effort. Not far from the south bank of the Perfume River, elements of the 4th NVA Regiment and supporting local force units opened an attack on the MACV compound with a short barrage of mortar and rocket fire. Under the command of Lieutenant (JG) Marvin L. Warkentin, USN, the 1st ARVN Division liaison/spot team billeted at MACV, like everyone else, scrambled to meet the attack.

A thunderous blast from an RPG rocket slammed into the structure of an old French barracks building, shocking Corporal Michael L. Smith out of a sound sleep and throwing him to the floor. On the other side of the room, team radio operator Lance Corporal Paul J. Desport's sleep was also interrupted by the deafening explosion still ringing in his ears. Waking to a disheveled room filled with smoke and dust, both stunned Marines struggled to alertness through a lingering fog of concussion and realized immediately they were under attack.

Fumbling in the darkness for gear, Smith and Desport armed themselves and scurried outside to their assigned defense post as mortars and rockets continued falling on the advisors' complex.

Waking to the sounds of chaos, team leader Sergeant Charles S. Darby quickly grabbed his weapon and proceeded to his assigned defensive post on the roof of the hotel annex within the compound where he was billeted.

Arriving at a bunker about twenty feet inside the concertina barrier anchoring the southwest corner of the perimeter facing west, Corporal Smith took charge, assigning U.S. Army communicators to man two M-60 machine guns prepositioned in the bunker. Finding only two boxes of linked ammo, the NCO cautioned his charges to observe fire discipline and conserve what ammo was on hand. Grabbing an M-79 grenade launcher, Smith and his intraservice unit braced for an expected ground assault. Lance Corporal Desport took position at a firing port. Shouldering his weapon, Desport too steeled himself for what he knew was coming.

Lieutenant Warkentin, with a few officers of the advisory staff, manned a bunker in the center of the line. As a Naval officer, he never dreamed he'd be defending an Army post from behind a machine gun.

From his rooftop observation site, Sergeant Darby, behind a makeshift stack of sandbags, opened a box of hand flares. Being two stories above ground level, he was shaken to see so many muzzle flashes blinking from various locations around the encampment.

Resigned to do what he had to do, Darby held his breath and waited.

It wasn't a long wait. Even as others were scrambling to the bunker line, green tracers and RPG fire erupted from beyond the wire barrier as North Vietnamese troops in full battle dress mounted a serious assault on the perimeter. A two-story building on the opposite side of the road occupied by North Vietnamese gunners provided an aggressive base of fire to cover the attackers. A furious crackle of outgoing fire met the assault troops head on as every weapon on the line sprang to life, pouring out an interlocking barricade of flesh-tearing cones of hot metal.

Taking his cue, Darby launched several flares over the western perimeter. Seeing the launch flashes, NVA gunners adjusted fire, sending RPG rockets sailing over his head, barely missing the sergeant.

Flares bursting overhead illuminated what appeared to be a company-sized NVA unit coming across the road, some already inside the wire trying to blow a path through the barrier. Defensive fire accelerated, sweeping the assault zone and inflicting heavy casualties. Corporal Smith launched grenade after grenade at almost point-blank range in a sweeping motion toward oncoming troops. Lance Corporal Desport likewise poured fire into the assault force left to right and back again as fast as his finger could move. Up and down the line, soldiers, sailors, airmen, and Marines were loosing a ferocious barrage; the outgoing bedlam drove the attackers back across the road.

At the same time on the north perimeter, a larger attack on the isolated outpost almost succeeded as members of the NVA 12th Sapper Battalion, supported by RPGs and machine guns, mounted a determined effort to breach the perimeter. The north perimeter degenerated to a literal brawl at close quarters. Only several individual heroic performances and the indomitable fighting spirit of the defenders held the assault in check despite taking many casualties.

With less than 200 occupants of various service affiliations and nationalities, officers and enlisted men alike manned every foot of the perimeter, tenaciously standing their ground and turning back assaults at all points of contact.

Not being able to penetrate any portion of the perimeter, the NVA pulled back and tried to reduce the compound with mortar and rockets, which continued off and on through midmorning. Through the remainder of the night, NVA forces continued seizing the rest of the city south of the Perfume River, leaving MACV headquarters the only real estate not under their control when the sun came up.

Daylight brought heavy sniper and machine gun activity from several nearby two- and three-story buildings, which kept movement around the compound to a minimum.

Not yet comprehending the full scope of the communist offensive, an operation to evacuate casualties was organized.

Stubbornly fending off at least two concentrated ground assaults and several probes on the compound was not accomplished without a price. Nothing could be done for the dead but several wounded men needed urgent medical attention beyond the capabilities of the camp dispensary. Not having an area within its perimeter large enough to serve as a helicopter pad, the MACV personnel would have to venture out from their enclave to secure a landing site.

At midmorning the most severe casualties were loaded into vehicles while a column moved out through the north gate to the LCU ramp some 100 meters northeast. The small column followed QL1 (National Highway 1 was refered to as QL1 in northern I Corps) to the bridge then turned right on approach to the ramp. Having experienced no resistance to this point in the operation, the small force fanned out to secure the intended landing zone.

Walking parallel to a ten-foot-high concrete wall, Corporal Smith was sure he heard voices on the other side. Reaching the end of the wall, Smith pivoted around the corner, ready for a confrontation. All hell broke loose from several rooftops and prepared ground positions. Every weapon in the NVA arsenal opened up on the small force approaching the ramp. Smith was soon on the ground with a bullet in his left thigh just above the knee. Lance Corporal Desport immediately ran forward through a torrent of fire to reach Smith. At an eighty-pound disadvantage, Desport found the strength to pull the larger man by his web suspenders back behind the safety of the wall.

Substantially outnumbered, the evac party loaded their newly wounded on the vehicles and hauled ass back to the compound.

Informed by radio of reinforcements from Phu Bai making headway toward Hue, the advisors remained in siege mode, awaiting relief. Crossing the An Cuu Bridge just south of the compound in early afternoon, Alpha Company, 1st Battalion, 1st Marines reached the embattled advisors at 1515, breaking the siege. After a brief foray across the Highway 1 Bridge and back again, the Marines by 2000 had a landing zone set up west of the LCU ramp and effected Medevacs of their own casualties as well as those of the MACV personnel.

In a meeting with the 1st Marines on 1 February, Lieutenant Warkentin offered up the services of Sergeant Darby to spot naval gunfire in support of Marine operations. Teaming up with a sniper detail, Darby occupied the roof of one of the university's campus buildings overlooking the Perfume River while the Marines were still securing the campus. Taking position on the north end using a concrete architectural retaining wall for cover, Darby aided Marine efforts by taking several targets in the south city under fire and remained in place until 13 February. When not engaged with naval gunfire missions, Darby pulled double duty spotting for the sniper.

During 14-17 February, additional naval gunfire was used in direct support of U.S. Marines participating in Operation Hue City. Detailed planning was required before naval gunfire could be used successfully against the entrenched enemy holding the Hue Citadel. Due to bad weather, an air spotter could not be utilized, and it was necessary to use ground spotters to direct gunfire on the Citadel wall. A survey of the south bank of the Perfume River, already secured by U.S. Marines, revealed the best available vantage point was a hotel used by the International Control Commission, but it was considered neutral territory; however, the field commander, Colonel Stanley S. Hughes, commanding the 1st Marines, asserted that this building would be occupied because of the military necessity to effectively employ the naval gunfire team.

The parameters restricting fire within the Citadel further complicated the employment of naval gunfire. The eastern portion of the wall targeted for bombarded occupied heavily trafficked ground as well as priceless historic sites venerated by the Vietnamese. Troops of the 1st ARVN Division occupying positions at their headquarters trapped inside of the Citadel were about 400 meters north, while U.S. Marines attacking from southwest were within 200 meters of the target. The imperial palace grounds just to the west were of primary political importance, thus making it imperative that no rounds fall within its perimeter.

Walls surrounding the Citadel enclose an area of some six kilometers square. The walls themselves are 700 meters long, six-meter-high earth-filled masonry that measure up to 75 feet thick in places.

Achieving the desired results without destroying Vietnamese historical treasures would require precision marksmanship. The major worry of course was the occasional long or short round, which all naval gunfire spotters dread. With so many friendly troops in such close proximity to the target, this concern is not overstated.

To solve this problem, a ship was stationed at anchor directly north of the city, whereby the gun target line was perpendicular to the wall. This innovative mission planning eliminated any chance of long or short rounds causing friendly casualties or impacting on structures that, because of their historic value, were designated as protected from destruction (see map).

On 14 February, an attempt was made to fire the mission by USS *Providence* (CLG-6). After walking fire in on target, a check fire was given because of friendly aircraft in the area. However, the last adjusting round heavily damaged the wall, convincingly demonstrating the effectiveness naval gunfire could have in later missions.

Early morning of 15 February, bombardment missions commenced with USS *Manley* (DD-940) firing in support of the operation. Between 0842 and 0946, forty-two rounds of five-inch/54 ammunition was fired against the wall, rupturing it in three places, heavily damaging a wall tower, destroying one structure, and damaging ten other structures adjacent to the wall. Each of these structures housed or was suspected of housing an enemy strong point.

On 16 February, in support of the 5th Marines, the I Corps NGLO, U.S. Navy Lieutenant Commander Philip B. Hatch, adjusted eight-inch howitzer fire in coordination with a Marine aerial observer, adjusting gunfire from USS *Providence* on enemy strong points on the citadel wall and within the Citadel itself.

On 17 February, USS *Providence*, again in firing position, delivered 139 rounds of six-inch/47 ammunition against the Citadel wall between coordinates YD 766228 and YD 764223, damaging 250 meters of the wall and several structures adjacent to it, silencing numerous enemy automatic weapons.

Through the remainder of Operation Hue City, naval gunfire was employed in harassing and interdiction missions supporting U.S. Marines clearing the city. The devastating effect of naval gunfire against hard-fortified targets during the operation proved to be a great asset for U.S. Marine and ARVN units involved.

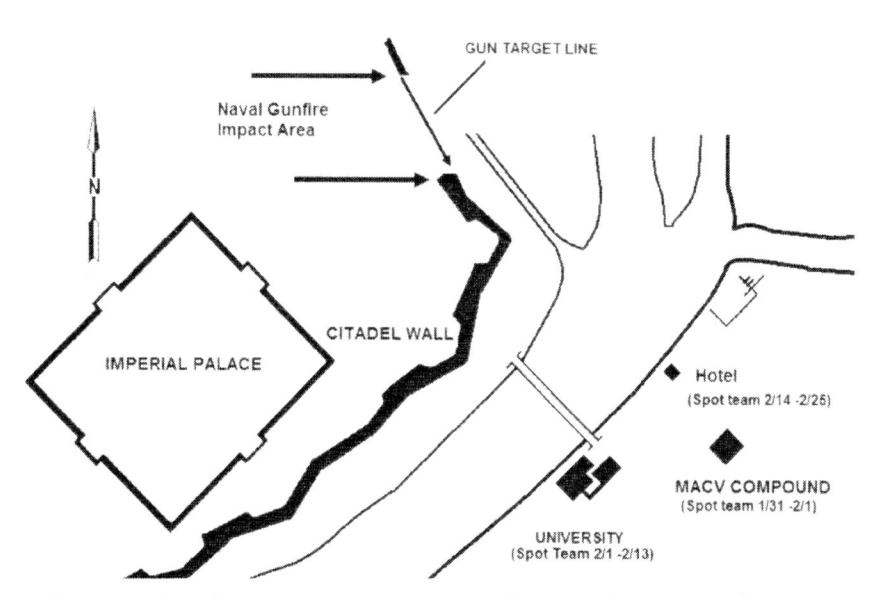

Outside the city, a second campaign for the liberation of Hue was taking shape. During the period from 4 through 29 February, gunfire ships in the Tonkin Gulf also became heavily involved as a supporting arm for elements of the 1st Air Cavalry Division operating north of the ancient capital. These were the same ships providing support for assault elements in the city pulling duty for both operations.

In support of U.S. Marine and ARVN forces attacking the Citadel from the south and east, 3rd Brigade, 1st Air Cavalry Division was given the mission of denying enemy troops access routes into the Citadel, interdicting its routes of egress, and locating and destroying enemy units north and northwest of Hue. Almost immediately after commencing its attack, elements of the brigade met stiff resistance from well-fortified positions 3,000 meters west of Hue and surrounding vicinity. In honor of the highly applauded Confederate cavalry officer, the operation was dubbed Jeb Stuart I.

Assigned as naval gunfire support for the 1st Air Cavalry, 1st Lieutenant Pasquale (Pat) J. Morocco and his team operating out of Camp Evans took to the air over the embattled 3rd Brigade.

From 4 through 6 February, Lieutenant Morocco directed the fires of USS *Lynde McCormick* (DDG-8) against enemy lines of communication. From 7 through 12 February, Morocco directed her fires in support of maneuver elements of the 1st Cavalry, neutralizing and destroying numerous well-fortified positions. On 12 February, controlled by U.S. Army spotters, she expended 1,077 rounds, making a significant contribution to suppressing NVA mortar fire and disrupting at least one assault on the 1st Cav.

The cruiser USS *Providence* (CLG-6), in company with destroyers USS *Hamner* (DD-718), USS *Johnson* (DD-821), USS *Manley* (DD-940), USS *Hoel* (DDG-13), and USS *Buchanan* (DDG-14), joined Morocco's armada from 12 through 18 February, providing highly effective fires against enemy units opposing the U.S. Army assault battalions.

On 21 February, the 3rd Brigade, now joined by the 2nd Battalion 501st Infantry of the 101st Airborne Division, initiated a concerted attack north of Hue to open Highway 1. The operational objectives were to eliminate enemy strongholds immediately west of the Citadel, establishing a blocking force while U.S. Marine and ARVN forces pushed through the Citadel from east to west. In preparation for the attack, in consideration of extremely heavily fortified positions, Lieutenant Morocco controlled the eight-inch guns of cruiser USS *Canberra* (CAG-2) with devastating effect. By nightfall, the aggressive assault of the U.S. Army successfully achieved all objectives. Using the eyes of U.S. Army observers, Lieutenant Morocco employed those eight-inch guns on interdiction missions, taking fleeing enemy troops under fire with good effect.

Back in the air on 23 February, Lieutenant Morocco directed five-inch/54 batteries of USS *Hull* (DD-945) on escaping NVA/VC troops attempting to cross the Inland Waterway. Friendly units sweeping through the area later that afternoon credited Hull with fifty confirmed KIAs. Again on the 25th the cruiser USS *Newport News* (CA-148) brought her main and secondary batteries to bear on a NVA/VC regimental command post, eliminating several automatic weapons sites.

Corporal Sean Hearn, on 27 February, flying in place of his boss Lieutenant Morocco, utilized the five-inch spin-stabilized (SS) rockets of USS *Carronade* (IFS-1) to engage a reported VC battalion west of Hue, causing fifty-three secondary explosions and an unknown number of casualties, having great effect on target.

In support of Operation Jeb Stuart I, U.S. Navy gunline ships controlled by Lieutenant Morocco and Corporal Hearn, with help from U.S. Army spotters, fired over 13,000 rounds of various caliber causing 397 NVA/VC fatalities (not counting 300-plus KIAs USS *Canberra* shared with artillery units). Additionally, Navy rifles were credited with damaging or destroying 128 enemy structures and bunkers, 3 mortar positions, 1 recoilless rifle, and several automatic weapons, and destroying or severely damaging thirteen sampans attempting to resupply NVA/VC elements in Hue City. These fire missions also neutralized two mortar attacks and two ground assaults.

Throughout the first two weeks of the operation, naval gunfire directed by Lieutenant Morocco and his team was employed to interdict enemy lines of communication and avenues of approach north, east, and south of the city. Reports by enemy prisoners taken during the fighting indicated naval gunfire inflicted many casualties among the enemy and had an extremely demoralizing effect. One prisoner reported that his battalion, which was infiltrating down the coast from Quang Tri into the Quang Dien area just north of Hue, had over 100 men killed by naval gunfire during the operation.

Sub Unit One's involvement in the Battle for Hue City has been casually alluded to in other accounts of this struggle, only by obscure references to naval gunfire, but Colonel Stanley S. Hughes, commanding officer of the 1st Marines, in his after action report cited the Hue City team as follows: "During the initial stage of Operation Hue City Naval gunfire support of the 1st Marines was arranged and controlled by members of 1st Air Naval Gunfire Liaison Company based in Hue City. Excellent coordination and cooperation by ANGLICO assisted in naval gunfire support for the 1st Marines for this period. Notable for this period was the use of the six-inch/47 guns of USS *Providence* (GCL-6) against the Hue City walls."

The "Battle for Phan Thiet" was the name given to combined U.S. Army/ARVN operations in the vicinity of Phan Thiet, a small coastal settlement in southern II Corps, during the Tet Offensive when the city was attacked in force by the 804th Viet Cong main force battalion. The north and eastern sections of the city were defended by the 3rd and 4th Battalions of the 44th ARVN Regiment, with the 3rd Battalion 506th (3/506th) Infantry Regiment of the 101st Airborne Division providing primary defense to the south and west. A naval gunfire liaison/spot team from Sub Unit One was assigned to the 3/506th, which conducted operations in the large TAOR west, north, and northeast of the city.

Prior to Tet, the Phan Thiet team had been actively supporting the 3/506th during Operations Byrd and McLain, which sought to destroy the elusive 804th and 482nd VC main force battalions as well as smaller local force units.

During the first days of Tet, a fire support ship was not available due to high priorities elsewhere. On 3 February, USS *Frank D. Evans* (DD-745) arrived on station and immediately began firing in defense of the city. During the early morning hours of 4 February, ANGLICO spotter Sergeant Allen D. Owen, using continuous illumination provided by C-47 flare ships, adjusted the extremely accurate fires of USS *Frank D. Evans* into the northern edge of Phan Thiet, repelling two companies of VC that had succeeded in penetrating the northeastern section of the city. The primary mission of this enemy force was to seize the eastern portion of Phan Thiet, which included the provincial headquarters, and to assassinate the province chief. With naval gunfire adjusted by Sergeant Owen to within 100 meters of friendly forces, the enemy became disoriented, fled the area, and was soon driven out by ARVN troops. Prisoners captured during this action reported that NGF had completely demoralized their company and disrupted their attack.

During follow-up operations from 5-13 February, additional naval gunfire controlled by the Phan Thiet team was employed in direct support of allied forces, clearing pockets of resistance in isolated sections of the city. These missions included LZ prep, modified illumination, destruction missions, and H&I fires.

At 0800, 18 February, enemy forces renewed their attack on Phan Thiet. An urgent call for fire support went out from the MACV Advisory Team. The 3/506th ANGLICO spot team responded by launching an airborne spotter, PFC Fallon, who requested and directed fires of USS *Frank D. Evans*. Once more, naval gunfire proved to be a decisive factor in the outcome of the battle. During the battle, naval gunfire scored a direct hit on the VC headquarters (as later reported by captured VC) and silenced an enemy mortar attack, directly contributing to neutralizing the assault. ARVN personnel monitoring the enemy's radio transmissions reported the Viet Cong complaining about of heavy casualties due to "mortars from the ocean."

On the following night, the Phan Thiet junk base was attacked, and once more naval gunfire provided by USS *Pritchett* (DD-561), adjusted under aircraft flares, and aborted the attack. Ten Viet Cong were driven into the open, where they were killed by allied forces. Throughout the following week, ANGLICO spotters contributed mopping up operations with counter mortar fire and illumination missions. Allied commanders lauded gunfire support, and USS *Frank D. Evans* in particular, for their instrumental role in saving the city.

Throughout the action from 5-19 February, ANGLICO spotters controlled and adjusted 5,908 rounds from USS *Frank D. Evans* and USS *Pritchett*, causing an undetermined number of enemy casualties. Naval gunfire destroyed or damaged 164 bunkers and other enemy structures, causing three secondary explosions. In addition, naval gunnery broke up three infantry assaults and silenced one mortar attack.

Over the next month, every allied maneuver battalion in I Corps was on the move, counter-punching the forces of Ho Chi Minh. By late February, allied forces were still engaged, putting the finishing touches on residual hot spots still smoldering from the month-long offensive. The siege of Khe Sanh was still being played out, holding center stage as the largest battle yet fought in the war, commanding first priority for all available aircraft, which were in great demand all over I Corps, creating a lot of stress in most areas within the Marine area of responsibility.

Ship Chungdae had been involved in Operation Mysterious Dragon 1 from the onset of the Tet Offensive and was running short on food and ammunition. Having secured Hoi An, the Brigade was on the hunt for the 31st NVA Regiment, still causing mayhem in the western TAOR. The company had been living off the land, shooting domestic livestock to fuel its sojourn through the coastal plains of Hoi An Basin the last several days. Corporals Richard (Vance) Hall, James Chally, and Charles Williams checked in with Brigade twice a day, trying to get choppers inbound to their location with needed supplies. The operation seemed to have a life of its own that just wouldn't end. One day melted into another. Dates and days of the week lost all meaning

One midmorning toward the last week in February, the company was traveling north on a dirt pathway close to the outskirts of a wooded area in single file. The ANGLICO team moved forward near the center of the column a hundred meters behind point when an ear-shattering explosion ripped a four-foot-deep cleft in the pathway a few feet behind the team. Engulfed in a shower of mud, nearly knocked off his feet, Corporal Hall spun around, retracing his last few footfalls around a bend in the pathway, only to behold a surrealistic scene that shocked his senses. His friend Boxie, a corpsman, was lying in a crater screaming. Looking on in horror at the sight of his comrade thrashing around in the crater cut in two at the hips, Vance remembers seeing Boxie's face twisted in pain. The corpsman's mouth contorted like a man screaming in agony, but no sounds escaped his throat. Vance couldn't hear a thing. Looking around in a trauma-induced stupor, Corporal Hall deduced many years later that the contour of the tree line at the bend probably saved his life, absorbing most of the blast. Within minutes, his hearing started returning.

In addition to Boxie, four other Marines scattered around the crater sustained moderate shrapnel wounds. Not knowing how this would play, Corporal Chally requested an emergency Medevac, which was accepted by the air wing. Twenty minutes later, with the evac operation complete, 10th Company continued on course.

Late in the afternoon, still traversing flat ground between hedgerows and tree lines, sporadic rifle fire slowed progress. Corporal Chally, with his immune system stressed, started complaining about flue-like symptoms. As routine Medevac requests were currently being ignored by the air wing, Chally knew he'd have to gut it out for a few days.

Emerging from direction of one of the many tree rows growing in their path, the company once again came under sniper harassment. A Marine caught sight of a muzzle flash in the window of a lone hut not far from another tree line off to the company's left front. Captain Yoon Choon Wong ordered a squad to flank the structure, cutting off the escape route. As grunts assaulted the building, a lone black-clad figure with no other options laid down his rifle, surrendering to the flankers.

As the man was still being bound, a second sniper further into the tree line sent a few errant rounds kicking up dirt in vicinity of the flank platoon on the eastern edge of the field. While the company advanced several hundred meters pursuing a retreating enemy, sporadic sniper fire continued then just as abruptly died off completely.

The lead platoon on the eastern flank, crossing a field some eighty meters wide, came to a shallow creek bed in front of a thick tree line. Advancing across the creek bed not ten paces from the wood line, a calamitous roar of gunfire erupted from an undetermined number of entrenched NVA just a few feet into the bush. Most members of 1st Platoon fell dead or wounded during the first few awful moments of a murderous volume of fire relentlessly streaming from the foliage. Machine guns and RPGs added more voices to the already deafening cacophony of ear-piercing thunder, forcing survivors to the ground. Tragically, platoon commander, Lieutenant Park Sung Jin, a longtime friend of Captain Yoon, was among the first to fall.

At just seventy meters away, the two remaining platoons and HQ personnel were quickly taken under fire, keeping the entire company pinned down. A Marine guarding the prisoner shot him and lent his rifle to the task of suppressing fire coming out of the tree line.

From above the din of battle, Captain Yoon contacted Brigade Recon on the west flank in a bid to coordinate rescue of his badly mauled platoon. Judging from the amount of fire gushing from the tree line, it was determined 10th Company was far outmanned.

Hustling forward to position itself for a flank movement on the tree line, *Suesecdae* (Recon Platoon) stopped forty meters from the objective, hidden by tall hedgerows. Corporal Ray Shawn, with Recon, had been dealing with the same problem of getting beans and bullets delivered; he wondered inwardly how much air support he could count on.

Captain Yoon, after receiving confirmation of *Suesecdae's* position, coordinated the assault by pouring fire into the tree line. As this action was just on the outer edge of the Blue Dragon area of responsibility, battalion artillery was out of range. This assault would have to be done the hard way. On command, *Suesecdae*—two squads online with one squad establishing a base of fire—launched their assault on the tree line from the west. The attack progressed only twenty or so feet when NVA guns opened up in a furious fusillade of chatter, immediately stalling further forward momentum. Four men on the assault fell wounded, as did the platoon leader, amid a storm of impacting bullets.

To the left front of 10th Company, a ten-foot break in the tree line allowed Marines to observe NVA shifting reinforcements to shore up their west flank. The line platoon furthest west took out several but could not stem the flow of men scurrying about to augment those facing the Recon Platoon. Captain Yoon's command group, located immediately south of this platoon, likewise continued pumping out fire in a bid to halt reinforcements rushing to stop Recon's advance.

Faced with massive torrents of fire by numerically superior defenders, Recon withdrew behind the hedgerow, still keeping up pressure on the tree line. Like Ship Chungdae, Recon was also experiencing dwindling ammo supplies.

At 10th Company, Vance Hall was on the radio requesting air support with any ordnance as soon as he could get it, as was Corporal Shawn with Recon Platoon. Captain Yoon was in contact with battalion, trying to get artillery of any caliber.

Captain Yoon also informed the ANGLICOs of an impending need for ammunition, as both his troops and Recon were down to just a couple magazines per man. Back up on the TAC net, Corporal Hall was begging battalion for helicopters, gunships, bombers: anything with wings or rotors. Corporal Ray Shawn on the other side of the tree line was also on the net seeking Medevac and resupply.

Outnumbered and outgunned Koreans repeatedly tried to reach the decimated platoon but were driven back by accelerating clamor of fire during each attempt. There was simply too much open ground to cover over established deadly fields of fire dominated by several well-placed machine guns. Ammunition shortages prevented any meaningful effort to match outgoing fire. One squad, however, did manage to cross the creek bed. In a heroic point-blank firefight, the squad did manage to evacuate some of the wounded, sustaining three more casualties. Captain Yoon was not a man easily discouraged, but he was not willing sacrifice any more men until he had the assets needed to suppress the devastating fire coursing from the trench line.

Corporal James Chally busied himself organizing an evac site to insure quick transfer of wounded once the Medevac touched down. He didn't have long to wait. Even as the staging was being completed, the team radio came alive with request for landing instructions from a CH-46 circling overhead. Corporal Williams directed the rotor craft to approach from the east, keeping the bird well away from the tree line firefight.

Once the craft was on the ground, Corporal Chally assisted the short-handed corpsmen, carrying casualties up the ramp. While the last man was being positioned on the deck, several bullets cracked through the fuselage, wounding one crewman. Reacting instantly, the pilot lifted his ship off the ground, trapping Chally and two Koreans inside, with no way to exit the ascending helicopter.

Several more rounds passed through the ship, heightening apprehension levels of all aboard. Clearing the tree line and gaining more altitude, the aircraft headed east out of range. Not long into flight, to the pilot's horror, the transmission chip light came on, indicating a catastrophic problem. Knowing he had less than one minute of flight to find a safe LZ, the pilot calmly put more power on the rotors while bottoming pitch. Both men in the cockpit scanned surrounding terrain for the closest friendly troops. Off to the northeast, 5th Battalion command post loomed a few thousand meters ahead. Altering course, the crippled bird raced on, managing to reach safe haven without much power to spare.

Captain Yoon, seriously concerned that some of his men may still lie wounded in front of the tree line, called an impromptu meeting. Believing any more rescue attempts without more ammo and supporting arms would be futile, Captain Yoon ordered everyone to hold position until nightfall, less than an hour away.

Corporal Hall asked for specific location of the battered platoon so he could facilitate evacuation of anymore possible wounded.

Studying the situation, Hall and Williams felt sure they had a good chance at reaching the trapped platoon by following the creek bed. Late afternoon shadows creeping over the landscape shrouded both Marines as they made their way to the creek bed, taking advantage of the east tree line. Being careful to not silhouette themselves against the skyline, the pair crawled slowly forward into the depression. Koreans manning positions along the way motioned them to go back. Pushing onward, the Marines put their fears aside, continuing on course toward the chewed-up platoon. Looking up over the berm periodically for reference, Williams and Hall zeroed in on the location of their objective. In the creek bed just in front of where the ambush was sprung, six or seven wounded Marines, who had managed to seek the safety offered by the berm, were happy as hell to see the Americans stumble in on them.

As quietly as could be arranged, Williams offered encouragement to the men, informing them more help would soon be on the way. He laid out a plan whereby he and Hall would take one man back with them and send more Marines to evacuate the remainder.

The senior Marine pointed out a corpsman with a bullet hole high on his thigh as the man needing care most urgently. With the corpsman between them, each Marine placed one arm of the wounded man on his shoulder. Keeping a low profile, retracing the circuitous creek bed back toward the command group, the injured medic was soon receiving long-needed field treatment.

After digesting the reconnaissance report from the Americans, Captain Yoon dispatched a detail to retrieve the rest of his casualties.

As stealthily as could be managed, two squads on the right flank moved into position to cover rescue teams proceeding down the creek bed. Within fifteen minutes, lead elements of the rescue party reaching the trapped Marines immediately set to work organizing evacuation efforts. As the berm of the creek bed was only about three feet tall, so many men stooped over in cramped posture could not help but make a little noise while attempting to maneuver injured men, who did not have control over their movements. This alerted NVA gunners in the tree line only fifteen feet away that something was up. One again, the trench came alive with the chatter of small arms and machine gun fire, which in turn drew fierce fire from Korean flank security. Managing to stay below the berm, recovery teams, braving a maddening swarm of lead lacing the air just overhead, pulled the wounded back down the creek bed out of harm's way.

In a triage established behind a tree line near the command group, evacuated Marines were handed off to corpsmen for field treatment. Thick foliage shielded the wounded from fire pouring out of the front tree line since the evacuation effort was discovered. This site was at the margin of an open area large enough for a landing zone. Soon after the first casualty was received, Hall and Williams requested one more emergency Medevac.

Soon after acknowledging the appeal, battalion advised both embattled teams that a request for next available aircraft had been approved. Due to current demand for air support, it was not possible to estimate time of arrival.

Just before dusk, Hall was ecstatic as battalion came up on net with news of one F-4 Phantom inbound to his position. Medevac helicopters without gunship escorts were expected to head for 10th Company soon thereafter. He was also informed the F-4 had but a single 1,000-pound bomb. It was the best they could do. Informing Captain Yoon of the newly available assets, a plan to coordinate the air operation was hastily put together.

Even as news of the impending air action was being passed around, battalion advised Hall of strike craft and Medevac now approaching his position. The Medevac also had ammo aboard for the beleaguered bush beaters.

As the airfield in Hoi An was not operational due to combat conditions, Kim Chi 1 and 2 were not available. This air strike would be coordinated through Battalion by radio relay. As jets are not equipped with FM radios, UHF-capable radios at battalion were needed to communicate with support jets.

Down to the last HE round for his M-79 grenade launcher, Corporal Hall identified this method of marking the target. Smoke or WP was more preferable but he only had what he had to do the job. As a precaution, so this one round could be easily recognized from the air with no smoke to obscure the pilot's vision, all outgoing fire into the tree line was suspended. As soon as Vance got the word from battalion that the F-4 was in position to observe target identification, Hall took careful aim then loosed his last remaining round. It landed a few feet long. Upon notification by battalion that the pilot did clearly observe the marker round impact, Vance called him down. He then hailed the Medevac bird, who was circling well south, to stand by. At just seventy meters from the strike zone, not knowing how much fallout could be expected from a 1,000-pounder at such close range, everyone lay pressed close to earth.

Coming in low over the pinned-down Recon Platoon, the F-4 made his one and only approach, then released his payload. Word was passed on to Ray Shawn with Recon, and to Captain Yoon, for everyone to get their heads down. Looking on from prone position, Hall and Williams held their breath as the big bomb arched its way to earth. As soon as he was satisfied the run was on target, Hall put his head down waiting for what he knew would be one thunderous blast.

Marines closest to the rear tree line were showered in wood splinters and palm fronds as shrapnel shredded and bent these tropical mainstays eight to ten feet off the ground. The earth shuddered from impact. No one in that field was totally prepared for the ear-splitting concussion that followed.

Looking up a little shaken, Hall observed a thick cloud of black smoke centered some thirty feet north of his marker, billowing back-spreading into the field from the tree line. Not bad! There wasn't a sound or a rustle coming out of the impact area.

Focusing attention on the Medevac operation, the Americans realized they had a problem. Lack of resupply over the past week had also levied a tax on the ANGLICO team. Without smoke or illumination grenades, the team had no choice but to identify the landing zone with a small campfire. Williams made contact with the evac chopper while Hall gathered wood and kindling from the surrounding brush.

As if life wasn't difficult enough, a light sprinkle began falling just before dusk, dampening most available fuel. Not an easily accomplished chore, Hall called upon his youthful experience in the Oklahoma countryside and made it work.

After the chopper properly identified the (fire) marker, Williams called him down.

With his ammunition replenished, Captain Yoon once more turned his attention to his KIAs in front of the tree line. Those Marines nearest the entrenched NVA unit were believed to have been killed. Nearer the creek bed that 10th Company controlled, it was thought that all the survivors had been recovered (or at least they hoped that they were). Nearby the creek, further efforts were made under the cover of darkness to find additional survivors, but without success.

Captain Yoon was surprised, to say the least, that no fire greeted them from the tree line, as it was not possible to pull off a rescue operation of this size under the noses of a numerically superior force without being discovered. Be that as it may, abandoned or not, the *Ship Chungdae* skipper wisely decided not to press his luck in the dark. Once what remains of the dead that could be reached were taken off the field, one platoon remained in place overnight, standing watch over the fallen Marines left in front of the creek bed.

In the morning, 3rd Battalion notified Captain Yoon that one artillery battery had been moved by truck overnight within range of his position and could offer fire support on call. With a favorable south breeze to his back, the Ship Chungdae skipper called for a barrage of white smoke to camouflage a reconnaissance of the open field and the recovery of the deceased Marines. He then ordered an assault of the bothersome wood line, which came off with no resistance, confirming Captain Yoon's assessment that the NVA did indeed abandon their positions last night.

Once within the former NVA position, evidence of that devastating 1,000-pound bomb was everywhere. Broken bodies of several North Vietnamese troops lay scattered throughout the wood line. (A formal body count was never established.) A pen occupied by cattle shredded by shrapnel was just to the west of three burning and smoldering hootches. The extensive trench works that were formerly occupied by NVA troops now lay partially collapsed and abandoned for a distance of forty or so feet each side of the crater. No signs of the enemy remained.

With the aftermath of Tet playing out all around them, for most of the morning, 10th Company Marines came across numerous NVA bodies spread out over a mile or more.

No one ever accused the Viet Cong of lacking imagination. By 1968, enemy forces turned their attention to make naval gunfire work in their favor. Early in March, the VC stopped a naval gunfire mission with a very effective trick. When an airborne spotter commenced a fire mission, a Vietnamese patrol in ambush position several kilometers away reported incoming rounds. The incoming stopped when the ship was directed to check fire. The ship checked her solution, then fire was resumed and the patrol again reported incoming. Although the spotter reported seeing the fall of shot and detonation of each round at the proper target location, the mission was cancelled by the friendly unit. Later investigation revealed that the enemy timed their mortar and rocket fire to coincide with the ship's firing, probably by listening in on the spot frequency or observing the ship's gun flashes. The VC tactic successfully stopped a naval gunfire mission and allowed their own gunners to escape unobserved. This incident precipitated Lieutenant Colonel Goodiel to step up his investigation of newly available cipher devices for secure communication.

One ongoing problem occurring throughout the country was that occasionally NGLOs of junior officer grade or NCOs in charge of small ANGLICO Detachments became somewhat restricted in access and opportunity to properly communicate with field-grade officers of supported units. Certain allied forces were more receptive to suggestions from a field-grade officer than that of a company grade officer and occasionally wouldn't even listen to an enlisted man.

To remedy this situation, Lieutenant Colonel Goodiel himself made visits to these commands with the appropriate Corps NGLO, educating their commanding officers on ANGLICO training and capabilities. The colonel's efforts did result in some improvement, but for many, the idea of listening to men of subordinate rank was never totally accepted. Many senior officers perceived having to deal with U.S. enlisted men as an affront to their professionalism, viewing these proceedings as American arrogance.

Lieutenant Colonel Frederick K. Purdum assumed command of Sub Unit One from Lieutenant Colonel Carlton D. Goodiel 5 August, maintaining current manning levels that had grown to 230 men at the turn of the year.

One of the more innovative contributions initiated by ANGLICO for improved supporting arms control was the establishment of an airborne FSCC. Having a Tactical Air Controller and Naval gunfire spotter in the same aircraft proved extremely efficient in coordinating artillery, naval gunfire, and tactical air, especially for prep and landing zone neutralization fires during early phases of ground operations. Artillery and naval gunfire controlled by the spotter was lifted or shifted to allow utilization of close air support with split-second timing. The procedures developed during these operations were soon adopted by the Marine Corps and improved upon, enjoying widespread use though the remainder of Marine involvement in the war.

Of the failed Tet Offensive, North Vietnam's General Vo Nguyen Giap, who planned and executed this operation, had this to say of the American fighting man in his memoirs:

"You defeated us! And we thought you knew it, but we were elated to notice your media was definitely helping us. They were causing more disruption in America than we could in the battlefields. We were ready to surrender". "You had won".

Royal Australian Navy

Naval Operations in Vietnam

Between 1965 and 1972, elements of the Royal Australian Navy (RAN) undertook continuous operational service in Vietnam. During this period, the Navy performed a variety of operational tasks at sea, ashore, and in the air. The RAN's primary contribution consisted of destroyers.

On the Gunline: HMA Ships *Hobart, Perth, Brisbane,* and *Vendetta.*

The largest single commitment by the Royal Australian Navy to Vietnam was the provision of destroyers on a rotational basis to the U.S. Navy's 7th Fleet for service on what became known as the gunline. RAN warships provided naval gunfire support from March 1967 to September 1971. They also participated in Operation Sea Dragon, the bombardment of North Vietnamese military targets, and the interdiction of supply routes and logistic craft along the coast of North Vietnam from the demilitarized zone to the Red River Delta, from April 1967 until it was suspended in November 1968.

The first RAN destroyers to deploy to Vietnam were Charles F. Adams class guided missile destroyers (DDG) HMAS *Hobart*, HMAS

Perth, and HMAS *Brisbane.* The Australian DDGs were well suited for the task of providing naval gunfire support. Armed with two five-inch/54 caliber gun mounts that fired a standard seventy-six-pound high explosive shell, they were capable of bringing down accurate five-inch gunfire at a nominal rate of twenty rounds per minute on targets at ranges beyond fourteen nautical miles in most conditions.

The Daring class destroyer HMAS *Vendetta* was also deployed for service on the gunline. Her main armament consisted of six 4.5-inch guns that were capable of providing accurate and rapid fire to a range of nine nautical miles at a rate of sixteen rounds per gun per minute. In good conditions, Vendetta's gun's were capable of expending up to 100 rounds per minute.

HMAS *Hobart* was the first DDG to join the U.S. Seventh Fleet on 15 March 1967, beginning the six-month rotation of RAN destroyers for service on the gunline. HMAS *Hobart* and HMAS *Perth* deployed three times to Vietnam, HMAS *Brisbane* twice, and HMAS *Vendetta* once. The destroyers carried out NGF missions in all of South Vietnam's four military regions. *Hobart* and *Perth* were actively involved in Sea Dragon. *Hobart* and *Perth* also came under fire on a number of occasions. HMAS *Perth* was hit once during her first deployment, and HMAS *Hobart* suffered two killed and seven wounded when she was mistakenly hit by missiles fired from a U.S. Air Force jet aircraft.

HMAS *Hobart* was awarded a U.S. Navy Unit Commendation in recognition of her service in Vietnam, while HMAS *Perth* received both the U.S. Navy Unit Commendation and the U.S. Meritorious Unit Commendation. This honor allowed both ships to fly distinguishing pennants known as "burgees" from their masthead when alongside for the duration of their commissions.

In their five years of service in Vietnam, the four gunline destroyers steamed over 397,000 miles and fired 102,546 rounds.

In April 1971, Prime Minister John Gorton announced that Australian forces in Vietnam would be reduced. This led to the withdrawal of the clearance divers in May and the RANHFV in June. The final RAN destroyer on the gunline, HMAS *Brisbane*, returned to Sydney on 15 October 1971.

HMAS *Jeparit* returned to Sydney from her final voyage on 11 March 1972, followed the next day by HMAS *Sydney*.

During the time RAN was involved in the war, eight officers and sailors were killed and another forty-six wounded. Dedication and professionalism shown by members of the Royal Australian Navy earned the service the respect of her allies and continued the valorous traditions established by Australian sailors in other wars.

Royal Australian Ships in Support of the Vietnam War

Gunline Destroyers	Logistic Support	Escorts
Hobart Brisbane Perth Vendetta	Sydney Boonaroo Jeparit	Anzac Derwent Duchess Melbourne Parramatta Stuart Swan Torrens Vampire Vendetta Yarra

We, who once found refuge under the protection of her guns, salute all the valiant ships and gallant crews of the Royal Australian Navy.

DIFFERENT WAR, SAME MESS

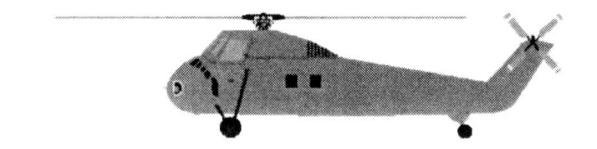

"Do not fear the enemy, for they can take only your life. Fear the media far more, for they will destroy your honor!"
Unknown

Even before the Tet Offensive began, the war in I Corps was recognized as the premier battleground in South Vietnam. U.S. Army Divisions began filling in behind U.S. Marines as the latter shifted its forces further North; General Westmoreland, having doubts about III MAF's capability to control an expanding war in the northernmost military region, initiated a change in the I Corps command structure. To this end, MACV forward came into being under Westmoreland's deputy commander, General Creighton W. Abrams, who established his headquarters at Phu Bai. This maneuver immediately became a source of irritation among senior Marine officers.

At a meeting on 17 February 1968, General Westmoreland informed Lieutenant General Robert E. Cushman, III MAF commander, and General Abrams of the creation of a Provisional Corps in northern I Corps, consisting of the 1st Air Cavalry Division, the 101st Airborne Division, and the 3rd Marine Division headed by U.S. Army Lieutenant General William B. Rosson. The Provisional Corps would, by year's end, assume the identity of XXIV Corps. Through a series of negotiations over the following weeks, most of the irritants were smoothed out as the new command moved forward, with General Cushman retaining control of Marine tactical assets. The 3rd Marine Division, while still under command of III MAF, was now under the operational control of the Provisional Corps, which in turn came under operational control of III MAF (see chart).

To this end, the ANGLICO I Corps NGLO, Lieutenant Commander Philip B. Hatch, Jr., USN, assumed additional responsibilities as NGLO for MACV forward on 5 February, relocating his team and equipment from the I Corps Tactical Operations Center (TOC) in Da Nang to Phu Bai.

I CORPS ORGANIZATIONAL CHART - 1968

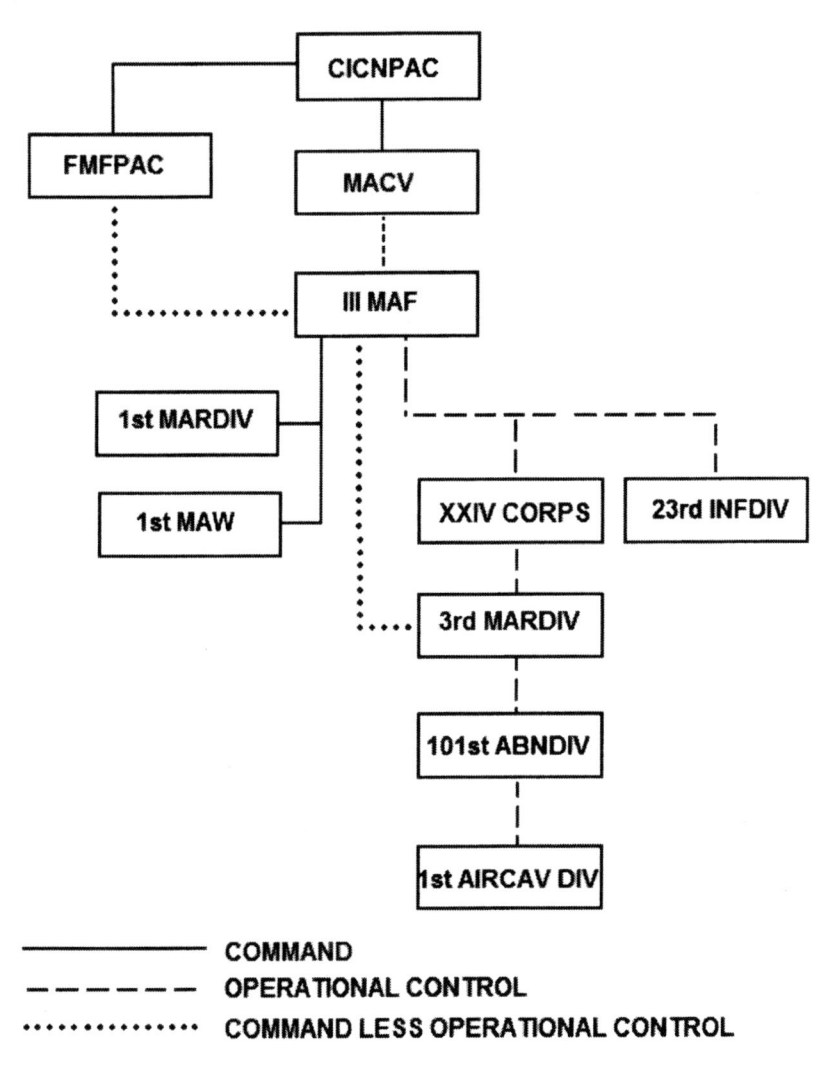

```
                    CICNPAC
                   /       \
           FMFPAC          MACV
              ⋮              ⋮
              ⋮............III MAF
                          /  ⋮  \
                 1st MARDIV ⋮   \
                         \  ⋮    \
                 1st MAW  \ ⋮     \
                           XXIV CORPS    23rd INFDIV
                                |
                           3rd MARDIV
                                |
                           101st ABNDIV
                                |
                           1st AIRCAV DIV
```

——————— COMMAND
— — — — — OPERATIONAL CONTROL
••••••••••••• COMMAND LESS OPERATIONAL CONTROL

President Lyndon B. Johnson announced a representative number of bombing halts in the spring of 1968 and opened preliminary negotiations with North Vietnamese representatives in Paris that May.

National elections held in November swept Richard M. Nixon into office as president of the United States. When the president-elect assumed office in January 1969, he immediately set in motion a strategy for winding down American troop involvement in Vietnam. His administration put forth a plan to advance the South Vietnamese government's ability to shoulder greater responsibilities for defense of their own country. As such, the term "Vietnamization" soon worked its way into the war vocabulary as part of the Nixon Doctrine.

At the Paris peace talks, the new administration sought to achieve a negotiated settlement and mutual withdrawal of all outside forces from South Vietnam, using the withdrawal pace of U.S. forces as a carrot.

Essentially, Vietnamization would be a gradual reduction and redeployment of American combat personnel in several phased stand-downs; hopefully with better trained and equipped Vietnamese units taking over their combat roles.

On 10 April, Secretary of Defense Melvin Laird was given directives to draw up a timetable for Vietnamizing the war. Complying with the directive, an initial plan was submitted to the Secretary of State by the Joint Chiefs of Staff in May.

Responding to requests for redeployment planning, the Marine Corps drew up a withdrawal schedule that was incorporated into a series of phased stand-downs, implemented under the Keystone series of operations. Operation Keystone Eagle was completed by August, redeploying 8,300 Marines of the 3rd Marine Division. Operation Keystone Cardinal, in two phases, pulled the rest of the division as well as significant assets of 1st Marine Air Wing (MAW) out of Vietnam before year's end. Corresponding units of other U.S. armed forces likewise ended their Vietnam service.

At the onset of 1970, III MAF in-country assets contained about 55,000 Marines, in contrast to an estimated 81,000 at the same period the previous year. By March, Keystone Blue Jay oversaw deployment of the 26th Marines, additional elements of the 1st MAW, and support units out of the war zone, leaving approximately 42,600 Marines awaiting further developments.

Redeploying within a dictated time frame created a very real necessity to alter management of the new alignment of Army/Marine units without sacrificing security or reducing pressure on the enemy. To this end, XXIV Corps changed roles with III MAF and now became the senior command for the five northernmost provinces under control of the U.S. Army.

I CORPS ORGANIZATIONAL CHART 1970

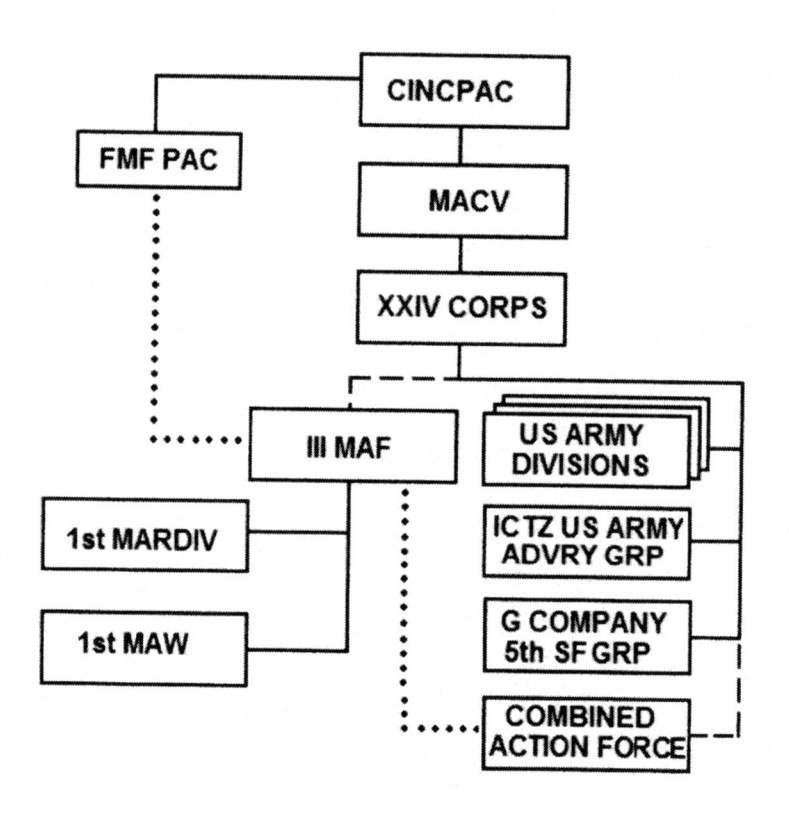

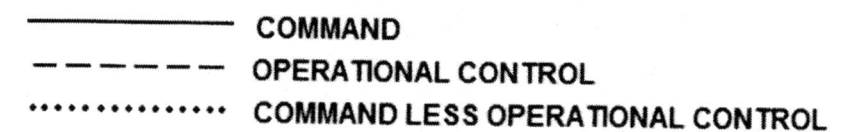

```
                        CINCPAC
        FMF PAC
                         MACV

                      XXIV CORPS

                                    US ARMY
              III MAF                DIVISIONS

                                   ICTZ US ARMY
    1st MARDIV                     ADVRY GRP

                                    G COMPANY
    1st MAW                         5th SF GRP

                                    COMBINED
                                   ACTION FORCE
```

———————— COMMAND
— — — — — OPERATIONAL CONTROL
•••••••••••••• COMMAND LESS OPERATIONAL CONTROL

III MAF, now subordinate to XXIV Corps, retained operational control of all Marine assets, keeping the air/ground team intact. The Combined Action Force (CAF), paired with Vietnamese local forces throughout the region, became the sole exception and functioned under operational control of XXIV Corps. As Vietnamization was the order of the day, XXIV Corps took over the III MAF headquarters in Da Nang, in part to maintain closer relations with ARVN I Corps commander, Lieutenant General Lam, who also headquartered at Da Nang.

Sub Unit One shifted its I Corps NGLO billet to XXIV Corps headquarters, being now in the position of coordinating all Naval gunfire missions in Vietnam.

Keystone Robin deployments beginning in July called for the withdrawal of 150,000 American troops in 50,000-man increments. Keystone Robin Alpha signaled the advent of the 1st Marine Division stand-down process, witnessing departure of the 7th Marines as well as representative air wing units and support personnel between July and October. Keystone Robin Bravo, completed by year's end, included only token Marine contributions to that segment. By the end of the first quarter 1971, the 5th Marines along with supporting units were withdrawn during the last phase, dubbed Keystone Robin Charlie, some only hours after disengaging from Operation Imperial Lake.

In February, the 3rd Marine Amphibious Brigade (MAB), incorporating 15,500 men consisting of the 1st Marines, as well as supporting artillery and air assets, came into existence to form a flexible rear guard. As the III MAF area of responsibility shrank in proportion to the exodus of its combat assets, it was a very prudent maneuver. By the end of June, these Marines would likewise depart.

Australia and South Korea were also making plans to pull their sizable troop contingents out of Vietnam.

North Vietnamese strategy gradually began to evolve away from matching U.S. troop buildup, shying away from seeking battlefield victories. Their own analysis of the crushing defeats suffered during Tet 1968 and post-Tet Offensives was a large dose of reality, raising grave doubts at the highest level about their ability to achieve military success.

In 1969, a new strategy emerged from Hanoi. Sensing the unpopularity of the war in the United States, a political victory, it was felt, would suit their purpose just as well. Now with American withdrawal on the table and actually witnessing U.S. forces leaving South Vietnam, a waiting game coupled with a protracted war of limited battlefield success looked to be a promising strategy.

One policy integrated into the overall approach was a war of attrition aimed at fueling antiwar elements in the United States for use as a negotiating lever at the Paris peace talks.

Emphasis on political maneuvering dominated North Vietnamese efforts to obtain what they couldn't achieve on the battlefield. Making the Americans pay in lives, equipment, money, and American public opinion, it was reasoned, could add more options in Paris. A shift to small unit actions designed to cause casualties and wreak havoc on Vietnamization efforts went into effect and continued well into 1971.

Politically motivated tactics increased in number and intensity during the first quarter of 1971. A concentrated effort was begun to go after the government of South Vietnam in the form of terrorism and propaganda. Kidnapping, murders, and general mayhem aimed at local government infrastructures, in a direct move to discourage Vietnamization, erupted in all four military regions. Even though U.S. presence at this point of time was a shadow of what it had been, no serious operations other than occasional shelling and ambushes seemed to be directed at American or ARVN troops. The war had actually gotten quieter, and it remained that way through most of the first quarter of 1972.

Much of the terminology of war also changed. I Corps, for instance, was now generally referred to as MR1, as were the other three regions, now widely spoken of as MR with their corresponding numerical suffix.

In 1966, Secretary of Defense Robert S. McNamara had proposed the naive idea to the Joint Chiefs of Staff of a wire barrier across northern South Vietnam backed by troops, which was not well received at any level in the chain of command. Through arrogance and his own sense of genius, he ignored opinions expressed by the military and used his high office to bring his useless idea to the forefront. Not being able to dissuade a "war manager" with absolutely no military experience, the project was negotiated by the military to a little better proposition but enjoyed absolutely no enthusiasm from any corner.

The final proposal called for a 600- to 1,000-yard-wide cleared trace to be carved out of the jungle just below the DMZ, extending west into the Laotian Panhandle. The trace would be augmented by electronic sensors, wire, lookout towers, and a Strong Point Obstruction System (combat bases).

When General Westmoreland directed III MAF to prepare the Marine portion of the concept, Lieutenant General Walt insisted a statement that III MAF disagreed with the barrier idea preface the proposal.

To make a long story short, the project was stopped in 1968 with the trace extending only between Gio Lihn and Con Thien, about 200 yards wide. The strong points designated with alphanumeric titles had by 1970 replaced the generic names of these locations. Con Thien was now referred to as Alpha 4, Gio Lihn as Alpha 2, and so on.

Sub Unit One also changed with the times, adapting to new command entities and structuring itself to continue its mission. Assets freed from supporting deployed American units were given other assignments, as emphasis shifted to providing more service to South Vietnamese Divisions. Pressure to downsize in keeping with Vietnamization directives did not affect the Sub Unit until late 1971, as ANGLICO was exempt from Keystone mandates.

USS New Jersey
(BB-62)
Iowa Class Battleship
Call Sign: Onrush

USS *New Jersey*'s third career began in April 1968, when she was recommissioned at Philadelphia Naval Shipyard, Captain J. Edward Snyder in command. Fitted with improved electronics and a helicopter landing pad, and with her 40mm battery removed, she was tailored for use as a heavy bombardment ship. Her sixteen-inch guns, it was expected, could reach targets in Vietnam inaccessible to smaller naval guns.

USS *New Jersey*, now the world's only active battleship, departed Philadelphia 16 May, calling at Norfolk and transiting the Panama Canal before arriving at her new homeport of Long Beach, 11 June. On 24 July, USS *New Jersey* received sixteen-inch shells and powder tanks from USS *Mount Katmai* (AE-16) by conventional highline transfer and helicopter lift.

Departing Long Beach 3 September, USS *New Jersey* touched at Pearl Harbor and Subic Bay before sailing 25 September for her first tour on the gunline in Vietnamese coastal waters. Near the 17th Parallel on 30 September, the dreadnaught fired her first shots in battle in over sixteen years. This first-ever fire mission for USS *New Jersey* in Vietnam was adjusted on target by an ANGLICO spotter flying a Marine TA-F4 from MAG-11. Firing against communist targets in and near the demilitarized zone, her big guns destroyed four gun positions and two supply areas. Ground data assessment confirmed one antiaircraft site silenced as well as one truck and four bunkers destroyed, causing eleven secondary explosions. She fired on targets north of the DMZ the following day, rescuing the spotter plane crew from the sea after their aircraft was forced down by antiaircraft fire.

For the next six months, the big ship settled into a steady pace of shore bombardment and fire support missions along the coast, interrupted only by brief visits to Subic Bay and replenishment operations at sea. In her first few months on the gunline, USS *New Jersey* directed nearly 10,000 rounds on communist targets; over 3,000 of these shells were sixteen-inch projectiles. She made a convincing argument of the effectiveness of naval gunfire capabilities.

Returning to Long Beach 5 May 1969, the ship took a well-earned rest. Through the summer months, USS *New Jersey*'s crew worked hard to make her ready for another deployment. Deficiencies discovered on the gunline were remedied, as all hands looked forward to yet another opportunity to prove the mighty warship's worth in combat. Reasons of economy were to dictate otherwise. On 22 August, the Secretary of Defense released a list of ships to be deactivated.

On 17 December 1969, USS *New Jersey*'s colors were hauled down, and she entered the inactive fleet at the Puget Sound Naval Shipyard.

We, who once found refuge under the protection of her guns, salute this valiant ship and her gallant crew.

THE BIG HURT

On Thursday, 16 May 1968, 57,200 tons of absolute bad ass slowly cleared the Delaware River at Cape May. The colossus made a slow wide turn to port, coming about to a southerly heading. Gradually accelerating to cruising speed, she began plowing a wide wake through the Atlantic; the "Black Dragon" was once again underway as the most formidable gun platform afloat. Having undergone a $21 million transformation at Philadelphia Naval Shipyard, the USS New Jersey (BB-62), now modernized with state-of-the-art electronics and a helicopter pad, was making steam for her new homeport of Long Beach. Her antiquated 40mm antiaircraft batteries had been removed. She now boasted a battery of twenty five-inch/38 newly refurbished dual-purpose guns in twin mounts; each gun having a nominal fire rate of 15 rounds per minute, providing her capability for delivering a devastating 300 rounds per minute on target.

For her Sunday punch, this behemoth was endowed with a main battery of nine sixteen-inch/50 Mark 7 guns, equipped with two types of ordnance. For shore bombardment, she employed high-capacity rounds weighing in at 1,900 pounds each that can reach targets up to 22.8 miles distant, traveling at 2,635 feet per second. Armor-piercing ammunition weighing 2,700 pounds, having a muzzle velocity of 2,300 feet per second and capable of achieving targets up to 21 miles away, provided a very lethal option. When she hit the waves during the later part of World War II, she and her sister battleships of the Iowa class had been the most sophisticated gun platforms to date. Her sixteen-inch/50 guns were an improvement over the sixteen-inch/47s of her predecessors, giving New Jersey's main batteries equal performance capabilities of the larger eighteen-inch guns of Yamato class battleships sent to sea by the Japanese Empire. She was pure gunship, and as nasty a customer as they come. Having been recommissioned a month earlier on 6 April, she was looking for trouble.

Before her arrival, B-52 Stratofortresses of the U.S. Air Force provided the most destructive power seen in Vietnam. Dispensing combined loads of 500- and 750-pound bombs, this delivery system would literally shake the earth for some distance from impact. As a comparison, thirty rounds of HC fired from *New Jersey's* massive sixteen-inch guns equaled an entire payload of one bomber.

Under the able command of Captain J. Edward Snyder, the "Big J" and her crew completed a training period in the waters off Southern California before setting sail for Vietnam.

Captain Snyder practiced a leadership style that captured the respect of all who served on the *New Jersey*. Frequently abandoning the officer's mess to interact with the crew at meal times like a common seaman, the New Jersey's skipper had a way of making all aboard feel like a valued member of a championship team. His genuine concern for the welfare of his crew is still remembered and cherished by all hands.

Officers from ANGLICO liaison teams attended a tactical planning conference on 16 July to identify targets and prepare a practical itinerary that would maximize her time on station. ANGLICO was given a major role in spotting and adjusting fire for the most powerful gunship afloat. In I Corps, gunfire spotters of the 1st and 3rd Marine Divisions would receive an equal opportunity to adjust her fires in the target-rich five northernmost provinces, but throughout the rest of the country she operated under the sole control of ANGLICO. One final conference was convened in Da Nang on 21 September to solidify planning in advance of *New Jersey's* imminent appearance in Vietnamese waters.

Arriving on the gunline 30,000 yards off the DMZ in the dark early-morning hours of Monday, 30 September, the newly arrived USS *New Jersey* turned her massive sixteen-inch gun turrets landward. For the first time in sixteen years, the Big J went to general quarters. Flying overhead in the back seat of a Marine TA-4F, ANGLICO spotter 1st Lieutenant Pat Morocco relayed target data to the big ship's fire control center. At 0630, the first sixteen-inch adjusting round sped toward an unsuspecting North Vietnamese supply area.

A fire-for-effect salvo of five sixteen-inch HC rounds covered the target in the biggest eruptions ever witnessed by the air crew, leaving craters gouged into a pockmarked terrain that was once a staging area. Moving through his list of preplanned targets, Morocco gave *New Jersey* gun crews a good morning workout.

For her first day on the gunline, USS *New Jersey* expended twenty-five sixteen-inch HC rounds and sixty-one rounds of five-inch ammunition on seven targets. The Big Hurt destroyed one antiaircraft site, four artillery batteries, and two supply areas, causing eleven secondary explosions and an unknown number of casualties, exerting devastating effect on all targets. Notice had just been served that life was going to be a little more hazardous for North Vietnamese soldiers.

After the morning fire missions, Lieutenant Morocco and pilot Captain John Clark came aboard by helicopter to discuss what they had witnessed with the embarked media. Captain Snyder greeted the pair as they stepped out of the aircraft, wanting anxiously to hear about the ship's real performance before they mesmerized the media with accounts of perfection. "It was a great entrance to the war," they assured him. "They know you're here and they wish like hell you weren't." Morocco and Clark were genuinely very enthusiastic in front of the press and spoke in positive terms of *New Jersey*'s accuracy and devastating effect of her fires.

During the evening of 7 October, surveillance aircraft reported a concentration of waterborne logistics craft moving south one mile offshore near the mouth of the Song Giang River. USS *New Jersey*, in company with USS *Towers* (DDG-9), closed on the convoy and took it under fire, destroying eleven before the surviving craft could beach.

Just north of the DMZ, communist engineers, seeking to improve logistic support for North Vietnamese operations against Marines positions just south of the divide, expanded natural cave formations at Vihn with an elaborate tunnel complex. Marine-directed artillery barrages and air sorties on a weekly basis were employed against this fortified natural feature, without much visible success. From 12 through 14 October, *New Jersey*'s main batteries sent salvo after salvo into the cave complex, causing several unprotected pieces of equipment to disappear, sealing one cave, and setting off several secondary explosions.

Further north of the DMZ about twelve miles from the mainland, artillery batteries on Hon Co Island had long been active and, on several occasions, came up on the losing end of artillery duels with ships of the gunline. Hon Matt Island on the windward side housed both artillery and early warning radar and was also known to fire on gunline ships when opportunity called. On 14 October, *New Jersey*, at direction of an airborne spotter from USS *America*, fired on Hon Matt, delivering a devastating salvo that literally blew a portion of that small landmass apart. Off and on over the next eight months, *New Jersey* returned from time to time to Hon Co and Hon Matt, leaving destruction and turmoil in her wake on each occasion.

ANGLICO spotters in II Corps received the next opportunity, as *New Jersey* steamed south to support operations in Phu Yen and Bihn Dihn Provinces, remaining on station until the 24th. Taking on a cave complex for the 173rd Airborne Brigade, she fired fifty rounds of sixteen-inch HC, then shifted support to the 9th ROK Army Division, expending fifty-seven more 1,900-pound payloads on four targets. Every mission received rave reviews by spotters and supported units.

On the 23rd, she was back in I Corps, escorted by HMAS *Perth*, supporting 1st Battalion of the 61st U.S. Army Mechanized Infantry Regiment, conducting operations just south of the Ben Hai River in Operation Rich. An NVA artillery site near the Mui Lay Peninsula just north of the demilitarized zone had the audacity to fire six rounds at the *New Jersey*, which never came closer than 500 meters. As soon as the salvo was complete, the NVA gunners moved quickly to get those guns away before the Big Hurt could level a broadside. From 28 October through 1 November, the Big Hurt remained on station, firing thirty-six missions into the eastern DMZ; taking out several artillery and antiaircraft sites; and pulverizing supply staging areas, troop concentrations, and three North Vietnamese base camps before traveling south to Da Nang in support of the 1st Marine Division.

She made one last trip to southern II Corps, firing in support of the Phan Thiet team and the 173rd Airborne Brigade, before retiring to Subic Bay for upkeep. Wherever she went, spirits were lifted and problem areas became a little less problematic.

By 23 November, the big ship was back in action near Chu Lai, firing in support of the U.S. Army's Americal Division and 2nd ARVN Division until the 26th. In three days, she destroyed or damaged 354 structures and bunkers, tore up 185 meters of trench line, caused eight secondary explosions, and took fifty-nine enemy soldiers out of the war.

New Jersey made one more trip to II Corps in December and finished out the year taking targets in and near the DMZ under fire of her devastating guns.

Shortly after the first of the year, the battleship once again departed for Subic Bay. Once upkeep was completed, she made wake for Yokosuka, Japan, for a goodwill visit then appeared back on gunline station 10 February, where she fired in support of the 1st Marine Division and 2nd ROKMC Brigade in the Da Nang Area of Operation (AO) for three days, then moved north.

Reacting to intelligence reports of a North Vietnamese rocket site being assembled in the DMZ about eleven miles northeast of Con Thien, the battleship under direction of a Marine ground spotter concentrated her sixteen-inch main battery on this ominous threat. Pouring on twenty-four rounds of high-capacity ordnance just prior to dusk, the Big Hurt put a big hurt on that battery, preempting NVA fire planning. Ground assessment damage reported twenty-five secondary explosions, causing seven fireballs climbing 500 feet into the night air.

Built to serve as a forward observation site, Outpost Oceanview sprang up amid sand dunes covering the northeast corner of Quang Tri Province. Located just inland from the surf line, Oceanview occupied a position less than 1,000 meters south of the DMZ and was as far north as any American was stationed during the entire war. One platoon of 1st AMTRAC Battalion Marines was assigned to defend the outpost housing a three-man naval gunfire spot team, for which Oceanview was established. The perimeter defense was augmented by two U.S. Army M-42 tracked vehicles armed with twin 40mm dusters, having a sustained rate of fire of 120 rounds per minute. Occasionally, one or two Marine tanks would be on station.

The only way in or out of Oceanview was Amtrac or helicopter. It was truly a very desolate and isolated location.

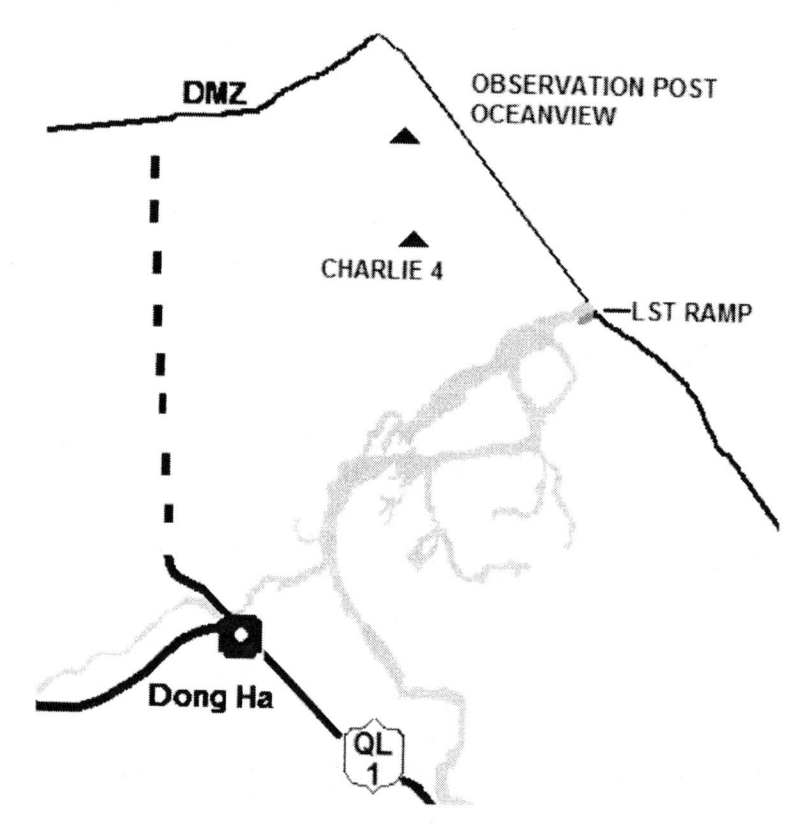

From the observation tower, spotters from 12th Marines, temporarily assigned to 1st ANGLICO, had a clear view of everything that moved as far north as the Ben Hai River some four miles up the beach. White sand interspersed with scrub brush dominated the topography for some two and a half miles west. So barren was the area that Hill 28 (twenty-eight feet high), less than 400 meters northwest, constituted the only recognizable terrain feature of the desert-like moonscape that was Oceanview.

In order to support combat operations, an LST ramp was built on the south bank of the Cua Viet River Basin in the spring of 1967. This ramp soon became the main logistic entrance port that funneled supplies down the Cua Viet River to the Marine combat base at Dong Ha and as far west as the artillery base at Camp Carroll. Cua Viet, prior to the arrival of the Naval Support Activity, was an unoccupied white sand beach. Once construction was finished, it became an active port complete with a small ship repair facility, warehouses, and a substantial fuel bladder farm. Here the supplies of war were offloaded then transported seven miles by LCU to Dong Ha.

The problem was Cua Viet was only six miles south of the DMZ and well within range of North Vietnamese gunners; hence the purpose of Oceanview. Spotters at that post had one function and only one function: Keep those NVA guns silent by generously pounding them with naval gunfire.

Lacking sufficient manpower to permanently station a fire control team at the observation post, several spotters from the 12th Marines were assigned to ANGLICO on a Temporary Assignment of Duty basis. As Sub Unit One had direct communication with ARVN command structures, it was in unique position of being able to acquire immediate call for fire clearances for any supporting arms mission anywhere in-country. Inasmuch as instantaneous reaction time was needed to address counter battery measures to thwart NVA attempts to disrupt the supply chain, volunteers from 12th Marine artillery batteries reported to ANGLICO I Corps headquarters for orientation and training.

From its inception, the defenders on a weekly basis were sent scurrying for cover to escape artillery, mortar, and rocket fire directed at the outpost, while the spot team scanned the landscape, trying to get a fix on firing locations and calling in counter battery coordinates. On several occasions, this small enclave on the South China Sea fended off probes on its perimeter from enemy troops looking for weak points. Having an unobstructed view all the way to the Ben Hai River and for some two and a half miles east, Oceanview presented a challenge to any would-be infiltrators. Daily patrols around the perimeter were mounted to detect enemy activity and scan nearby terrain for observation sites. However, at some point in mid- or late February, North Vietnamese work parties under cover of darkness dug several prepared fighting holes north of Oceanview and a series of L-shaped trenches less than 200 meters south. On 23 February 1969, the NVA made a concerted attempt to overrun and destroy that little thorn in their side.

At 2330 on 22 February, the AN/PPS-5 personnel radar equipment operator on base detected a group of ten to fifteen enemy troops moving east from the northwest toward Oceanview. A second sighting of four to six personnel was detected seconds later. Both tanks and M42s, joined by 12th Marine 105mm howitzers, took the dune-hopping NVA under fire, with unobserved results. One hour later, sappers under cover of small arms fire rushed the single-strand barbed wire perimeter with satchel charges and grenades. Springing to action, base defense met the initial attack with small arms and machine gun fire, holding the assault outside the wire. Every weapon within the small perimeter hammered out a rude greeting while spotter Lance Corporal Roger H. Clouse called for fire support. Artillery and mortar batteries from Fire Support Base (FSB) Charlie 4 and Camp Kistler responded within seconds, throwing up a curtain of steel around the beleaguered observation post.

By 0100, it became all too evident they were under attack by a much larger force than previously estimated. Pressing the defenders hard, NVA troops briefly penetrated the wire before being driven back by blistering Marine small arms fire at point-blank range, but not before suffering two killed and two wounded. In desperate need of more fire support, Lance Corporal Clouse came online with "Onrush" (*New Jersey*'s call sign). Pulling off a mission in progress, she responded with fire from two of her twin five-inch/38 mounts. The Big Hurt poured it on. Still in need of more firepower, two more mounts were thrown in action, giving Oceanview defenders benefit of eight guns now ringing the perimeter at danger close range. Also steaming nearby, the U.S. Coast Guard Cutter *Owasco* (WHEC-39) cranked up her five-inch 38s in support of twenty desperate Marines.

Lance Corporal Clouse was now controlling two Marine artillery batteries, four gun mounts from *New Jersey*, and two mounts from *Owasco*. Keeping a roster in his head as to who was firing where, Clouse skillfully adjusted fire where needed, keeping the NVA at bay all night. It is not possible to overstate the concentration and presence of mind required to control supporting fires that close from four different locations and eight separate batteries while in close contact with a numerically superior force, all the while dodging bullets and explosions.

As the sun peeked over the horizon, NVA forces disengaged from Oceanview at 0600 without achieving anything except taking casualties. Not once that entire night, while switching adjustments from one battery to another, did Clouse allow one round to fall within the outpost. More than 4,000 high-explosive shells fell around Oceanview over the course of six hours, including 1,710 rounds from USS *New Jersey*. Although enemy troops were observed to be dragging several bodies away from the battlefield, a body count was not possible, but with that much supporting fire, it's a safe bet there were more dead than alive.

New Jersey remained on station off the DMZ through 9 March, firing a variety of missions in support of the 3rd Marine Division, then set course for southern I Corps to assist the 2nd ARVN Division, and departed Vietnamese waters for her last scheduled upkeep at Subic Bay on 13 March, in preparation for the final leg of her first deployment.

On 22 March, *New Jersey* arrived back in Vietnam off the coast of II Corps, firing in support under direction of spotters from the Phan Thiet team, and continued steaming up and down the shoreline of Military Region 2 over the next seven days, leaving a path of destruction and carnage in her wake. Returning to the DMZ, where the great ship had fired her first mission of the war on the 28th, *New Jersey* in her curtain call once more made life less livable for communist activities in the demilitarized zone.

Firing her last mission on 31 March, she departed for homeport of Long Beach on 1 April 1969. The Big Hurt broke a lot of hearts as she cleared the combat zone. She fired over 10,000 rounds on a variety of targets including over 3,000 shells from her main sixteen-inch/50 caliber gun battery. During her time on station, the USS *New Jersey* was credited with saving the lives of an estimated 100 allied troops per month.

At arrival, USS *New Jersey* settled into a portside routine of upkeep and maintenance, preparing for her scheduled return to the gunline, tentatively set for 5 September. In a surprise announcement by the Department of Defense on 21 August, it was disclosed, much to the disbelief of her crew and thorough disgust of gunfire spotters, the USS *New Jersey* would be deactivated, along with several other ships, citing cost-cutting initiatives. In truth, she was sacrificed by the Nixon administration in yet one more of those inexplicably fathomless maneuvers that for political considerations gave away American tactical advantages. For a perceived show of good faith to clear away obstacles for the Paris peace talks, the lives of more grunts were put at risk. It seems the North Vietnamese considered *New Jersey* an impediment to negotiations. (It was too damaging to their war effort, hindering their ability to kill Americans, thus stagnating their strategy to fuel antiwar sentiments in this country.)

USS White River
(LSMR-536)
Landing Ship Medium Rocket

A total of 558 Landing Ship Medium (LSM) and Landing Ship Medium Rocket (LSMRs) were built during World War II. Because of their shallow drafts, particularly in IV Corps, where a shallow beach gradient kept deeper draft ships out of bombardment range, these ships found plenty of work. Ten twin continuous-loading five-inch spin-stabilized rocket launchers comprised the main armament, capable of delivering hundreds of rounds per minute on target. Additionally, USS *White River's* firepower was augmented by four 4.2-inch mortars, one single mount five-inch/38, two twin 40mm gun mounts, and four 20mm gun mounts. She truly was a formidable Inshore Fire Support Ship.

USS *White River* arrived off the I Corps tactical zone on 25 May 1966, immediately beginning gunfire support missions for Operation Mobile. Two days later, she concluded her support of Mobile and shifted support for the 2nd ARVN Division operating near Quang Ngai. She continued supporting that unit intermittently for the next two months, interrupting this duty only to provide gunfire and rockets for Operations Oakland, Deckhouse III, and Franklin.

Returning to Vietnamese coastal waters at the end of September 1966, USS *White River* continued gunfire support for troops ashore. During the next two months, she answered calls for fire in the northern portion of II Corps tactical zone. On 30 November, she terminated her second tour of duty in Vietnamese waters and headed to Yokosuka, where she spent the remainder of the year in upkeep.

She returned to the coast of I Corps tactical zone on 9 February 1967, immediately delivering gunfire for Marines ashore engaged in Operation Desoto. Concluding that assignment on 11 February, USS *White River* refueled at Da Nang and got underway to support Operation Deckhouse VI, an amphibious operation conducted by the Special Landing Force near Sa Huyen in the southern reaches of the I Corps zone. She finished her part in Desoto-Deckhouse VI operations on 23 February. USS *White River* returned to the Vietnam coast on 13 March, resuming shore bombardment duties in support of Operation Beacon Hill, a combined helicopter, waterborne-amphibious assault conducted near Dong Ha. On 23 March, released from Operation Beacon Hill, she proceeded to III Corps tactical zone, providing gunfire support for operations near the Rung Sat Special Zone (RSSZ).

Relieved by USS *Carronade* (IFS-1) on 2 April 1967, USS *White River* returned to Yokosuka on 17 April. After completing necessary repairs, she headed back to Vietnam on 29 May. The warship arrived back at I Corps tactical zone on 11 June, conducting shore bombardments until reassigned to II Corps until 21 July, when she departed Vietnamese waters to return to Subic Bay for upkeep. USS *White River* returned to the Vietnamese coast at the beginning of August, remaining on the gunline until 23 August. She began her last tour of 1967 off the Vietnamese coast on 31 October, remaining on the gunline until 27 December.

During 1968, USS *White River* continued operating out of her homeport, Yokosuka, and made four deployments to Vietnamese waters, rendering gunfire support for U.S. and ARVN troops. During January, *White River* relieved USS *Clarion River* (LSMR-409), providing gunfire support for South Korean troops during search and destroy Operation Meng Ho Kuho north of Qui Nhon (16-24 January and 27-29 January). Early the following month, the ship supported the 2nd ARVN Division in the same region (2-3 February). The gunboat began a working relationship with Korean units as she continued support of their operations through most of April and May. Subsequently returning to the gunline, USS *White River*, with an assist from an ANGLICO airborne spotter, on 15 July pounded suspected Viet Cong storage areas, a series of caves about ten miles southeast of Qui Nhon Bay, with over 1,000 spin-stabilized projectiles. Her fire set off more than forty-seven secondary explosions and nearly a dozen fires. Before she would return to Vietnamese waters, the ship was reclassified as an Inshore Fire Support Ship, LFR-536, on 14 August 1968. The ship then operated off IV Corps in December, supporting the 21st ARVN Division on four occasions (1-5 December, 12-14 December, 21-23 December, and 26-28 December) and Korean Marine Operation Victory Dragon IX on 28-29 December.

USS *White River* spent four days on the gunline in late January 1969, stationed off I Corps and IV Corps areas, supporting the 1st Battalion, 2nd ARVN Regiment. Responding to a call for gunfire support after the ARVN troops suffered fifteen killed while assaulting an enemy stronghold on 27 January, USS *White River* fired on communist positions eleven miles south of the Batangan Peninsula, Quang Ngai Province. A two-hour bombardment killed two Viet Cong, wounded one, leveled or damaged twenty-four structures, and started five secondary fires. The next day (28 January), the Inshore Fire Support Ship bombarded an enemy staging area a half mile from the previous day's target, killing fifteen VC and destroying fifty-four structures, eleven of which were of heavy masonry construction (six had been in use to store petroleum, oil, and lubricant products). Additionally, USS *White River*'s fire damaged twenty-one other structures and destroyed nine bunkers and thirty-five meters of trail, triggering five secondary explosions and starting forty-five secondary fires. "Still not content to rest on her laurels," a Pacific Fleet chronicler wrote later, "*White River* directed her five-inch spin-stabilized rockets at enemy positions in the same area on the 29th and silenced an antiaircraft site," killing or wounding eleven VC.

On 11 February 1969, a "multiple force operation" in the southern part of the Ca Mau Peninsula involved the deployment of air, ground, and sea forces, including ten Swift boats (PCFs). After a trio of PCFs conducted a psychological warfare operation on the Trum Gong River, four PCFs entered the Nang, only to encounter heavy communist automatic weapon and B-40 rocket fire that scored direct hits on two PCFs (one losing an engine and the other being badly damaged), wounding one sailor. Air Force fixed wing strikes destroyed some thirty bunkers and 200 meters of trench line. USS *White River* joined in the fray, unleashing a bombardment on enemy positions, exerting devastating effect of target.

During 1-5 May 1969, USS *White River* supported the 2nd ARVN Division, 2nd Republic of Korea Marine Brigade, and U.S. forces in Operating Daring Rebel, killing an estimated four VC, destroying twelve watercraft and thirty-five structures, damaging twenty-seven bunkers, triggering ten secondary explosions, and igniting thirteen secondary fires. Additionally, the Inshore Fire Support Ship set fire to 500 meters of tree line, damaging three rice storage bins. USS *White River*'s work prompted a response: The ship observed six-foot surface bursts, 800 to 1,000 yards short of the ship, from between eight and ten shells of unknown size being fired at her on the evening of 3 May.

On 16 June 1969, while operating in support of the 2nd ARVN Division eight miles northeast of Quang Ngai, she bombarded a Viet Cong assembly area, flushing out a squad of VC, who soon began setting up weapons to return fire. USS *White River* observed a twenty-foot surface burst some 200 yards off the bow, and numerous rounds of light weapons fire, all missing their mark. With coaching from an ANGLICO airborne spotter, the Inshore Fire Support Ship directed a ten-minute barrage of .30 and .50-caliber, 40mm, and rocket fire onto the enemy, who broke and took cover, leaving eleven of their number dead. USS *White River* continued to pound the area until inclement weather forced the spotter to head for home. In addition to eleven enemy corpses counted, the ship destroyed thirteen structures and ten bunkers, damaging twenty-one other structures triggered three secondary explosions, and started nine secondary fires. USS *White River continued* her bombardment the next day (17 June) and accounted for another two VC dead.

USS *White River* supported the 1st Australian Task Force in Phuoc Tuy Province, in the III Corps Zone, during the period 22-27 October 1969, unleashing a barrage of five-inch spin-stabilized rockets on twenty-eight enemy targets. Communist base camps, storage areas, bunkers, infiltration routes, and sampans all came under the ship's devastating fire; her "pinpoint accuracy" killed eighteen VC, wounded seventeen, destroyed some ninety-seven structures and bunkers, and damaged thirty-five; in addition, she destroyed two weapons sites and triggered thirteen secondary explosions. After supporting the 7th ARVN Division (2-5 November, 7 November) and the 9th ARVN Division (6 November) in the IV Corps Zone, USS *White*

River returned to III Corps again, working with the 1st Australian Task Force (8 November). "Along with deleteriously affecting enemy morale," one observer wrote, the Inshore Fire Support Ship killed fifteen communist troops, wounded seventeen, and destroyed four caves, forty-one bunkers, and forty-six structures. In addition, observers counted eighteen secondary fires and twelve explosions, and numbered damaged caves, bunkers, and structures among the ship's destructive handiwork.

USS *White River* returned to Vietnamese waters in January 1970. On 30-31 January, the ship operated off the Ca Mau Peninsula, in IV Corps, supporting the 21st ARVN Division, then lent her powerful ordnance to the same unit on three occasions the following month (1-4 February, 10-19 February, and 22-25 February). Additionally, she provided gunfire support for Sea Float operations in the same region (21 February). As she neared the end of her active service life, USS *White River* went out with style. On 17 March, accompanied by river patrol craft with an umbrella of air support, she "penetrated deep into the Rung Sat Special Zone, southeast of Saigon, in support of Operation Chuong Duong 11-70," steaming up the Long Tau River some eighteen miles to bombard suspected Viet Cong positions. Over a five-hour period, USS *White River* expended 2,526 spin-stabilized projectiles in the "deepest penetration inland of an NGFS [Naval Gunfire Support Ship] to date." Although the thick foliage canopy did not permit ready damage assessment, observers noted ten secondary fires burning upon the conclusion of the ship's bombardment. "This mission," a Commander in Chief, Pacific Fleet, historian noted, "also marked the final appearance of the LFR in active service." As the same chronicler noted, "A dramatic rise [for March 1970] in the expenditure of spin-stabilized rockets (16,083 in March) reflected the final efforts of USS *Clarion River* and USS *White River* as these intensely proud little ships concluded their last cruise before being stricken from the Naval Register."

Ultimately deemed "unfit for further Naval service" on 8 May 1970, USS *White River* was decommissioned at Yokosuka on 22 May 1970. Her name was stricken from the Naval Vessel Register that same day (22 May 1970), and she was sold in November 1970 to the Nissho-Iwai American Corp. of New York City for scrapping.

For her services in Vietnam, the USS *White River* earned honors in proportion to her valor: Combat Action Ribbon, three Navy Unit

Commendations, Meritorious Unit Commendation, RVN Gallantry Cross with Palm, RVN Civil Action Medal, First Class, with Palm, RVN Campaign Medal with 60's device, and the Vietnam Service Medal with ten Battle Stars.

We, who once found refuge under the protection of her guns, salute this valiant ship and her gallant crew.

MORE OF THE SAME

Since late 1968, the Blue Dragon Brigade kept busy with its Victory Dragon series of operations in and around their TAOR. Victory Dragon V, by the end of November, claimed no more than a disappointing twenty VC/NVA killed in action but did achieve great results for ANGLICO. This operation was the most heavily supported Sub Unit One action for the last quarter of the year. Sitting off the coast, three cruisers—USS *Providence* (CLG-6), USS *Galveston* (CLG-3), and USS *Canberra* (CAG-2)—along with destroyers USS *Towers* (DDG-9) and USS *O'Brien* (DD-752) and the rocket ship USS *Clarion River* (LSMR-409) combined as the naval gunfire arm of the operation for the best possible prep and support in the large sweep and clear activity. Controlled by ANGLICO spotters, they tallied up 785 structures and bunkers destroyed or damaged, eleven sampans destroyed, and triggered an incredible forty-eight secondary explosions.

Commencing on 1 December, Victory Dragon VI terminated on 1 January 1969, followed by Victory Dragon VII, both of which benefited from around-the-clock naval gunfire and close air support. When Victory Dragon VII came to an end on 2 February, Korean forces and ANGLICO combined for 301 VC/NVA KIAs and 22 enemy prisoners taken. Collective efforts of the ever-present gunline ships with assistance from TAC Air accounted for 300 enemy bunkers and structures destroyed or damaged and nineteen more secondary explosions.

Operation Victory Dragon VIII launched on 2 February, continuing through the end of the month, and ran up a confirmed body count of 231 enemy soldiers. In conjunction with this operation, the brigade conducted several company-size search and clear sweeps near the Suoi Co Ca River and Big Horseshoe area in their TAOR.

Slugging it out in the Que Son Mountains through winter and into spring, the ROKs launched Victory Dragon X on 1 April. The ROKMC Detachment stayed busy, providing heavy naval gunfire and TAC Air support as well as coordinating a helicopter assault to inaugurate the opening maneuver. When the dust finally settled, the ROKs claimed 258 more KIAs and 25 prisoners of war.

As Ba Lang An had been a major headache for the ROKs in Quang Ngai Province, so too had Go Noi Island become a festering boil on their ass at Hoi An. Like that problematic neighborhood farther south, the communists over many years cultivated a deep-rooted political infrastructure among the local population who, in turn, embraced and supported local Viet Cong units and participated in military operations. Intelligence reports traced to Tet 1968 indicate some suspicion that the Go Noi or someplace in close proximity served as headquarters for communist operations in Quang Nam Province.

Although not actually separated from the mainland as are most islands, this piece of turf derived its name because the area was not easily accessible most of the year except by watercraft. Centered in the junction of several rivers fed by yet more rivers and streams, it provided a safe haven for enemy troops, who used the favorable topography as a base of operations. The Que Sons just west of the district offered quick access to numerous mountain valleys where a man, or a division for that matter, could get lost in a hurry.

U.S. Marines, conducting operations on the Go Noi, deemed the area a real meat grinder. In June 1967, Operation Arizona conducted by 3rd Battalion, 7th Marines dubbed the land north of the Go Noi between the Song Tho Bon and Song Vu Gia and surrounding environment "Dodge City," as firefights and difficult tactical situations were not that difficult to come by, while the surrounding terrain was referred to as "the Arizona Territory." The Arizona occupying prime real estate between Da Nang and Hoi An demanded much attention. Control of this area had long been recognized as a necessity to maintain security for military installations and several I Corps command headquarters established in the Da Nang Vital Area, less than fifteen miles northeast.

Through the first quarter of 1968, the lion's share of III MAF's energy and assets were consumed in Tet-related actions and securing a lopsided victory at Khe Sanh. Once the dust settled, aggressive offensive operations resumed. Going after elements of the 2nd NVA

Division, now filtering back into southern Quang Nam Province, brought all three organic battalions of the 7th Marines back to the Arizona in Operation Allen Brook. From May through August 1968, the 7th Marines occupied center stage, slugging it out with a very aggressive enemy who had designs on re-establishing a presence in the area. A very grueling campaign yielded 1,017 enemy killed in action but not without a price. Casualties in that hard-fought summer offensive came in at 240 Marine deaths.

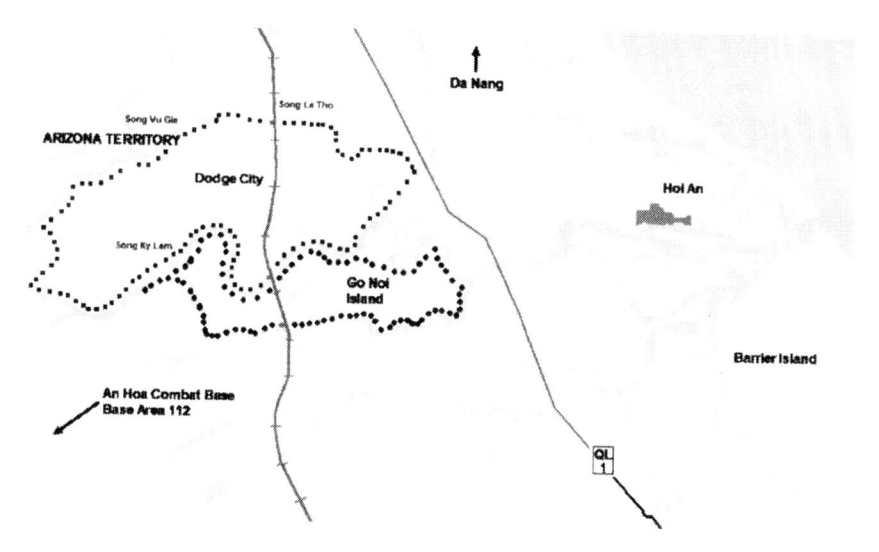

In the largest Marine air assault of the war, Operation Meade River was launched in November, utilizing almost every helicopter in the 1st Marine Air Wing's inventory. No less than six battalions descended on the Arizona, cordoning off the three- by five-mile area known to Marines as Dodge City, occupying land north of the Song Thu Bon/Song Ky Lam Rivers. Pushing on to their objectives, the Marines attacked a fortified position in a fierce battle that culminated in 130 enemy troops killed while attempting to flee north across the Song La Tho. In all, the Marines accounted for 1,023 enemy dead and 123 prisoners taken. One hundred eight Marines was the pricetag for Meade River.

Before Meade River ended, Operations Valiant Hunt and Taylor Common kicked into gear, sending all three battalions of the 3rd Marines, 5th Marines, two battalions of the 26th Marines, and 2nd Battalion 7th Marines (not all at the same time) swarming over the Arizona, Base Area 112, and An Hoa, southeast of Hoi An. The operation terminated in March 1969, stacking up a body count of 1,398 NVA while Marines suffered another 151 fatalities.

An oft-used strategy of communist forces to thwart complete defeat was to withdraw from an area when pressed, then infiltrate back to that area and re-establish a presence once the threat no longer existed. To this end, operations in the Arizona/Go Noi area were generally complemented by other phased-in operations, cutting off anticipated routes of withdrawal. Base Area 112, southwest of the target area, as well as Que Son Valley locations west became objects of interdiction by blocking forces or artillery/naval gunfire pursuit. In the larger picture, III MAF intelligence analysis identified elements of twenty-one enemy battalions operating in Quang Nam Province.

Like a pack of pit bulls, III MAF sent battalion after battalion into the Arizona meat grinder and Go Noi, relentlessly hounding battle-weary defenders, allowing them not one minute of peace. Every attack on this infested hell-hole came from a different direction, each with its own distinct maneuver scheme. For those who harbor notions that Vietnam lacked cohesive American strategy on the battlefield, one only need research combat operations in southern Quang Nam Province from May 1967 through December 1969. In addition to the operations chronicled here, smaller sorties of Marines in Operations Swift Play (July 1968), Sussex Bay (August-September 1968), Linn River (January-February (1969), Eagle Pursuit I and II ((March 1969), and Gallant Leader and Idaho Canyon (July-September 1969) all contributed to a tenacious struggle for denying access of the Arizona and adjacent terrain to enemy military designs.

The Blue Dragon Brigade also had its fill of the Arizona, as a good portion of the contentious turf overlapped into ROK territory. The eastern portion of Go Noi was less than four miles west of Hoi An and represented a continuous item on planning meeting agendas.

Enemy forces encountered in the Arizona were not deficient in a dogged determination of their own. Since 1967, NVA/VC forces suffered over 12,000 casualties in a test of wills to determine who owned the Arizona. In spite of escalating casualties in dozens of stinging defeats, the NVA showed no sign of backing off meeting Marine advances with determined resolve, fighting like hell for every inch. Combat in this cesspool on the Song La Tho was no picnic for the Marines either. Hardly a man in the 1st Marine Division was without some experience in the Arizona, and none of it was very pleasant.

Operation Pipestone Canyon launched on 26 May, with Go Noi getting the main focus of attention. Aside from routing an estimated six to nine enemy battalions out of the Go Noi and Dodge City, Pipestone Canyon was to be a major land-clearing project involving maneuver battalions of the 1st Marine Division, U.S. Army 23rd (Americal) Division, 2nd ROK Marine Brigade, and the 51st ARNV Regiment. An additional objective centered on opening Route 4 from Dai Loc to Dien Ban, running through Dodge City. Pipestone Canyon would continue through November, with extension operations phased in and out of various locations within the general objective area.

In parcels of 250 acres, land was to be cleared to a depth of six inches so as to render it useless for military designs and once and for all expel NVA/VC forces from the Go Noi. Other tag-on assaults complemented Pipestone Canyon in a "go for it all" effort to secure the Go Noi completely, putting a halt to all military activity. Over many years of communist occupation, the island had become a fortified oasis of bunkers supplemented with caves and extensive tunnels.

Arrayed against the allied incursion were three battalions of the NVA 36th Regiment, remnants of the disbanded 38th Regiment (April 1968), T-89th Sapper Battalion, D-3 Sapper Battalion, T-3 Sapper Battalion, and R20th Battalion; all inclusive of an estimated 2,500 troops poised to defend Go Noi and Dodge City.

On schedule, Marines of 1/26 launched east from Hill 37 into Dodge City. On their right flank further south, 3/5 stepped off in the western Go Noi, pushing east. During the first days, both battalions encountered booby traps and mines, taking several casualties as enemy fighters fled before the advancing Marines. As they neared the Go Noi, resistance stiffened, with enemy troops engaging the oncoming Marines with delaying and diversionary tactics. On 30 May, both battalions reached the railroad berm and began digging in to blocking positions.

North of Dodge City, the 1st and 2nd Battalions of the 1st Marines, ARVN 37th Ranger Battalion, and the 1st and 4th Battalions of the 51st ARVN Regiment crossed the Song La Tho River abreast on the 31st, entering Dodge City terrain. In advance of the attacking formation, naval gunfire and artillery raked the area in a bid to prematurely detonate expected surprise firing devices in the path of the five-battalion assault.

From southeast, Blue Dragons of the 1st and 2nd Battalions maneuvered to set up blocking positions, guarding southern escape routes along the Song Chien Son River.

Finding extensive bunker and tunnel complexes, the pace of advance from the north slowed as Marines and ARVN painstakingly searched and probed everything in their path. Frequent counter-sweeps and searches were conducted on all fronts to protect the rear, while artillery and naval gunfire continued raining on areas further downfield. On 2 June, ARVN rangers on the right flank, as well as elements of the 26th Marines at blocking points, turned fleeing NVA units away from western escape routes, forcing them to cross the Song Ky Lam onto Go Noi. The cordon was now complete.

By 5 June, elements of the 1st Marines reached the Song Ky Lam, which separates Dodge City from the Go Noi. Over the next three days, the remaining attacking forces closed on the river, then executed a counter-sweep in the direction they arrived from. Tactical air sorties dove on the eastern Go Noi, delivering 1,000- and 2,000-pound payloads, expending over 750,000 pounds of ordnance on suspected strong points.

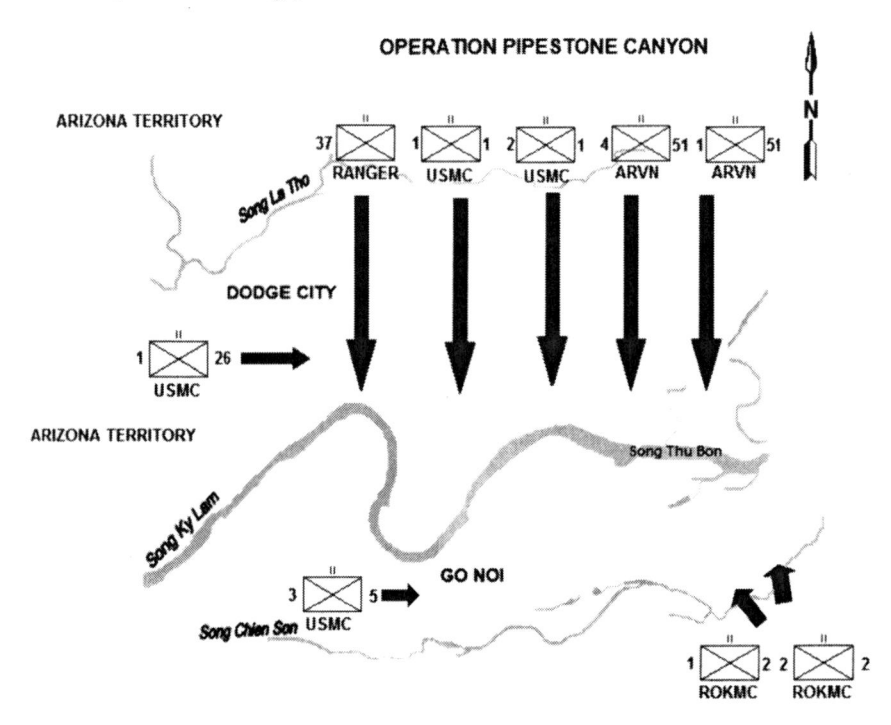

As the ROKs just south of the island had encountered nothing as of yet, it became evident that the NVA were not trying to escape south across the Song Chien Son, which indicated a possibility that there may be a battle looming ahead as the cordon neared completion.

On 10 June, TAC Air was back on station early in the morning, bombing and strafing two landing zones on the eastern Go Noi, then laying down a thick fog of smoke, dividing the island. Immediately after the attack craft cleared air space, a flight of twenty-two CH-46s began approach to the LZs. Assault troops consisting of 1st Battalion 1st Marines and 1st Battalion 2nd ROKMC Brigade debarked, formed up, and started sweeping north.

Koreans on the east flank encountered several extensive bunker and tunnel complexes one day into the push and requested permission to pull off assault to search the area, which was saturated with fortified positions.

Over the next ten days, the ROKs uncovered food and weapons caches and got down to the difficult business of rooting out communist troops guarding the supplies. For several days during the clearing operation, ANGLICO TACP teams were controlling up to ten TAC Air sorties a day, softening up hard targets for Korean infantry assaults.

Trapped between maneuvering elements and blocking forces, enemy troops broke into smaller groups, trying to evade detection, in an attempted escape south. A few did elude their pursuers but many were killed or captured as the noose tightened.

As June progressed, the 1st Battalion ROKMC began digging into the Go Noi, establishing two company-size base camps on the eastern portion of the island and initiating company-size sweeps going forth from the new outposts.

Surprise firing devices continued to plague the allied battalions fanning out over the area of operation, while the enemy avoided all possible contact. This operation witnessed what was possibly the largest concentration of mines and booby traps encountered at any time during the war. Almost on a daily basis, several Marines were killed or injured by these devices. G Company, 2nd Battalion 1st Marines, for instance; out of seventy casualties, fifty-nine were caused by surprise firing devices, and it was beginning to take its toll on troop morale.

Lieutenant Colonel Wendell P. Morganthaler, commanding officer of 1st Battalion 1st Marines, whose men suffered many casualties due to mines and booby traps, took a dim view of the Korean base camps. The colonel noted later that "the only way to avoid surprise firing devices was to avoid the area, which meant avoiding the mission. We did not stay inside our compounds like the Korean Marines to avoid casualties."

By mid-June, land clearing personnel and equipment supplied by the 7th and 9th Marine Engineering Battalions and the Army's 678th Land Clearing Company started work on reducing Go Noi, removing the tall elephant grass and bamboo thickets from the eastern portion of the island, also razing bunker complexes and collapsing tunnel works generously decorating the landscape. When work was completed on 20 July, over 8,000 acres of the former communist haven were flattened and denuded of cover. When Pipestone Canyon terminated, the Marines tallied 734 enemy dead and 55 prisoners taken, at a cost of 57 Marines killed in action and 394 seriously wounded, most by booby trap.

Major General Ormond R. Simpson, commanding officer of the 1st Marine Division, was determined that the Go Noi be permanently occupied to deny reintroduction of communist political infrastructures and military presence. To this end, with the help of engineers already in place, a combat base was constructed in eastern Go Noi and occupied by 3rd Battalion, 51st ARVN Regiment, and a second was built for 1st Battalion 2nd ROKMC Brigade. The U.S. Marines then crossed back into Dodge City, attending to the remnants of scattered NVA units.

Lieutenant Colonel Thomas H. Simpson replaced Lieutenant Colonel Frederick K. Purdum as commanding officer of Sub Unit One on 4 August, taking charge of 225 Marines and sailors. The tempo of activity remained constant for the new commander through the last quarter of the year.

With Korean participation on the Go Noi finished, final preparations for Operation Defiant Stand were completed in August. Korean battalions in a planned maneuver withdrew from Pipestone Canyon for participation in their first amphibious landing since the Korean War.

Earlier in 1969, Operations Daring Rebel (5-19 May) and Bolt Pursuit (25 June-6 July) conducted by the U.S. Marine Special Landing Force (SLF) hit Barrier Island in battalion strength. Aiming to disrupt a long-established Viet Cong infrastructure, the combined operations netted a disappointing total of 180 communist KIA. Seeking to avoid contact, the elusive enemy remained in hiding or withdrew from the area of operation. Employing occasional hit-and-run or diversionary tactics on each occurrence, local forces had no stomach for facing the Marines. Each time the Special Landing Force departed the island, communist units would return, re-establish control, and continue as though nothing happened.

Like the Go Noi, Barrier Island was not actually a separate land mass. Being cut off from the mainland by the Truong Giang River, it remained largely inaccessible to foot traffic except for the bridge at Route 534. Previous census estimates pegged the population at 20,000 inhabitants, but by September 1969, between 4,000 and 8,000 residents were all that was left of a once-thriving coastal community. Intelligence briefings identified elements of the Q-80th and V-25th Viet Cong Battalions as being active on the island, supported by an additional 295 unattached local guerillas.

On 5 September, Operation Defiant Stand was born, with two companies of 3rd Battalion, 2nd Republic of Korea Marine Brigade crossing the Song Thu Bon, while a third on the wings of HMM-265 was transported to positions west of the Truong Giang. To Viet Cong observers, it appeared to have the trappings of a search and destroy operation that posed little threat to Barrier Island. Conducting a cordon and search operation but finding only one VC killed by air, 3rd Battalion detained ten VC suspects and advanced rapidly toward their assigned blocking positions, settling into place on 11 September. The Koreans dubbed their part in these proceedings as Operation Victory Dragon XV.

During the dark morning hours of 7 September, ships of the Amphibious Ready Group once more appeared off the coast of Barrier Island with 1st Battalion 26th Marines, comprising Special Landing Force Alpha. Defiant Stand was destined to be the last Special Landing Force operation of the war. After waiting out poor weather, which threatened to cancel the operation, two companies of 1/26 aboard CH-46 helicopters from HMM-265 were inserted near the Truong Giang about midway of the north/south axis of Barrier Island at 0700; followed by an amphibious assault on Green Beach by the remaining two companies at 0840. Covering both troop movements, the destroyer USS *Taussig* (DD-746) and A-4 attack aircraft lit up both landing zones in a well-coordinated prep.

As both landings came off unopposed, Marines at each site quickly consolidated their positions and started moving north. Advancing with little resistance, the SLF secured and established its assigned blocking positions just south of the Route 534 Bridge by 11 September, claiming eight communist KIAs.

While SLF Alpha was coming ashore, elements of the Americal (23rd U.S. Army) Division slipped into blocking positions south and southwest of the AO, cutting off escape routes behind the landings and further isolating communists troops on the island.

For the first time in their history, Korean Marines were making preparations for an amphibious landing on foreign shores. Men of 5th Battalion embarked aboard USS *Iwo Jima* (LPH-2), while the 2nd Battalion was moved by LCUs to Amphibious Ready Group ships USS *Whetstone* (LSD-27), USS *Colonial* (LSD-18), and USS *Washtenaw County* (LST-1163) on 9 September. Shipboard drills, wet net training, and a turnaway amphibious evaluation were conducted with excellent results during the period from 10-11 September.

Historically, for Sub Unit One, this operation would mark the first time since Inchon, almost nineteen years to the day, that ANGLICO would perform its original mission in a combat amphibious environment. There wasn't a Marine in the ROKMC Detachment, however, who had one such experience under his belt with foreign troops.

At 0800 on the 12th, 5th Battalion Marines debarking from USS Iwo Jima were carried by HMM-265 to a landing zone on the northern edge of the island halfway between the coast and Truong Giang. Landing unopposed, the 5th Battalion moved out rapidly along the east bank of the Truong Giang, clearing out all resistance and establishing blocking positions a little inland from the river.

Red Beach welcomed 2nd Battalion with an unopposed landing at 0928, which was quickly consolidated. Maneuver schemes called for the 2nd to move north and south from Red Beach and set up for a westerly assault across the island, driving enemy forces into 5th Battalion to the west and the 26th Marines just to the south.

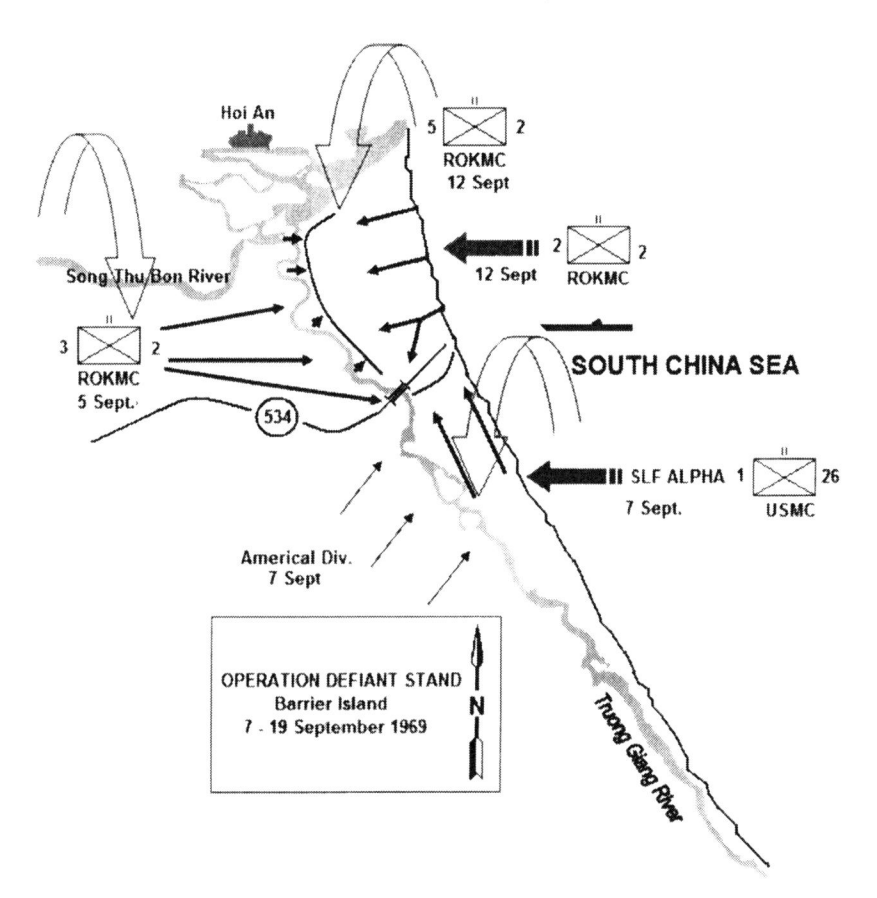

Map: Operation Defiant Stand, Barrier Island, 7 - 19 September 1969

As the Koreans moved south, VC caught in an ever-retracting cordon had no choice but to stand and fight. ROKMC grunts advanced on the trapped enemy, gunning down seventy-nine local force guerillas before sunset on the first day. Upon reaching the southernmost extent of their area of responsibility, the 2nd Battalion turned west and began pushing toward the Truong Giang River, where they encountered extensive tunnel works and fortified positions. On several occasions over the next three days, ANGLICO fire control teams were called upon to bring Naval gunfire missions and tactical air sorties to bear on dug-in militia, with devastating effect. Under cover of supporting arms, ROK Marines completed their sweep across the island, hooking up with 5th Battalion and bringing Defiant Stand to a successful conclusion on 18 September.

By 1700, 19 September, SLF Alpha back-loaded aboard their respective ships, officially terminating the operation while the Koreans remained on the island to root out and destroy Viet Cong infrastructure and remnants of the local force battalion who escaped the cordon.

Combined forces on Defiant Stand accounted for 293 enemy KIAs while detaining 2,552 suspects, of which 2,443 were released. The ROKs suffered one KIA and SLF Alpha five, with a total of forty-three Marines sustaining wounds. By any standard of success, Defiant Stand proved to be a well-planned and flawlessly executed operation, aggressively achieving all objectives.

Still determined to clean out Barrier Island, the Koreans pressed south, sweeping everything in their path. In the second week of November, ANGLICO TACPs controlled a series of air strikes that accounted for the destruction of forty enemy bunkers, causing five secondary explosions, and killing twenty-two additional communist troops. Again during the period from 16-22 November, ANGLICO-controlled air strikes destroyed twenty-nine more bunkers, adding sixteen more KIAs to Victory Dragon XV statistics.

Wanting no more of the 2nd Brigade, on 21 November, local force Viet Cong crossed the Truong Giang en masse, trying to escape the rapidly advancing Koreans. Southwest of the river, elements of the Americal Division intercepted the fleeing units, taking ninety prisoners while gunning down an additional sixty enemy soldiers. When the operation was terminated in early December, the communist infrastructure on Barrier Island had been dealt a severe blow.

With six years of service under his belt, Captain Carl Edwin Long was given responsibility for providing naval gunfire in support of special operations that were always ongoing in the Rung Sat Special Zone. Vietnamese Marines, Navy SEALs, and all the other tough guys who trod the RSSZ depended on quick, reliable supporting arms, and Captain Long made sure they always received their money's worth. "Rung Sat" in Vietnamese means "Forest of Death," and it never failed to live up to its name. Located southeast of Saigon near the coast, the Rung Sat was an especially nasty piece of turf that encompassed an area of some 480 square miles of dense parasite-infested mangrove swamps. Strategically, the Long Tau River, a vital waterway, ran through the Rung Sat. Being able to accommodate deep draft ships up to 720 feet long, it was a major supply artery to Saigon, and keeping that channel open to shipping was the only reason men where asked to endure the miserable conditions of this festering hell-hole.

Flying out of Vung Tau in southern III Corps, Captain Long spent much of his time plying space over the Rung Sat, doing what he could to ensure the safety of those operations he was assigned to support. Captain Carl E. Long sadly closed out 1969 on a tragic note. While patrolling the skies over the Rung Sat Special Zone southeast of Saigon, on 20 December, Captain Long's aircraft was brought down by antiaircraft fire, and his remains were claimed by the Forest of Death. Killed with him was pilot Lieutenant (JG) Joel A. Sandberg of the U.S. Navy's VAL-4. Although Lieutenant Sandberg's body was recovered, many years would pass before the Forest of Death relinquished Captain Carl Edwin Long.

At the turn of the year, with 21 Marine officers, 9 naval officers, 192 enlisted Marines, and 2 enlisted Navy corpsmen, Lieutenant Colonel Thomas H. Simpson commanded a force deployed in twenty-four locations from northern I Corps to the Ca Mau Peninsula. The Sub Unit looked forward to a very different cadence of war.

In keeping with directives on Vietnamization, the Commander of U.S. Naval Forces Vietnam (COMNAVFORV) opened discussions in January with Lieutenant Colonel Simpson on how to best turn over naval gunfire functions to the Vietnamese in IV Corps. Being of the opinion that there was no reason why Vietnamese couldn't be trained in the nuances of naval gunfire, the ANGLICO C.O. agreed. The Commander of the 7th Fleet (COMSEVENFLT) approved the plan on condition that ANGLICO provide training and coordinate naval gunfire, with all Vietnamese augmenting American spotters.

After a meeting in IV Corps on 30 March, Lieutenant Colonel Simpson, satisfied with preparations, gave his approval to launch the training program. Before the second week of April came to a close, Vietnamese FACs refused to proceed with training, as they had not yet obtained permission from higher authority within the Vietnamese Air Force. They had already been schooled on proper procedures and were ready to shoot, but the same old problem of Vietnamese reluctance to use their own initiative had not changed since the war began. With the Vietnamese, authority was never delegated down the chain of command, as senior officers and officials tended to hoard power. In order to save face, which was ingrained into Vietnamese culture, it was better to not make a decision than to be singled out for criticism after the fact. It's more or less akin to a co-worker who always consults his job description before doing anything asked of him, even if his refusal to cooperate could cost his job or, for that matter, bring down the company.

No sooner did that problem get ironed out when a new one instantly sprang up to take its place. Earlier in March, Lon Nol staged a coup, deposing Cambodia's supposedly neutral ruler Prince Norodom Sihanouk. The new government immediately attempted to expel the North Vietnamese from their base camps along the South Vietnamese border. With a now-hostile government in power, the North Vietnamese had to act in order to protect their supply routes and staging areas. In an effort to isolate Cambodia, the North Vietnamese attempted to cut off its capital, Phnom Penh, further west of Saigon by closing access from the Mekong River. Early in 1970, the oil tanker *Mekong* was sunk, prompting the new Cambodian government to call for assistance. As such the VNAF, already taxed to its limit, was now heavily committed to this added burden. Not being able to cut loose resources for commitment to naval gunfire well into June, no progress toward Vietnamization could be seen on the horizon. Vietnamization of naval gunfire was then delegated to the "things to do" list until such time as circumstance would permit continuance.

Early months of 1970 did not allow Lieutenant Colonel Simpson much respite, as he was constantly on the move, putting out one fire after another. The U.S. Navy decided to decommission the remaining LSMR rocket ships because of their advanced age. These Inshore Fire Support Ships, because of their shallow drafts, were able to operate quite efficiently in the shallow gradient littorals surrounding IV Corps. The LSMRs were basically LSM hulls outfitted with ten twin continuous-loading five-inch spin-stabilized rocket launchers, capable of delivering up to 380 rounds per minute on target. The LSMRs were redesignated as Inshore Fire Support Ships soon into their Vietnam service. Of the 500-plus LSMRs produced during

WW II, four were recommissioned in 1965 for service in Southeast Asia, rotating in and out of the war zone, providing great fire support. Destroyers, although very effective, had to remain in waters deep enough to navigate.

On 17 March, USS *White River* fired her last mission in Vietnam. Those rocket ships provided so much firepower that Lieutenant Colonel Simpson, not a man to mince words, noted in his monthly report: "March saw the passing of LFR rocket ships USS *Clarion River* (LSMR-409), USS *St. Francis River* (LSMR-525), USS *White River* (LSMR-536), and USS *Carronade* (ISF/LFR-1) as they were pulled off the gunline on the 17th. The gap which was left in IV Corps, where a majority of their firing is done, must be filled by destroyers assigned to IV Corps. HMAS *Vendetta* (D08) and USS *Orleck* (DD-886) have proven once more that destroyers can be used with good effect off the coast of IV Corps, but there were not enough [destroyers] available. The loss of the LSMRs does nothing but hurt the overall naval gunfire effort in IV Corps. If just one more destroyer had been added to offset the loss of the rocket ships the trade-off would have been fairly even."

Going back to May 1969, coverage on the gunline began developing a few glitches. The II Corps NGLO reported indiscriminant assigning and cancellation of naval gunfire units in his area of responsibility, making operational planning expectations for naval gunfire impossible. Utilization messages were usually superseded before addressees received them. As a result, ground commanders were unable to incorporate naval gunfire units into operational planning.

A first meeting was held with weapons officers from CGT 70.8 at a liaison visit to Sub Unit One Headquarters to discuss, among other agenda items, the problem of ships not keeping NGLOs informed of their intentions.

Voids in the gunline coverage continued into 1970, as the Sub Unit One skipper was forced to address an ongoing problem, whereby the current gunline commander also shifted ships between military regions without informing the NGLOs or spotters. This development resulted in the cancellation of several intended fire missions and relegated naval gunfire as an unreliable ground support weapon. In several instances, the gunline commander overrode the NGLOs request and further complicated the matter by not keeping anyone ashore informed of his intentions.

In a meeting with senior gunline officers at Sub Unit One Headquarters, Lieutenant Colonel Simpson pointed out, "It is the gunline commander's prerogative to put his ships in the best position to accomplish their assigned tasks; however, as the gunline commander is not familiar with the ground tactical situation, he should logically rely on the Corps NGLO's request for support to base his decision." The root cause of the problem, he felt, rested in frequent changes of gunline commanders, who typically served on station for a period of about three weeks. Therefore, the suggested solution was to increase the length of tour for each gunline commander; perhaps three months would be a minimum acceptable time. The Naval officers, in turn, did take up the matter with the 70.8 Task Group Commander (CGT 70.8).

On 14 March 1970, two American merchant seamen, Clyde McKay and Alvin Glatkowski, using guns they smuggled aboard, seized control of their ship, SS *Columbia Eagle*, in the first armed mutiny aboard an American ship in 150 years. The ship was sailing on a Department of Defense supply charter, carrying napalm to U.S. Air Force bases in Thailand for use in Vietnam.

To complicate Lieutenant Colonel Simpson's job even further, two U.S. Coast Guard Cutters, USCGC *Mellon* (WHEC-717) and USCGC *Chase* (WHEC-718), currently on Operation Market Time surveillance with Task Group 115, were diverted to guard the *Columbia Eagle* once it came back into American control. To fill the Market Time vacancies, the IV Corps gunline destroyers were assigned to replace the cutters. Even though the destroyers fell under operational control of Commander Task Group (CFT)-115, they were still assigned to the gunline on a no-interference basis. CFT-115 took this to mean that it controlled naval gunfire rather than ANGLICO NGLOs. This unfortunate turn of events resulted in calls for fire from the 21st ARVN Division that could not be honored because CTF-115 refused to allow the division NGLO to control the ship.

In spite of being one of the more junior officers embroiled in these crisis management exercises, the skipper stood his ground, within the realm of proper protocol, and did very well for his command.

That same month, XXIV Corps replaced III MAF as the senior command entity in Military Region 1. With that change in command structure, Sub Unit One now controlled all naval gunfire support in Vietnam. Subsequently, the III MAF billet was dissolved and moved to XXIV Corps headquarters. Although the 1st Marine Division still employed their spotters, the XXIV Corps NGLO function (a senior command) was assumed by ANGLICO.

With American combat assets disappearing from Vietnam and new command entities popping up all over the map, any thoughts that this war was going to get easier also disappeared.

For most of that spring, problems caused by U.S. troop withdrawal sprang up, creating difficulties procuring U.S. Army aircraft for airborne spotters in I and IV Corps. A pilot shortage and availability of repair parts affected support commitments for several Vietnamese operations. The problem was remedied through negotiation with the USAF 20th Tactical Air Support Squadron, which made flight hours available to affected teams.

Lieutenant Colonel Eugene E. Shoults, who relieved Lieutenant Colonel Thomas H. Simpson on 4 August, also wrestled with Vietnamization directives. As the new champion for the cause, in his first monthly report at the helm, the new C.O. noted, "The Coast Guard Cutter USCGC *Ponchatrain* (WHEC-70) has been doing an excellent job of providing NGF support to the Americal Division. The point of interest is that the fire control system for USCGC *Ponchatrain* is identical to the two cutters USCGC *Bering Strait* (WHEC-382) and USCGC *Yakutat* (WHEC-380) being turned over to the Vietnamese Navy (VNN). Preliminary opinions as to the effectiveness of these for naval gunfire support from NAVFORV were not optimistic. In actual firing, however, the USCGC *Ponchatrain* has done an outstanding job. It will be worthwhile to follow the reports on the USCGC *Bering Strait* and USCGC *Yakutat* when they get complete Vietnamese crews and start operational firing. They could possibly be a great asset for filling the gaps in the gunline."

Keystone Robin troop redeployments had, by early August, thinned out observation activities of the U.S. Marine 1st Recon Battalion, who were in the process of standing down, leaving only twenty-four teams available for patrol and surveillance missions. At best, 1st Recon was only able to field twelve teams at any specific time.

At its peak operating strength, the battalion on average had at least ten reconnaissance teams in the western Que Sons alone, providing timely intelligence reports on communist troop movements, concentrations, and other activities, which greatly benefited the Blue Dragon Brigade and other allied units as well.

Earlier in the year, the Recon Battalion instituted a series of three-week training programs for ARVN Rangers, the 51st ARVN Recon Company, and Recon Marines of the 2nd ROKMC Brigade. At completion of training, allied graduates accompanied live action patrols for evaluation and experience, which enhanced reconnaissance and intelligence capabilities for these units that would soon not be available from the 1st Marine Division. Scheduled for withdrawal beginning in February, 1st Recon Battalion would end its mission in Vietnam in May 1971, relocating to Camp Pendleton.

Among the most innovative and highly successful tactics adopted during the war were "Stingray Patrols." On 28 June 1966, a recon patrol led by Sergeant Orest Bishko observed between 150 and 250 North Vietnamese troops southwest of the Rockpile. The team adjusted artillery fire on the formation, killing approximately fifty enemy soldiers and forcing the unit to withdraw. Soon thereafter, owing to the success of that operation, Stingray teams were sent into the field, specifically to bring supporting arms to bear on communist formations.

Picking up on the successful marriage of reconnaissance and supporting arms, eight members of ANGLICO's ROKMC Detachment were sent to the Recon Battalion base camp for Stingray orientation and refresher training on 10 November. Later that month, the Blue Dragon Brigade launched extensive recon operations, focusing on the Que Son Mountains west and south of its TAOR. On each patrol, one ANGLICO Marine was inserted as a team member to apply his skills at bringing supporting arms to bear on observed enemy units.

As Marines of the 1st Recon Battalion shifted west, Blue Dragon recon teams joined Operation Imperial Lake, already in progress. The ROKs established a patrol base on Hill 322 in the northeast Que Sons. To take advantage of observations or to have assistance at the ready should a patrol run into trouble, the Koreans established a quick reaction force at LZ Baldy, ready to mount up. The ROKs continued these patrols throughout the remainder of their time in-county.

At year's end, Sub Unit One's manning level in December stood at 29 officers and 168 enlisted men, in contrast to January's 224-man unit strength.

USS Rupertus
(DD-851)
Gearing Class Destroyer
Call Sign: Search Party

In June 1965, USS *Rupertus* returned to Vietnamese waters, participating in Market Time operations, boarding and inspecting vessels off South Vietnam in search of contraband. She also took her turn on the gunline, providing naval gunfire support to U.S. and allied forces.

On 29 July 1967, USS *Rupertus* steamed in company with USS *Forrestal* (CVA-59) when a series of explosions temporarily disabled the giant carrier. USS *Rupertus* maneuvered to within twenty feet of the crippled ship, remaining alongside for a period of three hours, providing fire-fighting assistance, cooling magazines, and rescuing personnel thrown into the sea. USS *Rupertus* then participated in Sea Dragon operations, involving the interdiction of waterborne logistics craft emerging from North Vietnamese ports. Operating on Yankee Station, the ship drew enemy fire off Dong Hoi, North Vietnam, which resulted in minor shrapnel hits. Assigned once more to gunfire support off South Vietnam in October, she returned to Long Beach on 4 December.

Following overhaul and exercises off the California coast, USS *Rupertus* again found herself underway for WestPac in July 1968. On 22 July, she assumed naval gunfire support responsibilities off

South Vietnam. Taking up Sea Dragon duties on 29 August, she again came under fire from enemy coastal defense sites.

Continuing to operate throughout the Far East during 1969, part of that time off Vietnam, USS *Rupertus* returned to San Diego 15 August 1970. She remained in San Diego for the rest of 1970, spending much of the time in dry dock.

Both 1971 and 1972 brought USS *Rupertus* a WestPac cruise, each about six months' duration, alternating gunline duty with operations in the San Diego area. Soon after her return in the spring of 1973, she underwent an INSURV inspection, which resulted in her being declared unfit for further service. She was decommissioned on 10 July 1973.

We, who once found refuge under the protection of her guns, salute this valiant ship and her gallant crew.

SOLITARY REFINEMENT

As U.S. troop strength dwindled, the last remaining Marine combat elements organized under the command umbrella of 3rd Marine Amphibious Brigade (MAB) was activated in February 1971 to cover the scheduled departure of all III MAF assets still in country.

During the first half of the year, men of Sub Unit One bore witness to the slow trickle of U.S. forces leaving South Vietnam while awaiting their turn for stand-down. With departure of trailing elements of 3rd MAB on 26 June, they knew their time was not far off.

When Lieutenant Colonel D'Wayne Gray relieved Lieutenant Colonel Eugene E. Shoults on 25 July 1971, he assumed command of the only remaining Fleet Marine Force (FMF) element left on South Vietnamese soil. Aside from keeping to his mission of supporting what war effort still remained, it was expected he would also oversee redeployment of Sub Unit One somewhere down the trail.

A shortfall of artillery coverage, due to now-absent U.S. field batteries, became an ongoing challenge since American combat units began pulling out of Vietnam. Field commanders increasingly looked to naval gunfire as a bridge to fill the gap until South Vietnamese expanded coverage. While the U.S. armed forces, with its sophisticated weapons and experienced personnel, had developed advanced coordination concepts to effectively exercise control of supporting arms, the Vietnamese were not as capable, as they heretofore depended on U.S. tactical air, naval gunfire, and in many cases even artillery. One of the many problems that plagued the Vietnamese centered on power plays and political infighting among senior officers. The question of who was in charge when two services became involved with integrated operations always prompted rivalries and political intrigue among higher-ups trying to grab more prestige for their service affiliation or themselves.

This problem, with many U.S. coordination entities no longer in-country, soon transferred to the remaining American advisors. While Marine air/ground combat units were engaged, naval gunfire, artillery, and tactical air support, when under properly supervised coordination, complemented each other very well, contributing a powerful capability to offensive and defensive fire support requirements.

In the past, battalion and regimental FSCCs would broadcast save-a-plane reports when artillery or naval gunfire missions were in progress. Data such as target area, firing location, time of firing, and maximum trajectory ordinate would then be relayed by Division to the air wing and on to the pilots. This was all the information needed for an aircraft, fixed wing or helicopter, to avoid flying into an artillery round. Through the Marine tactical data system, all three weapons could be and were employed safely with devastating effect, using Marine-developed restrictive fire plans.

At this point in the war, artillery and naval gunfire were not permitted to fire coordinated missions with TAC Air. Lieutenant Colonel Gray addressed this problem daily, to no avail. Lieutenant Colonel Gray recalled that the U.S. Air Force "just refused to consider any alternative… and the U.S. Army, all the way to the top, let them get away with it."

As a consequence, when aircraft made their run on a target, artillery and Naval gunfire had to stop firing. Although it did create a lot of stress, it was tolerable, as nothing in the way of significant enemy tactical activity was going on.

The only other Marines still waging war in Vietnam were sixty-eight hand-picked members of the Marine Advisory Unit (MAU), who were disbursed throughout the Vietnamese Marine Corps. Like ANGLICO, MAU also established a headquarters in Saigon and were deployed in most regions of the country. These were professional Marines, most of whom returned to Vietnam to apply their skills and experience on second or third combat tours. As the war was being handed over to Vietnamese troops, the U.S. Marine Corps, knowing their time in-country was coming to a close, selected only the best of the best for this critical assignment. Since first establishing the command in 1954, fewer than 600 Marines collectively served the advisory unit.

The Vietnamese referred to them as "Covan," meaning "trusted advisor." The Covans breathed life into the fledgling Marine Corps of Vietnam, nurturing it into an organization that was now established as a force to be reckoned with. A junction was fast approaching when it would have to stand alone.

VNMC infantry was organized into Brigades 147, 258, and 369 adopting those designations to reflect the maneuver battalions assigned to a particular brigade at the time it was formed. Brigade 147, for instance, was at its inception composed of the 1st, 4th, and 7th Battalions. It was not unusual for a brigade to have a different alignment of maneuver battalions from month to month. The Vietnamese further organized each battalion with an Alpha and Bravo group, comprised of two companies each. Three artillery battalions were also part of the VNMC table of organization. No one who knew anything at all about this war doubted for one minute that these tiger-striped Marines were the most professional and aggressive component of the Vietnamese armed forces. They, along with ARVN airborne brigades, formed the Joint General Staff Reserve for the Republic of Vietnam. As such, Marine brigades or individual battalions were deployed in all four tactical zones. Being attached to individual army divisions or corps tactical zone commands as reaction forces played to their strength as shock troops, giving those ARVN divisions a powerful buttress. Late 1971 found two brigades, 147 and 258, operating in Quang Tri Province under operational control of the 3rd ARVN Division.

Colonel Joshua W. Dorsey, III, Senior Marine Advisor, like his ANGLICO counterpart, wrestled with developing procedures to judiciously stand down his command. Because many VNMC officers had been at this war for years, they were endowed with a confidence borne of experience and didn't really see a need for American advisors. A tour of duty for the average Vietnamese Marine amounted to a lifetime commitment that did not end in rotation out of the combat zone. Taking this into account, Colonel Dorsey set a course to withdraw his advisors from battalion level and establish brigade-based placement of his subordinates, thus establishing a sensible venue for eliminating enough billets to reduce his command.

Mid-August saw the departure of the U.S. Army's 1st Brigade, 5th Infantry Division from Vietnam, freeing up the spot team at Quang Tri for other assignments. This drawdown left the 6,000-man-strong 196th Light Infantry Brigade with the only tactical U.S. maneuver battalions left in Vietnam. As their time in-country was also short, the brigade remained close to Da Nang, operating more as a security force than a tactical asset.

Realizing a need for more muscle to replace deployed American units, the armed forces of South Vietnam activated the 3rd ARVN Division in November for service in MR1. Ai Tu combat base northeast of Quang Tri City would serve as division headquarters, assuming tactical responsibility for an area that was previously defended by nearly two American divisions.

Tactical assets of the new command were built around the 2nd Regiment, transferred from the 1st ARVN Division. It was a veteran, well-led unit that was considered by those in the know to be one of the best South Vietnam had. Creation of the 56th and 57th rounded out the organic infantry regiments of the new division, both of which would have to be built from the ground up. An artillery regiment and supporting units completed the division's table of organization.

Colonel Vu Van Giai, the very capable executive officer of the 1st ARVN Division, currently commanding that division's forward element at Phu Bai, was promoted to brigadier general, given command of the new entity, and established his headquarters at Ai Tu combat base adjacent to the airstrip at Quang Tri. His first order of business was to gather as much of an all-star cast as he could assemble. Reasoning that good leadership will balance out inexperienced troops, General Giai selected his former operations officer Lieutenant Colonel Pham Van Dinh to command the 56th. Both new regiments were heavily salted with under-trained Regional and Popular Force militia troops, who existed primarily as defensive forces at the local level. Deserters and hard-core discipline problems from other divisions also populated the organic battalions of each new regiment. Training pushed ahead as an ongoing process of on-the-job training, even as the 3rd Division filtered into combat bases formerly occupied by Americans. Several months would pass before the newly composed regiments approached anything near combat readiness.

In order to promote thorough familiarity with the division's area of operation, General Giai frequently rotated units within his command among the firebases under his control.

To increase combat effectiveness of mostly untried troops and fill manpower gaps created by vacancies of American combat assets, Brigades 147 and 258 of the Vietnamese Marines Corps was placed under operational control of General Giai and the 3rd Division.

Under the leadership of Colonel Donald J. Metcalf, U.S. Army Advisory Team 155 set up shop in Ai Tu with a lineup of experienced officers to lend their individual expertise to General Giai's staff. He in turn reported to Major General Frederick J. Kroesen at the Da Nang-based headquarters of Lieutenant General Hoang Xuan Lam, Military Commander of MR1. On 19 March, XXXIV Corps, having tactical assets consisting only of the 196th Light Infantry Brigade, was discontinued as a command entity and replaced with First Regional Assistance Command (FRAC) as the senior American military staff in MR1. In 1970, MACV, under the auspices of Vietnamization, instituted a program of reducing its advisory effort to regimental level. Seeing the experience and combat readiness infused throughout the 2nd Regiment, advisors were only assigned to the two new regimental entities.

Sub Unit One activated an NGLO team commanded by U.S. Navy Lieutenant (JG) W.H. Sadler in December to support the new combat element. The spot team already at Alpha 2 was transferred to the new command and remained in place. Airborne spotters out of Phu Bai began flying support for the maneuver battalions.

ANGLICO CHAIN OF COMMAND
1971 - 1973

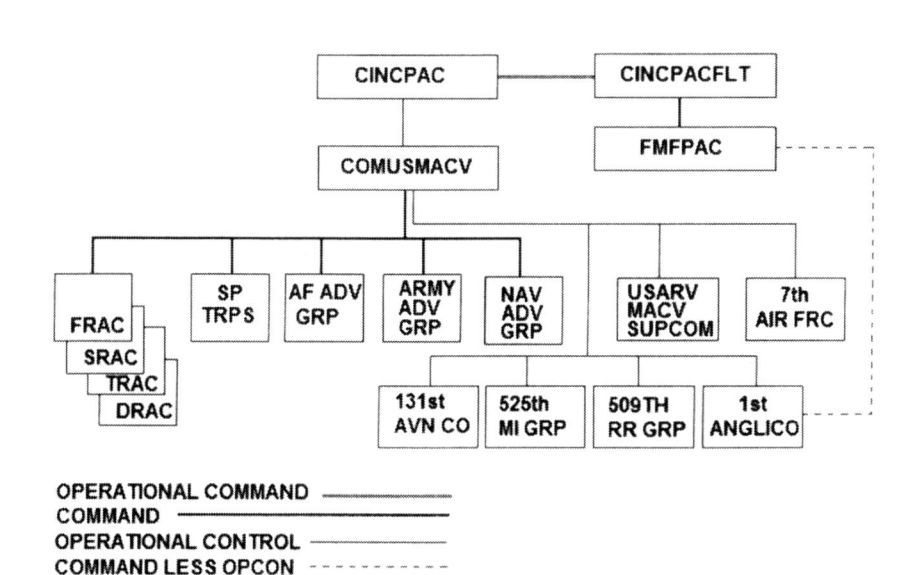

OPERATIONAL COMMAND ——————
COMMAND ————————
OPERATIONAL CONTROL ————
COMMAND LESS OPCON - - - - - - - - - -

Near the close of 1971, the Vietnamese Navy acquired four deep-draft ships with capability of providing naval gunfire support. The project of Vietnamizing naval gunfire, first attempted by Lieutenant Colonel Simpson, then bequeathed to Lieutenant Colonel Shoults, was now squarely in the lap of Lieutenant Colonel Gray. Although the Vietnamese embraced the concept and grasped the basics, gunfire ships, limited by poor gunfire control systems, fell short on their ability to employ indirect fire. As a result, close fire missions in support of friendly troops proved to be marginal at best. Using the Delta area of MR4 as the testing ground for an all-Vietnamese naval gunfire environment under these conditions panned out to be ineffective. Having no other choice in the matter, plans to cover the Delta with expanded ARVN firebases went ahead.

In mid-December, troop drawdowns by the government of South Korea pulled the Blue Dagon Brigade's 1st and 2nd Battalions out of Vietnam, cutting in half that organization's commitment in-country. The rest of the brigade was on schedule to withdraw after the first of the year.

USS Eversole
(DD-789)
Gearing Class Destroyer
Call Sign: Jolting Joe

On 8 October 1969, USS *Eversole* deployed from Long Beach Naval Station to the Western Pacific, stopping in Oahu, Hawaii, and Midway Island in transit to Yokosuka, Japan, before frequent deployments to the Tonkin Gulf for plane guard assignments with the carrier forces of the 7th Fleet and naval gunfire support duties for ground troops. Between combat deployments, Subic Bay Naval Station was used as the overseas homeport. Other R&R and maintenance visits were made to Sasebo, Japan, and Hong Kong. USS *Eversole* returned to Long Beach 8 April 1970.

Making a brief appearance on the gunline from 16-21 February 1970, USS *Eversole* fired in support of the 47th ARVN Regiment in II Corps, destroying several enemy bunkers and causing two secondary explosions and eight fires.

A command performance was turned in by USS *Eversole* during the 1972 campaign to recapture Quang Tri Province from the NVA. From 6-10 May and on 17 and 18 May, USS *Eversole* fired in support of the 2nd ARVN Division in southern MR1, then moved north in June to support Vietnamese Marines and remained on station, providing effective fire, in July and August, departing the gunline early in October.

We, who once found refuge under the protection of her guns, salute this valiant ship and her gallant crew.

THE LAST TANGO IN QUANG TRI

The year of 1972 made its debut as peaceful as was 1971's departure. Things were relatively quite considering a war was technically still in progress. As the Korean Marines were well into their stand-down schedule, only twenty-six men remained with the ROKMC Detachment, reducing total Sub Unit One assets remaining in-country to 142 Marines and Naval officers. With the departure of 3rd Battalion in January leaving only one maneuver battalion at Hoi An, the ROK Marine Detachment would soon be looking for work. The Blue Dragons conducted a stand-down ceremony on 26 January in preparation for relocating its long-absent colors back to Korean soil at Pusan.

Currently, the Sub Unit was providing support exclusively for South Vietnamese armed forces, with most activity centered in MR1. Alpha 2 on the DMZ still received sporadic to moderate rocket and artillery fire, answering back with counter battery missions from gunline destroyers, and found itself as the sole remaining ground spot team anywhere in-country by March.

Before the turn of the year, plans were well under way to close down operations in Military Regions 2 and 3, as activity for those teams was almost nonexistent. By March 1972, Sub Unit One for the first time since activation in1965 had not one fire control team deployed in either region, having pulled those personnel back to Saigon.

Military Region 4 was likewise much less busy as most gunfire missions were being taken over by Vietnamese artillery. A majority of naval gunfire activities now centered on providing security for new firebases being erected on southern Ca Mau Peninsula.

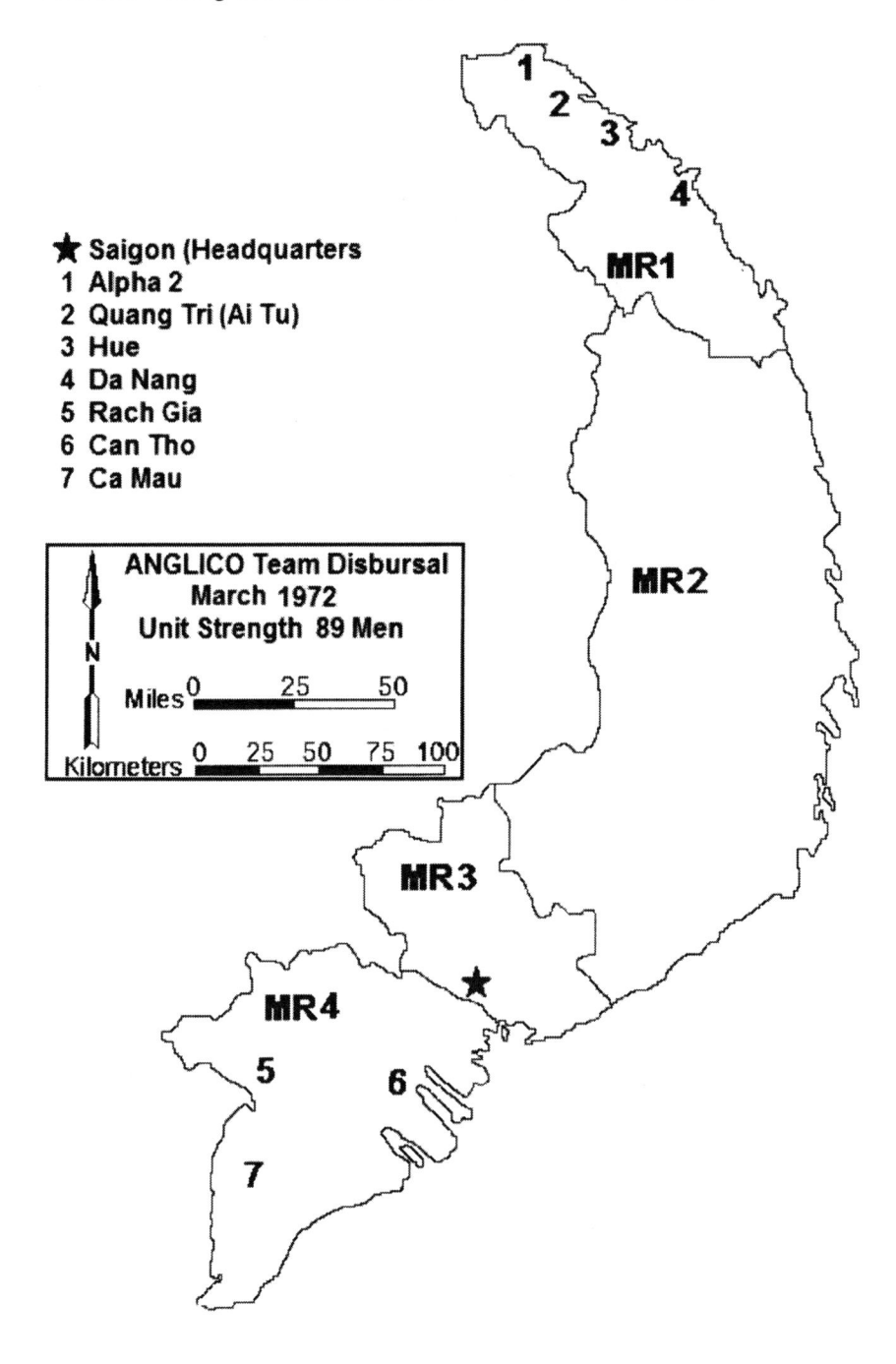

★ Saigon (Headquarters
1 Alpha 2
2 Quang Tri (Ai Tu)
3 Hue
4 Da Nang
5 Rach Gia
6 Can Tho
7 Ca Mau

ANGLICO Team Disbursal
March 1972
Unit Strength 89 Men

With departure of 5th Battalion, 2nd Republic of Korea Marine Brigade on 26 February, the ROKMC Detachment was dissolved, its personnel distributed to other locations. March saw reduction in manning levels for the Sub Unit to eighty-nine officers and men. As streamlining of personnel and reduction of support roles moved ahead, Lieutenant Colonel Gray and his staff had months ago prepared contingency plans to re-establish units, if and when needed, should shifting winds of war demand redeployment of the Sub Unit's combat assets. Pushing ahead with personnel reduction mandates, the Alpha 2 team was scheduled to be withdrawn on 1 May, followed by complete stand-down of all remaining human resources in July. Mobility and diversity would replace manning deficits in case unforeseen circumstance abruptly arose.

One such unforeseen circumstance was already looming on the horizon that would soon test the mettle of every man in the unit.

Heavy cloud cover and low visibility brought on by seasonal monsoons dominated meteorological events in the closing days of March, keeping allied aircraft close to their hangers. North Vietnamese planners, having patiently waited for just such a weather system favorable for limiting air activity, made their move.

At 1030 on 30 March, a platoon-size patrol from 1st Company, 4th VNMC Battalion made first contact about 1,000 meters northwest of Nui Ba Ho. At about the same time, elements of the 8th VNMC Battalion operating west of Fire Support Base Holcomb area also encountered the western spearhead of an advancing North Vietnamese Army. Before full assessments of the contacts now in progress could be ascertained, 120mm rockets and 130mm rounds from NVA artillery bases to the west began pounding Nui Ba Ho, Mai Loc, and Camp Carroll in blanket bombardments. At 1100, Captain Ray L. Smith, Marine advisor with 4th VNMC Battalion Bravo Group at Nui Ba Ho, observed three companies of North Vietnamese advancing to attack the outpost.

Even as elements of the 9th NVA Regiment began their assault of Nui Ba Ho, Fire Support Base Sarge, home of 4th Battalion's Alpha Group some 1,200 meters south, was also under the gun, receiving more than 500 rounds within its perimeter. Major Walter E. Boomer, Senior Adviser to the 4th VNMC Battalion, exposing himself to thunderous explosions within the chaotic confines of the base, located several enemy batteries. Calling for ARVN artillery support from Camp Carroll, he was able to successfully adjust fire on many of those sites before NVA field pieces drove South Vietnamese gunners into their bunkers.

Manning radio nets at Sarge, Spec 5 Gary P. Westcott and Sergeant Bruce A. Crosby, Jr., of the U.S. Army's 509th Radio Research Group were hard at work deciphering NVA radio transmissions when the bunker housing their operation took a direct hit. Racing to the fire-engulfed structure as soon as the incoming slacked off, Major Boomer, in a futile attempt to affect rescue, was driven back by intense flames now raging from inside the dugout. Realizing there were no survivors, the Marine reluctantly forced himself away from the inferno.

General Giai, in a planned rotation of operational areas, ordered the 2nd and 56th Regiments to affect a position exchange on Easter weekend in keeping with his policy of promoting familiarization of the division's AO and to avoid what he called firebase syndrome. The maneuver required 2nd Regiment to vacate the western firebases headquartered at Camp Carroll and occupy the northwestern firebases being headquartered from Charlie 2, while the 56th conducted the opposite deployment. Due to a shortage of trucks, both regiments mounted the operation simultaneously, with each headquarters company shutting down their communications centers for transportation to the new operational command sites on 30 March.

In the process of exchanging positions, which by noon was about half complete, elements of the 2nd and 56th Regiments in the vicinity of Route 9 near Cam Lo were caught out in the open. 3rd Battalion departed Charlie 2 bound for Khe Gio. 2nd Battalion, Colonel Phong commanding, remained at Charlie 2, along with Major Joseph Brown, assistant advisor to the 56th, to guard the firebase until the 2nd Regiment arrived. The 1st Battalion of the 56th was in transit from Route 9 to Fire Support Base Fuller when it became engulfed by torrents of falling artillery shells. Taking casualties by the second, the battalion was decimated. All communication was lost.

As neither regiment had a fully operational communications center, fragmented reports of current events coming into the 3rd Division TOC added more confusion to an already-chaotic situation.

Hundreds of artillery rounds impacting on other exposed troops also took a heavy toll on South Vietnam's newest regiment. The main body of the 56th, newly arrived at the Camp Carroll artillery base just south of Route 9, was now under a devastating barrage of fire. Senior Advisor U.S. Army Lieutenant Colonel William C. Camper and his counterpart Lieutenant Colonel Pham Van Dihn arrived at Carroll under fire around 1130.

A string of combat bases along the DMZ came under direct siege just past noon. Every base in northern I Corps within range of NVA field pieces to the west and just south of the DMZ was also taken under fire before sunset.

The long-anticipated offensive was now under way as North Vietnam sent its 304th Division (reinforced) into South Vietnam from Laos in a coordinated maneuver, coinciding with the 308th Division and three regiments of the B-5 Front, attacking south through the demilitarized zone. Communist forces were augmented by at least two tank regiments and three unattached infantry regiments. Rocket, artillery, antiaircraft artillery, and surface-to-air missile sites were set up at several locations just across the DMZ and west of Camp Carroll to support NVA maneuver elements. All over northern I Corps, the forces of South Vietnam were hard-pressed to meet this threat. The only tactical assets available for deployment against this incursion were the 1st ARVN Division in Hue (several miles south), the untested 3rd ARVN Division (deployed at several locations guarding the DMZ), and two Vietnamese Marine Brigades manning firebases south and west of Quang Tri City.

Intelligence agencies of South Vietnam and the United States had, for some time, expected a military campaign of significant strength in 1972. An illogical move across the DMZ in flat terrain fully exposed to U.S. and South Vietnamese air and artillery, right into the strength of the MR1 defense, was pondered but not given serious consideration. Thought of a conventional attack was never ruled out but was considered a high risk for an army geared to guerilla tactics. Inasmuch as North Vietnam clung to the 1954 Geneva Agreement to legitimize its aggression in the South, it was widely believed a blatant violation of the demilitarized zone wouldn't happen.

At Alpha 2, the former Gio Lihn combat base defended by 1st Battalion, 57th Regiment, a five-man ANGLICO team, call sign

Wolfman 5, commanded by 1st Lieutenant David C. Bruggeman, hunkered down under a constant deluge of missiles. Reporting his situation to 1st Lieutenant Joel B. Eisenstein, commanding officer and NGLO of the 3rd ARVN Division Detachment, Lieutenant Bruggeman and his team continued going about the dangerous business of defending the outpost.

Lieutenant Eisenstein, at his headquarters at Ai Tu combat base, adjacent to the airstrip in Quang Tri, was privy to similar reports from all over the affected battle area. Every radio in the Tactical Operations Center was, in fact, alive with reports of this ominous development. Additional radio transmissions from Lieutenant Bruggeman recounted Vietnamese artillerymen barricaded in their bunkers, making no attempt at responding to calls for fire. A worsening situation still, many militiamen had already deserted the base camp. With ARVN artillery batteries silent and defensive positions unmanned, naval gunfire directed by Bruggeman and his team was the only counter battery measures answering NVA bombardment anywhere along the DMZ.

Alpha 2 reeled under a constant bombardment. As the northernmost Marines in Vietnam, they were in position to hear outgoing rounds and observe muzzle flashes from across the frontier. Wolfman 5 instituted a radio relay to warn other affected areas to expect incoming whenever the big guns came alive. This gave Lieutenant Eisenstein and the entire TOC group a timely heads-up. Division staff personnel at Ai Tu by this time were dodging 1,000 shells per day at the command post and really came to appreciate those precious few seconds of warning.

Calling upon the 7th Battalion of VNMC Brigade 258, Major Hue was ordered to bring his unit north from Fire Support Base Nancy below Quang Tri City to keep Route 9, the major supply artery, open to Camp Carroll. Marine advisors Major Andrew D. De Bona and Captain Ronald R. Rice accompanied the battalion on its new mission.

Major Jim Joy, senior advisor to VNMC Brigade 147 departed Ai Tu in a Vietnamese helicopter at 1600, returning to Mai Loc, where the Brigade command element was located. As Mai Loc was under fire, Major Joy directed the pilot to let him down at Houng Hoa district headquarters, where he flagged down a Marine truck, which ran the gauntlet of falling artillery into the base.

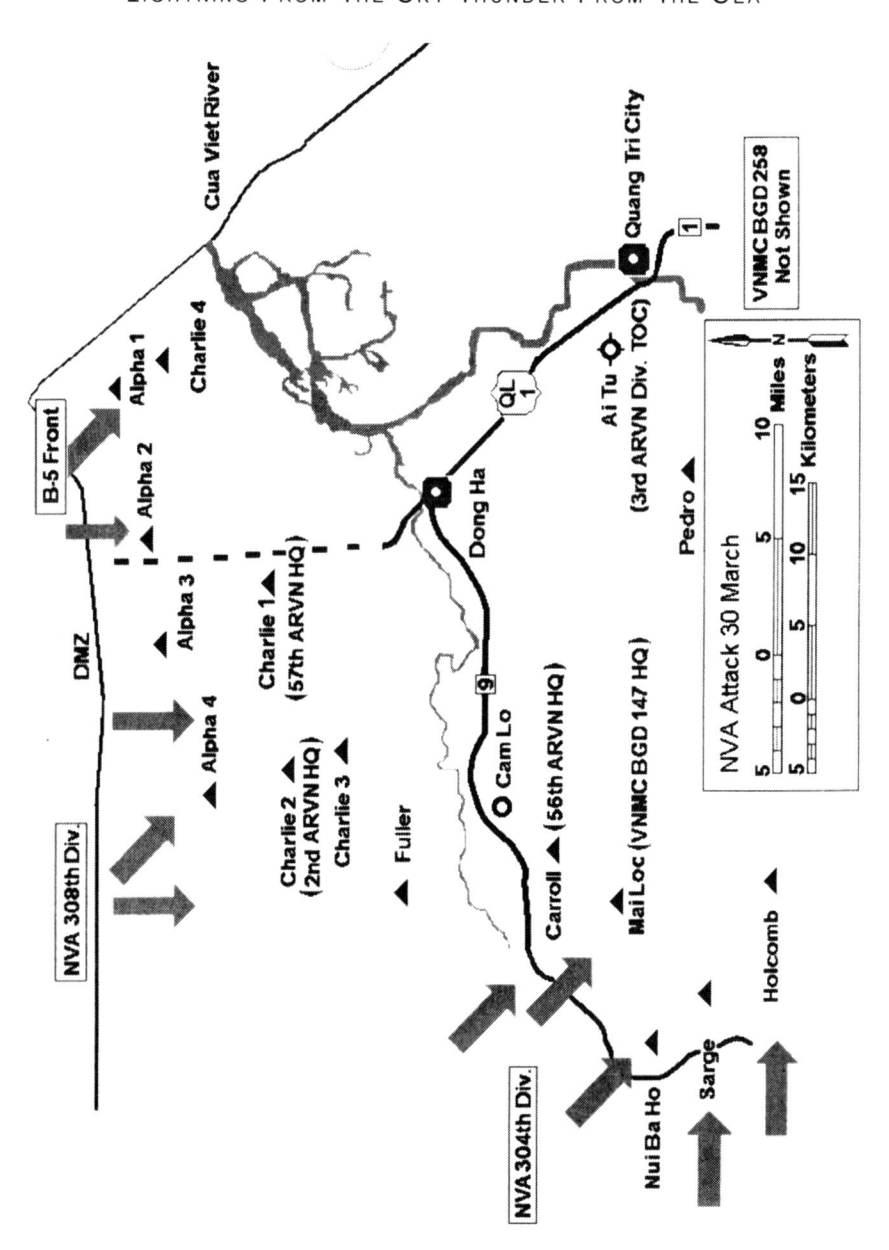

Once inside the wire, Major Joy made his way to the command bunker. He took his place with Brigade Commander Colonel Bao and Major Tom Gnibus, senior advisor to 2nd Marine Artillery Battalion, where he received a briefing on the unfolding tactical condition he just landed in the middle of. Colonel Bao was approaching critical mass trying to get fire support from the twenty-two guns at Camp

Carroll for his beleaguered 4th Battalion Marines at Nui Ba Ho and Sarge.

A platoon outpost 600 meters north of Nui Ba Ho was taken under intense small arms and RPG fire at 1700. Coming at the Marines in human-wave assaults to within grenade distance, NVA troops were violently thrown back three times.

Concurrently, a listening post manned by a squad of Marines just east of the combat base also came under ground assault. The NVA swarmed all over the listening post, driving seven wounded survivors off the position, all of whom managed to reach safety at Nui Ba Ho later that night.

Falling short of their main objective, NVA artillery resumed bombardment while infantry units maneuvered for position to resume the attack next morning.

Before the sun could fully peek over the eastern horizon on 31 March, NVA troops launched an all-out assault on the northern perimeter. Marines firing 106mm flechette rounds at point-blank range into oncoming NVA soldiers broke up the attack. Marine rifles and grenades turned back a determined enemy three more times before 1000. After the last failed attempt, 130mm rounds began impacting Nui Ba Ho once again, this time with more accuracy than the previous day. While artillery was making life hazardous for the Marines, enemy gunners brought 75mm recoilless rifles into action, which took a devastating toll on defensive structures, inflicting many casualties.

After several fruitless hours of trying, the battalion executive officer, Major Hoa, finally got through to Marine artillery at Mai Loc. Marine artillerymen, manning two 105mm howitzers, answered calls for fire in support of Bravo Group. Under bombardment themselves, the crews were pulling their lanyards from prone positions and did succeed in silencing two of those deadly 75s, causing an undocumented number of casualties. With only two guns in support of a major attack, it was like trying to swat flies with a toothpick.

In fact, every combat base in MR1 had been frantically calling for artillery the past two days, with no satisfaction. The lack of ARVN response allowed NVA gunners unrestricted access to every target they now had under fire.

For two days, Alpha 2 withstood a terrific pounding, while calling in counter battery fire from a U.S. Navy destroyer off the coast in an effort to silence NVA gunners, most of whom they could not see. Midmorning of 31 March, Lieutenant Bruggeman reported enemy troops massing north of his position. NVA units could be clearly observed on three sides. Small arms fire was now raking the outpost. Even under imminent threat of attack, South Vietnamese artillerymen were still not responding to calls for fire. Northern defense trenches remained unmanned as leadership and organization was nonexistent. Of major concern to Lieutenant Bruggeman's team, if ARVN troops would not even mount a token resistance, it was a foregone conclusion the outpost will fall. USS *Buchanan* (DDG-14), now joined by USS *Joseph P. Strauss* (DDG-16) just off the coast of the demilitarized zone, worked around the clock, placing their five-inch/54 batteries on call to Wolfman 5. 7th Fleet destroyers and cruisers from several locations on Dixie Station were now steaming for the coast of northern I Corps.

Knowing reinforcements could not be dispatched to his remote element, Lieutenant Eisenstein was confronted with an extremely daunting situation. He reasoned, if the Vietnamese were not even going to try defending Alpha 2, he was determined to get his fire control team the hell out of there. Fighting a losing battle is one thing, but allowing his people to remain with an outfit that wouldn't even fight is a totally different matter. Seeking approval from the senior 3rd Division U.S. Army advisor, Colonel Metcalf, Eisenstein presented his evacuation plan. Having a different view on the tactical situation, the officer in charge would not release needed assets for an extraction mission, as he needed that spot team's eyes on the DMZ. The lieutenant's requests were taken under advisement but approval remained in abeyance. For Eisenstein, there were no other options on the table. Concern for Wolfman 5 held his top priority.

Embattled Bravo Group Marines' spirits were lifted around 1730 when a brief break in the cloud cover allowed a flight of U.S. Air Force F-4 Phantoms to provide the only tactical air support Nui Ba Ho would receive. At Captain Smith's direction, the Air Force took out a large gun observed being hauled up the south slope and did manage to disburse an enemy formation supporting that gun. Under cover of darkness, the NVA resumed their attack. With renewed resolve, a determined enemy scaled the northslope in strength.

Marines on the perimeter met the assault with a furious storm of small arms fire. After two days of nonstop combat, the defense of Nui Ba Ho was by now reduced to only four squads. NVA assault troops now occupied position just below the wire.

A U.S. Air Force C-119 Stinger gunship arrived over the distressed outpost sometime around 2130, circling Nui Ba Ho and Sarge. By this time, the cloud cover closed in again, preventing the support ship from employing its miniguns. Major Walter Boomer at Sarge tried using a radar beacon to bring the ship's miniguns to bear on the target-rich landscape, but the airship could not get a lock on the transmitter. The quick-thinking Marine next tried using an infrared strobe light, with equally negative results. In one more attempt to get a position fix, the aircraft dropped flares, which due to an ever-increasing cloud cover, also came up empty.

When the 2 million-candlepower flares descended below the clouds, NVA troops could be seen swarming all over the landscape, massing to support attackers on the north perimeter, who now had a foothold in the wire of Nui Ba Ho. By 2205, North Vietnamese assault troops breached the perimeter. Captain Smith and his Vietnamese radio operator exited the command bunker to assess the situation. Four or five NVA troops appeared three meters in front of the bunker. They must have been disoriented, as Smith took the opportunity to slip past them unseen. The Marine moved cautiously toward the south perimeter, where he hooked up with several other unattached Marines. Major Boa arrived just seconds after Smith. It seems the Marines were afraid to go through the wire because of defensive mines augmenting the barrier.

Major Bao organized his men in single file and got them moving tentatively through the concertina barrier. From no more than five feet away, an NVA soldier suddenly emerged from the darkness, taking the stalled column under fire. Pivoting on instinct, Captain Smith shot the man dead. Knowing others would come to investigate, the Covan took the lead. Springing to the front of the column, Smith flung himself atop the wire on his back. Without hesitation, the others followed in trace, using the officer as a springboard to clear the perimeter. Extracting himself from the self-imposed snare, Captain Smith followed, leaving most of his uniform in the tangled wire and sporting numerous deep cuts. As soon as the last Marine was safely away, in fluent Vietnamese, the Covan called for artillery on the now-enemy-held combat base. At 2240, all radio contact with 4th Battalion Bravo Group ceased.

Major Boomer, with 4th Battalion Alpha Group at Sarge, faced the same situation of concentrated artillery fire and all-day infantry assaults from the NVA 66th Regiment. Several times that afternoon, in the face of fierce resistance, assault troops were forced back to regroup, taking heavy casualties, only to doggedly come back at the Marines again. Hearing Captain Smith's call for fire on his own position added more stressful overtones to an already-desperate situation. Aside from concerns for Captain Smith, Major Boomer was well aware that without Nui Ba Ho guarding the northern approach to Sarge, things were going to get much tougher.

NVA assaults coming against Sarge all night kept the embattled Marines immersed in a continuous fight. At 0345, NVA infantry finally penetrated the wire. The remnants of Alpha Group, along with Major Boomer, abandoned the outpost, using heavy rain as a partial shield to slip between two enemy units on a downhill escape from Sarge.

Earlier in the day, Firebase Fuller, manned by 1st Battalion, 2nd Regiment, was overrun, as was Khe Gio, defended by 3rd Battalion, 56th Regiment. Both units were now embroiled in a fighting withdrawal toward Cam Lo.

Lieutenant Colonel Gerald H. Turley, USMC, newly arrived for his second tour in Vietnam, was in the Ai Tu TOC keeping up on events and making himself useful since hostilities began on 30 March. Having recently assumed duties of assistant senior advisor to the Vietnamese Marine Corps, the colonel was on a brief tour of VNMC units in northern I Corps, meeting his U.S. Marine advisors and getting a feel for his new position. He was preparing to continue his tour when the NVA interrupted his itinerary. As a visitor in northern I Corps, he had no command responsibilities, but did pass on VNMC activities to the G-3 staff and offered to work under the guidance of the U.S. Army G-3 officer. The evening of 31 March, Colonel Metcalf pulled Turley aside and asked him to take over G-3 responsibilities in absence of his own officer, who was not up to the task. After a brief conversation, the two officers came to agreement and Turley accepted the responsibility.

The evening of 31 March, North Vietnamese infantry were reported closing on Alpha 1, 2, 3, and 4; Charlie 1, 2, 3, and 4; as well as Mai Loc and Camp Carroll.

Close to 0900 on 1 April, Lieutenant Eisenstein finally received tentative approval from Colonel Metcalf to organize an emergency rescue operation to Alpha 2, but was ordered to hold launch until final approval was given. Rushing to the airstrip to expedite transportation, Eisenstein couldn't find one U.S. helicopter on the tarmac. After an anxious wait, a single Huey from F Troop, 8th Cavalry finally set down. The pilot agreed to fly the mission but had to wait on his Cobra gunship escort. It was finally coming together. As soon as the gunship escorts arrived, Lieutenant Eisenstein lost no time briefing all three crews. Pointing out Alpha 2 on his situation map, Lieutenant Eisenstein didn't pull any punches while imparting the desperate tactical situation. Knowing full well that Alpha 2 was almost completely surrounded and heavy ground fire could surely be expected, none of the pilots showed any hesitation. All he needed now was launch approval.

Finding a field phone, the anxious lieutenant called the advisors G-3 section to get launch approval from Colonel Metcalf. This officer needed for launch authority, however, had departed Ai Tu along with General Giai to meet with ARVN commanders on the firebases to shore up confidence and gain first-hand understanding of the fluid tactical situation. Lieutenant Eisenstein then got Sergeant Joe D. Swift on the phone, ordering him to secure Lieutenant Colonel Turley's permission on the hot. Having been briefed by Lieutenant Eisenstein on his Alpha 2 team situation prior, the colonel was already up to speed. Faced with a decision that he really didn't have the authority to make, Lieutenant Colonel Turley weighed the request. After a few moments of collected thought, Turley gave the go-ahead. It was now approximately 1130.

None of the pilots comprising the rescue mission had ever flown that close to the DMZ and were not familiar with the area. Without hesitating, Lieutenant Eisenstein volunteered his services as guide and jumped aboard. Under overcast skies and threatening weather, the small armada lifted off the tarmac at Quang Tri.

Once airborne, the UH-1E and armed Cobra gunships set course for Alpha 2, flying north along the coast, hugging the ground. A call had already gone out, alerting Lieutenant Bruggeman to have Wolfman 5 assembled and ready for extraction. The accommodating guns of the USS *Buchanan*, now augmented by the batteries of the USS *Joseph P. Strauss* (DDG-16), commenced pounding the area immediately north of Alpha 2, danger close! Lieutenant Eisenstein took control of naval gunfire support assets while Wolfman 5 assembled their equipment and moved from their concrete observation tower to the landing pad some thirty feet away.

Approaching Alpha 2 from the east, staying south but still uncomfortably close to the gun target line of destroyers *Buchanan* and *Joseph P. Strauss*, Lieutenant Eisenstein could make out NVA troops maneuvering to surround the station. Both Cobras made repeated runs on target but were only partially successful at suppressing escalating ground fire, now directed at the approaching slick. From 200 meters out at treetop level, the oval-shaped outpost assumed a scene straight from Dante's Inferno. Shell craters pockmarked the entire landscape. Most trees within 100 meters of the perimeter were splintered and denuded of foliage. Explosions kicked up earth at a rate of two or three per minute on the ground below, as automatic weapons spewed green tracers crisscrossing the path of the solitary airship. Applying more resources to foil the mission, NVA artillery patiently waited until the Huey flared for descent then began to pour it on, blanketing the outpost with an intense shower of steel. Naval gunfire generously pummeling areas north and northeast around the outpost did little to disrupt NVA gunners.

Progressing closer to touchdown, Eisenstein was stunned to see numerous defensive bunkers heaped in rubble, guarding a half-destroyed concertina barrier that remained only a twisted portion of a once-formidable obstacle. A thick layer of gunpowder smog wafted effortlessly across a seemingly deserted ghost town atmosphere, emitting a heavy odor of cordite, completing an all-too-real illusion of descending into hell. Not one person was moving inside the perimeter. High-explosive shells continued falling on Alpha 2 unabated even as the skids made contact with the landing pad.

Minutes before the evacuation chopper touched down, Lieutenant Bruggeman was felled by shrapnel wounds to his head en route to the landing pad. He'd given up his own helmet to one of his Marines, whose own helmet had been stolen.

Springing from the door, Lieutenant Eisenstein sprinted to the team about twenty meters away, nestled behind a bunker. Not having time for pleasantries, he quickly got his people, loaded down with equipment, moving toward the waiting chopper. Sergeant James L. Newton, struggling under his own load, was also trying to carry his commanding officer. Eisenstein relieved the NCO of the wounded officer, ordering the equipment-heavy sergeant to get on the helicopter. The door gunner, noticing Lieutenant Eisenstein struggling with the wounded officer, bolted from the aircraft to help carry the wounded man.

Hard on the run, with impacting ordnance shaking the ground under their feet, the last three passengers scrambled aboard the UH-1E. Eisenstein immediately noticed only four team members in the helicopter. Corporal James F. Worth was not with the team. Fog of war, missed communication, no one knows, but he wasn't there. Ordering Wolfman 5 to remain in the helicopter, Joel Eisenstein gutted out a mad dash excursion to the observation tower, calling to his absent Marine through deafening explosions and mounting battle clatter. Worth was nowhere to be found. The pace of incoming fire now started picking up noticeably in intensity. Quickly moving among nearby bunkers and Quonset huts, still calling out to Worth, the determined officer knew he was running out of time. He also knew he had no choice but to get out what men he could. He silently said a prayer for James and hoped with all his heart he would soon be demanding an answer of his errant corporal in person: "Just where the hell have you been?"

Turning back to the helo pad scorched to his soul, the dejected lieutenant reluctantly gave thumbs-up to the pilot, who was already rolling in throttle.

By this time, a few Vietnamese troops still on station awakened to the fact that something was going on. Hearing familiar sounds of rotor blades slapping at the wind, some even garnered enough courage to venture out of their bunkers, gravitating toward the crowded aircraft. Lieutenant Eisenstein sprinted through the gathering throng and pulled two wounded Vietnamese aboard before the packed helicopter broke contact with earth. Terrified at the prospect of remaining at Alpha 2, several rushed the aircraft in a vain attempt to secure passage on the last train out of Dodge. Lieutenant Eisenstein was forced to lean out the door and kick two would-be stowaways off the skids.

Pivoting west, the aircraft pulled away from Alpha 2 still under covering fire from gunship escorts. North Vietnamese soldiers were observed breaking through the south gate even as the UH-1E cleared air space over the beleaguered outpost.

Somewhere between the aircraft and observation tower, Joel Eisenstein had picked up a few metal souvenirs and lacerations, which were of little concern compared to the condition of his friend Dave Bruggeman, whose head he held cradled on his lap. His heart was also seeped in remorse at not lifting off with his entire team.

En route to Quang Tri, via radio transmission an arrangement was made to have a Medevac chopper waiting to transport Lieutenant Bruggeman to the hospital in Da Nang. ANGLICO corpsman HM3 Thomas E. Williamson accompanied the wounded officer on his flight to Da Nang, applying all the life-saving skills in his inventory. Mortally wounded, the valiant lieutenant did not survive his flight, expiring in Doc Williamson's arms. For his valor at Alpha 2 through three days and two nights under constant fire, Lieutenant David C. Bruggeman was posthumously awarded the Silver Star.

More bad news from the west reached the TOC. Fire Support Base Holcomb, after three days of fending off continuous assaults, fell to the NVA at 1430.

General Giai, after consulting with Colonel Metcalf, ordered his units north of the Cua Viet to fall back to Dong Ha, where it was hoped he could mass his troops and stop forward momentum of the invasion. As the general's style of leadership was to be up front with his troops, instilling confidence and bolstering morale, he was absent from the TOC up to four or five hours at a time each day. This fall back and regroup order was issued from the field communicated directly to his battalion and regimental commanders. No one bothered to inform the advisors at the TOC until much later. As a result, there was no coordinated fire support plan to cover the withdrawal.

Affected units of the 57th Regiment began pulling out of their firebases, moving in the general direction of Dong Ha, mixing with panicked civilians moving south. NVA spotters, making no distinction between military and noncombatants, continued raining artillery on the mixed crowds. The intended orderly withdrawal soon lost focus as control slipped away from field commanders.

At Charlie 1, the regimental command center, things were a little more under control as the defenders waited in place for trucks to move the artillery. A plan was in motion to move off the firebase at 2400. 2nd Battalion of the 57th performed rear guard duties to cover the evacuation, while 3rd Battalion with the regimental headquarters fell back to Dong Ha.

Soldiers of the 2nd Battalion 56th with U.S. Army advisor Major Joseph Brown, withdrawing from Charlie 2 on the west flank, now joined by an ARVN armored cavalry squadron, was making progress toward the Cam Lo Bridge in a bid to reach Route 9 and eventually Camp Carroll. After a two-day journey, fighting every inch along the way, the battered but not defeated 2nd Battalion finally reached Camp Carroll in the early evening hours.

Marines of the 7th VNMC Battalion were pulled off their current mission of keeping Route 9 open and ordered to reinforce Mai Loc. The 7th moved out in convoy on trucks west on Route 9 toward Cam Lo. Coming under artillery attack twice, the column halted just west of Cam Lo. Reacting to reports of enemy armor, Major Hue dismounted his Marines and proceeded south by foot on Route 558, passing behind the east side of Camp Carroll. The Battalion arrived at Mai Loc under intermittent fire, passing through the wire at 1530.

At 1900, on orders from General Giai, headquarters personnel of the 3rd Division started relocating to Quang Tri City. In order to keep continuity in coordinating fire support, a skeleton crew of G-3 advisors remained in place at Ai Tu under command of Lieutenant Colonel Turley, on orders from General Kroesen. Lieutenant Eisenstein and his team chief, Sergeant Swift, stayed with the now 3rd Division forward.

When dawn broke on Easter Sunday, every fire support base north of the Cua Viet belonged to the enemy. Mai Loc and Camp Carroll were the only firebases guarding the western approach to Quang Tri City, still holding out under ferocious assaults and bombardment. Heightened activities of 2 April would quickly accelerate to a host of events, any one of which at any other time during the war would have dominated headlines for a week.

Major Boomer, with survivors of 4th Battalion Alpha Group, made his way to a village northeast of Mai Loc, where Captain Smith and surviving Marines of Bravo Group from Nui Ba Ho were already gathered. As each Covan thought the other to be killed in action, it was a surprise and joyful discovery for both.

Sometime that morning (not documented), Corporal Worth came up on radio to advise that he was going to try and make Dong Ha. (The source of this report is unknown. That broadcast did not come over the ANGLICO TAC net.) Corporal Worth never arrived in Dong Ha. The North Vietnamese claim they did not take him prisoner, and his fate is not known.

At 0854, the first confirmed report of communist tanks reached the TOC. Enemy armor was spotted at Alpha 2. At 0910, U.S. Navy destroyers reported tanks in the open north of the Cua Viet, which were taken under direct fire and destroyed. Further reports of tanks on Highway 1 between Alpha 2 and Charlie 1 sent every one's adrenalin levels over the top. A two-pronged armored attack moving south was confirmed by Vietnamese and American radio nets. Lieutenant Eisenstein and Sergeant Swift went to work mapping out fire control plans to deal with the tanks as well as defensive fires to support the onrushing confrontation at Dong Ha. Five ships comprising Naval Gunfire Support Task Unit 70.8.9 USS *Buchanan* (DDG14), Commander William J. Thearle, captain, assumed flagship responsibilities. In company with USS *Joseph P. Strauss* (DDG-16), USS *Waddell* (DDG-14), USS *Hamner* (DD-718), and USS *Anderson* (DD-786), the small armada in a massed display of naval power took the enemy armor under fire, destroying several while dodging fire and dealing with NVA shore batteries.

2nd Battalion of the 57th held in place through the night, guarding the Trouc Khe Bridge two miles north of Dong Ha, waiting for ARVN engineers with demolitions, who never arrived. Enemy tanks were reported just a few miles north at Charlie 1, and NVA troops were making a bid to outflank the battalion. As these troops were needed to complete defensive position alignments at Dong Ha, they were immediately ordered south.

With the VNMC Brigade 258 now in Ai Tu since 31 March as 3rd Division reserves, Lieutenant Colonel Turley could see no other option but to move them up to Dong Ha to reinforce the 57th. All the capital to stop the invasion was invested in holding the North Vietnamese north of the Cua Viet. Making a call to General Giai in Quang Tri for tactical guidance on committing the reserves, he spoke to the division deputy commander, Colonel Chung, in the absence of the general, who was out on one of his morale-boosting visits to the front lines. Refusing to make a decision, Colonel Chung denied the request and nothing would change his mind.

Seeing the situation slipping away, Turley then appealed to the 258th VNMC Brigade commander, Colonel Ngo Van Dinh, to commit his assets to Dong Ha. After some hesitation on the part of Dinh, the two Marines took it upon themselves to reinforce the 57th. Colonel Dinh commanded Major Le Ba Bihn and his 3rd Battalion to Dong Ha under orders to hold the city and its bridges "at all costs."

Armor of the 20th Tank Battalion under command of Lieutenant Colonel Ton Ta Ley, with U.S. Army advisor Major James E. Smock, hooked up with 3rd VNMC Battalion on approach to Dong Ha just south of the outskirts. As the column went forward, NVA artillery started pounding the city and ARVN defensive positions in a deluge of 120mm rockets and 130mm high-explosive shells.

At some point late in the morning, a rumor of NVA tanks on the bridge made its way through ARVN radio channels, causing panic among the battle-weary 57th. Hundreds of soldiers deserted their posts, mixing with an ever-increasing flow of fleeing civilians meandering south down Highway 1.

Seeing terrified throngs of soldiers scurrying past the column in the opposite direction, Major Bihn dismounted the tank he was riding, asking, to the effect, where the hell is everyone going? When one man who couldn't avoid the major answered, "It's no use, no use," the enraged officer pulled out his pistol and shot the man. To the others, it was a nonevent, as the disorganized mob seemingly ignored the incident, continuing helter-skelter away from Dong Ha.

At an unspecified location in or near the embattled city, only the presence of General Giai kept the remnants of the 57th from fleeing. Whatever traits historians may assign to the man, Vu Van Giai possessed good leadership instincts and an abundance of personal courage.

Once inside the city, two companies of Marines occupied position on either side of the bridge, while a third company deployed further west along Route 9 to cover the railroad span.

Closing in on noon, Captain John W. Ripley, advisor to the 3rd VNMC Battalion, arrived at Route 1 about 1,500 meters south of the bridge through an intense artillery bombardment with a small column of tanks from the ARVN 20th Tank Battalion. Ripley radioed the TOC that he was in position.

Soon after, North Vietnamese infantry appeared on the north bank of the Cua Viet. Lead elements of the 36th NVA Regiment had already started across the old French-built railroad span 300 meters west of the Highway 1 Bridge. Captain Ripley called in a fire mission, danger close, to interdict the north bank, railroad span, and bridge. Although they could not see the target, Lieutenant Eisenstein and Sergeant Swift had a fire support plan for Dong Ha already complete and knew what to do. Once the mission was passed on to the destroyers of Task Unit 70.8.9 lurking offshore, an intense one-hour bombardment kept both bridges and their respective approaches under fire. Captain Ripley then sent coordinates for fire support boxes 1,000 x 2,000 meters for each bridge approach and requested that fire be shifted between the bridges. The boxes proved to be just the right move, negating any further need for time-consuming coordinate checks and adjustments, just a request for more fire at box 1 or 2.

Four PT-76 amphibious tanks were observed traversing the north bank of the Cau Viet east of Dong Ha. Captain Ripley quickly shifted fire. U.S. Navy destroyers soon had 5-inch/54 help on the way, taking out all four.

Clearing skies allowed a flight of VNAF A-1 Skyraiders to dip below the clouds, bombing and strafing enemy armor formations within 1,000 meters of the bridge, taking out eleven tanks before expending all ordnance. More tanks kept coming. From high ground looking across the river, ARVN tanks acquired visual contact with the NVA armor column. At 2,500 meters, 1st Troop opened fire, taking six more tanks out of action. Getting closer to the river, NVA tanks soon disappeared from sight, covered by terrain features that offered a defilade approach to the bridge.

Developments of communist armor appearing north of the Cua Viet in strength presented a menacing new dimension of potential disaster to chaotic defense preparations being hastily put together at the bridge. Pitifully short of antiarmor weapons Captain Ripley radioed Ai Tu, requesting permission to blow the bridge. Telling Ripley to stand by, Colonel Turley called FRAC headquarters, summarizing the critical tactical situation and asking for authority to demolish the bridge. Permission to blow the bridge was denied, using the logic that it needed to remain standing for counterattacks. Over his strong objections, Turley received a direct order: "Do not destroy the bridge."

Knowing every minute counted, Turley weighed the severity of leaving the bridge intact. For the second time that morning, Lieutenant Colonel Turley took it upon himself to brush aside orders from above and told Captain Ripley to blow the bridge by whatever means he could.

At 1215, NVA artillery prep slacked off, and the lead tank moved onto the bridge. Sergeant Huynh Van Luom, a rocket squad leader attached to the 1st Company, in position at the bridge abutment, fired two M-72 disposable Light Antiarmor Weapon rockets at the tank, scoring a nondisabling bull's eye on the second attempt. For whatever reason, the tank commander backed his vehicle off the bridge.

Captain Ripley and Major Smock, riding tanks, advanced within 100 meters of the bridge, hidden from observation. On foot, the pair used cover of an old bunker and closed more ground. From the bunker to the bridge was open terrain. Both men ran the gauntlet under fire by small arms and occasional artillery rounds. Upon reaching the bridge, they found ARVN engineers at work applying explosives, but not in a placement that would get the job done.

Being schooled in explosives, Captain Ripley took it upon himself to move the charges where they would do some good. Explosives placement needed to be staggered to torque and lift the span upon detonation. Working in tandem, Ripley scaled the chain link fence, accepting the charges passed over the fence by Major Smock. The captain then transported the explosives to the bridge and carried them hand over hand across the steel girders and secured them in place. Ripley repeated this physically exhausting maneuver over a dozen times while under fire from the north bank. NVA gunners, sensing what he was up to, tried very hard to take John Ripley out of the war. Major Smock scaled the fence several times, dodging NVA shooters, to have charges ready for Ripley. Once the job was complete and charges ready, Captain Ripley went back under the bridge to set the fuses while Major Smock shifted his efforts to the railroad span, assisting ARVN engineers.

While the battle for Dong Ha was just getting started, North Vietnam's 304th Division kept pressure on Camp Carroll, now reeling under its fourth day of intense bombardment. By 1400, the 56th Regiment turned back two massive assaults on its western perimeter in the fiercest fighting since the opening volley. NVA bodies, now decorating the concertina barrier, offered gruesome testimonial on how close the fight had been. Almost succeeding in their last attempt, enemy troops fell by the hundreds to point-blank firing of Carroll's howitzers.

As the surrender of Camp Carroll has always been a topic of much discussion, generating as much controversy as any of the swarm of events occurring during the Easter Offensive, the following narrative from Andrew Wiest in *Vietnam's Forgotten Army* is offered in a condensed presentation of one of his interviews with Lieutenant Colonel Pham Van Dinh, commander of the 56th ARVN:

Soon after the second attack was beaten off...

Dinh received a call from the NVA. The caller said he was near and knew all about Dinh and his men and of their dangers. The caller went on to make this offer: If Dinh surrendered, he and his men would be welcomed by the NVA. If they did not, they would die. The transmission ended.

Dinh received a second transmission from someone who claimed to be the commander of communist forces in the area. He repeated the earlier offer and stipulated it was the last such offer that Dihn would receive. Dinh responded that he would need time to meet with his regimental staff and requested a cease fire. The NVA representative complied.

When Lieutenant Colonel Dinh polled his staff, a unanimous vote was taken to accept the NVA offer. (Lieutenant Colonel Camper, unaware of the meeting's agenda, did know a meeting was in progress but was denied entry when he tried to enter the bunker at around 1500.)

Dinh informed the NVA of the decision and arranged for a longer cease fire while his staff prepared for the surrender. The NVA officer had one last request: He wanted the U.S. advisors who accompanied the 56th Regiment. Dihn replied the advisors had long since left Camp Carroll.

Arriving at the American's bunker, Lieutenant Colonel Dihn informed the two officers of his decision to lay down arms. Lieutenant Colonel Camper and Major Brown received news of surrender in total disbelief and anger. Not being able to dissuade his counterpart, Camper in as civil a manner as he could muster ended their relationship. He then transmitted news of this event in an obscure coded message to Ai Tu (in case the NVA had ears). He then requested evacuation. Not being able to decipher the true meaning of the message, Lieutenant Colonel Turley sent a reply indicating that he was to hold position.

The advisors quickly gathered whatever classified materials were on hand and destroyed them. Joined by a few Vietnamese who wanted no part of surrender, the Americans and their small entourage gravitated to the south perimeter. On the way, Camper again contacted Ai Tu and repeated his message of minutes ago, this time in plain English, and again requested help. The small formation cut through the wire and started downhill.

From the TOC, U.S. Army Captain James Avery established contact with a U.S. Army CH-47, call sign Coachman 005, inbound to Mai Loc with an external load of ammunition. The pilot agreed to accept the mission. Once the cargo was deposited, the Chinook banked northeast, closing on Camp Carroll.

The escaping soldiers had not gone very far through the wire when they were spotted and taken under fire by NVA further downhill. In the midst of exchanging fire with an unknown number of communist troops, Coachman 005 contacted Colonel Camper, requesting landing instructions.

While transmitting the requested information, the Americans and Vietnamese loyalists scurried back inside Camp Carroll's perimeter. Within a matter of minutes, Coachman was on the ground. Several unarmed Vietnamese tried boarding but were barred by a very pissed-off Colonel Camper, who would only allow armed men who hadn't surrendered onto the waiting chopper. With a full load, Coachman 005 lifted off under cover from two Cobra gunship escorts, found a southeast heading, then sped off toward Ai Tu.

Afraid that Dihn was using the chopper for his personal departure, the NVA announced that it was prepared to open fire on the craft with artillery and antiaircraft guns. Dinh, though, reassured the NVA that he was still there and that the chopper was only a Medevac for his most badly wounded men, and stayed on the radio the entire time it took for the helicopter to come and go.

At 1530, the loss of Camp Carroll, along with 1,800 men and twenty-two field pieces, dispatched shock waves of alarm all the way to Saigon. As the anchor for the western line of defense fell, nowhere else did the sting of that event have more of an urgent impact than it did at Mai Loc, just 2,000 meters southwest of the fallen firebase. As Carroll and Mai Loc provided each other with reciprocal fire support, the Marines of VNMC Brigade 147 now stood alone. Viewing the position to be untenable without supporting fires and with dwindling ammunition stocks, Lieutenant Colonel Nguyen Nang Bao, commanding, requested and received permission to evacuate Mai Loc but reserved the actual decision to do so until conditions dictated that option as an action of last resort.

With all the charges in place, Captain Ripley crimped blasting caps onto communications wire, then attached the caps to his explosives. Providing an option to protect his investment, the resourceful Marine also ran a forty-five-minute timed fuse to his prepared demolition packages.

Clearing the fence, Captain Ripley ran the wire back to a burning utility truck near the road, then touched the wire to each battery terminal. Nothing happened. Braving the gauntlet of fire back to the bridge, Ripley ignited the timed fuse, then once more ran for cover.

After what seemed an excessive passage of time, the anxious Ripley and every ear in the area heard 500 pounds of explosives detonate. The span, in the manner expected, twisted and rose, shearing its anchor to the abutment. The 600,000-ton steel and concrete structure then dropped into the Cua Viet.

Seeing the opportunity slipping away, North Vietnamese began massing PT-76 amphibious tanks on the north bank. Four tanks crawled to the river's edge, preparing to enter the Cua Viet. Bridge or not, they fought too hard to be denied this prize. Calling back to Eisenstein, Captain Ripley requested fire. Calling on the USS *Buchanan*, who because of the distance had to brave enemy shore batteries to come closer, entered the five-fathom curve (minimum depth clearance for a DDG) and opened fire with devastating effect, causing all four amphibians to disappear. They were the last tanks to challenge her guns that day. In spite of North Vietnamese shore batteries trying very hard to take her out of the equation, the USS *Buchanan* stood her ground and became the deciding factor that day.

Still not ready to throw in the towel, having been turned back at Dong Ha and at the mouth of the Cua Viet, NVA armor advanced from the west, attempting to cross the Cam Lo Bridge. The American advisor with the 1st ARVN Armored Brigade called for air strikes to destroy the bridge. When the smoke cleared, the tanks were gone but the bridge still remained.

Through the night right up to dawn, the guns of USS *Buchanan*, USS *Joseph P. Strauss*, and USS *Waddell* hurled five-inch/54 shells into suspected NVA positions and approaches, interdicting enemy movement. Dong Ha was safe for the time being.

When, at 1800, the last 155mm rounds on the base were expended, artillerymen on Mai Loc spiked their guns. Colonel Boa made his decision to evacuate at 1815 and informed his Covan. Major Joy and his advisors began destroying all they had in the way of classified materials. In a coded message, Joy sent word to Major Boomer at Mai Loc Village of the impending evacuation.

During the resupply mission flown earlier by Coachman 005, the executive officer observed that his low approach from the east did not attract ground fire. Through the east gate, Headquarters Company in front, followed in trace by each unit in the designated order of march, Marines began their exodus from Mai Loc. Major De Bona and

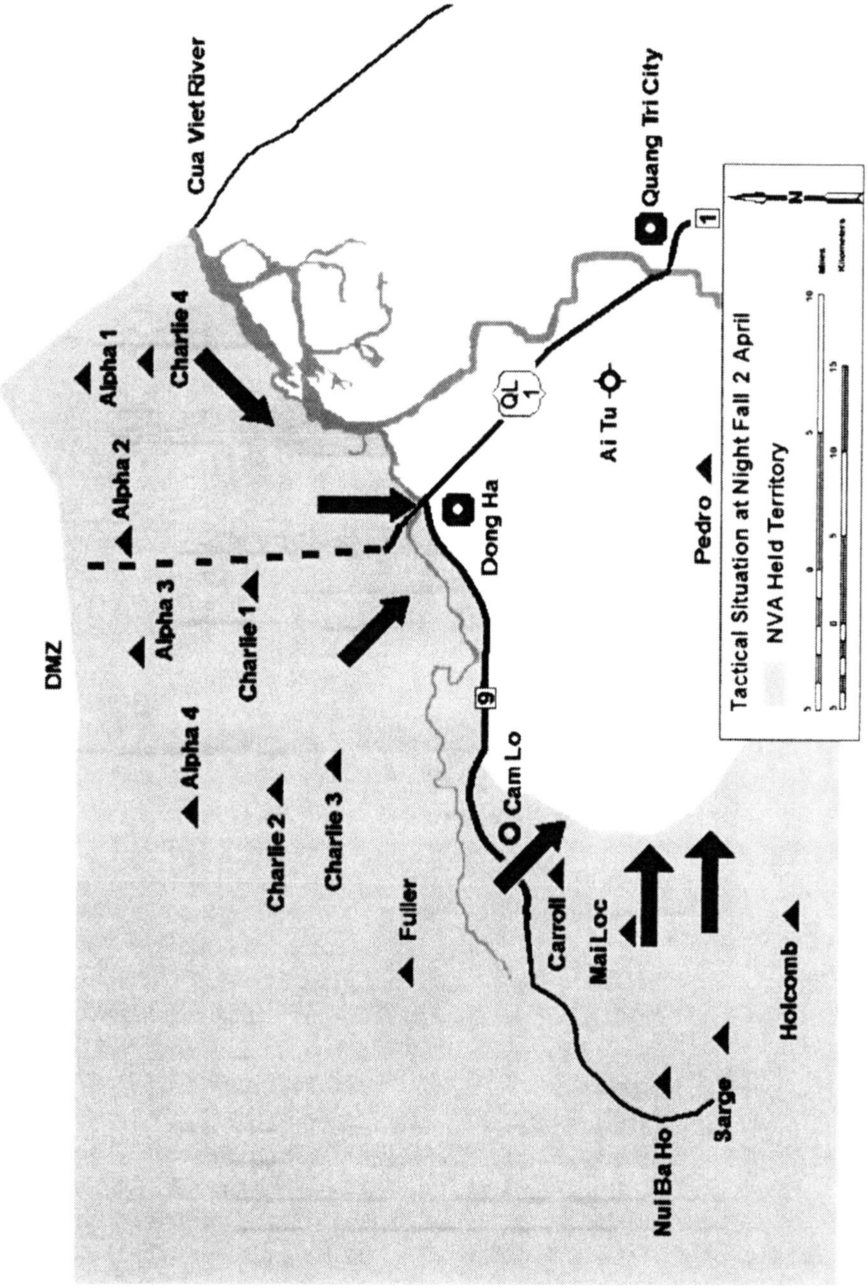
Cua Viet River
Quang Tri City
Alpha 1
Charlie 4
Alpha 2
DMZ
Alpha 3
Charlie 1
Alpha 4
Charlie 2
Charlie 3
Fuller
Dong Ha
QL 1
Ai Tu
Pedro
9
Cam Lo
Carroll
Mai Loc
Holcomb
Sarge
Nui Ba Ho
1
N
Tactical Situation at Night Fall 2 April
NVA Held Territory

Captain Rice with 7th VNMC Battalion were last to clear the outpost as rear guard. As two of its companies were still engaged holding the perimeter against attacking forces of the 66th NVA Regiment, there was some confusion on descent from the outpost. Considering the stress of this difficult maneuver at night, the 7th Battalion executed as orderly a withdrawal as could be asked.

The withdrawal through virgin jungle in driving rain can be capsulated, although very much understated, as one miserable night in a swampy hell. Most of these Marines, including the Americans, were running on empty, not having slept in over ninety-six hours on very little food.

The easterly trek to Ai Tu was divided into three groups of bone-weary Marines.

Major Joy, Major Gnibus, and Captains Randall, Kruger, and Evasick took point with Brigade 147 command group.

Major De Bona and Captain Rice followed the command group of Brigade 147 by an hour, picking up wounded and exhausted Marines on their journey east. After crossing the winding Song Dinh River three times, the wet and worn-out 7th Battalion stopped for the night around 1200 and continued on to Ai Tu in the morning.

Major Boomer and Captain Smith, with the surviving members of the 4th VNMC Battalion, departed Mai Loc Village per instructions passed on by Major Joy, taking a slightly different heading in the same general direction.

As if the calamitous events of 2 April hadn't yet caused enough stress, a USAF EB-66C/E electronics warfare aircraft, call sign Bat 21, escorting a B-52 strike mission, was brought down just north of Cam Lo by surface-to-air missiles. One of a crew of six men, Lieutenant Colonel Iceal E. Hambleton, emerged as the only crewman to survive the shootdown. Because of his extensive knowledge of radar and communications jamming and ballistic missile programs, it became very imperative he not be allowed to fall into communist hands. Events following that shootdown quickly mushroomed into the largest Search and Rescue operation of the war. A no-fire zone twenty-seven kilometers in radius, centered on Lieutenant Colonel Hambleton's position, was immediately imposed by the 7th Air Force, acting on authority from MACV. This no-fire zone extended almost to the coast and as far south as Ai Tu combat base. No air strikes, artillery, or naval gunfire missions could be conducted without approval of the Direct Air Support Center (DASC) in Da Nang, thus slowing an emergency situation demanding immediate reactions down to the speed of a bureaucratic two-step.

At a time when a critical battle was looming at the Dong Ha Bridge in an effort to halt further advance of so-far-unstoppable North Vietnamese Army columns, the use of fire support weapons was suddenly restricted. Men were dying, a war was about to be lost, and now some far-removed officer in Saigon restricted fire support without one word of consultation with battlefield commanders in the affected area. This decision should have been deferred to General Giai as ground commander. It wasn't that anyone in MR1 was not pulling for Lieutenant Colonel Hambleton's rescue, in fact all concerned hoped like hell he'd get out of this, but there were many more lives and even the fate of an entire country at stake.

A phone call was received at the 3rd Division TOC at 2115, informing the G-3 watch officer of this restriction. Immediate efforts to lift or reduce the restriction met with no success. The lunatics were now running the asylum.

At FRAC headquarters in Da Nang, Lieutenant Colonel Gray, who arrived earlier in the day to personally oversee his MR1 assets, flew into a rage upon being informed of the fire restrictions. As forceful as he was, the Sub Unit One C.O. could not convince the Air Force colonel in Da Nag to lift the restriction, nor could he convince the colonel's U.S. Army superiors to even try to convince him.

Calling on his artillery advisors, Lieutenant Colonel Turley was assured that ARVN artillery could be monitored and aborted if fire missions anywhere near the officer's vicinity were attempted. It was also determined that artillery could be safely employed within 1,000 meters of Hambleton should the need arise.

Once the location of the downed airman was learned, Lieutenant Colonel Turley, having had enough of the Air Force, set up a six-kilometer-radius safe zone around that position. On his own initiative, the lion of Ai Tu gave the order to resume supporting fires. He then contacted FRAC operations center in Da Nang, informing them of his actions and accepting full responsibility for them. Disobeying ill-advised orders to do the right thing was getting easier.

Of the whole affair, General Kroesen observed, "No commander in MR1 could change it and no command authority in Saigon could be convinced of the need to change it."

After the fact, Turley's decision was confirmed by history to be the only commonsense course of action taken anywhere in-country by anyone; but consider the courage required to shoulder the career-ending ramifications of going full throttle over orders from every senior officer involved. It will happen every time when you have a man in charge with a complete set of balls.

From 3 through 8 April, repeated attempts to capture Dong Ha were thwarted by the 3rd VNMC Battalion and 20th ARVN Tank Battalion. Under the protection of ANGLICO-coordinated naval gunfire from TU 70.8.9, communist forces were unable to secure a major beachhead on the south bank. As elements of the 2nd Regiment arrived, the defensive line at the Cua Viet gathered strength. VNMC Brigade 369, released as reserve from the Joint General Staff in Saigon, flew into Phu Bai and began filling in at firebases west and south of Quang Tri vacated by VNMC Brigade 258. Additional reinforcements of the 1st, 4th, and 5th ARVN Ranger Groups rushed to Quang Tri, adding more firepower to shore up thin defenses. B-52 ARCHLIGHT strikes and TAC Air, weather permitting, continued pounding North Vietnamese staging areas and avenues of approach.

As North Vietnamese Regiments poured across the border on 30 March, Amphibious Ready Group Alpha/31st Marine Amphibious Unit (MAU), consisting of Battalion Landing Team (BLT) 3/4 and HMM-165, had just departed Subic Bay, Republic of the Philippines, for operations in the South China Sea, where ARG/BLT 1/9 was already on station. When the situation along the DMZ boiled to crisis, ARG Alpha received direction to proceed at best speed to the vicinity of the demilitarized zone and await orders. Arriving on 2 April and keeping below the horizon, the Amphibious Ready Group stood by, making preparations to evacuate American personnel. The ARGs now on station served as advanced elements of the 9th Marine Amphibious Brigade, which was now being formed to address current events.

Twenty-four additional naval gunfire ships from all over the Pacific were also arriving off the coast. In addition to mainstay five-inch/38 and /54 destroyer guns, the light cruiser USS *Providence* (CLG-6) once more settled into the gunline, adding the weight of her six-inch /47 main batteries, as did the cruiser USS *Oklahoma City* (GLC-5). Sub Unit One spotters were now in communication with many familiar call signs of old friends making encore appearances off the coast as well as first-timers looking for a taste of blood.

In order to keep up with ever-increasing calls for fire and having more available ships to answer those calls, Lieutenant Colonel Gray transferred four air observers to Phu Bai flying back seat in L-19 Birddogs piloted by VNAF personnel. Still dealing with bad weather, the spotters performed mission assignments at great risk by breaking through cloud cover, flying at hazardously low altitudes, allowing spotters to direct gunfire where needed.

South Vietnam's Joint General Staff and their counterparts at MACV had always expected a major invasion, if one occurred, to come from the west, designed to cut South Vietnam in two. The early morning of 5 April validated intelligence analysis concerning this eventuality, as the 5th NVA Division, supported by the 203rd Armored Regiment emerged from Cambodia in Binh Long Province northwest of Saigon. By 7 April, after five attempts, the border outpost of Loc Ninh fell after heavy fighting, setting up events for the drawn-out battle of An Loc.

An OV-10A Bronco piloted by U.S. Air Force 1st Lieutenant Bruce C. Walker, call sign Covey 282, touched down at Phu Bai Airfield after a short hop from Da Nang. ANGLICO spotter 1st Lieutenant Larry Fletcher Potts quickly scrambled aboard. Around 1035, Covey 282 was airborne once more, heading north past Quang Tri City along QL-1.

Neither man was looking forward to this mission, as their flight path would cross the Cua Viet River, putting the aircraft well within range of NVA gunners. It was a fact of life that numerous surface-to-air missile sites and antiaircraft artillery pieces supporting the weeklong offensive were now operational inside and south of the DMZ, and they had been very active for the past week.

The now-famous Bat 21 shootdown just five days prior loomed as an ominous event, giving both men good reason to be concerned.

The EB-66 was a much more sophisticated aircraft, and it flew faster and operated at higher altitude than the OV-10A could ever hope to achieve. That shootdown occurred close to the area Covey-282 was currently on course to intercept. Later the same afternoon of Bat 21's demise, two of four helicopters dispatched to effect crew rescue were likewise knocked out of the sky. One chopper went down in the jungle, with its crew of four lost, while the other managed to reach an area still under friendly domain, making a controlled crash landing. On the following day, 3 May, an OV-10, call sign "Nail 38," was also brought down in the same general vicinity, looming only a few minutes ahead on Covey's flight path. Nail-38 had been piloted by Captain William Henderson, who was eventually captured. His back seater, Lieutenant Mark Clark, grandson of WWII General Mark Clark, evaded capture and was eventually rescued after several days of evasion, along with Lieutenant Colonel Hambleton. A few miles south near Quang Tri City, and that's really close to home, one more UH1-H, flying normal resupply missions, was taken out by enemy gunners.

Both men received daily briefings on current tactical events and were very well aware of North Vietnamese progress on their very aggressive push toward Quang Tri. The latest incident of concern for air crews had occurred only the day before, when an HH-53C just west of Covey's current position was lost with all hands while making a rescue attempt for Bat 21. Once north of the Cua Viet, things could get rough.

On this day 7 April, Larry Fletcher Potts was born twenty five years ago, taking position at the starting gate of life. What a way to celebrate a birthday. Clearing air west of Dong Ha where South Vietnamese forces still clung to a tenuous defense against a swarming enemy at approximately 1055, Covey was now braced for action.

An O2 Birddog on station some distance east observed a SAM launch from inside the DMZ at 1105. Minutes later, Lieutenant Walker was heard on the Guard channel, reporting his shootdown and current location. Within minutes, Search and Rescue aircraft arrived on station, establishing radio contact with Potts and Walker, who were separated from each other on descent, as indicated by the location of each parachute on the ground. The SAR craft soon verified each crewman as uninjured, reporting visual sightings on both. NVA troops in the vicinity reacted quickly, cordoning the area and driving off the SAR craft with heavy ground fire, effectively aborting any immediate rescue attempt.

Soon thereafter, voice and visual contact with Lieutenant Potts was lost. Frequent attempts to raise the gunfire spotter proved fruitless. Over the next several days, visual and voice contact with Lieutenant Walker continued to fuel promise for at least one successful operation. Aerial observers directed him east toward a more favorable extraction point. Taking an active role in his rescue, Lieutenant Walker several times employed his signal mirror as a visual reference for guiding airborne FACs in directing air strikes on enemy positions. Continuing to evade capture, Lieutenant Walker made good progress toward the intended extraction site.

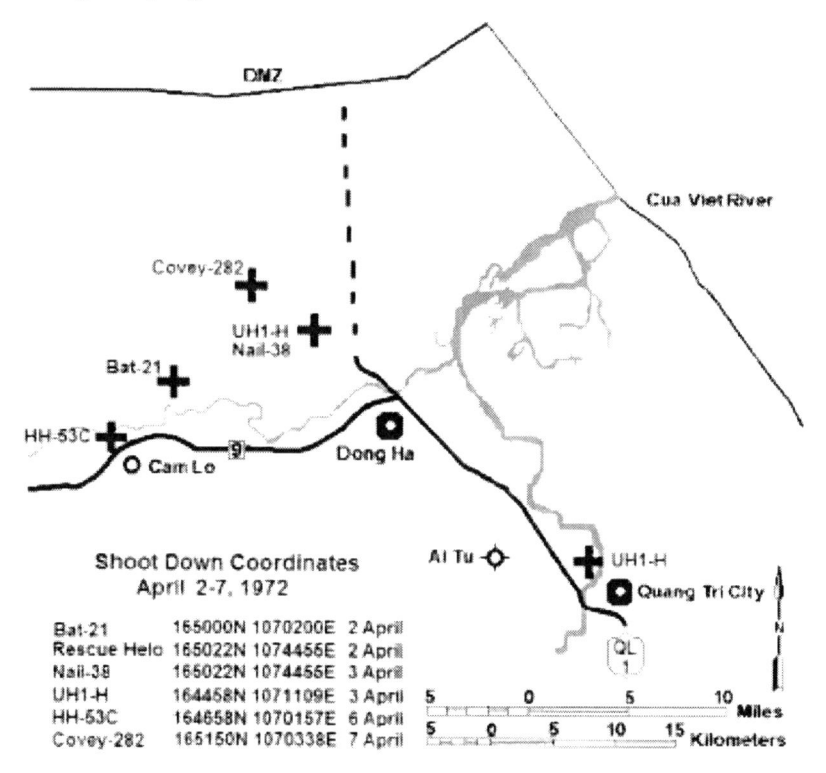

Shoot Down Coordinates
April 2-7, 1972

Bat-21	165000N 1070200E	2 April
Rescue Helo	165022N 1074455E	2 April
Nail-38	165022N 1074455E	3 April
UH1-H	164458N 1071109E	3 April
HH-53C	164658N 1070157E	6 April
Covey-282	165150N 1070338E	7 April

Early on the morning of 18 April, Lieutenant Walker, while on the move, was spotted and taken under fire by NVA soldiers. At 0718, Walker, realizing his evasion effort was finished, came up on his radio even as the NVA were on close approach, advising further rescue attempts be aborted.

From overhead, an airborne FAC, observing enemy troops positioned around Lieutenant Walker, requested an emergency air strike at close quarters in a bid to keep this rescue operation going. Arriving quickly on station, two F-4s did manage to brush back forces closing in on Lieutenant Walker. With 30,000 North Vietnamese running rampant between the Cua Viet and DMZ, it was like trying to plug a dam with a pencil. The FAC looked helplessly on once the F-4s, deplete of ordnance and running low on fuel, cleared air space as NVA troops closed in on Walker. On that day, Lieutenant Bruce C. Walker fought his last fight, his radio went silent, and, like Lieutenant Larry Fletcher Potts, has not been heard from again.

USS John R. Craig
(DD-885)
Gearing Class Destroyer
Call Sign: Assassin

On September 13, 1966, USS *John R. Craig* entered the Gulf of Tonkin for plane guard duty; ten days later, she provided naval gunfire support for Operation Golden Fleece in Quang Ngai Province. She was next assigned to Operations Sea Dragon and Traffic Cop, interdicting supplies from the North to the demilitarized zone. During this duty, she engaged enemy shore batteries and shelled North Vietnamese radar sites. On December 4, 1966, she departed the Gulf of Tonkin and returned home early in 1967 to prepare for future action.

Once again plying the waters of Vietnam on 7 August 1969, USS *John R. Craig* plunged into a tense situation. For more than sixty minutes of continuous gunfire support, her twin five-inch/38 caliber guns suppressed hostile fire, enabling rescue helicopters to pick up a team of trapped rangers. The *Craig* remained on station until August 22, firing at 289 targets during forty-eight missions. The ship was credited with four KIAs, eighty-five bunkers destroyed and seventy-eight damaged, ninety-five meters of tunnel collapsed, forty-four military structures destroyed, damaging eleven more, and causing seventeen secondary fires and two secondary explosions. USS *John R. Craig* headed for San Diego on 19 October, arriving there on 3 November 1969.

New Year's Day 1971 found USS *John R. Craig* on the gunline. Taking her turn on Yankee Station, she assumed SAR duties in the Gulf of Tonkin through most of March. On 25 March, she was once again on the gunline in Military Region 2 of the Republic of Vietnam for the second time this cruise, returning home to San Diego on 22 April.

In February 1972, USS *John R. Craig* was again in her familiar position on the gunline. Reassigned to the Gulf of Tonkin, on Sunday 2 April, the ship suffered a tragedy when FA Thomas Muren was lost overboard in the northern part of the Gulf of Tonkin. He wasn't reported missing from his watch station for some time, and the subsequent search by USS *John R. Craig* and other units was fruitless.

The very next Sunday, 9 April, USS *John R. Craig* was near the southern edge of the DMZ, conducting naval gunfire support operations against the North Vietnamese troops pushing south in the Easter Offensive. Approaching an assigned target that was well inland, the ship positioned herself close to the beach to close range when shells from North Vietnamese shore batteries began splashing to port and starboard. Knowing she had been bracketed, the ship turned to speed for open water when one shell found its mark, penetrating the fantail, damaging the aft gun mount and starting a fire that threatened the missile magazine.

With the USS *Rowan* (DD-782) speeding alongside and artillery shells kicking up water spouts all around both ships, the dauntless crew managed to get the fires under control and make port at Da Nang.

Awards, Services Ribbons, and Battle Stars for the USS *John R. Craig* (DD-885):

China Service Medal, National Defense Service Medal with one star, Navy Occupational Service Medal with "Asia" clasp, United States Korean Service Medal with three stars, United Nations Korean Service Medal, Republic of Korea War Service Medal, Korean Presidential Unit Citation, Armed Forces Expeditionary Medal with one star, Navy "E" Ribbon, Vietnam Service Medal with seven stars, Combat Action Ribbon with five stars, Navy Unit Commendation, Navy Meritorious Unit Commendation, RVN Gallantry Cross Unit Citation Ribbon with one star, and the Republic of Vietnam Campaign Ribbon.

We, who once found refuge under the protection of her guns, salute this valiant ship and her gallant crew.

NOT ON MY WATCH

Having to make do with what assets he had on hand, on 7 April, Lieutenant Colonel Gray transferred underutilized MR4 personnel, with only twelve hours' notice, to reinforce his hard-pressed MR1 assets. When a second front opened in Binh Long Province (MR3), the commanding general of Delta Regional Assistance Command (DRAC-MR4) frantically called for re-establishment of ANGLICO support teams on the 11th. Knowing if this war got any hotter he'd be strung too tight, Lieutenant Colonel Gray had the foresight to have already requested additional personnel from FMFPac on 8 April to augment the manpower drain needed to shore up this unexpected and most urgent crisis.

At the urging of Lieutenant Colonel Gray, the Seventh Air Force command, upon request from MACV, agreed to provide up to forty-two daily OV-10 flight hours, continuous dawn-to-dusk air coverage for the 1st and 3rd ARVN Divisions. On 10 April, four OV-10s were made available. Air observers at Phu Bai were transferred to Da Nang and began flying with the U.S. Air Force 20th Tactical Air Support Squadron.

From 12 through 19 April, in answer to Lieutenant Colonel Gray's call to arms, Marines from duty stations throughout the Fleet Marine Force arrived in-country many for second and third rotations into the Sub Unit. Having eighteen more officers and twenty-one additional enlisted Marines available for assignment, the ANGLICO skipper re-established Sub Unit One detachments where needed, shifting assets to satisfy all requests for support. Three detachments were quickly reintroduced to MR4 at Nihn Thuy, Can Tho, and Rach Gia, staffed by a total of four officers and nine enlisted Marines.

The NVA turned up the heat again. On 5 April, the opening rounds of Phase III of the offensive really put a strain on support commitments. In MR2, communist forces quickly overran several ARVN positions in coastal Binh Dihn Province in an attempt to close Highway 1. This proved to be a ploy for drawing ARVN forces from the highlands, where the communist B-3 Front, consisting of the 320th and 2nd NVA Divisions with supporting armor, swept in from Laos on 12 April. In the lowland, the 3rd NVA Division opened yet another thrust in an attempt to cut South Vietnam in half.

Receiving directives from MACV, naval gunfire teams were re-established in MR2 on 23 April. Headquartered at Qui Nhon, Captains U.S. (Sam) Grant and Frank L. Turner, having arrived from Okinawa on the 13th, began flying out of Phu Cat Airbase, providing much-needed gunfire support over the new battleground. Fighting became extremely heavy near the coast, presenting lucrative targets, which were taken under fire and destroyed. Alternating with VNAF pilots and those of the 20th TASS, the two spotters were in the air continuously, doing what they could to exert some influence over the fluid tactical situation along the coast of northern MR2.

To better manage crisis events at the Cua Viet, the NGLO detachment at FRAC headquarters in Da Nang was augmented by extra personnel. Major James E. Dyer, executive officer of Sub Unit One, came up from Saigon to take charge. An additional team was established at FRAC Forward in Hue, and spot teams were also installed at Camp Eagle for service with the 1st ARVN Division, which was now heavily engaged against elements of the NVA 324 B Division, coming at the ancient capital from the west. In a matter of two weeks, the Sub Unit expanded coverage from six locations to thirteen.

In need of help, the beleaguered 3rd ARVN Division team received a much-needed shot in the arm in the personage of Major Glen Golden. Having a reputation as being an expert fire support coordinator, he arrived for duty at the 3rd Division TOC, assuming responsibilities as naval gunfire officer for MR1 on 24 April. Before his first week, Major Golden proved his worth. Finding 155 Advisory Team and ARVN TOC officers located in different bunkers about fifty yards apart, which made fire support coordination difficult to say the least, having to run back and forth to disseminate information and obtain clearances. Taking charge, the Marine had a direct phone line installed to the ARVN artillery officer, speeding up call for fire clearances and streamlining coordination. This simple but effective move allowed him to process fire requests from anywhere on the battlefield, firing massed time on target missions of naval gunfire and ARVN artillery.

Protecting an ever-increasingly smaller perimeter around Quang Tri City, VNMC Brigade 369 aggressively patrolled west of Highway 1. Since the fall of Mai Loc and Camp Carroll, these Marines now formed the forward defense west and southwest of the TOC, knowing somewhere out there the 304th NVA Division was advancing. On 8 April, two companies of the 5th Battalion, under command of the executive officer, Major Tran Ba, while probing for contact 1,200 meters west of Fire Support Base Jane, encountered dug-in NVA troops. Mortars and well-placed machine guns erupting in unison, extracted a heavy toll, killing Major Ba and most of his command staff. Being greatly outnumbered, Captain Marshall R. Wells, Marine advisor, assisted in command control efforts to disengage from the superior force and withdraw back to FSB Jane. Pursuing NVA troops close on their heels had to be chased off with artillery from the firebase as the retreating companies came within view.

VNMC 3rd Battalion, after one full week defending Dong Ha, was pulled back to Ai Tu for reorganization, freeing 6th Battalion (Brigade 258) to assume control over abandoned Fire Support Base Pedro. Of 700 Marines deployed with 3rd Battalion valiantly keeping the NVA from crossing the Cau Viet, only 200 remained.

That same afternoon of 8 April, 6th Battalion arrived at FSB Pedro. Acting on intelligence reports of anticipated armor attacks from the west along the axis of Route 557, only one company occupied Pedro, positioning one platoon at a blocking position 600 meters west of the outpost. One company dug in east of the road, while the remaining two comprising the Alpha Group set up an arch-shaped position on high ground overlooking a mine field northwest of Pedro, intersecting the supply road from Ai Tu. Marine advisors Major William R. Warren and Captain William Wischmeyer elected to stay together with the Alpha command group.

Shortly after midnight, 9 April, NAV artillery prep began pounding Pedro and surrounding area, continuing through the night. In the early light of morning, two tanks were observed approaching Pedro, then eight more appeared east of Route 557, coming on at fifteen miles per hour. Infantry emerging from the wood line deployed behind eight tanks already moving on Route 557. Within minutes, eight more tanks crawled into view.

Marine artillery FOs called in fire missions on the formation. Exposed infantry, estimated to be regimental strength, was forced to seek shelter in the wood line from which they moments earlier emerged, while the tanks closed their hatches and pressed forward.

The two lead tanks attacked the platoon blocking position west of Pedro, killing the entire unit in a swift but violent fight then turned toward the outpost.

Only half an hour after launching the assault, tanks penetrated Pedro's scant defenses. In their first experience against armor, the Marines experienced difficulty properly employing their only defense, LAW rockets, and were soon forced to withdraw. NVA tanks pursued the retreating Marines by fire. Two tanks remained, tearing up Pedro's defense, while the rest moved forward into the mine field recently prepared by the Marines.

Monitoring radio traffic from the TOC, Colonel Dihn and Brigade advisor Major Jon Easley began mapping out plans for a counterattack. Within thirty minutes, a reaction force of two companies from the 1st VNMC Battalion and a column of twelve M113 armored personnel carriers supported by eight M-48 tanks from 2nd Troop, 20th Tank Battalion broke for Pedro.

A rare break in cloud cover allowed a flight of four Vietnamese A-1s to come down for a shot at the tanks. Losing one plane to antiaircraft fire, the air strike roughed up the armor but scored no hits. The air show did, however, occupy the enemy's attention long enough to allow the reaction force, accompanied by Marine advisor Captain Lawrence H. Livingston, to move closer to Pedro.

Enemy tanks moving past Pedro now concentrated on 6th Battalion and advanced on the command group. Within 300 meters, the lead tank exploded from one of the mines. Others mixed in with Marine units, causing mayhem until the shock effect wore off and Marines began standing their ground, fighting off the armored attack with LAW rockets. Several other tanks that bypassed the 6th Battalion entered the liberally sown mine field, a few becoming disabled or outright destroyed.

Colonel Dinh, commanding officer of VNMC Brigade 258, gave the order for the relief force to attack. Because of rolling hills between the reaction force and Pedro, ARVN armor deployed online unobserved. As the reaction force came to a halt on the last hill overlooking the mine field, the M-48s opened fire at 1,500 yards, scoring several first-round hits, destroying three T-54s. Enemy tanks maneuvering to return fire in the mine field triggered several antiarmor devices, taking more casualties. Marine artillery ratcheting up fires drove what infantry still remaining on the field to withdraw, leaving the tanks fully exposed, which soon fell prey to ARVN tanks, LAW rockets, and another flight of A-1s. Every communist tank committed to Pedro was burning except for two abandoned in the mine field, which were taken as prizes by the Marines.

Persistent in building strength west of Pedro, North Vietnam's 304th Division continued coming against the Marines. NVA tanks and infantry again mixed with 1st and 6th VNMC Battalions on the 10th, with the same results.

In an effort to extend bombardment range, 130mm guns moved further south from the DMZ and were now able to take Quang Tri City under fire. Refugees from Cam Lo and Dong Ha, mixing with Quang Tri City residents, clogged Route 1 in a maddening race to get out of range. NVA gunners having no regard for these unfortunate migrants, maimed, crippled, and killed hundreds of terrorized men, women, and children alike on their flight south.

Dozens of daily B-52 ARCHLIGHT strikes continued raining 750-pound payloads on suspected troop concentrations, avenues of approach, and known enemy positions. Weather permitting, tactical air took to the skies, taking out observed targets around Quang Tri Province. U.S. Air Force Major David A. Brookbank, 3rd ARVN Division ALO, worked around the clock, planning and coordinating the air show in a superb show of skill.

On 14 April, General Hoang Xuan Lam, MR1 military commander, ordered a counterattack on a broad front to re-establish the western defense line right at the strength of a stubborn enemy, who unleashed massive artillery bombardments on ARVN assault troops. By the end of the first week, no unit had advanced beyond 500 meters from its line of departure. Dubbed Operation Quang Trung 729, the initiative soon degenerated into a battle of attrition, succeeding only in reducing several ARVN battalions.

NVA continued to probe defensive positions and kept up daily artillery fires, effectively destroying large portions of Dong Ha, which was by now denuded of its civilian population. Employing the as-of-yet still standing Cam Lo Bridge, the NVA moved supplies, troops, and armor south of the Cua Viet, building up to a major push on Dong Ha.

On 27 April, monsoon weather once again socked in tactical air support. At 0600, NVA artillery began pounding the ARVN defenses along the Cua Viet and defense positions west of Highway 1. Fifteen minutes later, the 4th Ranger Group on the western defense line was hit hard by massed infantry assaults. At 0715, the 5th Ranger Group on the right flank of the 4th came under attack by armor-reinforced infantry. Soon, every unit along the northern portion of the western defense became embroiled in an all-out massed offensive supported by tanks and artillery.

ARVN lines continued to hold firm against a very aggressive, well-executed attack. At 0900, NVA artillery scored a direct hit on a command vehicle, killing senior officers of 2nd Troop, 20th Tank Battalion. Within minutes, newly deployed Soviet wire-guided Sagger missiles took out three tanks. For reasons not understood, 3rd Troop, observing the burning M-48s, pulled offline and bolted for Highway 1. Seeing their armor suddenly leave the field, infantry and rangers witnessing this exodus also left position, leaving the flank of 38th Battalion, 5th Ranger Group exposed. Almost on cue, a massive surge aimed right at the 38th began to develop and extended across the area defended by the 30th Battalion of the 5th. By 0915, NVA infantry broke through the 38th, exposing the right flank of the line held by the rangers, which was enough to force this unit to pull back.

Unit commanders on the western front were losing control as a once-solid defense began to fall apart. That part of the line defended by the 5th Rangers retracted now, exposing the left flank of the 20th Tank Battalion and the right flank of the 4th Ranger Group, but somehow both managed to hold. The battle raged on into early afternoon, when at 1400, Sagger missiles took out two tanks supporting the 4th Rangers, causing a critical shortage of morale-boosting armor in that sector. At 1630, enemy infantry fell upon the 4th Rangers, overrunning its 43rd Battalion, which abandoned its fighting holes, fleeing east. No one bothered to communicate the withdrawal up the chain of command.

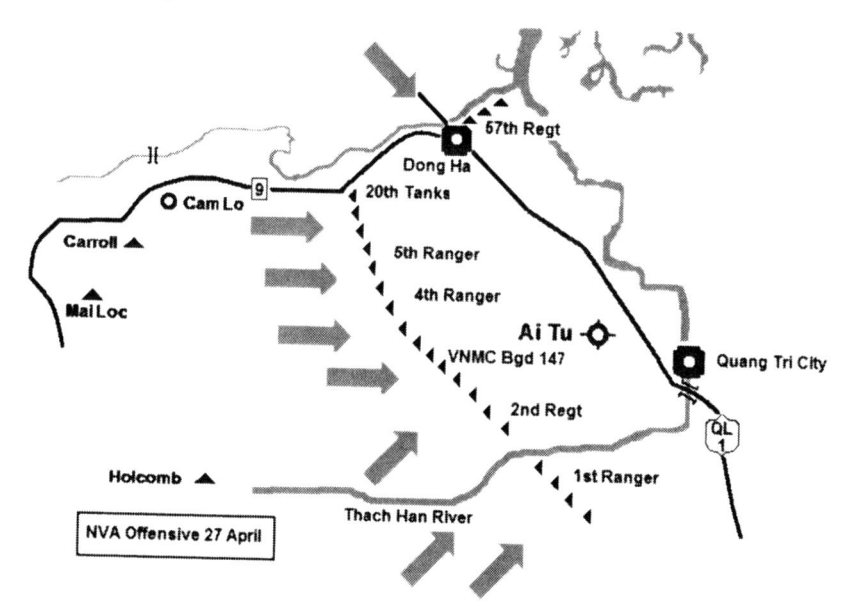

Fear of being cut off prompted Colonel Luan, commanding officer of the 20th Tank Battalion, holding position just south of the Cua Viet, to order his tanks withdrawn to Route 1—again, without informing anyone up the chain of command. This was all it took to instill a panicked infantry to follow the tanks east. Confusion now took command; the battle was lost. Not discovered until later that evening, the 57th Regiment withdrew, without orders, from its assigned defensive positions on the Cua Viet, leaving the northern defenses unmanned and the city of Dong Ha completely open.

South of the 4th Rangers, VNMC 1st and 8th Battalions were ordered to pull back, as no one was protecting either flank. Immediately south of the Marines, the 2nd ARVN Regiment, up to this point not under infantry attack, started receiving accelerated artillery fire. Guarding the southern approach to Quang Tri City and the vital Thach Han River Bridge, Lieutenant Colonel Camper and Major Brown, reassigned to the 2nd after the fall of Camp Carroll, became concerned when a firefight broke out at the river. As no one was sure of the exact location of the battalions, both Americans exited the command bunker to check on the firefight. While scanning wood lines near the river, an artillery round exploded in the tree they were standing under, peppering Colonel Camper with shrapnel to the face and neck. As blood was collecting in his throat, Major Brown laid Camper on his side to improve air passage. Having no success in getting ARVN vehicles to stop, Major Brown radioed the TOC for assistance.

Word of a wounded advisor reached Quang Tri City, where an improvised dispensary manned by personnel from the U.S. Naval Advisory Unit was providing medical care to ARVN casualties. Discovering the area was cut off from air and road access, the intrepid ANGLICO corpsman HM3 Williamson immediately stepped forward to offer his services and go out to the wounded officer. U.S. Army Sergeant Roger Shoemaker procured an ARVN M-113, forcefully persuading its Vietnamese driver's cooperation, while Williamson gathered his medical bag.

Racing south out of the city across the Thach Han River Bridge, Williamson and Shoemaker, augmented by a newly arrived medical corpsman and an unidentified ANGLICO Marine, then dismounted the APC. The corpsman and Marine remained to ensure the APC driver's continued cooperation, while Williamson and Shoemaker proceeded 600 meters on foot, braving intense small arms and artillery fire, finally arriving at the side of Colonel Camper, some 200 meters north of the river bank. Doc Williamson went to work under fire, doing what he could to stabilize the injured advisor, applying field dressings and slowing blood loss. With Shoemaker's and Major Brown's help, Camper was carried back over fire-swept terrain to the waiting APC and on to Quang Tri for advanced care and evacuation.

Constant artillery bombardments continued on through the night and into the next day. Content for the time being at consolidating hard-won new gains, communist forces mounted no serious attacks on Ai Tu or the capital but did continue moving closer, as defenses constricted nearer to the CP. Supported by TP-76 amphibious tanks, NVA infantry advanced south along the coast, overrunning regional force positions northeast of Quang Tri City, and now occupied real estate less than three miles from the TOC. By nightfall, the 4th Rangers occupied the north sector of Quang Tri airstrip, while 5th Ranger Group and two battalions of the 2nd Regiment covered the bridges and Highway 1 south of the city. 3rd Division's 57th Regiment and 1st Armored Brigade assumed defense inside Quang Tri City. Marines of the 7th VNMC Battalion were ordered north from FSB Nancy to reinforce 147 Brigade. Enemy forces, having cut the highway at several locations, inflicted heavy casualties on the northbound Marines but they did come through, fighting every inch of the way in what can only be described as a suicide mission.

During the dark hours, at 0200 on the 29th, an artillery prep followed by armor infantry assaults at the Thach Han Bridge was repulsed by 18th Cavalry APCs and FAC-controlled air strikes under flare light. South of the city, Highway 1 was cut off from My Chanh north, effectively shutting down resupply efforts and further isolating Quang Tri Province.

Light of day found thousands of civilians, mixed with ARVN soldiers, frantically pushing south on Highway 1. Once more these frightened souls became sport for NVA gunners, indiscriminately pouring fire into crowds of helpless people doing nothing more than trying to get out of the way.

A check of assets revealed that most troops of the 57th Regiment, who were supposed to be guarding Quang Tri City, had managed to slip away, rendering the unit combat ineffective. Two battalions of the 2nd Regiment last reported as holding positions at the Thach Han Bridge could not be located. The 4th and 5th Ranger Groups were then given the mission to hold this bridge, vital to Highway 1 access. Both units dutifully took the bridge, crossed over to the south bank, and kept going. There were no longer any friendly troops west of the bridge. Armor assets, while willing to hold, had been reduced to less than twenty operational tanks and APCs. VNMC 147 Brigade was the only infantry asset standing between the capital and three NVA divisions.

With dwindling combat assets available for assignment and with the NVA threatening to cut the combat base off from the city, General Giai reached a decision to evacuate Ai Tu, pulling his forces tighter around Quang Tri City. Enemy artillery continued reducing Ai Tu and the capital, as NVA armor and infantry closed to within 3,000 meters northeast and 4,000 meters west by 1 May. Under cover of continuous naval gunfire barrages and air strikes, VNMC 147 Brigade, last to abandon the base, withdrew across the Thach Han and dug into defensive positions around the capital soon after sunset.

General Giai, seeing the inevitable, laid out another plan to withdraw south and establish a defense line at the My Chang River. General Lam in Da Nang, however, reacting to political pressure and not having the first clue of the reality of the tactical situation, countermanded this order as soon as it reached his ears. He insisted that Quang Tri City not be allowed to fall, giving Giai a direct order to stand and die. General Giai then informed his subordinate units to disregard his first order and directed them to prepare to defend the capital. Unit commanders either refused to obey or just disregarded the latest directive. Most battalions had, in fact, already abandoned the fight and were in various stages of withdrawing, some having already left. In light of the countermanded order, there wasn't enough time to recall the original order and reorganize defenses. Colonel Bao, commanding VNMC Brigade 147, out of exasperation flat-out told Giai the Marines were leaving with or without him. Naval gunfire and TAC Air continued unabated to hammer approaching NVA units, but without infantry support, it wasn't enough to put off the inescapable fate of Quang Tri.

Recognizing the futility of staying any longer, at noon on 2 May, General Giai released Brigade 147 to breakout. The general and his staff then mounted two ARVN APCs and sped out of the city. Around 1400, General Giai and his entourage returned to the Citadel after being attacked by NVA, forcing the APCs to turn back.

The morning before, Lieutenant Colonel Metcalf had called the advisory staff together, making final preparations for the inevitable evacuation. Arrangements had been made for U.S. Air Force SAR helicopters to come in and pick up the eighty or so Americans still remaining. Not wanting to have to fight off the Vietnamese for a seat, Colonel Metcalf astutely elected to evacuate after all the Vietnamese left, leaving the American advisors last out of Quang Tri. USAF Major David A. Brookbank performed magnificently as Air Liaison Officer from the onset of the offensive, providing TAC Air coordination and ARCHLIGHT planning; he worked closely with Major Golden, expertly setting up a wall of supporting fire to box in the Citadel. Major Joy declined aerial evacuation for his advisors, electing to take his chances with 147 Brigade's breakout to the My Chang River.

At 1430, Major Brookbank, working with three airborne FACs, covered Brigade 147's withdrawal south. At 1500, each FAC received four more flights of F-4s, working the surrounding terrain in support of HH-53C Jolly Green Giants inbound for the extraction. In some of the heaviest use of TAC Air since the offensive began, Brookbank pulverized the west bank of the Thach Han, keeping NVA at a distance. Arriving at the Citadel even as NVA forces were already in the city, at 1630, with A-1 Skyraiders providing fire suppression, the extraction went as planned. Lifting off in the last sortie was Colonel Metcalf, Major Glen Golden, and the ANGLICO team. From the door of the helicopter, Major Golden continued directing naval gunfire bombardment on advancing NVA right to the last.

As a tribute to their honor, courage, and loyalty, even though they had been offered an opportunity for aerial evacuation, American advisors assigned to the 3rd ARVN Division's 1st Armored Brigade and VNMC Brigade 147 elected to stay with their counterparts and slug it out overland. Fighting almost every inch of the way, all managed to make the fifteen-plus-mile trek after an exhausting and brutal journey.

USS Samuel N. Moore
(DD-747)
Allen M. Sumner Class Destroyer
Call Sign: Macaroon

From 13 March to 2 October 1964, USS *Samuel N. Moore* was away from Long Beach on another deployment to the Western Pacific. In August, during the crisis following the Tonkin Gulf incident, USS *Samuel N. Moore* supplied ammunition to USS *Maddox* (DD-731) and transmitted documents from USS *Turner Joy* (DD-951) and USS *Maddox* to USS *Ticonderoga* (CVA-14).

Sailing from the West Coast to the Western Pacific on 28 September 1965, she took her turn on the gunline, providing fire in support of allied forces, then acted as plane guard in the South China Sea. She again assumed position on the gunline, firing on targets in the Mekong Delta, before returning to Long Beach on 8 April. Getting underway again for her third deployment to the war zone on 28 March 1967, she patrolled waters off North Vietnam as part of Operation Sea Dragon, where she protected carriers in Tonkin Gulf. She was back at her homeport of Long Beach on 20 September. Underway once more on 28 July 1968, she spent her fourth deployment guarding carriers in the Tonkin Gulf until mid-February 1969 before returning to Long Beach.

In April, she was designated as a Naval Reserve training ship at Tacoma, Washington, until decommissioned on 24 October and struck from the list.

We, who once found refuge under the protection of her guns, salute this valiant ship and her gallant crew.

NOT ONE MORE INCH

Having lost confidence in his senior military command, President Nguyen Van Thieu, on recommendations from MACV, appointed Lieutenant General Ngo Quang Truong to assume responsibility for turning around the catastrophe that was brewing in MR1. Truong, with a hand-picked staff, traveled to Da Nang on 3 May, exuding a professionalism and military competence that had long been missing. Now that Quang Tri was lost, his first order of business was to secure Hue, which now occupied full focus of NVA commanders as the next objective in the month-long offensive.

Looking over the tactical disaster now unfolding around the ancient capital revealed three NVA Divisions with supporting armor closing in from the north and one division with supporting armor pressing his defenses from the west. To meet this threat, all three VNMC brigades for the first time in South Vietnam's fledgling history had assembled together at one place under a unified divisional command and were assigned responsibility to maintain the integrity of the My Chanh Line on the extreme northern border and provide security on northwest approaches to the Hue perimeter. Under the able command of newly promoted Brigadier General Bui The Lan, this would be their Guadalcanal.

Defensive preparations west of Hue focused on halting further advance of the NVA 29th and 803rd Regiments, which on 28 April, after two weeks of intense fighting, captured FSB Bastogne. This event left FSB Checkmate vulnerable, and it was abandoned, leaving Route 547 open as an invasion route to the capital. As the 1st Division's 54th Regiment, heavily blooded in that hotly contested action, was rendered combat ineffective, the 1st Division had only two regiments to hold down its area of responsibility, stretching from the Bo River south.

Inasmuch as the tactical situation in Quang Tri became the main focus of events, 1st ARVN Division efforts at containing the 320B NVA Division has been widely overlooked. Major General Pham Van Phu reacted quickly and decisively to disrupt enemy offensive buildups in the long-standing NVA sanctuary of A Shau Valley. Acting on intelligence reports, General Phu actually went on offense west of Hue in mid-February, throwing the 320B Division off balance. Having stalemated NVA tactical aspirations in Thua Thien Province, with all the reinforcements going north to Quang Tri, the division acquitted itself very well, giving ARVN forces retreating from the northernmost province a secure place to fall back.

Fortunately, NVA assaulting divisions, having advanced so quickly, had outrun logistic capability to fuel further incursions and were forced to pause while supplies needed to sustain the offensive reached front line units. All news was not good news, however, as the NVA now had six full-strength divisions closing in on Hue. The 304th and 308th Divisions received needed replacements and were reinforced with the presence of 312th, 324B, and 325th Divisions, plus additional supporting armor and artillery.

Not having time to totally digest all aspects of the Quang Tri debacle, Truong, acting on advice from General Kroesen, polled senior American advisors and Vietnamese staff officers for their opinions. Command and control inefficiencies from corps to battalion level dominated each critique, which the general quickly addressed in a reorganization of command elements. His first move brought about establishment of a forward headquarters in Hue, sending the message to his demoralized troops that they no longer had a rear echelon commander. Having a corps-level command post at the front transferred confidence to the men that leadership would be on top of tactical developments.

Lieutenant Colonel Gray forcefully expressed a need for improved fire support coordination, pointing out a superfluity of disconnects in events of the past month. To this end, Fire Support Control Centers, with U.S supporting arms integrated into these control structures, were organized at corps and divisional commands. The Sub Unit One skipper established a larger presence for his command in MR1, boosting ANGLICO assets to thirty-five officers and seventy-four enlisted Marines, reintroducing ground spot teams at battalion and regimental levels, with corresponding NGLO activities in all major corps and divisional headquarters.

General Tuong was on familiar ground, having personally commanded the 1st ARVN Division garrisoned in Hue from 1966 through 1970. Here he was a known commodity, well respected within South Vietnam's military community. Having served under General Lam in that capacity, Truong was painfully aware of military inadequacies prevalent throughout his new command and acted swiftly, replacing underperforming staff officers who had obtained their position through political connections.

In order to keep pressure on North Vietnamese and disrupt attempts to organize offensive initiatives, Operation Loi Phong (Hurricane and Thunder) was launched on 5 May in a bid to buy time for development of a defense in depth. Massive amounts of ordnance impacting on advancing units, staging areas, supply lines, and troop movements fell on communist troops in the form of B-52 ARCLIGHT strikes, artillery, naval gunfire, and tactical air sorties. For seventy-two straight hours, every available weapon of high destruction was employed in concentrated bombardments of death-dealing furry.

Soldiers of the 1st Ranger Group having been reorganized and replenished in Da Nang reported for assignment on 7 May. On 8 May, the 2nd Airborne Brigade, 1st Airborne Division arrived from MR3 fresh from the battle of Kontum and was immediately sent north, reinforcing the thinly spread Marines. Other Airborne units already committed were making preparations to follow and would be in MR1 by month's end.

U.S. Marine combat air assets from MAG-15 arrived in Da Nang from Iwakuni, Japan, late evening of 6 April, adding more muscle for the ARVN offensive thrust, now poised to take the field.

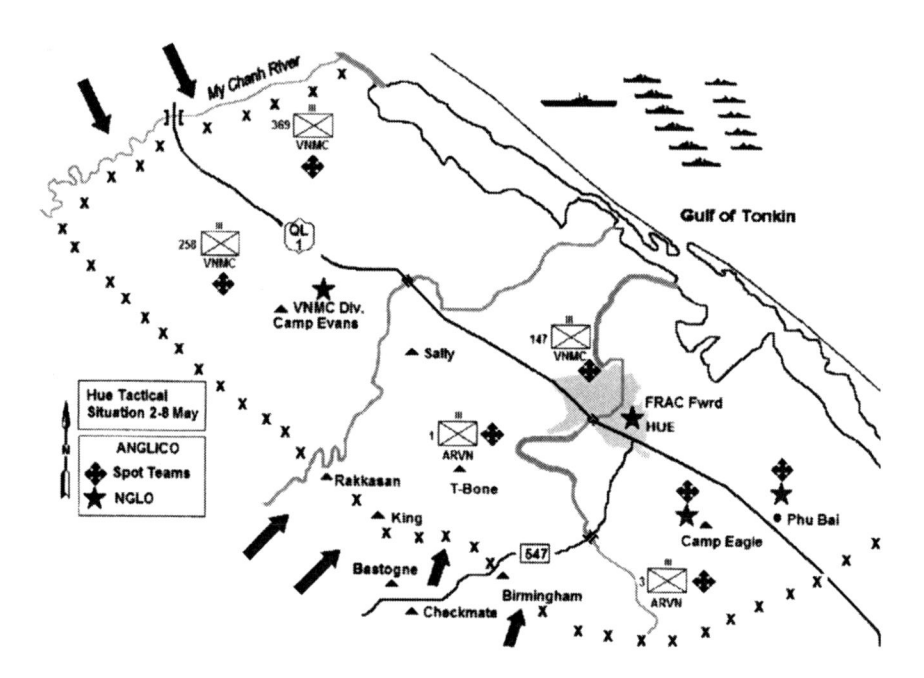

On 9 April, 9th MAB was activated, assuming control of four Amphibious Ready Groups—Alpha, Bravo, Charlie, and Delta—currently assembled off the coast of South Vietnam. Brigadier General Edward J. Miller, in his third war, assumed command and readied his force. Initially, his projected mission was to evacuate U.S. personnel under threat from the unexpected success of North Vietnam's Easter Offensive. By the time the MAB arrived off the coast, an improved tactical situation belayed a need for imminent evacuation operations. Functioning as the landing force component of the 7th Fleet, 9th MAB now stood ready to provide MACV with assistance as directed. From his flagship, USS *Blue Ridge* (LCC-19), Rear Admiral Walter D. Gaddis commanded a flotilla of sixteen U.S. Navy ships, providing transportation and support. On authority of the president of the United States, a mission was accepted by Commander Task Group 79.1 (CTG 79.1) in early May to support Vietnamese Marine Corps operations and ARVN initiatives in retaking lost territories.

USS *Newport News* (CA-148) arrived on the gunline 11 May, adding her eight-inch main batteries in support of MR1 activities, bringing more firepower and additional range, which had long been lacking. Naval gunfire ships continued to receive heavy counter battery fire in northern MR1, several receiving direct hits from enemy artillery. But being more than a match for North Vietnamese gunners, at no time was any ship disabled. The stage was now set, and the worm was about to turn.

With an in-depth defense now protecting Hue and more tactical assets arriving every day, General Truong prepared to seize the initiative and shift to limited offensive operations, designed to disrupt NVA offensive intentions. He had turned things around 180 degrees in only two weeks.

Under cover of darkness, Recon Company Marines of VNMC 369 Brigade clandestinely crossed the My Chang River on 12 May. Leading a communications detail, the patrol arrived at destination three hours before dawn, where a command and control site was quietly placed into operational readiness.

Just before sunrise, ground prep fires from USS *Newport News* (CA148), USS *Providence* (CLG-6), USS *Davidson* (DE-1045), USS *Cecil* (DD-835), and USS *Rowan* (DD-782) impacted on Landing Zones Delta and Tango. At first light, TAC Air arrived on station, working over both LZs some two miles distant from each other.

At 0800 on 13 May, ship-born helicopters from HMM-164 departed USS *Okinawa* (LPH-3), bound for the Vietnamese mainland to embark waiting Marines. Lifting off on schedule from FSB Sally, the assault force arrived over Tango with 3rd VNMC Battalion and made the insertion unopposed under cover from AH-1G, UH1-E, and OH-6A gunships of F Troop, U.S. Army 4th Cavalry, at 0934.

At 1130, while inbound to LZ Delta with 8th VNMC Battalion, gunship escorts declared the landing site hot, as the first ship in took ground fire. Command and Control then shifted the insertion location toward the southern edge of the zone. Orders were passed for troop waves to continue. Machine gun and small arms fire covered every inch of ground as CH-46s landed, discharged cargo, and departed. Several airships took hits coming and going, as successive flights braved fire while putting Marines on the ground. One CH-53 became disabled and was destroyed by gunships to prevent its capture once the crew was rescued.

As soon as sufficient troops were in place, Marines attacked across 400 meters of open rice paddies, driving NVA gunners from their entrenched positions and consolidating the LZ.

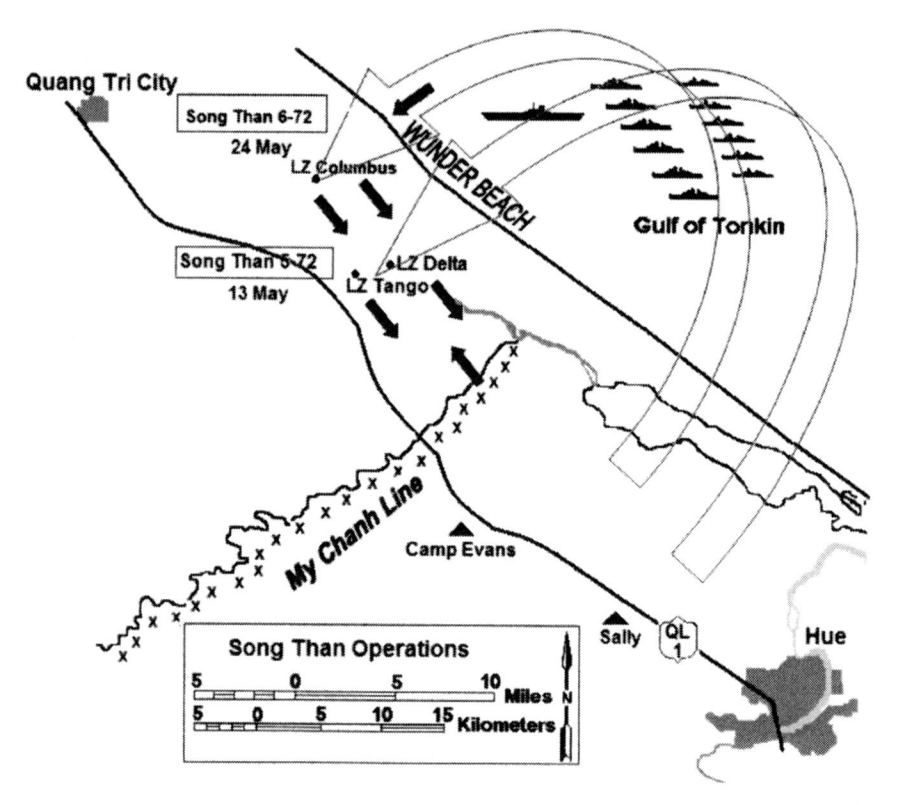

Marines from both locations per plan attacked south, while the 9th Battalion crossed the My Chanh driving north, signaling operation Song Than 5-72 was now fully deployed. For the first time in a long time, three ANGLICO spot/TACP teams accompanied Marines in the field, providing fire support in coordination with Major Glen Golden, MR1 NGLO flying airborne spot position overhead.

Lasting only one day, the operation achieved its goal of throwing the NVA off balance. General Truong made a strong statement through this bold move, inflicting over 240 enemy casualties, destroying three tanks and two of those bothersome 130mm guns.

Concentrating on shoring up the western perimeter, the 1st ARVN Division launched an assault to recapture Fire Support Base Bastogne on 15 May. Securing the high ground in lighting-quick attacks, the 1st Division rolled into Bastogne on the 17th then turned south, retaking Fire Support Base Checkmate on the 20th. The invasion path offered by Route 547 was now secure.

Caught totally off guard, the NVA, wanting to regain the initiative, launched an armor-supported infantry attack, crossing the eastern extent of My Chanh River early morning on the 21st. Hard-pressed regional force troops holding that sector could not stand up to the onslaught and fell back, exposing the right flank of the 3rd and 9th VNMC Battalions, which in turn forced those units to withdraw. After regrouping, the Marines counterattacked with support of ARVN armored cavalry assets. Getting assistance from Marine TAC Air in an all-day fight, the Marines took back lost ground and restored the line by nightfall.

A well-timed assault by North Vietnamese armor, less than six hours later at 0100 on the 22nd, hit the 3rd VNMC Battalion hard. Twenty-five tanks supported by infantry quickly punched through Marine lines. Fighting back with LAWs and point-blank fire from 105mm howitzers, Marines made the NVA pay for every inch; destroying eight tanks while giving ground. First light found headquarters group frantically fighting off tanks not 400 meters from the command post. Newly arrived in-country, TOW missiles (wire-guided antitank missiles) operated by U.S. Army personnel made their world combat debut, scoring a direct hit on a PT-76, then took out four more in quick order. Cutting across the battlefield from the west flank, 8th VNMC Battalion mounted a fierce counterattack, pushing NVA soldiers back across the My Chanh. By 0930, what began as a well-executed attack collapsed into an "every man for himself" rout as enemy dead and wounded were abandoned on the battlefield along with ten burning tanks.

Taking the initiative to relieve pressure on the My Chanh line, Operation Song Than 6-72 was born after many hours of detailed planning aboard the Blue Ridge. This area of operation would be north of the previous assault, nearer to Quang Tri City

Arriving at the Tan My naval facility on 23 May, the 7th VNMC Battalion boarded landing craft and was transported to amphibious force ships USS *Cayuga* (LST-1186), USS *Duluth* (LPD-6), USS *Manitowoc* (LST-1180), and USS *Schenectady* (LST-1185). For many, this would be their first amphibious landing.

That same evening, Marines of 6th Battalion assembled at a collection point south of the My Chanh along Route 597 for transportation the next morning to LZ Columbus.

In the early hours just before dawn on 24 May, massed naval gunfire prep from the largest concentration of gunships so far in the war started pounding Red Beach and LZ Columbus. ARVN artillery joined the bombardment, intermixing 105mm, 155mm, and 175mm explosions with naval gunfire. ARCHLIGHT strikes and TAC Air also lit up both assault objectives, as well as avenues of approach to the target area.

At 0750, *Cayuga* and *Duluth* launched twenty LVTP-5 amphibious tractors carrying 580 Vietnamese Marines from 3,600 yards off the coast. During launch, both LSTs came under fire from NVA coastal artillery. USS *Hanson* (DD-832), observing her own fall of shot, had the last word in that argument, pounding the artillery site into silence. When the Amtracs closed to within 2,000 yards a final flight of B-52s scattered sand all over Red Beach in a perfectly executed support sortie. Breaching the surf line at 0832, Marines were greeted with scattered mortar and small arms fire. Assaulting across the sand dunes under continuous ANGLICO-controlled naval gunfire and TAC Air support, the Marines killed fifty enemy defenders while consolidating VNMC's first-ever beachhead.

One hour later, a mixed flight of eighteen CH-46 and CH-53 helicopters from HMM-164 set course for LZ Columbus with 550 Marines. Vietnamese artillerymen fogged in the LZ north and west with smoke rounds, screening the treetop-level approaching flight as U.S. Army gunships raked the objective with suppressive fires.

From both locations, Vietnamese Marines attacked south toward the My Chanh in a coordinated movement, becoming heavily engaged with surprised enemy soldiers of the newly committed 18th NVA Regiment, 325th NVA Division. From prisoners taken, it was learned that Song Than 6-72 preempted this unit's attack on the My Chanh line. During the ensuing battle, Marines claimed 369 NVA soldiers and three more tanks, while suffering 35 fatalities.

Under pressure by superiors to regain lost momentum, NVA field commanders mounted an attack on the northwest sector of the Hue perimeter defended by VNMC Brigade 258. A regimental-size force with heavy armor support launched its assault at 0530 on 25 May. In almost two continuous months of contact with enemy tanks, Vietnamese Marines had lost their fear of armor and, by this time, had developed exceptional skill employing M-72 LAW weapons. A combination of having relied upon shock effect, which had lost its fear factor, and being relatively unfamiliar with classic armor tactics did not generate the desired affects for the NVA. North Vietnamese commanders prematurely committed infantry units, exposing NVA soldiers to devastating supporting arms fire. Leaving hundreds of casualties and more than two dozen burning tanks in front of Marine lines gave mute testament of a stinging defeat.

Again on the 26th, a reinforced NVA battalion once more came at Brigade 258 out of the early morning darkness. Exploiting a weak point in the line, enemy attackers forced Marines of the 9th Battalion to pull back 1,000 meters. Two additional battalions of the NVA 88th Regiment, with supporting armor behind a heavy artillery and mortar barrage, then hit 1st Battalion Marines on the flank, threatening to overrun that sector. Marine advisor Captain Lawrence H. Livingston, acting quickly, brought tactical air to bear on a determined enemy, causing the attack to disintegrate. At VNMC 9th Battalion, a counterattack behind TAC Air and naval gunfire directed by Captain Robert K. Redlin re-established the perimeter but only after a brutal fight.

During the period from 8 through 21 May, enemy activity substantially increased in the vicinity of the Cua Viet River, as North Vietnamese logistics planners began making extensive use of the U.S. Navy-built LST ramp and port facilities. As such, it soon became a permanent fixture on the target list of ANGLICO aerial observers. Shoulder-fired SAM-7 heat-seeking missiles were also confirmed to be tactically deployed south of the Cua Viet. This ominous new development posed an even greater danger to low, slower flying spotter craft. To this end, normal spotting altitude of 3,500 feet was increased to a 7,000-foot minimum, making target observation all the more difficult.

Four weeks into his third tour with Sub Unit One, WO2 William E. Thomas, Jr., once again found himself in Vietnam, performing in his familiar role as airborne naval gunfire spotter. Based out of Da Nang this time around, he did enjoy a few more creature comforts and much better chow than the Spartan existence he once coped with during his stay with the Korean Marines. Life, however, was just as hazardous.

After finishing breakfast and attending to some personal responsibilities the morning of 19 May, Gunner Thomas made his way to the day's mission and intelligence briefing at 1000, where he hooked up with mission pilot U.S. Air Force Captain David P. Mott, call sign "Covey 248." Gunner Thomas would be operating under his usual *nom de guerre*, "Wolfman 3-1." That day, Covey drew an afternoon Search and Destroy assignment that would keep them on station over hostile territory from 1200 to 1600 hours, carrying enough fuel for six hours of flight. The area of operation for this patrol encompassed the entire Easter Offensive killing grounds, from just north of Hue City up to the demilitarized zone.

The war had changed quite a bit in his absence, as did technology for waging that war. Making its combat debut in late 1967, the twin-engine OV-10A Bronco now prowled the skies in place of the outdated O1 bird dog. Developed as a multipurpose, light attack and observation craft, the OV-10 was much improved and more versatile than its predecessor. Armed with up to 3,600 pounds of assorted bombs, machine guns, cannon, and missiles on five weapon attachment points, this aircraft was something to fear.

Mission capabilities of the Bronco included observation, forward air control, helicopter escort, armed reconnaissance, gunfire spotting, utility, and limited ground attack; however, the USAF acquired the Bronco primarily as a forward air control platform.

Lifting off the landing strip at 1130, Covey 248 was right on schedule, assuming a northerly course that would take it over Quang Tri Province. Per established procedure, Gunner Thomas checked in with ANGLICO ground control: "2-6 Charlie, Wolfman 3-1 is airborne, feet wet" (over water).

Once on station, 2-6 Charlie transmitted the afternoon targets. A U.S. Navy destroyer, call sign "Bright Penny," was standing by to receive fire missions. Normal protocol allowed an airborne spotter to prioritize the targets and determine his own sequence of bringing the objectives under fire, unless urgency dictated otherwise. This system permitted the air crews to select and stagger their destinations, thus limiting the enemy's ability to predict anticipated flight paths.

From the cockpit, the crew, looking east over South China Sea, could see the destroyer USS *Berkeley* (DDG-15), Commander Jerry

A. Dickman, Captain, cruising parallel to the coast. Observing each target in relation to the ship, Covey would take position to spot and control the fire mission well outside the gun target line. Proceeding on mission, Gunner Thomas went to work, taking out targets as they appeared on his strike list, giving USS *Berkeley* gun crews a full afternoon of quality trigger time.

At approximately 1445, Covey approached the Cua Viet LST ramp at the mouth of the Cua Viet River. The NVA were now employing that ramp to offload their supplies from North Vietnam. Spending forty-five minutes on target, the USS *Berkeley*, through the eyes of Wolfman 3-1, took the LST ramp under fire, causing one secondary explosion, destroying several boats, and causing an undetermined number of KIAs, exerting good effect on target.

Having completed that mission at approximately 1535, Covey closed in on the next target, which was reported to be an NVA command post operating out of a village. Some of the NVA were reported to be attired in civilian clothes. Scanning the village with binoculars, Warrant Officer Thomas confirmed the target's legitimacy. Once the target check was complete, Captain Mott climbed to altitude, while Thomas jotted down notes on his knee board, preparing for the fire mission.

Not long into ascent, an ear-popping explosion jarred the senses of both crewmen. There was no mistaking that sound, a sinister decibel of racket neither man ever wanted to hear. The left engine was hit. Captain Mott, monitoring his instrument panel, observed every emergency gauge light in the cockpit blink to life. Noticing the left propeller blade was not rotating, Gunner Thomas instinctively hit his ICS (intercom) button, informing Mott of what they both already knew: "We're hit!"

Captain Mott, already up on UHF, sent out a broadcast informing USAF ground control of his impending crash along with coordinates and situation brief.

Gunner Thomas came up on the gunfire net. "Bright Penny, this is 3-1. We're hit! We're going down!" Thomas then switched to ANGLICO TAC, repeating the same broadcast for 2-6 Charlie.

Captain Mott fought the controls hard, keeping his crippled Bronco on an easterly heading, hoping to get out over open water. In spite of his best efforts, Covey 248 was losing altitude fast. Keeping the nose pointed east, the pilot kept course, employing every skill in his inventory to stay aloft until the plane reached the lowest safe bailout altitude.

The ICS system went dead, severing crew communication within the craft. Gunner Thomas could do no more than sit back in nerve-racking suspense and wait for Captain Mott to activate the ejection system, terminating this white-knuckle ride through hell.

Keeping an eye on his altimeter, Captain Mott, at the right moment, pulled up on the ejection handle, filling the crew cabin with smoke as jettison rockets ignited, setting a timed sequence in motion. Gunner Thomas's seat slowly raised from its moorings a few inches, then accelerated instantly to full velocity, sending the salty gunner through the glass dome. 12 to 14 *g*'s pulling at his body drained just enough blood from his brain to cause blackout.

A couple heartbeats later, Captain Mott rocketed free of the powerless aircraft.

Seconds after clearing the aircraft, Thomas re-entered the conscious world, experiencing the shock of chute deployment. Instantly alert and cognizant of his situation, the Marine shifted his psyche to survival mode. A veteran of countless jumps, Gunner Thomas started hauling in riser, climbing to the silk border of his parachute, trying just by force of will to get that damned canopy moving east. Knowing full well he wouldn't make open water didn't do a thing to deter his effort.

Bullets ripping past the exposed Marine from several directions gave him something else to think about. No sooner had he become aware that he was now a sporting clay for NVA soldiers, a bullet glanced off his leg, ripping away some skin he was fighting so desperately to save.

During his bone-jarring ejection, Captain Mott's sidearm worked loose from its holster. Now on hostile ground, unarmed and in the middle of who knows what, too many thoughts to deal with raced through his consciousness, demanding immediate attention. Being in survival mode, the captain found his hand radio, alerting ground control of his situation and condition. He quickly became aware of

Thomas, still fifty or so feet overhead on course to settle not twenty feet away.

Still clinging on the edge of his canopy, Gunner Thomas released the risers, bouncing to earth on his ass before the chute could oscillate. It wasn't one of his better landings, but he was unhurt and able to function. He found himself in a small clearing, supporting generous growth of high grass. The hulk of the burning OV-10 couldn't have been thirty feet to his right. Captain Mott was just to his left front, looking straight at him. What are the odds that he, Mott, and the ship would all come to ground so close?

Gaining his feet, the gunner's .45 was in already in his hand before he stood fully erect. Gravitating to where Captain Mott was hunkered down, the pair quickly put together a no-brainer evasion plan to move east, east, east, and keep moving east.

One problematic condition of moving through high grass during an evasion maneuver was the tendency of this particular vegetation to become matted once it's bent. As speed was imperative to rescue, both fighting men knew they'd either get out of this quick or they wouldn't get out at all. Not having the luxury of time to avoid tramping down the grass, they may just as well have hung up a sign, "We went that way." Having no choice in the matter, speed was more desirable than gardening, as the pair moved east under a veil of caution.

On the move, several times both men became aware of NVA search parties in their immediate area. From the sounds of unseen men moving about nearby, Gunner Thomas suspected the NVA already picked up their trail and were in anticipation of the direction of movement, trying to get ahead of the pair and cut them off from the east.

Knowing the NVA were closing in, the Americans stopped to think things out. Captain Mott once more got on his radio to check on SAR efforts and report their progress and situation. Hearing the sound of voices startlingly close, Gunner Thomas cautiously rose above the grass line to have a look. AK fire from a young NVA soldier not more than twenty yards distant hammered out a rude greeting to the surprised Marine. Bullets zipped past just overhead, cutting a swath through the tall grass. Before Thomas could get his head back below the grass line, one of those rounds took a piece of his ear.

Observing at least a full platoon, the gunner realized there were more of those monkeys than he had rounds for his weapon. In a quick huddle, the pair realized they had only seconds to decide if they would live or die. Prospects of escaping this mess appeared to be nonexistent. There was absolutely no doubt they were surrounded and out of options. If the gunner fired one round, they were both going down for sure. Surrender was not part of the code either man lived by, but then neither was suicide.

Figuring the odds at 50/50 versus no chance at all, both men agreed to give it up. Reluctantly, Gunner Thomas laid his automatic down, still a little shaken by the near miss just seconds ago. Each then raised his hands above the grass. Both men were gripped in foreboding anxiety, fighting to suppress frightening expectations of dread; they stood up slowly and waited in suspense. This was it and they both knew it.

Quickly surrounded by several soldiers, the pair was immediately separated. Shoved off to the side by one Vietnamese, another produced a knife while angling behind Thomas. Thinking it was all over, the Marine steeled himself to his fate. However, much to his relief, the NVA busied himself cutting Thomas's flight suit from collar to crotch. While this was going on behind his back, another soldier took the watch off his wrist. Gunner Thomas was then made to step out of the suit, now clad only in boots and skivvies.

Surrounded by guards, Thomas was soon on the march. After a while, the detail entered a campsite, where a bandage was applied to his bleeding ear.

Some ten minutes later, Dave Mott entered the campsite, accompanied by his own entourage. The camp inhabitants huddled around a radio, presumably reporting their trophies to higher authority. After a short interval, the pair found themselves once more on the hoof.

When darkness fell, the Americans were forced to take off their boots. The laces were tied together, then the boots were hung around their necks. Continuing on, the pair now had to negotiate almost blind through a war-torn landscape littered with shrapnel and other debris of battle. Considering the amount of ordnance expended over this area in the course of seven years of combat in countless operations, they were lucky to have any skin at all still left on their feet.

In their sojourn, the Americans couldn't help but notice huge numbers of NVA troops engaged in various activities. By Gunner Thomas's reckoning, they were somewhere in an area that in times past was known as Leatherneck Square. The people living there used to love Marines, but that wasn't the case now, as the Americans soon found themselves targets of kicks, frequently having to shield their bodies from stick-wielding villagers.

Considering the thousands of local inhabitants who had been callously murdered and maimed by indiscriminant NVA field artillery and rockets barely six weeks earlier, it's difficult to fathom how these unfortunate victims were now acting out of hatred toward Americans.

Finally arriving at their destination near midnight, wherever that was, the Americans were shown to a concrete building, where they remained four days.

On day five of their captivity, Thomas and Mott moved further north. At the Ben Hai River, which runs through the DMZ, Gunner Thomas was impressed into service by one of his captors to repair a boat beached on the river bank. It seems no one could start the engine. Not knowing the first thing about boats, Thomas explained to deaf ears that he couldn't do a damned thing for them.

After a token dry run of pretending to fiddle with the motor, both Americans were put in the boat and paddled across the Ben Hai. Once on the north side, after a half-hour walk from the river, they settled in to spend the night in a bamboo hut.

Throughout the ordeal since capture, the duo had not yet encountered anyone who spoke English. That situation changed in the DMZ. Once more the Americans were separated. As Thomas sat alone in the hut, an official-looking Vietnamese and his guard entered, disturbing the gunner's solitude. His first interrogation was now in session.

Bill Thomas knew this moment would come sooner or later. Since capture five days ago, he'd been preparing and rehearsing for this inevitable event. He knew he'd have to tell them something. Not knowing for sure what the NVA would be digging for, the Marine figured he'd just have to play it by ear until he was told what they wanted to know. To backtrack a little, Captain Mott had in his pocket a letter from his wife, which contained his unit and address in Vietnam. Since that NVA soldier cut off Thomas's flight suit at the capture site, he gambled that they wouldn't be able to correlate that he was a Marine. As the only source of identification he had on his person was a wedding ring, this was all the information his interrogator could possibly have at his disposal in the way of physical evidence. Having reasoned this out days ago, Gunner Thomas was as ready for this interview as he was ever going to be.

Picking up on the fact that his interrogator, knowing the two were in the same aircraft, would most likely assume that he was in the same unit as Mott, the crafty warrant officer hatched a scheme. Not knowing a great deal about aircraft, the Marine did feel he could put up a good act as an aerial photographer who didn't know squat about tactical particulars. That night and through the next ten months, that's just what Gunner Thomas became.

USS Blandy
(DD-943)
Forrest Sherman Class Destroyer
Call Sign: Exclamation

USS *Blandy* joined the gunline off the coast of Vietnam in May 1968 and returned four more times that year. While on line her responsibilities regularly put her in the thick of combat operations where she was constantly exposed to enemy artillery fire. Six times she was the target of intense enemy fire, often straddled and bracketed by incoming rounds. USS *Blandy* proved too elusive for enemy gunners and returned completely unscathed, as her crew functioned smoothly, maneuvering their ship out of range and bringing her guns to bear on the menacing shore batteries. After eighty-three days, her guns fired 28,000 rounds, claiming 148 enemy lives, wounding 22, silencing sixty-nine artillery pieces, and destroying or damaging well over 105 bunkers. She took a devastating toll on other military structures and boats, and made fourteen bridges and seventy-six roads impassable. In her six-month tour, she fired on 622 observed targets, 1,820 H&I targets, and 145 coastal defense sites. She received fire on five different occasions by coastal defenses. While on Sea Dragon operations, she sank twenty-two waterborne logistics craft and crippled twenty-five others, collapsed three North Vietnamese bridges, and damaged eleven more.

By 23 November 1972, the destroyer was again in Vietnamese waters, near the mouth of the Cua Viet River, firing at enemy positions north of Quang Tri City. Her gun crews manning their weapons around the clock fired an average of more than 200 rounds a day from just 5,000 yards off the beach. By the end of the year, USS *Blandy*'s guns fired 5,687 rounds, destroying numerous enemy bunkers, mortars, 130-mm guns, and other targets.

New Year's Day 1973 was quiet on the gunline until 1800, when USS *Blandy* initiated an attack on an enemy gun emplacement near Cap Lai. At 1802, the ship came under hostile fire, which she responded to with accurate counter battery measures. After thirty-two rounds, the enemy guns went silent. As the cease fire drew near in late January, the pace of enemy activity increased. So did USS *Blandy*'s response. On 28 January, she fired her 10,000th round during her final fire mission in Vietnam, on the last day of official support for South Vietnamese forces.

We, who once found refuge under the protection of her guns, salute this valiant ship and her gallant crew.

WHOOP ASS IN TIGER STRIPES

THUY QUAN LUC CHIEN

Through the remaining days of May, MR1 forces gathered strength as the 3rd Airborne Brigade arrived under operational control of General Truong. Replacement equipment, particularly armor and artillery newly arrived from the United States, added more muscle for the dangerous work ahead.

Launching Operation Song Than 8-72, four VNMC battalions crossed the My Chanh on 8 June, establishing a permanent beachhead on the north bank. Taking advantage of improved supporting arms control, Vietnamese Marines cleared the heavily defended coastal area east of the Triple Nickel (Route 555). Although the fight was tenaciously contested by a well-dug-in North Vietnamese resistance, the Marines suffered relatively few casualties, evicting stubborn defenders, who left behind eight more Russian-built tanks along with 230 dead comrades. ARVN engineers followed in the wake of the attack, erecting several pontoon bridges across the river to fuel offensive ambitions with armor, artillery, and logistic support.

Once the bridgehead was consolidated, Operation Song Than 8A-72 kicked off with battalions of all three Brigades once again pushing north. VNMC Brigade 147 continued slugging it out along sandy coastal areas east of Route 555. Brigade 258 on the left flank moved out along QL1. Attacking across open rice paddies, Marines of Brigade 369 held down anchor position in the center. With over a month to get organized, communist forces had prepared a formidable defense in depth. Going about this dangerous enterprise with a methodical but aggressive approach, the Marines overran several trench lines and fortified positions, doggedly pressing their advance into enemy territory.

While Marines moved north, elements of the 1st ARVN Division struck west from Bastogne and Checkmate toward A Shau, in a brutal struggle behind heavy artillery and TAC Air support.

Alarmed by these sucessful Marine and ARVN incursions, NVA forces during the night of 20 June sent a reinforced battalion with armor support, under cover of intense artillery preps, against 6th VNMC Battalion's sector. Still not having learned to suitably deploy, enemy infantry and tanks were again not properly coordinated. Massed Marine artillery directed on each tank swept the field of armor and stalemated the infantry. In spite of devastatingly accurate supporting fires, a platoon-size unit, however, was able to penetrate to the 6th Battalion command area, scattering the command group. In the ensuing confusion, Major James M. Tully, senior advisor, and his ANGLICO spot team became separated from the Marines. Battalion commander Lieutenant Colonel Do Huu Tung, while moving about his command group, began organizing his troops and found the Americans. Over the next eight hours, the embattled command staff rallied and, with help from naval gunfire, succeeded in restoring the perimeter.

Forging ahead, scratching and clawing for every inch against an entrenched enemy harboring not the least intention of withdrawing, the Marines extended their defensive lines four miles north of the My Chanh during ten days of fierce bloody combat.

Preparing the battlefield is a time-honored military doctrine dating to antiquity. One commander, as much as he would like to, obviously cannot position his opponent's troops where it would be advantageous to his plan, but manipulating the other commander to do it for him is a military art that had been applied by field commanders for centuries.

On 11 June, four parachutes and one dead man with a code book on his person were placed in the countryside near Route 548, which winds through A Shau Valley. Members of a South Vietnamese SOG (Special Operatrions Group) team deposited the props to look as though they'd been partially hidden in haste. An NVA patrol discovered the plants and passed them on to intelligence operatives on the 12th. In the pages of the code book, radio frequencies (dedicated networks) and authentication codes of two other actual teams were recorded. The code was just difficult enough to make NVA cryptologists work to decipher it. That same day, North Vietnamese radio operators monitoring the frequencies began picking up transmissions from those teams, one located west of Khe Sanh the other near Dong Ha. Those transmissions correctly identified NVA artillery sites and reported on actual troop movements and other items of military interest, convincing NVA ears that they really had in that code book a genuine intelligence coup.

Two defectors from the NVA 304th Division, now members of South Vietnamese SOG operations, were captured in the A Shau on 19 June. As if following an elaborate script, through interrogation, the NVA was led to another site near Khe Sanh, where radio batteries, medical supplies, and other items needed to sustain long-range covert patrols were discovered. Just in time to react, on the 25th, radio transmissions intended for the team near Dong Ha were intercepted, ordering that team to coordinate with a combined airborne and amphibious landing northwest of Dong Ha scheduled for early morning of the 27th.

On 27 June, Task Force 76 assembled off the coast parallel to the Cua Viet River. Vietnamese Marines, having been embarked from Tan My Naval Station, were already aboard amphibious assault ships, giving every indication of an impending seaborne operation. In a strategy to fix and hold in place any forces north of the Cua Viet that could possibly be in position to reinforce units south of the river, 9th MAB planners orchestrated an amphibious feint aimed at the north bank of the Cua Viet.

Just prior to dawn, gunfire ships commenced a vigorous barrage of preparatory fires on beaches just north of the river. Assault craft were already on course, heading for the beach, at 0800 when helicopters from HMM-165 launched from USS *Tripoli* (LPH-10) and passed over the LVTP-5s on the same heading. At 0806, HMM-165 closed to 5,000 meters of the beach; slower moving LVTPs were still 10,000 meters out when both airborne and surface formations suddenly turned away, leaving North Vietnamese commands in a state of confusion. Later intelligence reports confirmed just how successful the deception worked.

As was witnessed during a prior landing conducted for Song Than 6-72, NVA shore batteries attempted to thwart the invasion, unleashing salvos of 130mm rounds at the surface ships and actually bracketing several, including the USS *Blue Ridge*. Springing to action in lightning-quick precision that only the U.S. Navy could muster, counter battery fires from gunship escorts soon had active coastal artillery sites under fire before adjustments could be made and kept the surface ships from being hit. USS *Newport News*, boasting the most firepower in the fleet, came about, charging straight at Hon Co (Tiger) Island, bringing main and secondary batteries to bear with devastating accuracy. Nothing more was heard from Tiger Island.

Following a very successful feint, Operation Lam Son (Total Victory) 72, designed to seize and hold a line along the Thach Han River, launched on 28 June. For six days prior to jump-off, every available supporting arm within range mercilessly pounded NVA defenders, logistics, collection points, and every avenue of approach in Quang Tri Province. Behind a curtain of thunder, the 1st ARVN Airborne Division, striking out west of QL1, and Marines advancing on a front extending from QL1 to the coastal plains on the east flank took the first steps of an offense in force.

Stepping off with both airborne and Marines battalions, ANGLICO fire control teams were once more in the field, primed and ready to assert full extent of their death-dealing tactical capabilities. Flying out of Phu Bai and Da Nang with the U.S. Air Force 20th Tactical Air Support Squadron, airborne spotters also applied their deadly trade over the battleground. Flying on average seven missions daily, affording fire support coordination availability around the clock, airborne spotters provided invaluable service to their land-locked teammates and field commanders maneuvering below them.

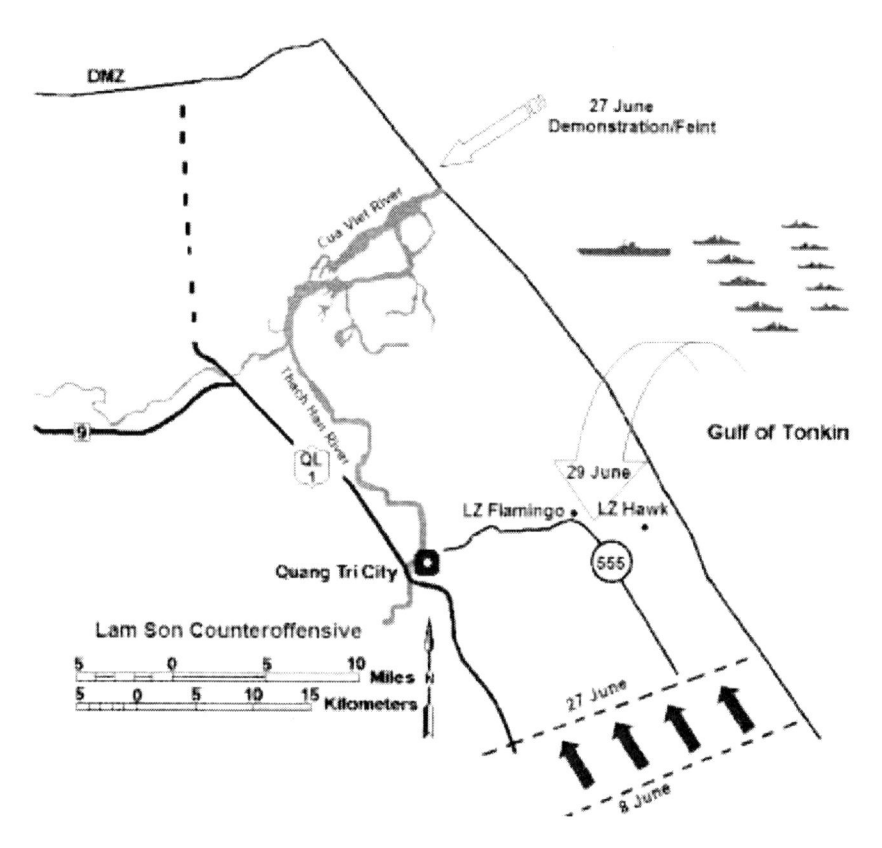

Map labels: DMZ; 27 June Demonstration/Feint; Cua Viet River; Thach Han River; Gulf of Tonkin; 29 June; LZ Flamingo; LZ Hawk; 555; QL 1; Quang Tri City; 9; Lam Son Counteroffensive; 27 June; 8 June; Miles; Kilometers

Lam Son 72 was now a two-division offense on a broad front, pressing NVA defenders with the largest attacking force yet seen in MR1.

Lieutenant Anthony P. Shepard and Lance Corporal Michael Jurak, comprising an ANGLICO fire control team, moved north with the 2nd Brigade, providing supporting arms coverage west of the highway.

Lieutenant Shepard was struck by these observations: *"When we started north on the counter-offensive in late June, we moved across the My Chanh River for the first time. Shortly after we got across, we saw the remnants of what had been a huge massacre during the initial push. From what I pieced together, the fleeing ARVNs and civilians clogged the road and made it to a bridge just north of the My Chanh (I believe it was pronounce 'Okay,' but I don't know the spelling), which had been destroyed. At that point, everything became a huge traffic jam and the NVA began shelling the turmoil. When we crossed, the brigade engineers had already used heavy equipment to bulldoze the vehicles to one side of QL1. There was every kind of vehicle you can imagine: Peugeot cars, 6x6s, buses, bicycles, you name it. This mess was consolidated around three to six vehicles wide and probably several hundred yards distant on the west side of the road. There were human remains still in the wreckage, some skeletal and some mummified. The place stunk something awful. It was like a scene from Dante's Inferno."*

Marines on the east flank quickly gained momentum; although heavily opposed, VNMC continued a steady advance. Seizing an opportunity to exploit the surge and help accelerate Marine progress, an aerial assault north where Route 555 bends west to Quang Tri City was put in play on the 29th. A scheduled sequence of preparatory fires commenced at 0600, including ARCHLIGHT strikes. Per plan, the first actual insertion would occur forty-five minutes after the last B-52 sortie on the landing zone.

Insertion of the first wave at LZ Flamingo at 0918, in spite of moderate ground fire, came off on schedule. With great supporting cover from F Troop, 4th Air Cavalry U.S. Army Cobras, the 4th VNMC Battalion secured the LZ and readied for attack.

Appearing over LZ Hawk at 1104, crews from HMM-164 and HMM-165 made their descent through moderate ground fire. As was the case at Flamingo, U.S. Army Cobra escorts covered the insertion with devastating suppressive fire, allowing 1st Battalion Marines to gain a foothold. While the Marines fanned out to consolidate the landing site, Cobra gunships, staying on task, destroyed an enemy T-54 not far from the insertion point.

Shortly after insertion, scattered enemy units made a haphazard attempt to block 1st Battalion's advance from Hawk. NVA tanks and armored personnel carriers, off and on through the afternoon skirmish, tried unsuccessfully to flank the Marines by rushing armor down the surf line. The Marines were fortunate to have brought ANGLICO's 1st Lieutenant Stephen G. Biddulph and Corporal Jose F. Hernandez along, who had voice com with 7th Fleet gunline ships. Lieutenant Biddulph, declaring everything north of his position a free-fire zone, gave blanket clearance for the offshore gun platforms to fire on any observed targets. Positioned just 4,000 meters offshore, gunline ships, able to observe their own fall of shot, took the armored units under direct fire, breaking up the attacks and leaving several vehicles burning in place.

Before sunset, over 1,450 Marines were on the ground due east of Quang Tri City, giving NVA commanders one more headache to deal with.

Over the next nine days, until relieved, the spot team directed call for fire missions at enemy gun emplacements and, on more than one occasion, expertly utilized fires from offshore gunships to break up probes and attacks on their position.

Flying in support of Lam Son 72 on 29 June near dusk, an OV-10A crew—USAF Captain Steven L. Bennett, pilot, and naval gunfire spotter Captain Michael B. Brown—answering a call for support, arrived over a platoon desperately fighting off several hundred enemy soldiers. Judging the contact at quarters too close for naval gunfire and with air support not readily available, Captain Bennett, seeing no other way, lined up his craft for a strafing run. Five dives on target gave the embattled Marines a little breathing room, brushing back the determined attackers. Climbing out of his fifth pass, the OV-10 was violently jolted on impact with a SAM-7 striking the aircraft from behind. One engine was disabled, exposing the damaged left landing gear, which had popped out of its well. The explosion wounded Captain Brown slightly and set the aircraft on fire.

Knowing a dry landing wasn't possible, Captain Bennett steered his crippled craft out over open water, where the crew had a much better chance of rescue after bail-out. While preparing for ejection, Captain Brown noticed his parachute was damaged. Captain Bennett had a good chute, but could not leave Brown in the back seat without a pilot, and made ready to ditch, realizing full well that no OV-10 pilot had ever survived a water landing. He had to know he was giving his life to allow Brown a chance to live.

Upon contact, the plane cartwheeled end over end, coming to rest nose down on its back. Captain Brown painfully exited the cockpit and pulled himself along the fuselage toward the front seat. Not known for its buoyancy, the plane and Captain Bennett slid below the waves as Captain Brown could do no more than look helplessly on. For his selfless act of giving his own life for that of his crewman, Captain Steven L. Bennett was posthumously warded the Congressional Medal of Honor.

Facing a concerted attack from the south and now cut off from the north, the pace of Marine advances up Route 555 gained momentum, exposing the flank of NVA units trying to hold back the 1st Airborne, soon forcing those troops to give ground.

West of QL1, on 30 June, the 3rd ARNV Airborne Brigade encountered stiff opposition just south of Quang Tri City. Corporal John E. Parton, ANGLICO spot team member, advanced to confront a machine gun that had slowed progress, pinning down Airborne troopers to his immediate front. Finding his prey, Parton extended his M-72 LAW. While positioning himself for a good shot, he exposed his body just long enough to be taken under fire by the machine gunner before the Marine could launch his missile. Mortally wounded by multiple hits of flesh-tearing cones of death, Corporal Parton painfully shouldered his weapon once more, then let fly a rocket, obliterating the machine gun and crew. Corporal Parton's selfless act of valor enabled the assault to continue through the enemy position and closer to the capital.

As South Vietnamese forces closed on Quang Tri City, resistance from dug-in NVA troops stiffened, slowing the advance. By 4 July, the 2nd Brigade, 1st ARVN Airborne Division, in sight of the capital, encountered heavy defensive fires from a well-entrenched enemy. Under cover of darkness, the ANGLICO spot team of 1st Lieutenant Anthony P. Shepard and Lance Corporal Michael Jurak, under guidance of U.S. Army advisor 1st Lieutenant Terry A. (Buddha) Griswold, made their way with ninety soldiers of the Brigade Recon Company to a position on the southwest outskirts of the city. With black-painted faces and uniforms sporting leaves and other camouflage vegetation, the recon troops went forth into the night, observing clandestine practice.

Movement to the line of departure brought the patrol in grisly contact with evidence of the ARVN retreat south. Everywhere, badly decomposed corpses of civilians intermingled with dead ARVN soldiers still littered QL1, from indiscriminant NVA shelling during the Quang Tri exodus some weeks before. Those vivid memories, in spite of many years separating the event, still remain with Lieutenant

Griswold from that long-ago assignment. Thirty-seven years later, Lieutenant Shepard recalled:

When we pushed north, we could see the evidence of an Army en route. When the ARVN ran south in April, they dropped enough gear to outfit an entire NVA division, I swear. There was so much of it that there was still lots of stuff left when we moved north because, I'm sure, the NVA just didn't have a way to cart it all off!

From south to north, we saw uniforms and boots: A little further north, weapons and ammo belts. Further still, boxed ammo, loose grenades, helmets, and 782 gear. Further yet, boxed grenades, crates of small arms ammunition, claymore mines, LAWs, and rucksacks.

The recon team linked up with a battalion at the forward edge of battle. Lingering for a conference with the battalion adviser to coordinate movement, the team waited while ARVN troops engaged a number of enemy positions blocking their path north. NVA troops, under pressure from the airborne advance, were fighting a rear-guard action using a 37mm antiaircraft gun to inhibit progress. As the ARVN were so close, enemy gunners were unable to level the weapon low enough for effective fire, as rounds exploded harmlessly to the rear. Soon after the action subsided, the reconnaissance in force cautiously stepped off.

Infiltrating from the 2nd Brigade's forward perimeter, at midnight, the patrol progressed north on QL1, then filtered into the suburban setting on the outskirts, under cover of artillery barrages. At one point in the mission, the team was forced to crawl across 1,000 meters of open rice paddy. Frequently, progress was halted as illumination rounds bursting overhead forced the infiltrators to freeze in place until darkness once again settled over the landscape.

Once inside city limits, the company split into three groups and moved forward. The command group cut east, until coming to a suitable observation site just north of where QL-1 bends west at the junction of a north/south access road. Arriving at a partially bombed-out two-story building at 0300, the command group established a control center. Lieutenant Griswold moved to the second floor, where he positioned a VS-17 signal panel on the roof, giving spotter planes a reference point on the team's location. When the sun came up on 5 July, from their vantage point, the team discovered they were located on the flank of an NVA battalion. Undaunted, the team later moved forward under a shroud of caution. Finding a two-story cinder block house within 300 meters of the Citadel wall, the team once more set up shop and continued on with their mission.

From here, Lieutenants Griswold and Shepard directed numerous air strikes and naval gunfire missions on the Citadel walls and defensive positions on its approach. On several occasions over the next four days of their stay, NVA soldiers occupying structures just across the street would come out to relieve themselves and scratch their asses. It was a most unnerving position, as all concerned hoped like hell that no one would get curious enough to venture over to the harbor site.

Remaining at the observation post in spite of enemy activity in such close proximity, the team went about the dangerous business of reducing several fortified strong points and sending back intelligence reports on enemy strength and activities.

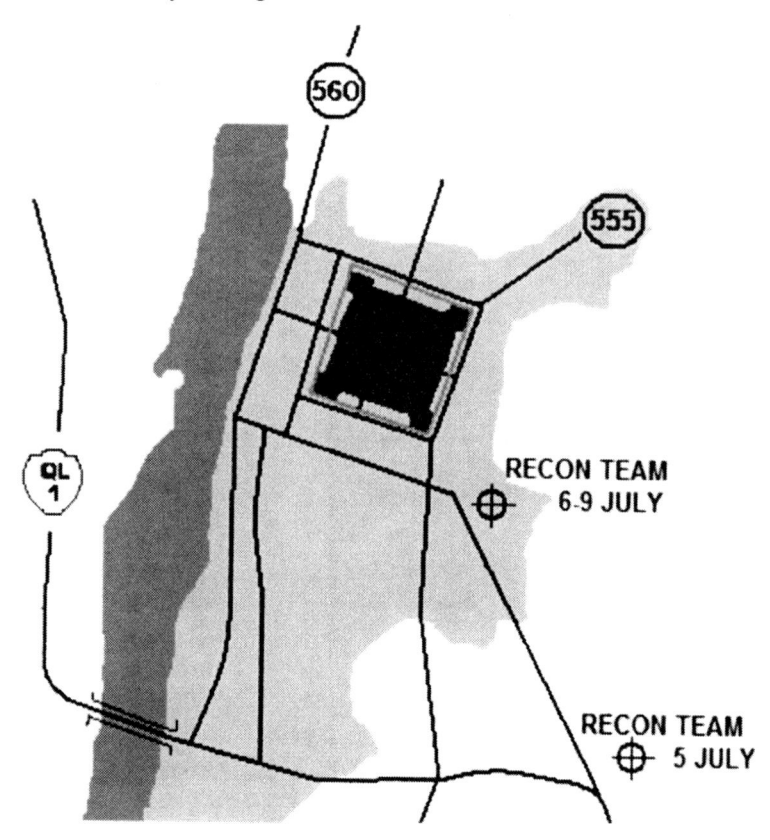

On 9 July, security elements reported enemy troops advancing on the observation post. Reconnaissance commander Captain Tran Ut ordered his exposed unit to fall back. Even as the team was exiting the rear of the building, NVA search parties were pouring through the front door. As a rude welcoming gesture, the last man out rolled a hand grenade toward the front entrance, greeting the new occupants with an M-26 house-warming gift. North Vietnamese artillery began impacting the immediate area, as the team made its way down a series of rubble-strewn side streets. Behind a cordon of supporting Vietnamese artillery, the reconnaissance teams withdrew. Throughout the rest of that night, NVA units remained hard on the hunt as the recon party skillfully evaded their pursuers in a high-stakes game of hide and seek. Under intense small arms, mortar and artillery fire, the recon soldiers fell back in good order, threading their way east through the suburban rubble and out into surrounding rice paddies. The Airborne troopers, having successfully eluded their pursuers, broke contact around midnight.

As extraction plans for remaining in place to await the Airborne Division advance was no longer viable, and since moving around amid enemy defenses was obviously not too smart, Captain Ut ordered a halt, deciding to logger in until morning.

At 0500, the reconnaissance men, on very little sleep, rose and made ready for the ARVN advance to move through their location, tentatively timed for 0630. The 3rd Brigade, moving forward under constant sniper harassment, fell behind schedule. Being lulled into a false sense of security, a relaxed atmosphere of relief at the impending hook-up settled over the patrol. No one bothered to station listening posts around the perimeter. At 0700, an unmistakable sound of mortar rounds leaving their tubes filled the air with expectations of dread. It seems an NVA company still at war had moved in on them during the night. As he was diving for cover, Lieutenant Shepard can still recall the exact thoughts racing through his head:

"We screwed up and let our guard down, we're going to die, and we deserved to."

Recovering from the initial attack, the command group moved to the rear while security teams fought a delaying action. After a quick conference with Captain Ut, Lieutenants Griswold and Shepard crawled forward into an open area, establishing radio contact with an Airborne FAC. Panels were immediately displayed, while Shepard employed a signal mirror to confirm his location. Calling out enemy positions relative to the panels, the FAC was quickly brought up to speed on tactical particulars. Directing a flight of A-7s on suspected enemy locations, the attack was prematurely pre-empted with 500-pound payloads. With a renewed sense of alertness, the recon company remained in place until relieved later that morning.

By 7 July, elements of the 1st Airborne Division clawed and scratched their way to the outskirts of Quang Tri in force and became embroiled in a violent standoff with enemy defenders, supported with massed artillery and mortar fire. From the fierce resistance encountered, it became all too evident that NVA forces were determined to fight to the death in order to remain in control of the provincial capital. The battle now reverted to house-to-house fighting, reminiscent of the fight to retake Hue City during Tet 1968. After turning back an armor/infantry attack on the 9th with the help from TAC Air, the Airborne troopers once more advanced on the Citadel. Still in its infancy, a 2,000-pound laser-guided bomb, delivered on the wall by a U.S. Air Force plane, put a gaping hole in the structure. Advancing to within 200 meters of the Citadel, the Airborne troopers dug in. Both sides attempted to pulverize the other, with artillery reverting to a type of World War I trench-style warfare. Not even sortie after sortie of TAC Air could break the standoff.

The Marines, still bogged down east of the city at the juncture where Route 555 bends west toward Quang Tri, were in no position to launch an assault from the rear to mitigate pressure on the Airborne. Well-entrenched enemy, occupying fortified positions along the Vinh Dinh River, kept the Marine drive in check. In order to relieve pressure on the Airborne and allow the Marines to advance, another chopper assault was planned 2,000 meters north of the city to interdict Route 560, given the mission of keeping reinforcements from reaching resisting elements already in place.

Beginning at 0600, naval gunfire and TAC Air prep commenced fire. As in the previous assault, three waves of B-52 strikes, the last scheduled fifteen minutes before L-Hour, pounded the landing zone in sequence. Thirty-six helicopters from HMM-164 and HMM-165, skimming the treetops at maximum speed to avoid SAM-7 antiaircraft missiles, followed six U.S. Army gunship escorts toward touchdown. Carrying 840 Marines within their fuselage and 12,000 pounds of ammunition and C-ration external loads, everything was ready for a single-wave insertion, with enough beans and bullets for a sustained operation.

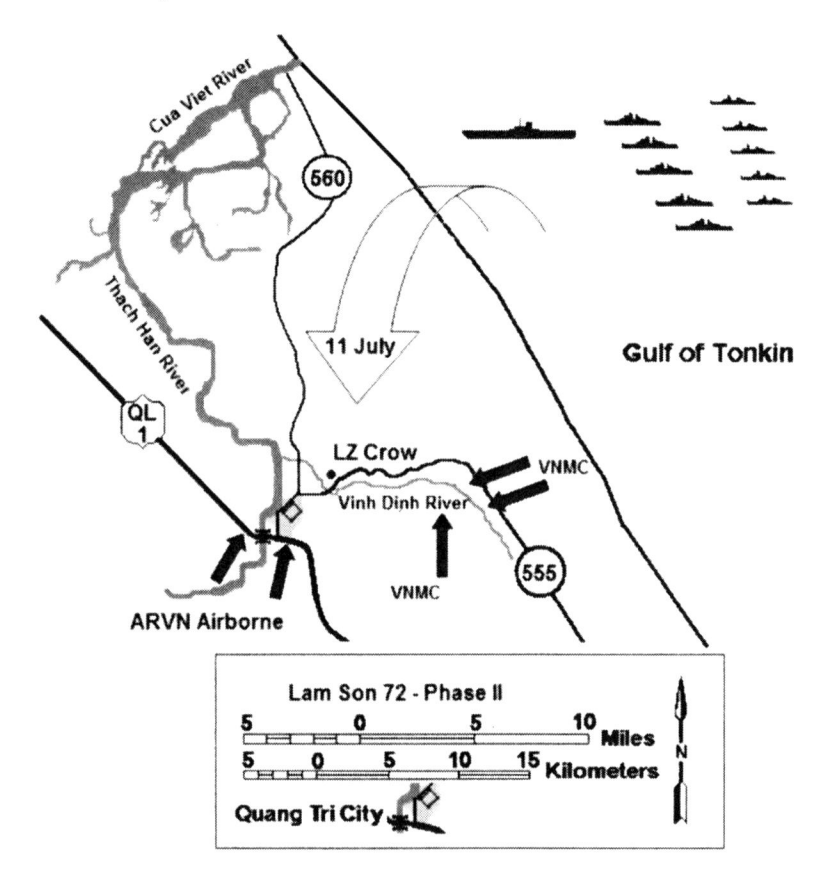

[Map: Lam Son 72 - Phase II, showing Cua Viet River, Thach Han River, QL 1, LZ Crow, Vinh Dinh River, Gulf of Tonkin, Quang Tri City, with markers 560, 555, and arrows indicating ARVN Airborne and VNMC movements on 11 July]

At 1200 on 11 July, the mixed flight of CH-53s and CH-46s flared for descent on LZ Crow. One of the first birds in, a CH-53 barely avoided landing on a T-54 tank. Reacting quickly, an AH-1 Cobra gunship rolled in hot, firing a TOW antitank missile before the surprised tankers could react. Gunfire erupted from all directions as each helicopter landed, discharged its cargo, and departed. In a staggering, surprise development that almost any battle is capable of producing, the landing zone was occupied. One CH-46, in fact, came to ground right on top of an NVA command post. Almost every craft in the operation, including gunship escorts, took hits as the landing zone and surrounding area was awash in gunfire. One CH-53 only 100 feet from landing was hit by a SAM-7, killing its crew of two U.S. Marines and all but seven passengers. Two more CH-47s became disabled, remaining on the ground until extracted later. Both crews were recovered by helicopters of the U.S. Army's 4th Air Cavalry, braving intense fire to lift out the Marine airmen.

Marines exiting aircraft became embroiled in a close-quarter firefight as soon as boots hit the ground. 1st Lieutenant Biddulph and Corporal Hernandez sprinted in serpentine fashion toward the far side of the LZ, then lay prone on the ground, trying to establish contact with fire support ships. While trying to secure communications, Lieutenant Biddulph sustained gunshot wounds in both legs. Seeing the downed officer, Captain Lawrence H. Livingston, 1st VNMC Battalion advisor, sprinted to Biddulph through a maelstrom of fire and explosions, pulling the injured Marine to safety.

Seeing casualties on the exposed LZ, Biddulph's radio operator, Corporal Hernandez, with complete disregard for his own safety, made repeated forays over the fire-swept real estate, helping several wounded Marines to reach cover in a nearby depression.

Pinned down and barely able to move, Captain Livingston organized nearby Marines and led an assault on an enemy trench line fifty meters away. Leaving the protection of their trenches, NVA soldiers sprang forward to meet the Marines. Livingston was knocked off his feet by an explosion but was back on attack, as both sides collided in front of the trenches in a brutal hand-to-hand brawl that favored the Marines.

Major Nguyen Dang Hoa, a leathered veteran, rallied his men and personally led them on assault, overrunning two trench lines and killing over 125 defenders, enabling his Marines to gain more control.

Somewhat recovered from the shock of injury, Lieutenant Biddulph regained limited mobility and, with the help of Corporal Hernandez, kept up with advancing Marines. Hernandez briefly took over spot duties under guidance from Lieutenant Biddulph, calling fire mission after fire mission to keep reinforcements away from the landing zone, pounding every known avenue of approach. With a lot of fight still remaining in him, the intrepid lieutenant resumed his mission, providing very effective fire support plans throughout the battle for LZ Crow. Biddulph kept on the move, securing vantage points to observe and adjust gunfire on an enemy that showed no sign of backing off. Wounded and in unspeakable pain, Lieutenant Biddulph epitomized the fighting spirit of a U.S. Marine throughout that bitterly contested free-for-all.

Once consolidated, the Marines expanded the enclave and pressed toward objective. In three days of brutal nose-to-nose fighting, turning back several counterattacks, the 1st Battalion stubbornly succeeded in cutting Route 560. Quang Tri City was now isolated. This event forced NVA units opposing the 1st Battalion to withdraw. Because of the unrelenting intensity of fire that would not let up, Medevacs on three occasions were unable to effect evacuation of wounded warriors. On 14 July, when the fighting finally tapered off, 150 casualties, including Lieutenant Biddulph, were at last on the way to medical facilities. For their valorous performances at LZ Crow, both Biddulph and Hernandez were awarded Silver Star medals, and Captain Livingston was honored with a Navy Cross.

Over the same three-day period, the 7th VNMC Battalion started moving west. Enemy resistance diminished as communist forces withdrew closer to the capital, trying to avoid being cut off. So swift was the Marine advance, an enemy regimental command post, not able to withdraw fast enough, was overrun, suffering the loss or capture of several armored vehicles. By 20 July, Marines were firmly established in positions just northeast of the city.

Brigade 147 doggedly advanced through stiff resistance, establishing position on the outer fringes of town and making preparations to continue the attack the next morning. Heated artillery duels continued, with both sides dishing out as much punishment as received. A battalion ANGLICO team of Lieutenant Edward G. Hayen, II, and Corporal Terry L. Willis were in conversation with VNMC advisor Captain David D. Harris, concerning fire support plans for the next day, when a massive barrage engulfed the trio, setting ablaze the hut they occupied. Lieutenant Hayen was killed instantly, taking the full force of a 152mm round that landed just to the trio's rear. Both Harris and Willis were peppered with shrapnel and seriously wounded by the same round. Although badly injured, Captain Harris was able to establish radio contact and arrange medical evacuation.

ARVN Airborne, still engaged in house-to-house fighting, managed at one point to claw their way to within fifty meters of the Citadel walls before being forced back. Employing tanks, naval gunfire, air strikes, and every direct and indirect weapon available, the ARVN could make no further progress against heavily fortified resistance points. TAC Air managed to blow three gaps in the walls, to no avail. The NVA put up a savage defense at these breaches, denying even the least bit of ground to troops who were running out of steam.

Earlier in July, the arch-bitch of Hanoi, Jane Fonda, had arrived in the capital of her communist heroes. In her entourage was a pipsqueak pock-marked draft dodger named Tom Hayden, who to this day likes to pretend he's a man.

While real men were dying a few miles south, they toured the Hanoi prisons, where American heroes were being tortured, then proclaimed to the world how humanely these *"criminals"* were being treated. Led around like dogs on leashes, they were taken to selected locations to view what was advantageous for the communist strategy of assisting efforts of the antiwar crowd in the United States. These useful idiots were introduced to politburo members, wined, dined, and treated like royalty. They did not, however, meet survivors from the exodus from Quang Tri Province, whose friends, neighbors, and families had been mercilessly killed, crippled, and maimed by deliberately aimed "humane" NVA artillery several weeks past.

On 17 July 1972, this calculating bitch actually made the first of several seditious propaganda broadcasts over Radio Hanoi. Her targeted audience was none other than courageous American warriors fighting and dying in a ferocious battle less than 200 miles south. While they were doing their best to keep communism from being inflicted on people who wanted no part of it, Jane Fonda did her treacherous best to thwart that honorable undertaking.

"This is Jane Fonda speaking in Hanoi, and I'm speaking privately to U.S. servicemen who are stationed in the Gulf of Tonkin...Seventh Fleet, in the ANGLICO Corps. You are very far away, perhaps, and removed from the country you are being ordered to shoot shells at and bomb, and the use of these bombs, or condoning the use of these bombs, makes one a war criminal.

"The men who are ordering you to use these weapons, according to international law, and in the past in Germany and Japan who were guilty of these kinds of crime were tried and executed."

Again on 22 July 1972: *"This is Jane Fonda in Hanoi. I'm speaking to the men in the cockpits of the Phantoms, in the B-52s, in the F-4s; those of you who are still here fighting the war, in the air, on the ground, the guys in the ANGLICO Corps, on the Seventh Fleet, the* Constellation, *the* Coral Sea, *the* Hancock, Ticonderoga, *the* Kitty Hawk, *the* Enterprise . . . *All of you, in your heart of hearts, know the lies, cheating on body counts, falsified battle reports, the numbers of planes that are shot down, what your targets really are. Knowing who was doing the lying . . . should you allow these same liars to decide for you who your enemy is? Should we examine the reasons given to justify the murder you are being paid to commit? If they told you the truth, you wouldn't fight, you wouldn't kill."*

How did that arrogant, useful idiot know of ANGLICO, a very small unit that received absolutely no press coverage and was all but completely unknown to the American public? She was hand-fed that information by her "humane" communist hosts, that's how.

Seizing an opportunity to exploit a weak point in NVA field positions along the coast just south of the Cua Viet River, and to further isolate enemy defenders in the city, Vietnamese Marines once again took to offense. Since May, the Marines had been able to do just about as they pleased: amphibious assaults, helicopter envelopments, and just plain ol' smashmouth straight-up-the-middle infantry attacks.

Song Than 9-72 was launched after sunrise, behind the usual cast of supporting arms bombardments. Brigade 147 committed two battalions, supported by armor, to attack north astride Route 603. The 5th Battalion Alpha Group was transported by HMM-164 to LZ Victor two and a half miles north of the line of departure at 0938, followed by insertion of Bravo Group further north at the junction of Routes 560 and 603 a half hour later. Experiencing relatively moderate opposition, Marines at both landing zones moved out quickly, hooking up with the two-battalion ground force.

During the next two days, Marines attacked west then south, encountering light to moderate opposition that netted 133 NVA killed, three tanks destroyed, and two captured. Quang Tri City, now completely isolated, became the sole focus of MR1 planners.

Being fed into Lam Son 72 just days after standing down from a grueling battle at Kontum, the Airborne troopers had been under the gun for almost three consecutive months, and it was starting to show. Spent and exhausted, the 2nd Airborne Brigade was relieved in place by VNMC Brigade 258 under continuous mortar and artillery fire on the 27th.

Over the next three days, NVA artillery and mortar crews persisted in sending over 1,000 rounds a day, raking Marine positions. Allied artillery and naval gunfire reciprocated by mercilessly pounding the isolated defenders in a shroud of iron. All through the month of August, Airborne ANGLICO spotters relentlessly braved SAM-7 threats, hunting the surrounding area in search of NVA artillery. Hundreds of TAC Air sorties and naval gunfire missions, seeking to silence the troublesome guns, met with limited success. Enemy gunners, reverting to guerilla tactics, dispersed their field pieces in groups of two, keeping them constantly on the move to improve survivability. Well over 58,000 Naval gunfire shells were fired in support of the operation during the month of August. Inside the capital, engaged in a never-ending cycle of house-to-house fighting in neighborhoods south of the Citadel, Brigade 258 continued methodically but painfully exterminating festering pockets of resistance.

North of the city, Brigade 147 was forced to fend off several enemy attempts to break the blockade along Route 560 by elements trying to rush reinforcements and supplies to their desperate comrades. As this avenue represented the only practical lifeline to defenders inside the Citadel, NVA field command committed the entire 325 Division to open the road. Heavily outnumbered, Brigade 147, with help from ANGLICO-directed supporting arms, stood firm, forcing the enemy to ferry supplies across the Thach Han River by barge, which made them easy prey for allied pilots.

During the first three days of August, gunfire ships controlled by ANGLICO spotters expended over 9,000 rounds of various calibers in and around Quang Tri City.

Back on the hunt again, Airborne spotters relentlessly called mission after mission, directed north and northwest of the city,

LIGHTNING FROM THE SKY THUNDER FROM THE SEA

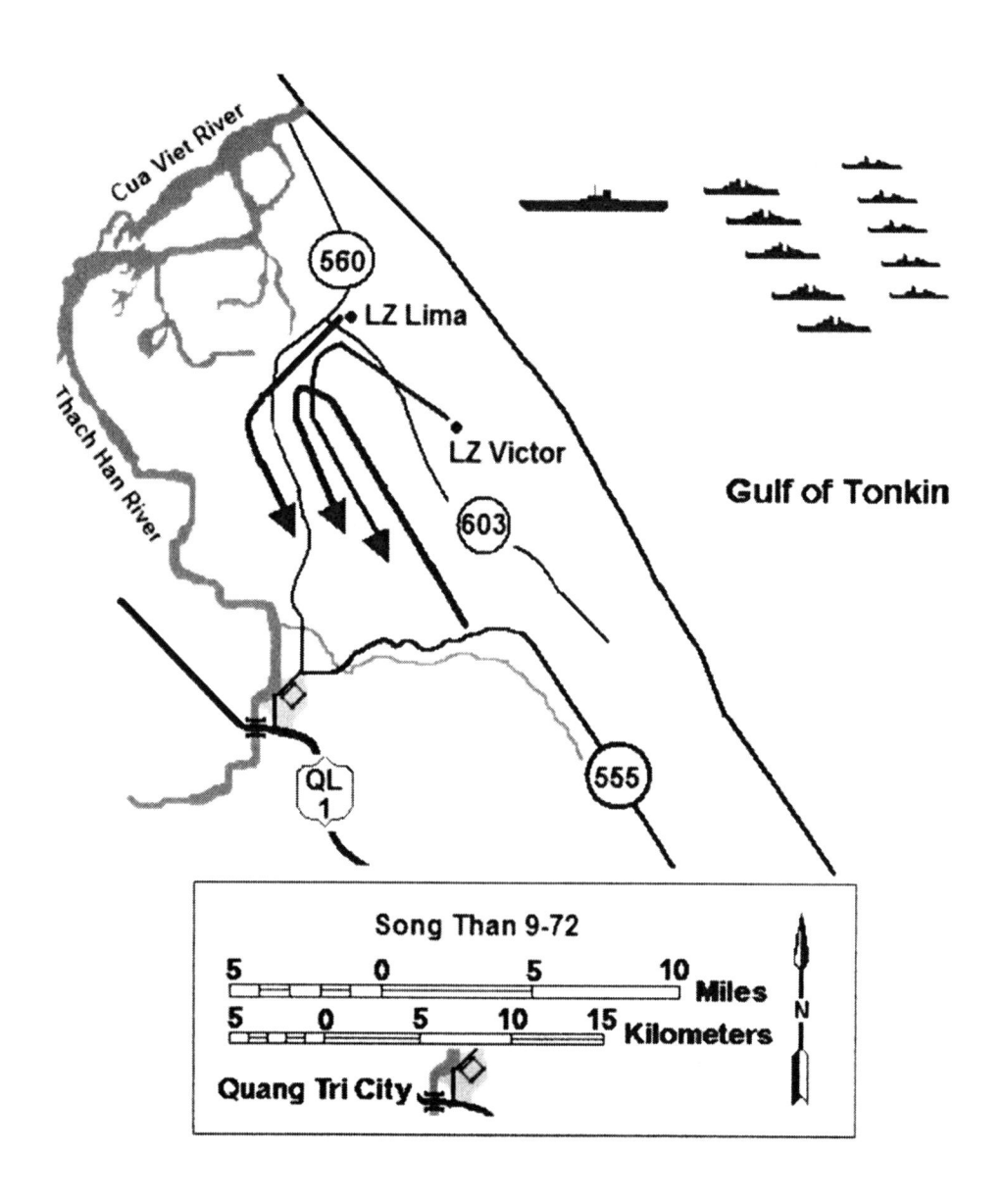

Song Than 9-72

hammering NVA attempts to bring supplies and reinforcements to their beleaguered comrades.

In a failed attempt to break out of the Citadel the night of 22 August, an NVA regiment under cover of artillery advanced on VNMC 8th Battalion behind an armored spearhead. After recovering from the surprise attack, the Marines took a terrible toll on the NVA, driving the survivors back inside the battered fortress.

The battle progressed into the early days of September, under a constant rain of artillery. Marines continued rooting out the enemy house-to-house, inching closer to their objective. On a daily basis, elements of the NVA 308th Division launched counterattacks against forward positions, desperately seeking a way out of the Citadel, but the Marines would not allow passage, making the NVA pay a terrible price.

Offshore, an impressive array of gunships crowded each other for position on the gunline. From 1 through 9 September, no less than twenty-five ships rotated position just off Wunder Beach, taking turns at pounding defensive positions and routes of egress to the embattled ancient capital.

Escalating political pressure from Saigon demanding a solution prompted a strategy meeting late in August between General Truong and Brigadier General Lan, Marine Division commander, to develop a plan that would once and for all end the siege. It had been obvious to both men for some time that more troops were needed to mount a serious attack on the Citadel, but they were already stretched to the limit. Brigadier General Lan pointed out that with elements of five communist divisions still active in Quang Tri Province, the risk of pulling troops out of current position would open the vacated area to attack. If he were to commit Brigade 369 several miles south, he would be depleting his only reserves and lose reaction options for unforeseen developments. As the 1st Airborne Division was still not up to par, the southern sector of the province would be vulnerable without the Brigade's presence. General Truong was in complete agreement, but he also understood that if more troops were not made available, the standoff could continue on into fall. General Truong reasoned since he could not get more troops, the job would have to be done by using the best troops he had at his disposal. For that purpose, the 1st Ranger Group took over Brigade 147's blocking position north of the city on 8 September, freeing up that unit for an all-Marine assault on the Citadel.

When North Vietnam committed its 325 Division to Quang Tri operations, in so doing they depleted their last reserves. There were no more divisions north of the DMZ to commit. Knowing communist forces faced the same manpower problems as did South Vietnamese units in their endeavor to manage economy of force principals, the MR1 brain trust once more turned its attention to preparing the battlefield. An actual amphibious landing was asked for, approved and planned in late August but was subsequently cancelled. To draw NVA forces trying to reinforce Quang Tri City north of the Cua Viet, and divert enemy artillery coverage away from attacking forces, General Truong then requested another amphibious landing feint from 9th MAB, which was approved. Due to a suspected leak in the ARVN chain of command, the cancellation of the previous assault was not formally announced but kept secret among a very select few. In this way, if word of the assault was passed on to North Vietnamese operatives, it could only enhance the feint.

As any poker player knows, once a player bluffs, everyone at the card table is now aware that player is capable of bluffing. If it is then assumed that every time this player raises a bet, he is bluffing, then when the other players see a raise, they are leaving themselves open to being wiped out by a strong hand. This was the dilemma about to confront NVA field command. They had been faked out of their shoes on 29 June. On the other hand, Vietnamese Marines actually came ashore and did pretty much as they pleased in May during Song Than. If they failed to react to the amphibious threat and 9th MAB actually came ashore north of the Cua Viet, communist forces in Quang Tri City would then be forfeit. The thing with a bluff, it only works when the stakes are high. The higher the stakes, the more viable a strategy it becomes, as the other side dare not ignore a possible catastrophic battle-ending maneuver. For North Vietnamese field commanders charged with holding Quang Tri, the stakes couldn't get much higher. Inasmuch as NVA reserves had already been committed, the only option open was to pull troops from someplace else on the battlefront to oppose this invasion. General Truong understood this when opting for this maneuver and he had just introduced his opposite number to the proverbial pressure cooker.

Early morning of 9 September, massive artillery fires began pounding the Citadel, pausing only occasionally to allow tactical air strike sorties.

Simultaneously, naval gunfire and B-52 missions dispensed tons of ordnance in and around the targeted feint objective in volumes not seen before. Three hours before H-Hour, bombardment intensified to a maddening crescendo and kept this pace until landing craft approached the demarcation zone. LVTP-5s formed online, making headway toward the beach as a flight of B-52s in now-familiar succession delivered the final prep sortie. On schedule, when Marine helicopters launching from USS *Tripoli* passed over the LVTPs, gunfire escort ships ceased fire. Knowing from experience this event heralded a beach landing, North Vietnamese defenders left fortified positions in the tree line, preparing to halt the pitifully predictable "puppet troop" assault forces in the surf. As in the previous demonstration air and surface formations suddenly turned away at 5,000 and 10,000 meters, respectively, leaving stunned defenders in a state of déjà vu. Milling around the beach, scratching their asses and trying to figure out what the hell was going on, NVA soldiers were immediately caught in the open by massed naval gunfire and took a terrible pounding.

As hoped for, the NVA did shift troops and artillery to defend against the projected threat, reducing available assets for support of Quang Tri City. As a result, incoming artillery previously directed at the Marines diminished, allowing for rapid advancement on the Citadel.

One ongoing obstacle throughout the assault were three forts occupied by NVA troops that prevented allied forces from gaining position to launch an assault against the ancient stronghold. These forts just south of the Citadel afforded communist troops a crossfire defense for any attacks against the Citadel walls. It was a Catch-22 proposition, as fire from the Citadel prevented attacks on the forts, providing reciprocal cross-fire defenses. On 9 September, 3rd Airborne Brigade took advantage of reduced artillery support, and a coordinated attack by the Marines against the Citadel was finally able to break the deadlock, storming those forts and neutralizing their protective fires.

Attacking the northern portion of the Citadel, Brigade 147 had first to clear out enemy troops occupying buildings in front of the wall. Brigade 258, already entrenched south of the fortress, pressed forward, its 6th Battalion taking up assault position at the southwest corner of the wall. Although heavily damaged, a good portion of the thirty-inch-thick, fifteen-foot-high barrier still remained intact, standing guard over crumbling rubble that was once the garden spot of Quang Tri Province.

Due to an intricate labyrinth of connecting tunnels and fortifications erected by the mole-like defenders since occupation, Marine advances slowed but maintained continuous progress all day. At nightfall, a recon team from 6th Battalion was close enough to successfully infiltrate inside the Citadel and slip out again. At 2100, 10 September, Lieutenant Colonel Do Huu Tung, 6th Battalion's commanding officer, directed his troops in a night assault. Although tenaciously defended, his men were able to establish a small enclave atop the wall at the southwest corner. Seeing this as his inch to go for a mile, a platoon assault the next morning penetrated the Citadel. In spite of fanatical resistance, the platoon was able to expand its penetration, allowing a company-size force to push its way over the wall, establishing a foothold that would not be relinquished.

News of the breach reached NVA field command, prompting a series of desperate counterattacks to reinforce the Citadel. VNMC 1st Battalion at the QL1 Bridge over the Thach Han River faced the brunt of these thrusts, turning back each assault while inflicting heavy casualties. Naval gunfire controlled by ANGLICO spotters with the 1st Battalion, as well as Airborne spotters plying the skies over Quang Tri, emerged as the deciding factor in stopping these last-ditch reinforcement efforts. From the ground and in the air, spotters pounded barges, tanks, troop concentrations, artillery, and mortar positions in an unending shower of five-, six-, and eight-inch projectiles from an armada of gunline ships eagerly responding to calls for fire.

Doggedly hanging on to the hard-won bridgehead inside the wall, 6th Battalion tenaciously fended off several counterattacks over the next four days in a viciously contested struggle. The battalion's fierce determination drained enough manpower and caused enough casualties among the defenders to allow VNMC 3rd Battalion to punch through on the north side at 1015 on the 15th. Running out of options, NVA artillery began hammering both battalions in the Citadel, who by now controlled the entire eastern portion of the ancient structure. Calling in fire of their own, with victory in sight after eight-plus weeks of gut-wrenching combat, the Marines were not about to let anything get in their way. By 1700 that afternoon, with resistance and the will to fight among NVA defenders extinguished, the Battle of Quang Tri City was added to the long list of Vietnamese Marine Corps victories.

South Vietnamese armed forces, all of which saw action throughout all four military regions, earned a well-fought victory, turning back the Easter Offensive at all points of conflict. Quang Tri Province was the last territory taken by the NVA still not under ARVN control. For the VNMC, victory did not come without a price. Having sustained 3,638 casualties, amounting to one of every four Marines in the service of South Vietnam, the time had come to replenish and regroup.

Sub Unit One also paid a price, surrendering three killed and four missing in action, while fourteen personnel were officially listed as sustaining wounds. Many ANGLICO Marines assert that fifty percent wounded is more in line with reality.

Soon after conquering the Citadel, VNMC officers from each battalion underwent training in tactical air control and naval gunfire spotting techniques, reducing critical needs for both ANGLICO and MAU participation requirements. The day was not far off when Vietnamese warriors would have to stand alone. Having proven themselves time and again, these Marines were as self-sufficient and experienced as any Marines on the planet.

General Truong did manage to regain all conquered territory south of the Cua Viet River but could make only token gains west of the Thach Han before the cease fire in January 1973. Having been continuously under the gun since March, his troops were understandably running out of steam and in need of a well-deserved rest.

USS Towers
(DDG-9)
Adams Class Guided Missile Armed Destroyer
Call Sign: Peg Leg

On 4 June 1966, USS *Towers,* with COMDESDIV 72, Captain J.K. Lesley, USN, embarked for WESTPAC in company with USS *Buck* (DD-761) and USS *Wiltsie* (DD-716) as units of TG 70.8.9. She assumed station 1 July off the III and IV Corps area and Rung Sat Special Zone, participating in Naval gunfire support operations. USS *Towers* proceeded with USS *Wiltsie* to Da Nang for counter PT boat training, arriving on Northern Search and Rescue patrol on 1 August.

USS *Towers* remained on station for thirty days. During this period, operations often took the ship within visual range of the area around Haiphong Harbor and the North Vietnam coast. After a month on station, USS *Towers* and USS *Wiltsie* were relieved on Northern SAR by USS *Hoel* (DDG-13) and USS *Gurke* (DD-783), proceeding to Hong Kong for five days of well-deserved liberty from 4 to 8 September. USS *Towers* with COMDESRON 7 and USS *Wiltsie* proceeded to Northern SAR station, remaining at that post until relieved on 31 October by USS *Hoel* (DDG-13) and USS *Southerland* (DD-743). The ship returned to Subic Bay a last time on 3 November.

Returning to Vietnamese waters on 29 September 1968, USS *Towers* conducted naval gunfire support in company with USS *New Jersey* (BB-62). On 6 October, the ship assumed duties as a unit of Operation Sea Dragon. Through the remainder of this deployment,

USS *Towers* performed on the gunline, delivering effective fire support as well as steaming off the coast of North Vietnam, wrecking havoc wherever she went.

1 January 1969 found USS *Towers* of the coast of South Vietnam, operating in support of 4th Ranger Group, 42nd Ranger Brigade and 21st Division of the Army of the Republic of Vietnam. Throughout this deployment, USS *Towers* was a mainstay on the gunline, delivering fire support for U.S. Army, Marine, and ARVN armed forces as well as Korean Marines. Her crew also experienced more action on Yankee Station as a Naval unit in Operation Linebacker.

At the onset of the massive North Vietnamese Easter Offensive into Quang Tri Province, ships of the Pacific Fleet assumed a new and expanding role in the Vietnam conflict. USS *Towers*, scheduled to deploy in late September 1972, was given two weeks' notice to deploy and went into a hectic preparatory period in late May and early June of 1972. The deployment began on 20 June, when USS *Towers* got underway. Once on the gunline, the ship applied heavy commitments and long hours, firing in support of ARVN forces involved in Operation Lam Son 72. From 29 July to 5 August, with COMDESRON 31 embarked, in company with the USS *Henry B. Wilson* (DDG-7) and USS *F.B. Parks* (DD-884), *Towers* conducted Linebacker strikes against the coast of North Vietnam. USS *Towers* qualified for the Combat Action ribbon after being subjected to hostile enemy shore fire on numerous occasions. During the period of 22-23 September, *Towers* provided naval gunfire for Lam Son 72 and for 1st ARVN Division in the vicinity of Hue City. On the nights of 24 and 25 September, *Towers* fired night Linebacker strikes as a unit of TU 77.1.2. From 26 to 30 September, *Towers* returned to MR2, providing support for the 1st ARVN Division. From 21 October to 16 November, *Towers* provided NGFS for ARNV forces near Qui Nhon and Quang Tri.

After a well-earned stand-down, USS *Towers* arrived in San Diego 20 January 1973. During her last deployment, *Towers* fired 12,500 rounds and spent eighty percent of the deployment underway, replenishing, rearming, and refueling at sea countless times. In more than 220 fire missions, spotted and unspotted, *Towers* inflicted heavy damage upon the enemy.

We, who once found refuge under the protection of her guns, salute this valiant ship and her gallant crew.

SHUT IT DOWN WHEN?

Realizing the failed offensive was all but dead, by the end of September, North Vietnamese diplomats in Paris saw their perceived negotiating leverage neutralized and appeared to be more amenable to serious negotiation than they were at the end of March.

Believing progress toward a negotiated settlement was within reach, the Nixon administration ordered a cessation of bombing in the vicinity of Hanoi in mid-October. Washington, in a gesture to the North Vietnamese, further limited allied strikes below the 20th parallel. Not yet willing to concede one demand, the North Vietnamese again stalled negotiations in Paris while strengthening air defenses around Hanoi and Haiphong, restoring the bombed-out rail lines to China and stockpiling war reserves.

Behind the scenes during the ongoing failed offensive, while North Vietnam was suffering an estimated 100,000 casualties along with half its tanks and artillery, General Vo Nguyen Giap, the military brain trust of Ho Chi Minh who engineered the communist victory over France, was quietly fired and replaced by General Van Tien Dung. To this day, the communist government of Vietnam claims that Giap never was in charge of that military catastrophe, in order to propagate the myth of invincibility surrounding Uncle Ho's favorite commander, but intelligence sources say different.

While negotiators negotiated and politicians politicked, USAF Lieutenant Colonel Carl O. McCormick and ANGLICO spotter WO2 Bruce E. Boltze had been flying armed reconnaissance and directing gunfire missions near Da Nang; the OV-10A they were flying suddenly disappeared from airbase radar on 6 October. The aircraft was flying a visual reconnaissance and gunfire missions

Thomas Petri

parallel to the coastline over water between Da Nang and Hoi An when observers reported to have witnessed the aircraft to explode (cause unknown) and fall into the South China Sea. Later, some of the wreckage and partial human remains were recovered but could not be conclusively identified as either man. In all likelihood, these two heroes will continue to populate the roster of men missing in action. And the negotiators negotiated and politicians politicked.

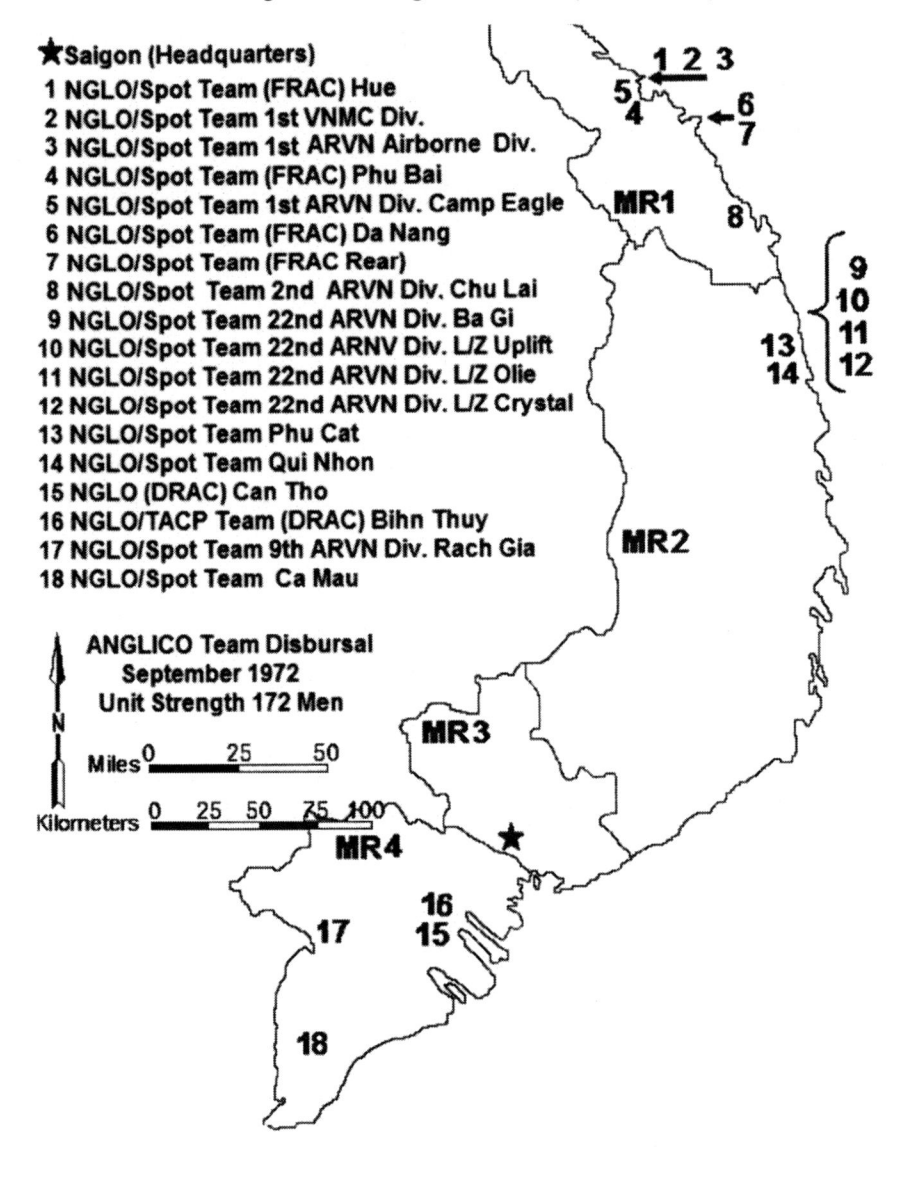

★Saigon (Headquarters)
1 NGLO/Spot Team (FRAC) Hue
2 NGLO/Spot Team 1st VNMC Div.
3 NGLO/Spot Team 1st ARVN Airborne Div.
4 NGLO/Spot Team (FRAC) Phu Bai
5 NGLO/Spot Team 1st ARVN Div. Camp Eagle
6 NGLO/Spot Team (FRAC) Da Nang
7 NGLO/Spot Team (FRAC Rear)
8 NGLO/Spot Team 2nd ARVN Div. Chu Lai
9 NGLO/Spot Team 22nd ARVN Div. Ba Gi
10 NGLO/Spot Team 22nd ARNV Div. LZ Uplift
11 NGLO/Spot Team 22nd ARVN Div. LZ Olie
12 NGLO/Spot Team 22nd ARVN Div. LZ Crystal
13 NGLO/Spot Team Phu Cat
14 NGLO/Spot Team Qui Nhon
15 NGLO (DRAC) Can Tho
16 NGLO/TACP Team (DRAC) Bihn Thuy
17 NGLO/Spot Team 9th ARVN Div. Rach Gia
18 NGLO/Spot Team Ca Mau

ANGLICO Team Disbursal
September 1972
Unit Strength 172 Men

During all the turmoil in South Vietnam, November elections in the United States saw Richard Nixon breeze to victory by the largest margin to date in American history. November also witnessed the conclusion of American withdrawal of combat troops, as the 196th Light Infantry Brigade completed its stand-down.

Seeing the rebuilding and replenishing effort continuing north of the DMZ, President Nixon ordered massive air assaults against military targets in Hanoi and Haiphong by U.S. Air Force B-52 bombers, Marine and Air Force tactical aircraft, and the Navy's carrier attack units. On 18 December, the intraservice operation, designated as Linebacker II, fell on the enemy capital. On that night and succeeding nights, wave after wave of bombers and supporting aircraft struck Hanoi, hitting command and communication facilities, power plants, rail yards, bridges, storage buildings, ship repair complexes, and other targets of strategic importance. The North Vietnamese met Linebacker II operations by launching 1,250 surface-to-air missiles, which brought down fifteen of the big American bombers and three supporting aircraft; antiaircraft defenses and MIG interceptors destroyed another four carrier planes.

The loss of six B-52s on 20 December, however, called for a change in tactics and placed more reliance on technologically superior equipment. Thereafter, the American air forces employed the most advanced precision-guided weapons and electronic countermeasures, target acquisition, and other advanced equipment in the U.S. inventory. They also concentrated on destruction of the enemy's missile defense network, including command and control facilities, missile assembly and transportation points, and the missile batteries themselves. To spread thin communist defenses, the American command broadened operational areas to include not only Hanoi, but Haiphong and several other areas of military and industrial logistics interest as well.

While negotiators continued negotiating and politicians continued doing whatever it is they were doing, Sub Unit One's 1st Lieutenant Dwight G. Rickman, piloting a O1 bird dog, took off from Phu Bai Airfield at the onset another day in a long war. He was flying a familiar visual reconnaissance mission with a back seat Vietnamese observer on Christmas Day, 1972. That day's mission assignment brought them west of Dong Ha over the Cam Lo River, where the craft was brought down by a SAM-7 missile (author's guess) fired from an unknown location. Official crash site coordinates place Rickman's aircraft just south of the location where Bat 21 had come to earth on Easter

Sunday earlier that year (in fact, not far from the reported location where teammate Lieutenant Larry Potts was last seen on 7 April). After the fact, intelligence reports suggest both men were either killed in the crash or died shortly after (died of injury, combat, or execution not called out) and were buried at the crash site by unidentified persons. The fate of either man really isn't known and most likely never will be.

As Linebacker II intensified, North Vietnamese, seeing their infrastructure coming apart, sent word through channels that they were ready to talk.

Peace negotiations between U.S. Secretary of State Henry Kissinger and communist politburo member Le Duc Tho reconvened on 8 January 1973. The two sides laboriously, but quickly hammered out terms and conditions that were agreed upon the next day. President Thieu, objecting vehemently to the terms, was eventually forced by the American administration to accept the agreement under threat of having all United States aid to his government discontinued. Thieu called the treaty, which allowed the estimated 150,000 North Vietnamese soldiers then in South Vietnam to remain in place, as indistinguishable from surrender. Once the political smoke settled, a formal cease-fire agreement was worked out, scheduled to go into effect at 2400 Greenwich Mean Time, 27 January 1973 (0800 28 January in Vietnam).

Since 19 May the previous year, Emilia Thomas, wife of WO2 William E. Thomas, did not know the status of her husband. Under terms of the agreement, North Vietnam made public for the first time the names of POWs being held by the communist regime. No one associated with 1st ANGLICO had more reason to celebrate than she, after receiving the first official confirmation that her husband was alive and in line to be released. His homecoming was not far off. Bill Thomas is the only ANGLICO who came up missing in action during the war returned to U.S. control.

At 0745, 28 January 1973, USS *Turner Joy* (DD-951), a much-storied ship that was involved in the first naval engagement against North Vietnam in the Tonkin Gulf incident on 4 August 1964, fired the last officially admitted-to naval gunfire mission of the war. At 0800, the cease fire went into effect, curtailing the activities of all fire control teams in country. Sub Unit One, 1st ANGLICO ceased all operations in support of South Vietnamese armed forces in all four military regions.

Fire support teams remained at post, holding field position until 17 February, before being pulled into Saigon.

For Lieutenant Colonel George E. Jones, the last commanding officer of Sub Unit One, who relieved Lieutenant Colonel D'Wayne Gray on 17 July 1972, the task of shutting down operations became sole focus of his remaining days in-country. Although he was given a timeline, the accelerated stand-down schedule took on the trappings of a deadline. Under terms of the peace accord, all American military activities were to complete their stand-down in sixty days.

FMFPac assumed operational control of its long-absent asset from MACV on 6 March. Eight days later, on 14 March 1973, Sub Unit One, 1st ANGLICO, after eight continuous years of gut-wrenching combat, was deactivated in Saigon, finally completing its long road to stand-down.

The occasion was solemnly noted by Lieutenant General Louis H. Wilson, Jr., then Commanding General of FMFPac.

"The completion of Sub Unit One, 1st ANGLICO's combat support mission in South Vietnam, ends more than eight years of continuous Naval gunfire support to Free World Forces throughout South Vietnam. From the initial entry of Sub Unit One in May 1965 through the recent NVA invasion in March 1972, the outstanding support provided by this small but highly professional unit has been noted at all levels. The aggressive spirit displayed by ANGLICO airborne and ground spotters, combined with the firepower of the 7th Fleet naval gunfire ships, was given considerable credit for stemming the tide of the NVA invasion in MR1 during March/April 1972. The professionalism and esprit de corps of the officers and men of Sub Unit One these past eight years are an indication of what a few good men can do when faced with a challenge."

The remaining members of Sub Unit One were again reunited with the Fleet Marine Force and redeployed to a Marine Corps without a war.

EPILOGUE

The Blue Dragon Brigade saw continuous action in Vietnam from September 1965 through February 1972. A total of 312,000 South Korean warriors served in Vietnam, rotating in and out on one-year tours of duty. Over 5,000 South Koreans were killed in action in Vietnam and over 17,000 received wounds while in-country (statistics are not available by branch of service).

In the aftermath of the Battle of Tra Bihn Dong, where the dauntless Marines of the 11th Company prevailed in an all-night battle against a mixed reinforced regiment of Viet Cong and North Vietnamese regulars, honors in proportion to the accomplishment were awarded to the entire company.

The morning of 15 February 1967, the commanding generals of III MAF— 2nd ROK Marine Brigade, Commanding Officer of I Corps, and the Commanding General of ROK Forces Vietnam—all traveled to Tra Bihn Dong to personally congratulate Captain Jung and all Marines under his command.

President Park Chung Hee of South Korea directed all enlisted Marines of Ship II Chungdae to receive a promotion of one grade in rank. It was the first promotion en masse for any unit in the armed forces of *Dae Hon Minh Guk* since the Korean War. In a formal proceeding on the brigade parade ground some six weeks after the battle, a ceremony was held to honor the 11th Company. President Park dispatched to South Vietnam the prime minister, the commandant of the Korean Marine Corps, and Defense Minister Kim Sung Eun to preside over the formalities. Kim Sung Eun was also a former commandant of the ROK Marine Corps and had commanded the only other unit to have been so honored with a mass promotion. During the Korean War, Kim Sung Eun earned the mystique as a larger-than-life legend in Korean Marine Corps lore, rivaling the reputation of our own Chesty Puller in his homeland.

The government of South Korea awarded more personal decorations for the battle of Tra Bihn Dong than in any other action involving Korean Forces in Vietnam. Captain Jung and Lieutenant Shin received the Korean equivalent of the Medal of Honor, the

Taeguk. Through many years of Korean involvement in the war in Vietnam, only eleven Taeguk medals were awarded, Tra Bihn Dong being the only instance of multiple awards. Other decorations too numerous to catalog were also awarded for the countless acts of individual valor performed that night. Included in those honors are Presidential Unit Citations from both the Republic of Korea and the United States of America.

In all the accounts of that night, never before in print, voice, or video media have the names Dave Long and Jim Porta been associated with the victory they both made contributions to in no small manner. They are not bitter from the lack of recognition. They know, and now we all know, the valor of both, and we couldn't be any prouder of them. Several months later, they were each presented with Bronze Star medals, which we all feel strongly should have been Silver Stars.

Upon being honorably discharged from the Marine Corps in June 1970, Jerry Becker, one of a trio of Marines who prowled Nha Trang during the opening rounds of the 1968 Tet Offensive, enrolled in college and earned a degree in accounting. After graduation, he accepted a job with a CPA firm in his hometown of Cumberland, Maryland. During his employment, he successfully passed the CPA exam and rose to the level of partner in the firm. Leaving his firm in June 1984, the Becker family relocated to Hagerstown, Maryland.

Jerry and Susan, his wife of thirty-six years, still reside in Hagerstown with their son Jason, daughter-in-law Deanna, and granddaughter Isabelle. He currently works for a regional CPA firm as a manager in the audit department.

Willis McBride received his rotation orders on October 8th and was very anxious to get home to his wife. The next morning, rain and poor visibility grounded all but emergency helicopter traffic. John Biehn, in a bid to help his friend and speed his journey home, signed out a Jeep to drive Willis to Chu Lai for a flight to Saigon and on to Tazewell, Virginia. With monsoon season firmly re-established in I Corps, exceptionally heavy rains flooded the Song Tra Bong River and rice paddies just south of the Tra Bong River Bridge. Tragically, the Jeep was washed off the road, drowning both. Their bodies were found in close proximity to each other. Investigative evidence suggested that one was trying to save the other. We'll never know which way it was, but we are to a man certain either one would have willingly given his life for the other. John and Will truly were friends to the end. The death of two close friends so near to going home really demoralized the original ROKMC Detachment and took much of the exhilaration out of leaving Vietnam.

USAF Captain Steven L. Bennett, in a gallant effort to save the life of ANGLICO naval gunfire spotter Captain Michael B. Brown, while attempting a maneuver he knew no OV-10 pilot had ever survived, was killed trying to bring his crippled plane to rest in the South China Sea. Captain Brown's parachute had been damaged when the plane was hit, and even though Captain Bennett had an operable chute, he elected to remain in the plane for the sake of his back seat passenger, even though it meant certain death. For his heroic and selfless act of valor on 29 June 1972, Captain Bennett was posthumously awarded the Congressional Medal of Honor.

The following citation documents that action:

Capt. Bennett was the pilot of a light aircraft flying an artillery adjustment mission along a heavily defended segment of route structure. A large concentration of enemy troops was massing for an attack on a friendly unit. Capt. Bennett requested tactical air support but was advised that none was available. He also requested artillery support but this too was denied due to the close proximity of friendly troops to the target. Capt. Bennett was determined to aid the endangered unit and elected to strafe the hostile positions. After 4 such passes, the enemy force began to retreat. Capt. Bennett continued the attack, but, as he completed his fifth strafing pass, his aircraft was struck by a surface-to-air missile, which severely damaged the left engine and the left main landing gear. As fire spread in the left engine, Capt. Bennett realized that recovery at a friendly airfield was impossible. He instructed his observer to prepare for an ejection, but was informed by the observer that his parachute had been shredded by the force of the impacting missile. Although Capt. Bennett had a good parachute, he knew that if he ejected, the observer would have no chance of survival. With complete disregard for his own life, Capt. Bennett elected to ditch the aircraft into the Gulf of Tonkin, even though he realized that a pilot of this type aircraft had never survived a ditching. The ensuing impact upon the water caused the aircraft to cartwheel and severely damaged the front cockpit, making escape for Capt. Bennett impossible. The observer successfully made his way out of the aircraft and was rescued. Capt. Bennett's unparalleled concern for his companion, extraordinary heroism and intrepidity above and beyond the call of duty, at the cost of his life, were in keeping with the highest traditions of the military service and reflect great credit upon himself and the U.S. Air Force.

WO2 Bruce Edward Boltze was shot down over Quang Nam Province on 6 October 1972. Evidence strongly suggests that he was killed, but his body has never been recovered and quite possibly never will be. The time has long since passed for Bruce Boltze to come home.

Lieutenant David C. Bruggeman died of wounds received at outpost Alpha 2 while being transported to the field hospital in Da Nang on 1 April 1972. For his numerous acts of valor in a gallant attempt by him and his team to defend the outpost, Lieutenant Bruggeman was posthumously awarded the Silver Star medal.

Several attempts at trying to locate Sergeant Kenneth C. Campbell yielded negative results. Most former ANGLICO teammates who had some prior contact with him since Vietnam were certain that he and his wife Patricia were living somewhere in the state of Oregon. Kenny, if you are reading this, please pop some smoke and send your coordinates. The war is over; you can transmit in the clear.

James Chally, upon discharge from the Marine Corps, went back to college and graduated from CSU Chico. He then moved to Seattle for a couple of years, eventually getting a teaching certificate at Seattle University. He and his wife then relocated to Oklahoma, where he taught school, then went back to the Pacific Northwest to Portland, Oregon. Jim retired this past summer and he and his well-traveled wife moved to Boise, Idaho, to be close to their children and grandchildren.

Several years after discharge, Charles Darby became a budget analyst, then supervisory budget analyst, for the Marine Corps Stock Fund in the Installation and Logistics Division, Headquarters Marine Corps. He worked in that capacity for ten years and had the opportunity to travel throughout the Marine Corps, meeting with senior-level military and civilian commanders and also participated in numerous trips with the Inspector General. He currently operates his own law practice in Maryland and is very proud of his association with 1st ANGLICO and the incredible men he was privileged to have served with.

Lieutenant Colonel Pham Van Dihn, who surrendered the 56th Regiment at Camp Carroll on 2 April 1972, accepted equivalent rank in the army of North Vietnam. The once-staunch patriot and hero of Hue City, who led the final assault on the Imperial Palace, restoring South Vietnam's colors over the ancient capital in February 1968, remained in the service of North Vietnam throughout the remainder of the war. While his former heroic deeds have all but slipped from the memory of his associates, his treasonous act of capitulation, for whatever reason, will always be associated as his legacy in the hearts of those who loved their country.

Gary Fiedler entered law enforcement after separation from the Marine Corps. He worked his way up through the Teaneck, New Jersey, police force and retired after achieving the rank of captain. Gary is still active with the ANGLICO Association. After frequently flirting with mischief and rarely passing up a chance for mayhem during his Marine Corps enlistment, we are encouraged by Gary's example that there may be a chance for the rest of us to stay out of jail.

Unfortunately, Hanoi Jane Fonda, for reasons that are well beyond comprehension and common sense, has never been brought to justice for her treasonous activities in open support of her communist fellow travelers. She has gone on to enjoy a wonderful acting career and has been graciously honored by like-minded Hollywood liberals, who enjoy making a mockery of the greatest country this world has yet seen. For the men and women who so honorably served this great nation in Vietnam, she will indelibly remain a seditious, treasonous bitch who will unwittingly be responsible for the greatest celebration of our generation on the occasion of her death. Grass will most likely never grow on her grave until the last surviving Vietnam Veteran is too old to make the pilgrimage to piss on it.

Brigadier General Vu Van Giai, who commanded the 3rd ARVN Division during the early days of the 1972 Easter Offensive, was recalled to Da Nang after the fall of Quang Tri City, where he was placed under arrest. Courageous and dedicated, General Giai, who did the best he could but was constantly undermined by his superiors, was cast in the position of designated scapegoat: charged with desertion, put on trial, and sentenced to five years of imprisonment. He was still serving out that sentence when he was discovered by North Vietnamese victors in 1975 after the fall of Saigon. Vu Van Giai spent the next twelve years imprisoned by the new masters of his country in the guise of re-education camps. His inept superior, Lieutenant General Lam, commander of Military Region 1, who had been appointed to that position because of his political connections rather than military skills, was dismissed from that post and replaced by Lieutenant General Ngo Quang Truong. As was always the normal mode of conduct in the corrupt confines of Saigon politics, President Thieu's good friend, Lieutenant General Lam, who should have taken the fall, contacted friends in high places, called in a few markers, and was actually promoted to head the ministry of defense's anticorruption campaign for his incompetence in a complicated maneuver known as the Nguyen Tenet (Vietnamese version of the Peter Principle).

Lieutenant Colonel D'Wayne Gray, who commanded Sub Unit One, 1st ANGLICO through some very dangerous times in Vietnam, particularly the 1972 Easter Offensive, went on to enjoy a colorful career in the Marine Corps. He first saw action in Southeast Asia in 1965 as advisor to the Vietnamese Marines and finished that tour as executive officer of 2nd Battalion, 3rd Marines. As a young officer in the Korean conflict, Lieutenant Gray had received his baptism of fire as an artillery forward observer attached to Battery A, 1st Battalion, 11th Marines. Retiring in 1987 after thirty-five years with rank of lieutenant general, he remains an active member of the ANGLICO Association.

Terry A. (Buddha) Griswold retired from the U.S. Army as a major after twenty years of service and now resides in Kansas, where he runs a consulting company. During the 1972 Easter Offensive, Lieutenant Griswold saw continuous action with 2nd ARVN Airborne Brigade Reconnaissance Company. He, along with the 2nd Airborne, pulled out of the grueling fight for Kontum once that battle was won and was pitched headlong into the struggle to retake Quang Tri City without much stand-down time. Buddha still maintains contact with Tony Shepard, with whom he spent four days under the gun not 300 meters from the Citadel wall during that long-ago recon patrol.

Vance Hall came home from Vietnam and resumed his education at the University of Oklahoma on the GI Bill, earning a B.S. degree in geology. While at OU, he met and married Marilyn, an education major. After straightening him out, she taught school for two years, and then focused on being a mother.

While enrolled in graduate school at the New Mexico Institute of Mining and Technology, Vance then received an offer that he couldn't refuse, working for a famous coal geologist in the San Juan Basin. Much later, he finally earned an M.S. in geology at Oklahoma State University in 1993 after finishing night school. For the past thirty-six years, he's explored for coal, oil, and gas, and had a great time doing it.

Tom Hayden, who accompanied his future wife Hanoi Jane Fonda to the capital of his communist heroes and is just as guilty of treason as she is, has led a life of inspiration for all wild-eyed liberals aspiring to become as naive a useful idiot as he grew up to be. Remaining true to his calling as a mature professional protestor, Haden has been involved with, among other things, the herd mentality issues of protesting the 1968 Democrat convention in Chicago, anti-Iraq War protests, World Trade Organization protests, global warming, and the really important earth-shattering issue of animal rights. Isn't that precious? He has successfully run for and won election to a few local and state political offices and failed at a few others as (you won't believe it) a Democrat. And yes, this obnoxious punk, who has not earned even one of the rights he enjoys as a citizen of this great country, still likes to pretend he's a man.

John Houghton was awarded the Silver Star for his heroic actions in the paddy fight of 10 January 1967. He is now retired from the U.S. Postal Service, currently residing in Camden, New Jersey. He keeps telling everyone about how much he's slowed down, but no one this author knows really believes him.

Captain John Lavish, commanding officer of the 3rd ROKMC Battalion Detachment, was killed in action on 1 August 1967, while on Operation Dragon Head V, west of National Highway 1.

General Lee Byong Chul retired from service after completing a turn as commandant of the Korean Marine Corps.

Captain Carl Edwin Long, while flying back seat on a naval gunfire spot mission, was shot down over the Rung Sat Special Zone on 20 December 1969. Twenty-three years later, on 16 December 1992,

Captain Long's remains were returned to the United States but were not conclusively identified until 3 May 2004. He is interred at Arlington National Cemetery, where he now rests with countless other heroes of our great country who gave all they had to give.

Dave Long, who participated in the battle of Tra Binh Dong, is currently residing in West Virginia, where he leads the life of a retired hell-raiser after many years of service with the Army Corps of Engineers.

Dave Lucht recovered from wounds received in the paddy fight of 10 January 1967 and returned home after several months of rehab. He still remembers the hell of lying in that paddy most of that rainy afternoon and has yet to experience more discomfort than he underwent in that long-ago firefight.

Sergeant Calvin McGinty, the seasoned veteran, in the tenth month of his tour, was killed in action on 1 August 1967, while on Operation Dragon Head V, west of National Highway 1.

Captain David P. Mott, who was shot down over Quang Tri on 19 May 1972 with WO2 William E. Thomas, Jr., was released from the North Vietnamese prison system during Operation Homecoming on 27 March 1973. Dave Mott retired from the Air Force as a colonel, now residing in Colorado with his wife Liz. The colonel and his wife have two grown children.

Retiring from the Marine Corps in 1975 with rank of captain after twenty-three years of service, Pat Morocco settled into civilian life in Southern California, where he became self-employed in the landscaping business and still keeps a hand in it, more or less as a hobby.

Pat and Norie, his wife of forty-six years, have two daughters and a son, who blessed them with seven grandchildren, which manages to keep Pat's travel itinerary very active. He still maintains contact with many of the Marines he served with over the years and volunteers a lot of time at the local hospital.

Larry Oswalt recovered from wounds sustained in the paddy fight of 10 January 1967 and retired from the Marine Corps after twenty years of service with the rank of major. He also retired from a second career with Gannet. He is now settled in Virginia with his wife, who was his former nurse at Great Lakes Naval Hospital, where he was transferred for advanced medcal care for injuries received in the paddy fight. Larry now operates a small business and enjoys staying active.

As a side note: Two years after Larry Oswalt was evacuated from the paddy fight, he experienced the personal satisfaction of piloting an A-4 Skyhawk in a flight participating in an air strike on the two wooded hillsides surrounding that same paddy were he lay wounded for over six hours. He was elated to be on the giving end and flew that mission with an absolute vengeance.

Sergeant Allen D. Owen, the Airborne naval gunfire spotter whose spotting and adjusting skills were given credit for breaking up the attack of Phan Thiet in February 1968, was killed in a sky-diving accident near the North Pole on September 9, 1981. He was employed as a career smoke jumper at the time of his death, living the life he dreamed. Allen Owen, at four feet, ten inches tall (officially listed at the Marine Corps minimum height of five feet on his personnel records), was considered by all who knew him as one of the most courageous individuals encountered during their stint in the Marine Corps. He was a totally unflappable Marine who always managed to remain calm, even in the most hair-raising of combat situations. Allen always found a way to complete difficult assignments that would pose a problem for lesser men.

Corporal John Edward Parton was mortally wounded on 30 June 1972, while silencing an NVA machine gun during 3rd ARVN Airborne Brigade's advance on Quang Tri City in Operation Lam Son 72. After putting up a good fight, the intrepid Marine quietly passed away in the hospital at Da Nang on 4 July. For his courageous act of valor on 30 June 1972, Corporal Parton was posthumously awarded the Silver Star medal.

Lance Corporal Terry John Perko was killed in action. The twenty-year-old kid from Maple Heights, Ohio, while participating in Operation Giant Dragon, was tragically felled by a bullet in a heated firefight on 21 February 1967, in an area southwest of the Tra Bihn Dong killing ground, less than a week after the epic stand of the 11th Company.

It didn't really seem that long ago when Terry and I picked up a couple wahines along the strip in Waikiki one Friday night. In an alcohol-induced moment of brilliance, we convinced them to go skinny dipping in one of the resort hotel pools. When we arrived at the hotel around 3:30 a.m., we found the beachside pool already occupied by six other nude swimmers of mixed gender. We simply dropped our clothes and crashed the party. For about fifteen minutes, the ten of us frolicked and played, not having a care in the world. No one noticed Terry get out of the water and collect all our clothes. No one really noticed when he picked up a brick and heaved it through a plate glass patio door that opened into the hotel lobby. We did, however, see him take off with our clothes speeding down the beach as hotel security came pouring through the broken door, storming into the pool area. Terry was laughing all the way down the beach as though he'd just pulled off the biggest "I Gotcha" of his young life. It probably was. He didn't stop laughing for three days. As furious as I was, I couldn't help but join in on his merriment when I caught up to him. That was a great "I Gotcha," buddy.

Of all the memories still with me from those fun-filled days in Hawaii, that incident never fails to bring a smile to my face and remorse to my heart.

Lieutenant (now Captain) Larry Fletcher Potts was shot down over Quang Tri Province on 7 April 1972, while on an armed reconnaissance and naval gunfire support mission. He is known to have survived his crash via radio and visual contact, and he is still listed as missing in action. The North Vietnamese never claimed Lieutenant Potts and USAF Lieutenant Bruce C. Walker, who was his crewmate, as prisoners of war. Two unconfirmed reports concerning the fate of Larry Fletcher Potts continue to be associated with his history. An NVA prisoner taken later on in April 1972 told his interrogators of a Negro crewman who, while trying to escape captivity some seven miles north of the shootdown site, was killed during the attempt. One additional unconfirmed report by an unknown source tells of a wounded Negro crewman who died while in captivity around July 1972 at camp K4 located in Quang Bihn Province, North Vietnam. A joint American/Vietnamese effort to investigate that reported burial site in Quang Tri Province came up empty. Locals reported the body was removed several years later. That same team was not permitted to visit the site of K4 prison to continue their investigation. If either report has the least factual basis, then it is reasonable to assume the North Vietnamese, who claim he was never in their custody, know full well what happened to this American hero. Where is Captain Larry Fletcher Potts?

Jim Porta survived the Battle of Tra Bihn Dong and is now living with Barbara, his bride of forty years, in Tucson, Arizona, where he has worked as a supervisor for the city transit system the past thirty-four years. Jim recently made a soul-healing pilgrimage back to Vietnam, where it gladdened him to see healthy people working the fields, with nobody trying to kill them. Reflecting back to the battle of Tra Bihn Dong, Jim has developed quite a bit of empathy for the defenders at the Alamo, who, in a similar situation, facing overwhelming odds, never gave up the fight. Both he and Dave Long felt sure they too would be fighting to the death that night long ago.

Captain Albert J. (*Nam Doe Khe Be*) Ransom retired from the Marine Corps as a full colonel after thirty years service and now resides with his wife in Southern California, where they enjoy operating a small wedding business and raising grapes for vintners. He is still very proud of his Korean nickname and to this day is still referred to by many of us as Nam Doe Khe Be.

1st Lieutenant Dwight Gary Rickman was shot down over Quang Tri Province on Christmas Day, 1972, while flying an O1 Bird Dog on a visual reconnaissance mission. Neither Lieutenant Rickman nor his Vietnamese passenger has ever been accounted for. Intelligence reports (of unknown origin) indicate he was killed in the crash or shortly thereafter. His remains have not been recovered and most likely never will be. Is it not time for Dwight Gary Rickman to come home?

Major Richard E. Romine, commander of the original Sub Unit One deployment to Vietnam in 1965, returned to Vietnam, where he distinguished himself as a Navy Cross recipient for valorous performance of duty after being shot down during heavy fighting 3 June 1967, while commanding an emergency helicopter extraction mission with HMM-165.

The following citation documents that action:

Citation:

Thomas Petri

The Navy Cross is awarded to Major Richard E. Romine, United States Marine Corps, for extraordinary heroism as Helicopter Pilot, Troop Commander, and Tactical Air Controller with Marine Medium Helicopter Squadron 165 in the Republic of Vietnam on 3 and 4 June 1967. When his transport helicopter was hit during an emergency retraction of a besieged combat team from an enemy-surrounded bomb crater, Lieutenant Colonel (then Major) Romine displayed exceptional aeronautical skill in maneuvering his crippled aircraft away from enemy concentrations prior to crash- landing into the mountain forest. Directing his crew to bring all the battle equipment that they could carry, he fought and led them through the almost impassable and enemy-populated forest back to the besieged forces position. With darkness closing, illumination flares were requested and adjusted to pinpoint accuracy. He exposed the advancing enemy, brought them under fire, and prevented surprise attacks. Awake throughout the cold, rainy night, Lieutenant Colonel Romine resumed calling in air strikes at dawn. Without thought of personal risk, he exposed himself along the barren crater rim to direct the strikes within ten meters of his position. Faultlessly, for twenty-four torturous hours, he gallantly controlled air operations and directed his nearly decimated ground forces against insistent, overwhelming enemy attacks until their guns were silent, the enemy beaten, and the trapped men were helicopter-lifted to safety. Lieutenant Colonel Romine's dynamic leadership, indomitable fighting spirit, and relentless exposure to the enemy to control ground and air operations that saved the lives of his men, reflected great credit upon himself and the Marine Corps and were in keeping with the highest traditions of the United States Naval Service.

Major Ross E. Rowell made history at Ocotal, Nicaragua, commanding the first-ever close air support mission, and served the Marine Corps with distinction for forty years, retiring as a lieutenant general in 1946. Seeing the United States was safely through WWII, Lieutenant General Ross E. Rowell, a highly decorated Marine aviator, died in the U.S. Naval Hospital in San Diego on September 6, 1947.

Raymond R. Roughton, III, remained in the Marine Corps. Retiring to his native Georgia with rank of sergeant major after twenty-three years of service, Rick, as he is now known, enjoys archeology and spends quite a bit of time in the Georgia countryside, excavating Indian graves and old settlements. He is still pissed off over the incident in Nha Trang when he, Sandoz, and Becker were abandoned by their so-called cover fire while clearing a house of enemy infiltrators.

After separation and a homecoming in time to watch the moon landing on TV, James Sandoz married Shirley, the girl of his dreams, and earned a bachelor's and master's degree in biology. He spent about thirty years pretty much pretending he never served in the Marine Corps or in Vietnam. Jim and Shirley raised four children and are currently spoiling two grandchildren. Jim is currently a senior lecturer in biology at the University of Maryland, Baltimore County. His life is richer for having recently gotten back in touch with some of his brothers in arms, and he recommends this to all veterans.

Lance Corporal Stanley Seavers was killed in action on 1 August 1967, while on operation Dragon Head V west of National Highway 1. He had been looking forward to his tour with 1st ANGLICO and the ROK Marines and surrendered his young life in the company of two of the best.

Lieutenant Christian F. Schilt, after receiving the Medal of Honor for his actions at Quilali, Nicaragua, made history once again during World War II as one of the few men who have ever worn the uniform of U.S. Marine to obtain the rank of four-star general. After forty years of service, General Schilt retired from the Marine Corps, providing service to his country in three major wars. General Schilt died on 8 January 1987, at age ninety-one, in Norfolk, Virginia, and was buried with full military honors in Arlington National Cemetery.

Corporal Ray Shawn was killed in action on 4 July 1968 while participating in a Search and Destroy operation near Hoi An. He was a man of action who could always be counted on in any situation, and his presence on the battlefield was greatly missed by his 3rd ROKMC Battalion teammates.

Following his return from the recon mission in July 1972, Lieutenant Anthony P. Shepard was reassigned to the ANGLICO team at VNMC Division (Fwd.) at Houng Dinh, and later to the team at Ca Mau in MR4. He returned to his permanent duty station with the 1st Battalion, 12th Marines in September 1972. In 1990, on completion of twenty years of service, he retired in the grade of major.

Since his retirement, Tony Shepard has worked for a national laboratory as a decision systems support engineer, specializing in command and control systems, and is currently a field support engineer for several system engineering tools and automation products. He currently resides in Gig Harbor, Washington, where he and his wife Mary relocated on his retirement from active duty.

On 3 April 1967, we lost Lance Corporal Bobby Sherwood. While being transported to a hot LZ by helicopter, Bobby sustained a lethal wound from heavy ground fire. He passed away quietly in the hospital at Charlie Med soon after surgery. Having a well-developed sense of humor, everyone in the detachment really enjoyed being paired with Bobby.

Lawrence C. Smith retired from the Marine Corps as a master sergeant after twenty-three years of service. He currently resides with his wife Carole in Colorado, where he spends quite a bit of time restoring vintage automobiles.

Michael L. Smith recovered from wounds received in the battle for Hue City and earned a master's degree in counseling from the University of Central Florida. He was employed as a counselor at the Vet Center in Orlando, where he helped fellow veterans and their families deal with Vietnam-related issues and, in the process, exorcized a few ghosts of his own. Retired now, living in Orlando with his wife Judith, Mike spent the last ten years of his professional career in the schools, helping at-risk children and their families. The couple has two children, one of whom is still in college working toward a law degree, while the eldest is off and running, having completed college.

Captain J. Edward Snyder, Jr., who commanded the USS *New Jersey* during her Vietnam tour in 1968-69, retired from the U.S. Navy as a rear admiral. The admiral passed away after one last fight with prostate cancer on 4 November 2007. He is interred at Arlington National Cemetery with other notable heroes of our great country.

William E. Thomas, Jr., retired from the Marine Corps as a chief warrant officer in 1985, after thirty-one years of faithful service. He currently resides with his wife Emilia in Hawaii, where both of them spent many happy years during Bill's active duty days. Bill returned to Vietnam during the hectic days of the Easter Offensive on his third tour of duty, where he was shot down while on a naval gunfire mission in the skies over Quang Tri Province on 19 May 1972. After a two-month journey from near the DMZ, he and pilot USAF Captain David P. Mott endured the next nine months in the prison system as guests of the North Vietnamese. Both he and Captain Mott were repatriated in March 1973 during Operation Homecoming, giving the gunner the unofficial distinction of being the last ANGLICO to stand down from Vietnam. As his leadership talents are still as strong as ever, we are all grateful for the four years he served as president of the ANGLICO Association.

Lieutenant General Ngo Quang Truong, who took charge of MR1 after the fall of Quang Tri and pushed the North Vietnamese back across the Cua Viet River, remained as military commander of that region until the final North Vietnamese offensive in 1975 toppled the government of South Vietnam.

Shortly before the fall of Saigon, an American officer arranged for the general and his family to board a U.S. Navy vessel, which eventually brought them to the United States. The general settled in Falls Church, Virginia, where he wrote extensively about ARVN military history during the war.

From 1955 through to the end, General Truong served his country well, gathering a reputation as the best officer in the armed forces of Vietnam. He did not grow wealthy from rank, as did many of his politically appointed colleagues, but remained a true patriot and always maintained his honor. At the time of the 1968 Tet Offensive, General Truong was in command of the 1st ARVN Division in Hue, where he and his command was the sole contingent of troops in the city not captured or defeated during the lightning-fast attack on the ancient capital. Through his leadership and tactical genius, he played a major, if overlooked, role in the eventual hard-won victory that expelled communist forces from Hue City.

The man who was described by General Norman Schwarzkopf as "the most brilliant tactical commander I've ever known" passed away after a long fight with cancer on 22 January 2007.

Lieutenant Colonel Gerald H. Turley, whose leadership and tireless efforts through the early days of the 1972 Easter Offensive were critical to stabilizing the tactical situation and blunting the NVA advance in I Corps, retired from the Marine Corps as a full colonel after thirty-two years of service. No one this author has spoken with who was involved in any aspect of those turbulent times has anything but praise and respect for this officer, who was impressed into service as a division-level G-3 officer doing a job well beyond exemplary. His well-written and thoroughly documented book, *The Easter Offensive*, proved an invaluable guide for the events chronicled in the last several chapters of this book. As events from March through the end of April 1972 were tumultuous, to say the least, sorting through mountains of documents to present his work in correct sequential order is an accomplishment of no small nature. As chaotic as any episode of the Vietnam War, being in the position he was, Colonel Turley is one of the few men who knows the entire story. Without his efforts to present this campaign in order of events and his commentary on behind-the-scenes perspectives of major personalities involved, even the most experienced historians would most likely have pulled their hair out trying to piece together this last American involvement in a very long war.

William L. Vandiver, whose fire control planning was given considerable credit for the successful defense of Nha Trang during the opening shots of the 1968 Tet Offensive, served in the U.S. Navy for twenty-three years, mostly as an enlisted man. To hear him tell it, he was the last of the gray-haired ensigns. Vandiver retired as a lieutenant commander in 1970. He held the office of personnel director for the city of Shreveport, Louisiana, for many years before retiring for good (we think).

Lieutenant Bruce C. Walker, pilot of an OV-10A, call sign Covey 282, was shot down over Quang Tri Province on 7 April 1972, along with naval gunfire spotter Lieutenant Larry Fletcher Potts. Both were known to have survived the crash. Lieutenant Walker was in radio and visual contact with SAR craft over several days and aided in rescue efforts by helping to direct air strikes at enemy positions. He was also visually seen by SAR craft as North Vietnamese soldiers closed in on him the morning of 18 April. The North Vietnamese claim he was not taken prisoner, nor do they know where his body may be. If this is true, how did Lieutenant Walker's ID card find its way into a museum in Hanoi? His fate is still not known. Where is Lieutenant Bruce C. Walker?

Thomas E. (Doc) Williamson continued his service in the U.S. Navy for twenty years, rotating between assignments with the submarine service and Fleet Marine Force units, before retiring with the rank of HMCS8 to Connecticut. For his selfless act of valor on 27 April 1972, when he voluntarily braved intense small arms and artillery fire to render medical assistance to the wounded Lieutenant Colonel Camper, was awarded the Silver Star medal. Every Marine this author interviewed went out of their way to make a point that Tom Williamson, many times throughout the month of April 1972, went above and beyond to take care of his Marines and anyone else who was in need of help. There is no way to calculate how many men, American and Vietnamese, survived that hectic month because Tom Williamson was there to make a difference.

Captain Yoon Choon Wong, commanding officer of ROKMC 10th Company during the 1968 Tet Offensive, eventually immigrated to the United States and obtained American citizenship and settled in the Los Angles area where he passed away in 2005.

Corporal James Fredrick Worth was heard transmitting over his radio on 2 April 1972, the day after he was separated from his team when outpost Alpha 2 was overrun. Corporal Worth reported that he was trying to make Dong Ha overland on foot (the source of this report is not known). Corporal Worth never showed up at Dong Ha. His body has never been recovered, and there is no evidence whatsoever to suggest that he was, in fact, killed in action. On 17 December 1977, the Secretary of the Navy approved a presumptive finding of death. Inasmuch as his remains have not been repatriated or even seen, for that matter, we are astounded with that finding. General John W. Vessey, former head of the Joint Chiefs of Staff, who conducted countless hours of investigation into MIA status, categorized Corporal Worth on his list of 135 discrepancy cases. General Vessey's list was capsulated from a December 1992 report by Senator Bob Smith (Vice Chairman, Senate Select Committee on POW/MIA Affairs) of an estimated of 324 men who may have survived in captivity. Where is James Fredrick Worth?

For their selfless act of bravery on 19 August 1967, the incredible crew of Klondike Medevac flew into Marine Corps history. In December 1967, while on an abbreviated visit to South Vietnam, President Lyndon B. Johnson presented the Navy Cross to Gunnery Sergeant Leroy N. Poulson. One month later, Captain Rupert E.

Fairfield and Lance Corporal John G. Phelps were likewise honored with Navy Crosses for their heroic actions on that desolate beach. On 17 June 1968, Captain Stephen W. Pless was honored with the Helicopter Heroism Award, presented by the Aviation/Space Writers Association. At a White House ceremony on 16 January 1969, Major Stephen W. Pless was presented with the Congressional Medal of Honor by President Lyndon B. Johnson.

The following citation documents that action:

For conspicuous gallantry and intrepidity at the risk of his life above and beyond the call of duty while serving as a helicopter gunship pilot attached to Marine Observation Squadron 6 in action against enemy forces. During an escort mission Major Pless monitored an emergency call that four American soldiers stranded on a nearby beach were being overwhelmed by a large Viet Cong force. Major Pless flew to the scene and found thirty to fifty enemy soldiers in the open. Some of the enemy were bayoneting and beating the downed Americans. Major Pless displayed exceptional airmanship as he launched a devastating attack against the enemy force, killing or wounding many of the enemy and driving the remainder back into a tree line. His rocket and machine gun attacks were made at such low levels that the aircraft flew through debris created by explosions from its rockets. Seeing one of the wounded soldiers' gesture for assistance, he maneuvered his helicopter into a position between the wounded men and the enemy, providing a shield which permitted his crew to retrieve the wounded. During the rescue, the enemy directed intense fire at the helicopter and rushed the aircraft again and again, closing to within a few feet before being beaten back. When the wounded men were aboard, Major Pless maneuvered the helicopter out to sea. Before it became safely airborne, the overloaded aircraft settled four times into the water. Displaying superb airmanship, he finally got the helicopter aloft. Major Pless's extraordinary heroism, coupled with his outstanding flying skill, prevented the annihilation of the tiny force. His courageous actions reflect great credit upon himself and uphold the highest traditions of the Marine Corps and the U.S. Naval Service.

It cannot conclusively be stated as a fact, but until evidence to the contrary is brought forward, the unbendable crew of Klondike Medevac stands out as the most decorated helicopter crew of the Vietnam War. In the newly dedicated Marine Corps Museum in

Washington, D.C., the helicopter they flew into history has been restored and proudly put on display in the presence of the greatest of the great.

On 20 July 1969, the U.S. Marine Corps lost one of its brightest stars. We don't know for sure all the circumstances surrounding the event, but while attempting to jump a drawbridge separating Pensacola, Florida, from Pensacola Beach on a motorcycle, the military career of Major Stephen W. Pless came to a tragic end.

"Up to a point a man's life is shaped by environment, heredity, and the movements and changes in the world around him. Then there comes a time when it lies within his grasp to shape the clay of his life into the sort of thing he wishes to be. Only the weak blame parents, their race, their times, lack of good fortune, or the quirks of fate. Everyone has it within his power to say, *'This I am today; that I will be tomorrow.'* The wish, however, must be implemented by deeds."

Louis L'Amour, *The Walking Drum*

ADDENDUM I
ANGLICO IN VIETNAM

Non Multa Sed Multum
(Not Many, But Much)

Sub Unit One, 1st ANGLICO was continuously deployed in Vietnam from May 1965 through March 1973. Not at any time during those eight years of deployment did the unit have more than 235 men in-country at any specific period. Typical in-country strength was approximately 175 to 185 men on average. Because of yearly rotation, fill-in replacements due to casualties, tour extensions, and multiple tours by many individuals, it is not possible to accurately determine the exact number of Marines and sailors who served Sub Unit One. By this author's count, no more than 1,325 men can lay claim to membership in this unit during its entire eight years of continuous deployment in Vietnam, giving this organization the distinction of being the smallest (or surely one of the smallest) tactical force to see action in that war. Fire control teams of this organization operated in all four tactical zones, providing control of close air and naval gunfire in support of South Vietnamese Army and Marines; South Korean Army and Marines; Thai, Australian, and New Zealand Armed Forces; as well as U.S. Army and Marine combat units. Marines of Sub Unit One were the last tactical Marines (and most likely the last tactical unit overall) to stand down from the war.

Throughout the war, Sub Unit One, 1st ANGLICO had the distinction of being the only Marine combat asset tied directly into the chain of command of MACV. Although not officially employed as Special Operations troops, many of the assignments drawn by members of this small force certainly did qualify. Either in the air or on the ground, fire control teams of this unit operated at one time or another with SEAL Teams, Rangers, LRRPs, (Long Range Recon Patrol) and every other tactical or advisory activity conducting combat operations in Vietnam in all four military regions.

Honors earned by the 1st ANGLICO in Vietnam include the Vietnam Service Streamer with two silver stars (each silver star indicating five additional awards) and two bronze stars (each bronze star indicating one additional award), Navy Unit Commendation Streamer with one bronze star, Meritorious Unit Streamer with one bronze star, and the National Defense Service Streamer. Men of Sub Unit One were awarded personal decorations and honors, both foreign and domestic, too numerous to chronicle. Those personal decorations awarded to the unit include the Presidential Unit Citation awarded to the 1st Marine Division and all attached units. The 1st Marine Division is the only military organization to have received that honor twice during the war. Members of that organization are also authorized to wear the Republic of Vietnam Armed Forces Meritorious Unit Citation (Gallantry Cross) with palm and gold frame.

Casualty figures resulting in direct cause of involvement by 1st ANGLICO due to effects of close air support and naval gunfire controlled by Sub Unit One personnel were credited, for the most part, to the gunline ships and units being supported. No accurate figures are available for this statistic. Naval gunfire spotters controlled countless fire missions, exceeding delivery of 2,816,000 three-inch caliber rounds or larger on intended targets. Tactical Air Control Parties, primarily in support of the Blue Dragon Brigade, controlled countless sorties of fixed wing air strikes, delivering over 16,610,170 pounds of ordnance on target. The TACP teams controlled 4,361 medical evacuations and countless resupply and other logistic sorties, with combined cargos of over 100,000,000 pounds for the Korean Marines. There are no records detailing A/C130 and C-47 Spectre gunship missions, as these statistics were kept by the U.S. Air Force.

Of special note, and a source of disquieting concern to those of us who served 1st ANGLICO, not all Marines of Sub Unit One returned home from Vietnam, as five our teammates remained unaccounted for when Sub Unit One was deactivated on 14 March 1973.

The following data was compiled from Command Chronologies of Sub Unit One, 1st ANGLICO, May 1965 through March 1973.

NAVAL GUNFIRE SUMMARY

Year	Rounds Fired	Ave./Month
1965		
1966	462,002	38,500
1967	436,844	36,404
1968	528,608	44,051
1969	364,333	30,361
1970	218,006	18,167
1971	113,609	9,467
1972	613,453	51,121
1973	79,752	79,752
Total	2,816,607	
1965	No Data Available	
1966	Estimate: No figures available for last half of year	
1967	Estimate: No figures available for last half of year	
1973	Only one month of active NGF ops.	

Only three-inch projectiles or larger

AIR SUPPORT SUMMARY

	Fixed Wing			Helicopter	
	Bombs (Lbs)	Napalm (Lbs)	Rockets	Medevacs	Logistics (Lbs)
1965					
1966	425,000	125,000		219	4,251,160
1967	3,249,600	579,500	3,569	1,143	16,128,000
1968	3,838,320	665,500	12,926	1,255	14,433,996
1969	4,861,350	771,000	31,467	954	18,273,404
1970	896,000	860,500	37,566	565	22,588,175
1971	233,000	105,500	23,429	444	25,520,048
Total	13,503,270	3,107,000	108,957	4,361	101,194,783

1965 No TACP assets in-country
1966 Estimate: TACP operations started in September
1967 Estimate: Figures for first half of year not available
1971 Air operations ceased in October

ADDENDUM II
KOREAN INVOLVEMENT IN VIETNAM

Republic of Korea's Blue Dragon Brigade saw continuous action in Vietnam from September 1965 through February 1972. In December 1971, the Korean Marine Corps recalled the 1st and 2nd Battalions. 3rd Battalion withdrew in January 1972, followed by the 5th Battalion stand-down a month later, thus ending the long commitment to Vietnam of one of the most formidable fighting forces to see action in that war.

Over 1,200 Republic of Korea Marines lost their lives in action during the Vietnam War, and over 4,000 sustained wounds while in-country. A total of eleven Taeguks (Korean equivalent of the Medal of Honor) were awarded to Korean fighting men of all service affiliations in Vietnam.

A total of 312,000 South Korean warriors served in Vietnam, rotating in and out on one-year tours of duty, suffering over 5,000 killed in action. Over 17,000 received wounds while in-country, roughly equivalent to U.S. casualty statistics.

Korean troop strength in Vietnam by year (total includes all branches of the Korean military):

1965   21,031
1966   41,809
1967   42,743
1968   45,729
1969   43,408
1970   42,349
1971   42,602
1972   33,177
1973 No figures available.
Total   312,853
Total KIAs   5,066 All branches.

ADDENDUM III
1ST ANGLICO HONORS

NAVY UNIT COMMENDATION STREAMER WITH TWO BRONZE STARS
Vietnam, 18 February 1968–31 July 1969
Vietnam, 1 April 1972–10 September 1972
Southeast Asia, 14 August 1990–16 April 1991

MERITORIOUS UNIT COMMENDATION STREAMER WITH THREE BRONZE STARS
Vietnam, 1 September 1969–31 May 1970
Vietnam, 14 April 1971–27 June 1971
Vietnam, 1 August 1981–30 June 1983
Vietnam, 10 December 1996–10 January 1998

NATIONAL DEFENSE SERVICE STREAMER WITH THREE BRONZE STARS
2 March 1951–27 July 1954
1 January 1961–15 August 1974
2 August 1990–30 November 1995
11 September 2001–Present

VIETNAM SERVICE STREAMER WITH TWO SILVER AND TWO BRONZE STARS
Vietnamese Counteroffensive, Phase II, 1 July 1966–1 May 1967
Vietnamese Counteroffensive, Phase III, 1 June 1967–29 January 1968
Tet counteroffensive, 30 January 1968–1 April 1968
Vietnamese Counteroffensive, Phase IV, 2 April 1968–30 June 1968
Vietnamese Counteroffensive, Phase V, 1 July 1968–1 November 1968
Vietnamese Counteroffensive, Phase VI, 2 November 1968–22 February 1969
Tet 1969 Counteroffensive, 23 February 1969–8 June 1969
Vietnam Summer-Fall 1969, 9 June 1969–31 October 1969
Vietnam Winter-Spring 1970, 1 November 1969–30 April 1970

Consolidation, 1 July 1971–30 November 1971
Consolidation, 1 December 1971–29 March 1972
Vietnam Ceasefire Campaign, 30 March 1972–28 January 1973

SOUTHEAST ASIA SERVICE STREAMER WITH TWO BRONZE STARS
1 September 1990–16 January 1991
17 January 1991–11 April 1991

GLOBAL WAR ON TERRORISM EXPEDITIONARY MEDAL Iraq 2003

PRESIDENTIAL UNIT CITATION – Iraq 2003

IRAQI CAMPAIGN MEDAL WITH TWO BRONZE STARS
August 2005–March 2006
September 2006–March 2007
February 2007–Present

"It is foolish and wrong to mourn the men who died. Rather we should thank God that such men lived."
General George S. Patton

ADDENDUM IV

Honor Roll of those heroic members of Sub Unit One, 1st ANGLICO who did not survive their tours of duty in Vietnam

Clair Lowell	Hayner	1st Lt.	1965	October 22
James William	Eisner	PFC	1966	November 3
Terry John	Perko	L/Cpl.	1967	February 21
Robert James	Sherwood	Cpl.	1967	April 3
Charles Elbert	Thomas	L/Cpl.	1967	May 25
Calvin A. Jr.	McGinty	Sgt.	1967	August 1
John Larry	Lavish	Capt.	1967	August 1
Stanley Joseph	Seavers	PFC	1967	August 1
John William	Telford	Cpl.	1967	August 17
Bartley Thomas III	Stokes	L/Cpl.	1967	September 6
Willis Leonard	McBride	Cpl.	1967	October 9
Maurice John	Biehn	PFC	1967	October 9
Marvin Royce	Davis	Sgt.	1967	December 15
Charles John	Eisenacher	SSgt.	1968	February 6
William Edward	Ranc	SSgt.	1968	February 6
Russell Jay Jr.	Fauser	Cpl.	1968	February 15
James Gordon	Smith	L/Cpl.	1968	June 2
Raymond Ben	Shawn	L/Cpl.	1968	July 4
Dan Ross	Moore	L/Cpl.	1968	October 10
Randolph Jr.	Brown	L/Cpl.	1969	February 12
George Richard	Dover	1st Lt.	1969	June 19
Carl Edwin	Long *	Capt.	1969	December 20
Clifford Gerald	Burdette	L/Cpl.	1970	October 30
David Charles	Bruggeman	1st Lt.	1972	April 1
James Frederick	Worth *	L/Cpl.	1972	April 1
Larry Fletcher	Potts *	Capt.	1972	April 8
John Edward	Parton	Cpl.	1972	July 4
Edward Gardner II	Hayen	1st Lt.	1972	July 20
Bruce Edward	Boltze *	WO2	1972	October 6
Dwight Gary	Rickman*	Capt.	1972	December 25
Donnie Ray	Conner	L/Cpl.	1973	February 14

* Denotes Missing in Action

GLOSSARY OF MILITARY ACRONYMS AND TERMS

A-1	Douglas Skyraiders, Korean War vintage
A-4	Single-seat attack jet
ALO	Air Liaison Officer
ANGLICO	Air Naval Gunfire Liaison Company
AO	Area of Responsibility
ARG	Amphibious Ready Group
ARVN	Army of the Republic of Vietnam
BLT	Battalion Landing Team
C-47	Douglas C-47 Skytrain (prop-driven transport) Used as a gunship when modified with miniguns
CH-46	Sea Knight, Marine transport helicopter
CH-47	Chinook, Army transport helicopter
CAF	Combined Action Force (USMC and Vietnamese)
Charlie	Slang for Viet Cong
Charlie Med	A hospital in Chu Lai
CINCPac	Commander in Chief, Pacific
Claymore Mine	Command-detonated directional mine
CTF	Commander, Task Force
CTG	Commander, Task Group
COMNAVFORV	Commander, Naval Forces Vietnam
COMSEVENFLT	Commander, 7th Fleet
DH4B	Biplane, 1920s era
DMZ	Demilitarized zone
DRAC	Delta Regional Assistance Command
FAC	Forward Air Controller
Feet wet	Over water
FM	Frequency modulated
FMFPac	Fleet Marine Force, Pacific
FSB	Fire Support Base
FO	Forward Observer
FRAC	First Regional Assistance Command
FSCC	Fire Support Control Center
FSCE	Fire Support Control Element (U.S. Army FSCC)
F8U	Crusader, attack jet
III MAF	Three Marine Amphibious Force
HMM	Marine Medium Helicopter Squadron

LAW	Light Antiarmor Weapon (disposable)
MAB	Marine Amphibious Brigade
MACV	Military Assistance Command Vietnam
MCAS	Marine Corps Air Station
MR	Military Region
NGF	Naval gunfire
NGLO	Naval Gunfire Liaison Officer
O-1	Cessna L-19, spotter plane
OV-10	Bronco, twin-engine attack/spotter plane
O2-B1	Biplane, 1920s era
O2-U1	Biplane, 1920s era
NVA	North Vietnamese Army
PAVN	Peoples Army of Vietnam (NVA)
ROK	Republic of Korea
RLT	Regimental Landing Team
SAM	Surface-to-Air Missile
SAR	Search and Rescue
SFCP	Shore Fire Control Party
SLF	Special Landing Force
Sub Unit One	ANGLICO assets in Vietnam
TAC	Tactical Air Controller
TACP	Tactical Air Control Party
TAOR	Tactical Area of Responsibility
TA-F4	A-4 Skyhawk Trainer, used for gunfire spotting
T/E	Table of Equipment
T/O	Table of Organization
TOC	Tactical Operations Center
UHF	Ultra High Frequency
UH-1E	Bell light attack/observation helicopter
UH-34D	Sea Horse, single-rotor helicopter
VMO	Vertical Marine Observation Squadron
VNAF	Vietnamese Air Force
VNMC	Vietnamese Marine Corps
VNN	Vietnamese Navy
XXXIV	Command element in MR1
Five inch/38	Older model five-inch naval gun
Five –inch/54	Newer model rapid fire naval gun
Sixteeen inch/50	Main armament of USS *New Jersey*

GLOSSARY OF KOREAN TERMS

Chung Yong Bodae	Blue Dragon Brigade
Dae Hahn Min Guk	Republic of Korea
Dae Han Min Guk Haebyong Dae	Republic of Korea Marine Corps
Ediwa	Come here
Haebyong Dae	Marine Corps
Hahn Guk	A Korean national
Hahn Guk Oh	Korean language
Hyong-je haebyong	Brother Marines
Jung	Commander
Kae sa Gya	Roughly translated: Son of a bitch
Kkolabaga	A form of discipline
Maek-ju	Beer
Maek-ju monta mashida	Drink massive quantities of beer
Mi Guk Haebeyong	American Marine
So-da	Fire! (or Shoot!)
So-ji mara	Don't shoot!
Tae Kwon Do	A Korean martial art

UNIT DESIGNATIONS

Suesecdae	Recon Company
Il Chungdae	1st Company
E Chungdae	2nd Company
Som Chungdae	3rd Company
Oh Chungdae	5th Company
Yuk Chungdae	6th Company
Cheel Chungdae	7th Company
Ku Chungdae	9th Company
Ship Chungdae	10th Company
Ship Il Chungdae	11th Company
Pundae	Squad
Sodae	Platoon
Chungdae	Company
Taedae	Battalion
Bodae	Brigade

BIBLIOGRAPHY AND DOCUMENTATION

Chapter 1 Good Ole Boys
The Marines in Vietnam 1954-1973: An Anthology and Annotated Bibliography, History and Museums Division Headquarters, U.S. Marine Corps, 1974.
Personal map of Quang Ngai Province.

Chapter 2 Blue Dragons
Personal recollections and conversations with Korean Marines while still in Vietnam.

Chapter 3 Super Grunts
Personal recollections.
Historical Division Headquarters, U.S. Marine Corps.
Semper Fidelis: History of the United States Marine Corps, by Allen R. Millet, Macmillan, 1980.
U.S. Marines in Vietnam: An Expanding War 1966, by Jack Shulimson, History and Museums Division Headquarters, U.S. Marine Corps, 1982.
U.S. Marines in Vietnam: Vietnamization and Redeployment 1970-1971, by Graham A. Cosmas and Lieutenant Colonel Terrence P. Murray, USMC. History and Museums Division Headquarters, U.S. Marine Corps, 1986.
http://web.meganet.net/kman/nfv3.htm.

Chapter 4 Hyong-je Haebeyong
Personal recollections.

Chapter 5 Nam Doe Khe Be
Interview with Colonel Albert J. Ransom, USMC (Ret.), September 18, 2005.

Chapter 6 The Lost Platoon
Interview with Chief Warrant Officer William E. Thomas, Jr., USMC (Ret.), November 11, 2007.
Interview with Master Sergeant Lawrence C. Smith, USMC (Ret.), November 18, 2007.

Sergeant Kenneth C. Campbell, one of the actual survivors, could not be located for an interview. Chief Warrant Officer Thomas and Master Sergeant Smith are two of only three Americans who were actually in the vicinity of this event capable of providing documented commentary of details concerning events in the village where the Koreans lost a platoon from the 2nd Company. The Koreans, for their part, tried to keep the incident quiet, as it offended their honor. As this event is pivotal and has significant impact on then future events, the proceedings of this episode are crucial. Several particulars of this chapter were more or less ad libbed to provide literary commentary gathered from what known details the author was able to pull together from all sources. The results, however, are very factual, as one platoon was, in fact, swallowed up in the village that day. As we could not reach a consensus on the actual time frame of this event, it is offered here as taking place in late 1966, although it could have taken place early in 1967.

Chapter 7 The Friends
Events recalled from long-ago discussions held with the participants during a rare get-together while still in Vietnam. Although the events of this chapter did not occur in such close proximity to each other as described, the author has combined four episodes for literary convenience. (He's too old to remember the correct sequence of events.) As these incidents were relayed to the author so long ago, Korean units involved in events of this chapter have long since lapsed from the author's memory (if he ever did know). Units attributed to the actions described herein are in all probability not the actual units involved in those long-ago events. As the four participants in this chapter did not survive their tour in Vietnam, follow-up interviews with Terry J. Perko, Willis Leonard McBride, Calvin A. McGinty, Jr., and Maurice John Biehn were not possible.

Chapter 8 Will the Last Man Standing Please Call a Medevac?
Interview with Colonel Albert J. Ransom, USMC (Ret.), September 20, 2005.
Interview with Major Larry Oswalt, USMC (Ret.), October 19, 2005.
Interview with David Lucht, October 22, 2005 and November 12, 2005.
Interview with John Houghton, October 8, 2005.
A History of Marine Observation Squadron Six, by Lieutenant Colonel Gary W. Parker, USMC, and Major Frank M. Bartha, Jr.,

USMC. History and Museums Division Headquarters, U.S. Marine Corps, 1982.

Chapter 9 What the Hell Happened to You?
Interview with John Houghton, October 8, 2005 and November 20, 2005. Interview with Colonel Albert J. Ransom, USMC (Ret.), September 18, 2005.
Interview with Major Larry Oswalt, USMC (Ret.), November 4, 2005.
Interview with Dave Lucht, November 22, 2005.
A History of Marine Observation Squadron Six, by Lieutenant Colonel Gary W. Parker, USMC, and Major Frank M. Bartha, Jr., USMC. History and Museums Division Headquarters, U.S. Marine Corps, 1982.

Chapter 10 Transition
Background information to set up Chapter 11.
Documents (not examined by the author) recovered from dead NVA officers littering the ground at Tra Bihn Dong.

Chapter 11 You're Here to Deliver a Valentine from Ho Chi Who?
Interview with Jim Porta, July 26, 2005.
Interview with Dave Long, October 30, 2005 and December 4, 2005.
Interview with Master Sergeant Lawrence C. Smith, USMC (Ret.), November 10, 2007.
"The Battle of Tra Bihn Dong and the Origins of the U.S. Marine Corps Martial Arts Program," by Lieutenant Colonel James F. Durand, USMC. *Marine Corps Gazette.*2005
Online article that appeared in www.vietvet.co.kr, No Title. by Jae-Sung Chung.
Documents (not examined by the author) recovered from dead NVA officers littering the ground at Tra Bihn Dong.

Chapter 12 Rampage of the Giant Dragon
Interview with Gary Fiedler August 20, 2007.
Interview with Master Sergeant Lawrence C. Smith, USMC (Ret.), November 18, 2007 and December 19, 2007.
Interview with Timothy Cioti, August 16, 2006.

The Marines in Vietnam 1954-1973: An Anthology and Annotated Bibliography, History and Museums Division Headquarters, U.S. Marine Corps, 1974.
Personal map of Quang Ngai Province.

Chapter 13 An Incident on Mui Ba Lang An
Personal verbal account of the action made to the author by Captain Stephen W. Pless in October 1967 and November 1968.
"Beyond the Call: Saga of Major Stephen Pless," by Kevin O'Rourke. *Vietnam Magazine.*
"Marine Chopper Battles 50 Reds," by John Dittman. *Stars and Stripes*, August 22, 1967.
Valor Remembered http://www.valorremembered.org/
Verbatim statements from the participants: Captain Stephen W. Pless, USMC, Captain Rupert E. Fairfield, USMC, Gunnery Sergeant Leroy N. Poulson, USMC, Lance Corporal John G. Phelps, USMC, Warrant Officer Ronald L. Redeker, U.S. Army, Warrant Officer James P. Van Duzee, U.S. Army, Staff Sergeant Lawrence H. Allen, U.S. Army, Captain Donald D. Stevenson, USAF.

Chapter 14 Unruly Party Guests
Interview with Vance Hall, November 26, 2007.
Interview with James Chally, January 14, 2008.
Interview with James Sandoz, January 27, 2008.
Interview with Sergeant Major Raymond R. Roughton, III, USMC (Ret.), January 29, 2008.
Interview with Lieutenant Commander William C. Vandiver, USN (Ret.), January 31, 2008.
Interview with Charles Darby, June 2, 2008.
Interview with Michael L. Smith, June 30, 2008.
Interview with Captain Pasquale J. Morocco, USMC (Ret.), May 22, 2008.
U.S. Marines in Vietnam: The Defining Year 1969, by Jack Shulimson.
Lieutenant Colonel Leonard A. Blasiol, USMC, Charles R. Smith, and Captain David A. Dawson, USMC. History and Museums Division Headquarters, U.S. Marine Corps, 1997.
Command Chronologies, Sub Unit One, 1st ANGLICO, 1 January through 28 February 1968.
Task Force X-Ray, After Action Report, Operation Hue City.

Chapter 15 Different War, Same Mess
U.S. Marines in Vietnam: High Mobility and Stand-Down 1969, by Charles R. Smith, History and Museums Division Headquarters, U.S. Marine Corps, 1988.
Command Chronologies, Sub Unit One, 1st ANGLICO, 1 January through 31 December 1969.

Chapter 16 The Big Hurt
Interview with Captain Pasquale J. Morocco, USMC (Ret.), 5/22/08.
http://www.fas.org/man/dod-101/sys/ship/bb-61.htm
http://www.navweaps.com/Weapons/WNUS 16-50 mk7.htm
http://www.ussnewjersey.org/1969_narrative.htm
http://www.history.navy.mil/seairland/index.html
Command Chronologies, 3rd Marines, 1 through 28 February 1969.
Command Chronologies, 1st Amphibian Tractor Battalion, 1 through 28 February 1969

Chapter 17 More of the Same
U.S. Marines in Vietnam: High Mobility and Stand-Down 1969, by Charles R. Smith, History and Museums Division Headquarters, U.S. Marine Corps, 1988.
Command Chronologies, Sub Unit One, 1st ANGLICO, 1 January through 31 December 1969.
After Action Report of Operation Defiant Stand, 2nd Republic of Korea Marine Brigade (undated), by Colonel Koh Kwang Soo.
Command Chronologies, 1st Battalion 26th Marines, September 1969.
U.S. Marines in Vietnam: Vietnamization and Redeployment 1970-1971, by Graham A. Cosmas and Lieutenant Colonel Terrence P. Murray, USMC. History and Museums Division Headquarters, U.S. Marine Corps, 1986.
Command Chronology, Sub Unit One, 1st ANGLICO, 1 January through 31 December 1970.

Chapter 18 Solitary Refinement
U.S. Marines in Vietnam: Vietnamization and Redeployment 1970-1971, by Graham A. Cosmas and Lieutenant Colonel Terrence P. Murray, USMC. History and Museums Division Headquarters, U.S. Marine Corps, 1986.

U.S. Marines in Vietnam: The War that Would Not End, 1971-1973, by Major Charles D. Melson, USMC, and Lieutenant Colonel Curtis G. Arnold, USMC. History and Museums Division Headquarters, U.S. Marine Corps, 1991.
The Easter Offensive of 1972, by Lieutenant General Ngo Quang Truong, U.S. Army Center of Military History, 1979.
Vietnam's Forgotten Army, by Andrew Wiest, New York University Press, 2008.
Command Chronologies, Sub Unit One, 1st ANGLICO, 1 January through 31 December 1971.

Chapter 19 The Last Tango in Quang Tri
Interview with Joel Eisenstein, September 4, 2007.
Interview with Joe D. Swift, June 30, 2008.
The Easter Offensive of 1972, by Lieutenant General Ngo Quang Truong, U.S. Army Center of Military History, 1979.
Vietnam's Forgotten Army, by Andrew Wiest, New York University Press, 2008.
The Easter Offensive, by Colonel Gerald H. Turley, USMC (Ret.), Presidio Press, 1985.
U.S. Marines in Vietnam: The War that Would Not End, 1971-1973, by Major Charles D. Melson, USMC, and Lieutenant Colonel Curtis G. Arnold, USMC. History and Museums Division Headquarters, U.S. Marine Corps, 1991.
FMFPac Operations of U.S. Marine Forces, Southeast Asia, July 1971 through March 1973, by Lieutenant Colonel Thomas H. Simpson, USMC.
Command Chronologies, Sub Unit One, 1st ANGLICO, 1 January through 31 December 1972.
Lieutenant Larry Fletcher Potts: www.taskforceomega.org.
www.warbirdalley.com/ov10.htm
http://www.ussberkeley.com/

Chapter 20 Not On My Watch
Interview with HM3 Thomas E. Williamson, USN (Ret.), October 16, 2008.
Command Chronologies, Sub Unit One, 1st ANGLICO, 1 January through 31 December 1972.
The Easter Offensive, by Colonel Gerald H. Turley, USMC (Ret.), Presidio Press, 1985.

The Easter Offensive of 1972, by Lieutenant General Ngo Quang Truong, U.S. Army Center of Military History, 1979.
Trial by Fire, by Dale Andrade, Hippocrene Books, 1995.
FMFPac Operations of U.S. Marine Forces, Southeast Asia, July 1971 through March 1973, by Lieutenant Colonel Thomas H. Simpson, USMC.

Chapter 21 Not One More Inch
Interview with Chief Warrant Officer William E. Thomas, Jr., USMC (Ret.), November 11, 2007.
The Easter Offensive, by Colonel Gerald H. Turley, USMC (Ret.), Presidio Press, 1985.
Trial by Fire, by Dale Andrade, Hippocrene Books, 1995.
The Easter Offensive of 1972, by Lieutenant General Ngo Quang Truong, U.S. Army Center of Military History, 1979.
Vietnam's Forgotten Army, by Andrew Wiest, New York University Press, 2008.
U.S. Marines in Vietnam: The War that Would Not End, 1971-1973, by Major Charles D. Melson, USMC, and Lieutenant Colonel Curtis G. Arnold, USMC. History and Museums Division Headquarters, U.S. Marine Corps, 1991.
FMFPac Operations of U.S. Marine Forces, Southeast Asia, July 1971 through March 1973, by Lieutenant Colonel Thomas H. Simpson, USMC.
Command Chronologies, Sub Unit One, 1st ANGLICO, 1 January through 31 December 1972.

Chapter 22 Whoop Ass in Tiger Stripes
Interview with Terry Willis, September 8, 2008.
Interview with Major Anthony P. Shepard, USMC (Ret.), September 13, 2008.
Interview with Major Terry A. Griswold, U.S. Army (Ret.), September 17, 2008.
FMFPac Operations of U.S. Marine Forces, Southeast Asia, July 1971 through March 1973, by Lieutenant Colonel Thomas H. Simpson, USMC.
U.S. Marines in Vietnam: The War that Would Not End, 1971-1973, by Major Charles D. Melson, USMC, and Lieutenant Colonel Curtis G. Arnold, USMC. History and Museums Division Headquarters, U.S. Marine Corps, 1991.

The Easter Offensive of 1972, by Lieutenant General Ngo Quang Truong, U.S. Army Center of Military History, 1979.
Trial by Fire, by Dale Andrade, Hippocrene Books, 1995.
Command Chronologies, Sub Unit One, 1st ANGLICO, 1 January through 31 December 1972.

Chapter 23 Shut It Down When?
U.S. Marines in Vietnam: The War that Would Not End, 1971-1973, by Major Charles D. Melson, USMC, and Lieutenant Colonel Curtis G. Arnold, USMC. History and Museums Division Headquarters, U.S. Marine Corps, 1991.
FMFPac Operations of U.S. Marine Forces, Southeast Asia, July 1971 through March 1973, by Lieutenant Colonel Thomas H. Simpson, USMC.
Warrant Officer 2 Bruce Edward Boltze http://www.pownetwork.org/bios/b/b214.
1st Lieutenant Dwight Gary Rickman: http://www.chadduck.com/ymarines/pow-mia/main.htm

Addendum I ANGLICO in Vietnam
Command Chronologies, Sub Unit One, 1st ANGLICO, May 1965 through 14 March 1973.

Addendum II Korean Involvement in Vietnam
Korean Vietnam Veteran web site: www.vietvet.co.kr

Addendum III ANGLICO Honors
ANGLICO Association website: www.anglicoassociation.org//home.htm

Addendum IV ANGLICO Honor Roll
U.S. Marine Corps Museums and History Division
Former members of Sub Unit One.

Abbreviated Ship Histories (Tonkin Gulf Yacht Club)
Copyright Tin Can Sailors, Inc. Used with permission. All abbreviated destroyer ship histories preceding chapters of this book have been condensed from Tin Can Sailors, Inc. from their web site at http://www.destroyers.org/index.html. Other facts of these ships' involvement were found at the following ship association web sites. *The Dictionary of Naval Fighting Ships (DANFS)* and Sub Unit One,

1st ANGLICO Command Chronologies were also a big help in sorting through the storied histories of these great men o' war.

Destroyers
USS *Henry B. Wilson* http://www.usshenrybwilsonddg7.com
USS *Berkeley* http://www.usberkeley.com/
USS *Buchanan* http://www.uss-buchanan-ddg14.org/
USS *Waddell* http://www.usswaddell.com/
USS *Ozbourn* http://www.ozbourn.org/
UAS *Goldsborough* http://www.ussgoldsborough.com/
USS *Turner Joy* http://www.ussturnerjoy.org/info.html
USS *Higbee* http://en.wikipedia.org/wiki/USS_Higbee_(DD-806)
USS *Mullinnix* http://www.ussmullinnix.org/
USS *Rupertus* http://www.hazegray.org/danfs/destroy/dd851txt.htm?
USS *Eversole* Sub Unit One Command Chronologies
USS *John R. Craig* http://www.ussjohnrcraig.com/History.htm
USS *Samuel N. Moore* http://www.destroyers.org/DANFS/h-DD-
USS *Blandy* http://ussblandy.org/
USS *Towers* http://64.226.139.28/474.htm

Cruisers
USS *Saint Paul* http://www.mindspring.com/~gtakisatlcom.net/history.html
USS *Providence* http://www.navsource.org/archives/04/082/04082.html
USS *Oklahoma City* http://okcity.com/history.html

Battleships
USS *New Jersey* http://www.ussnewjersey.org/

Inshore Fire Support Ships
USS *White River* http://www.history.navy.mil/danfs/w7/white_ri.html

Services
ROYAL AUSTRALIAN NAVY http://www.navy.gov.au/spc/history/vietnam.html

U.S. COAST GUARD http://uscg.mil/historyh_militaryindex.axphttp://www.uscg.mil/history/default.asp

Lightning Source UK Ltd.
Milton Keynes UK
177407UK00001B/122/P